Elements of

SOLID & HAZARDOUS WASTE MANAGEMENT

OM PRAKASH GUPTA

Ex DGM, HRD

Bokaro Steel Plant

Steel Authority of India Limited (SAIL)

KHANNA BOOK PUBLISHING CO. (P) LTD.

Publisher, of Science, Technology and Engineering Books

4C/4344, Ansari Road, Darya Ganj, New Delhi-110002

Phone: 011-23244447-48 **Mobile:** +91-99109 09320

E-mail: contact@khannabooks.com

Website: www.khannabooks.com

Dear Readers,

To prevent the piracy, this book is secured with HIGH SECURITY HOLOGRAM on the front title cover. In case you don't find the hologram on the front cover title, please write us to at contact@khannabooks.com or whatsapp us at +91-99109 09320 and avail special gift voucher for yourself.

Specimen of Hologram on front Cover title:

Moreover, there is a SPECIAL DISCOUNT COUPON for you with EVERY HOLOGRAM.

How to avail this SPECIAL DISCOUNT:

Step 1: Scratch the hologram
Step 2: Under the scratch area, your "coupon code" is available
Step 3: Logon to www.khannabooks.com
Step 4: Use your "coupon code" in the shopping cart and get your copy at a special discount
Step 5: Enjoy your reading!

Thanks,
Khanna Publishing House

Price: ₹ 450.00

ISBN: 978-93-82609-75-9

ELEMENTS OF SOLID & HAZARDOUS WASTE MANAGEMENT
by O.P. Gupta

First Edition: 2019
Reprint: 2023

To view complete list of books, please scan the QR Code:

Published by:
Khanna Book Publishing Co. (P) Ltd.
CIN: U22110DL1998PTC095547

Visit us at: www.khannabooks.com
Write us at: contact@khannabooks.com

Printed in India by: SPS Printers

PREFACE

Solid & Hazardous Waste Management is an integral part of the degree, postgraduate & diploma curriculum of various branches of engineering. Besides, it is also a compulsory paper for various associate membership examinations conducted by professional bodies like Institution of Engineers (AMIE), Indian Institute of Metals (AMIIM), Indian Institute of Chemical Engineers (AMIIChE) etc. This book has been prepared strictly as per the syllabus of these examinations.

This book covers the entire syllabus of Solid & Hazardous Waste Management which includes the following topics:

- Introduction to Solid Waste Management
- Municipal Solid Waste (MSW) Management
- Industrial Solid Waste Management
- Hazardous Waste Management
- Radioactive Waste Management
- Bio Medical Waste (BMW) Management
- e-Waste Management
- Integrated Solid Waste Management (ISWM)

Besides, Short questions & answers and multiple-choice questions & answers drawn from the examination papers of various engineering colleges and professional bodies examinations given at the end of the book enhances its utility for the students.

This book is targeted to benefit the following:

- Diploma in engineering students
- Degree in engineering students
- Postgraduate in engineering students
- AMIE, AMIIM, AMIICHE Students.
- Faculty members and teaching staff
- Practicing engineers/professionals /Consultants

Subject matter has been presented in simple, lucid and easy to understand language. I hope that the book in its present form will be useful for the students.

Constructive suggestion for the improvement of the book are welcome.

—Om Prakash Gupta

CONTENTS

CHAPTER

1

INTRODUCTION TO SOLID WASTE MANAGEMENT

1.1 INTRODUCTION

Solid wastes are all the wastes arising from human and animal activities that are normally solid and are discarded as useless or unwanted. Solid waste includes domestic wastes, municipal wastes, commercial wastes, garbage, rubbish, ashes, construction and demolition wastes, industrial wastes, hazardous wastes, hospital wastes and sewage.

Sources and Types of Solid Wastes

There are different sources and types of solid wastes as tabulated below.

S.N.	Sources	Typical waste generators	Types of solid wastes
1.	Residential	Single and multifamily dwellings	Food wastes, paper, cardboard, plastics, textiles, leather, yard wastes, wood, glass, metals, ashes, special wastes (*e.g.* bulky items, consumer electronics, white goods, batteries, oil tires), and household hazardous wastes.
2.	Industrial	Light and heavy manufacturing, fabrication, construction sites, power and chemical plants	Housekeeping wastes, packaging, food wastes, construction and demolition materials, hazardous wastes, ashes, and special wastes.
3.	Commercial	Stores, hotels, restaurants, markets, office buildings, etc	Paper, cardboard, plastics, wood, food wastes, glass, metals, special wastes, hazardous wastes
4.	Institutional	Schools, hospitals, prisons, government centers	Same as commercial

5.	Construction and demolition	New construction sites, road repair, renovation sites, demolition of buildings	Wood, Steel, concrete, dirt, etc.
6.	Municipal services	Street cleaning, landscaping, parks, beaches, other recreational areas, water and wastewater treatment plants	Street sweeping; landscape and tree trimmings; general wastes from parks, beaches, and other recreational areas; sludge
7.	Process (manufacturing, etc.)	Heavy and light manufacturing, refineries, chemical plants, power plants, mineral extraction and processing	Industrial process wastes, scrap materials, off- specification products, slay, tailings
All of the above are called as "municipal solid waste (MSW)".			
8.	Agriculture	Crops, orchards, vineyards, dairies, feedlots, farms	Spoiled food wastes, agricultural wastes, hazardous wastes (*e.g.* pesticides)

Definition of Some Types of Solid Wastes

Domestic wastes: These wastes are generated by household activities such as cooking, cleaning, repairs, redecoration, empty containers, packaging, clothing, old books, newspapers, old furnishings, etc.

Commercial wastes: Solid wastes generated in offices, wholesale stores, restaurants, hotels, markets, warehouses and other commercial establishments. These are further classified into garbage and rubbish.

Institutional wastes: Wastes generated from institutions such as schools, colleges, hospitals, research institutions. The waste includes garbage, rubbish and hazardous wastes.

Municipal wastes: Wastes generated due to municipal activities and services such as street waste, dead animals, market waste and abandoned vehicles. Generally, the term is used in a wider sense to incorporate domestic wastes, institutional wastes and commercial wastes.

Garbage: It includes animal and vegetable wastes due to various activities like storage, preparation and sale, cooking and serving. These are biodegradable.

Ashes: Residues from the burning of wood, charcoal and coke for cooking and heating in houses, institutions and small industries. Ashes consist of a fine powdery residue, cinders and clinker often mixed with small pieces of metal and glass.

Rubbish: Apart from garbage and ashes, other solid wastes produced in households, commercial establishments, and institutions are termed as rubbish.

Bulky wastes: Bulky wastes are large household appliances such as cookers, refrigerators and washing machines as well as furniture, crates, vehicle parts, tyres, wood, trees and branches. The bulky metallic wastes are sold as scrap metal but some portion is disposed as sanitary landfills.

Street wastes: Street wastes include paper, cardboard, plastic, dirt, dust, leaves and other vegetable matter collected from streets, walkways, alleys, parks and vacant plots.

Dead animals: It includes animals that die naturally or accidentally killed. It does not include carcass and animal parts from slaughterhouses as these are considered as industrial wastes.

Construction and demolition (C&D) wastes: Construction waste consists of unwanted material produced directly or indirectly by the construction or industries. This includes building materials such as insulation, nails, electrical wiring, as well as waste originating from site preparation such as dredging materials, tree stumps, and rubble. Construction waste may contain lead, asbestos, or other hazardous substances.

Major components of the construction materials are cement, bricks, cement plaster, steel, rubble, stone, timber, plastic and iron pipes. C&D wastes can be as high as 10 to 15 % of the materials that go into a building.

Industrial wastes: These are discarded solid material of manufacturing processes and industrial operations and are considered separately from municipal wastes. However, solid wastes from small industries plants and ash from power plants are frequently disposed off at municipal landfills. Major producers of industrial wastes are the thermal power plants producing coal ash, integrated iron & steel plants producing blast furnace slag & steel melting slag, non-ferrous industries like aluminium, zinc & copper producing red mud and tailings, sugar industries generating press mud, pulp & paper industries producing lime and fertilizer & allied industries producing gypsum. Management of industrial solid waste (ISW) is not the responsibility of local municipal bodies. Industries generating solid wastes have to manage by themselves and are required to obtain prior permission from the respective state pollution control boards under relevant rules.

Mining Solid Waste: Waste from extraction and processing of mineral resources, which is one of the largest waste streams in many countries.

Slaughterhouse Waste: India has the world's largest population of livestock. According to the Ministry of Food Processing, a total of 3616-slaughter houses slaughter over 2 million cattle & buffaloes, 50 million sheep & goat, 1.5 million pigs and 150 million poultry annually, for domestic consumption as well as for export purposes. The waste generated here are liquid and solid in nature. Slaughtering of animals generates waste consisting of non-edible organs, stomach contents, dung, bones and sludge from waste water treatment.

Hospital waste: Hospital waste is generated during the diagnosis, treatment and immunization of human beings or animals. It may include wastes like sharps, soiled waste, disposables, anatomical waste, cultures, discarded medicines, chemical wastes, etc. These are in the form of disposable syringes, swabs, bandages, body fluids, human excreta, etc. This waste is highly infectious and can be a serious threat to human health if not managed in a scientific manner. It has been estimated that out of the 5 kg of waste generated in a hospital at least 1 kg would be infected.

Bio-medical waste: Bio-medical waste means "any solid and/or liquid waste including its container and any intermediate product, which is generated during the diagnosis, treatment or immunisation of human beings or animals or in research pertaining thereto or in the production or testing thereof."

Bio-medical waste consists of human anatomical waste like tissues, organs, body parts, animal wastes generated during research, from veterinary hospitals, microbiology and biotechnology wastes, waste sharps, hypodermic needles, syringes, scalpels, broken glass, discarded medicines and cyto toxic drugs, soiled waste, such as dressing, bandages, plaster casts, material contaminated with blood, tubes, catheters, liquid waste from any of the infected areas, incineration ash and other chemical wastes.

Several health hazards are associated with poor management of bio-medical wastes like injury from sharps to staff and waste handlers associated with the health care establishments, Hospital Acquired Infection (HAI) of patients due to spread of infection, occupational risk associated with hazardous chemicals, drugs, unauthorized repackaging and sale of disposable items and unused/date expired drugs.

Occupier in relation to any institution generating bio-medical waste, which includes the hospital, nursing home, dispensary, clinic, veterinary institution, animal house, pathological laboratory, blood bank, means a person who has control over that institution or its premises.

Every occupier must set up bio-medical waste treatment facilities like incinerator, autoclave and microwave system to treat and dispose such waste.

- For human anatomical waste (human tissues, organs, body parts) the recommended treatment is incineration or deep burial.
- Wastes such as needles, syringes, scalpels, blades, glass, etc., are required to undergo chemical treatment, autoclaving or shredding.
- Solid waste items contaminated with blood and body fluids including cotton, dressing, soiled plaster casts, bedding and other materials are to be treated by incineration, autoclaving or microwaving.
- Solid wastes generated from disposable items such as tubes, catheters, intravenous sets are to be disinfected by chemical treatment or microwaving mutilation or shredding.

Bio-medical waste must not be mixed with other wastes and shall be segregated into containers or bags of different colours like yellow, red, blue and black depending upon the type of waste. The untreated bio-medical waste should not be stored in the premises beyond a period of 48 hours and shall be transported only in such vehicles authorized for the purpose by the Government.

Special wastes: Special wastes are those types of solid waste that require special handling, treatment, and/or disposal. The reasons for separate consideration include: 1) their characteristics and quantities (either or both may render them difficult to manage if they are combined with "typical" municipal solid waste); or 2) their presence will or may pose a significant danger to the health and safety of workers and/or the public, to the environment, or both.

These wastes are very different from each other, so they should be managed and handled separately if feasible. Typically, in developing countries, special wastes are set out for collection, collected, and/or disposed along with wastes from commercial, businesses and residential generators. Ideally, these wastes should not enter the municipal solid waste stream, but quite frequently they do in developing countries.

Some examples of special types of wastes are given below.

- Pathological or infectious medical waste from hospitals, clinics, and laboratories
- "Hazardous" waste in the household waste stream (*e.g.*, oil-based paints, paint thinners, wood preservatives, pesticides, household cleaners, used motor oil, antifreeze, batteries)
- Discarded tires
- Used oils
- Electronic waste (e-waste)
- Wet batteries
- Construction and demolition debris
- Municipal wastewater treatment (sewage) sludge, septage, and slaughterhouse wastes
- Industrial hazardous waste, and some types of industrial solid waste (*e.g.*, metal cuttings from metal processors or cannery waste).

Physical Characteristics of Solid Waste

Physical characteristics of Solid Waste are density, moisture content, size of the waste constituents *etc.*

The density of solid waste may vary during transportation of waste from its source to disposal points. Density of waste is an important measure which is used to define all the elements of the solid waste management system such as storage, transportation and disposal facilities required. Compaction of waste increases the density in order to accommodate larger quantities of waste within the available space.

The bulk density can be measured by filling a container of known volume with wastes and then weighing the loaded container. (The container should be constantly shaken during filling) The bulk density is calculated by dividing the net weight of the refuse(weight of loaded container minus weight of empty container) by its volume. The result is expressed as kg/m^3.

Bulk densities of solid wastes obtained in various countries are given below.

Country	Density (kg/m^3)
United Kingdom	150
United States	100
Egypt	330
Nigeria	250
Singapore	175
Tunisia	175
Bangladesh	600
Burma	400
India	400 to 600
Indonesia	400

Mexico	300 to 500
Nepal	600
Pakistan	500
Paraguay	390
South Korea	200 to 450
Sri Lanka	400
Thailand	250
Tanzania	330

Bulk densities of mixed MSW and various components of MSW are given below.

Component	Density (kg/m^3)
MIXED SOLID WASTE	
Mixed MSW	
Loose	90 to 178
After dumping from compactor truck	207 to 237
In compactor truck	297 to 416
In landfill	475 to 772
Shredded	119 to 237
Baled	475 to 712
Mechanically-Recovered Fractions (Loose)	
dRDF	481 to 641
Aluminium scrap	224 to 257
Ferrous scrap	369 to 417
Crushed glass	1,042 to 1,363
Powdered RDF (Eco-Fuel)	417 to 449
RECOVERED MATERIALS	
Loose	
Corrugated	16 to 32
Aluminium cans	32 to 48
Plastic containers	32 to 48
Miscellaneous paper	48 to 64
Garden waste	64 to 80
Newspaper	80 to 112
Rubber	209 to 258
Glass bottles	193 to 305
Food waste	353 to 401
Tin cans	64 to 80

Densified	
Baled aluminium cans	193 to 289
Cubed ferrous cans	1,042 to 1,491
Baled corrugated	353 to 513
Baled newspaper	369 to 529
Baled high grades	321 to 465
Baled PET	209 to 305
Baled HDPE	273 to 385

For comparison purposes, the densities of virgin materials are given below.

Component	Density (kg/m^3)
Wood	593
Cardboard	689
Paper	705 to 1,154
Glass	2,501
Aluminium	2,693
Steel	7,855
Polypropylene	898
Polyethylene	946
Polystyrene	1,042
ABS	1,026
Acrylic	1,186
Polyvinylchloride (PVC)	1,250

Size of waste constituents is important in the design of mechanical separators and **shredders and also in waste treatment process.**

Size distribution may be determined with the use of a set of manually manipulated screens. The screens should have square openings, particularly those with large openings, and the sizes of the openings included in the set should be 100, 50, and 25 cm. The screens, particularly those with large openings, can be easily made with lumber and wire. The sample size should range from 150 to 300 kg.

Representative waste from the sample is placed on the largest of the screens (100 cm). The screen is shaken until particles of refuse no longer pass through the openings. Material remaining on the screen (oversize) is collected and weighed. The material that has passed through the screen (undersize) is placed on the screen with the 50-cm openings, which is shaken as in the preceding step. The process is repeated until all three screens have been used. The fractions that are sized are weighed, and the weight values are used to plot a size distribution curve. Typically, the size distribution is plotted as cumulative percent passing versus screen size.

Physical Composition of Solid Wastes

Knowing the characteristics of the physical component of a community solid waste is important for the following purposes:

- For the selection and operation of equipments and facilities.
- To assess the possibility for resource of energy recovery.
- To design and analyze disposal facilities.

The types (components) of solid waste may be different from country to country by season, economic condition, developmental level, etc.

The individual component study involves to achieve the present composition of solid waste by volume and by weight. Volume measurements although difficult to measure are essential to disposal methods, *e.g.* to calculate incinerator sizes and landfill areas and to limit hauling capacity of refuse trucks, etc.

Moisture content of solid wastes is usually expressed as the weight of moisture per unit weight of wet material. Moisture increases the weight of solid waste, thereby increasing the cost of collection and transportation. Therefore moisture content is a critical component in the economic feasibility of waste treatment and processing methods by incineration.

The moisture content is determined as follows: The sample is weighed as received ("wet weight"). It is then allowed to stand until it is air-dry, *i.e.*, its moisture content is in equilibrium with that of the ambient air. The percent moisture content is then obtained through the following formula:

$$\text{Moisture Content (\%)} = \frac{W_W - W_D}{W_W} \times 100$$

where:

- W_W = wet weight of sample, and
- W_D = dry weight of sample.

Typical moisture content of components of municipal solid waste is tabulated below.

Component	Moisture Content, % by weight	
	Range	Typical
Food wastes	50 – 80	70
Paper	4 – 10	6
Cardboard	4 – 8	5
Plastics	1 – 4	2
Textiles	6 – 15	10
Rubber	1 – 4	2
Leather	8 – 12	10

Garden trimmings	30 – 80	60
Wood	15 – 40	20
Misc. organics	10 – 60	25
Glass	1 – 4	2
Tin cans	2 – 4	3
Nonferrous metals	2 – 4	2
Ferous metals	2 – 6	3
Dirt, ashes, brick, etc	6 – 12	8
MSW	15 – 40	20

Chemical Characteristics of Solid Waste

Knowledge of chemical characteristics of waste is essential in understanding the behavior of waste all through the waste management system and also in selecting and determining the efficiency of any treatment process. Further, the characteristics of leachate that could potentially contaminate the surrounding water resources depend on the waste characteristics.

Chemical characteristics include (i) chemical; (ii) bio-chemical; and (iii) toxic characteristics.

- Chemical characteristics include pH, Nitrogen, Phosphorus and Potassium (N-P-K), total Carbon, C/N ratio, *etc.*
- Bio-Chemical characteristics include carbohydrates, proteins, natural fibre, and biodegradable factor, *etc.*
- Toxicity characteristics include heavy metals, pesticides, insecticides, Toxicity test for leachates *etc.*

Knowledge of chemical characteristics is essential in selecting and designing the waste **processing and disposal facilities.**

Chemical Composition

Information on the chemical composition of solid wastes is important in evaluating alternative processing and recovery options. For example, the feasibility of combustion depends on the chemical composition of solid waste. If solid wastes are to be used as fuel, the four most important properties to be known are:

1. **Proximate analysis:** Proximate analysis for combustible components of municipal solid waste includes the following tests:
   (a) Moisture (loss of moisture when heated to 105°C for 1h) .
   (b) Volatile combustible matter (additional loss of weight on ignition at 950°C in a covered crucible).
   (c) Fixed carbon (combustible residue left after volatile matter is removed).
   (d) Ash (weight of residue after combustion in an open crucible).

2. **Fusion point of ash:** It is defined as the temperature at which the ash resulting from the burning of waste will form a solid (clinker) by fusion and agglomeration. Typical fusion temperature for the formation of clinker from solid waste ranges from 1100 to 1200°C.
3. **Ultimate analysis:** The ultimate analysis of a waste component typically involves the determination of the percent of C (carbon), H (hydrogen) O (oxygen), N (nitrogen), S (sulfur) and ash. The results of the ultimate analysis are used to characterize the chemical composition of the organic matter in municipal solid waste.

Typical ultimate analysis of the combustible components in municipal solid waste in Percent by weight (dry basis) is tabulated below.

Component	C	H	O	N	S	Ash
Food waste	48.0	6.4	37.6	2.6	0.4	5.0
Paper	43.5	6.0	44.0	0.3	0.2	6.0
Cardboard	44.0	5.9	44.6	0.3	0.2	5.0
Plastic	60.0	7.2	22.8	-	-	10.0
Textiles	55.0	6.6	31.2	4.6	0.15	2.5
Rubber	78.0	10.0	-	2.0	-	10.0
Leather	60.0	8.0	11.6	10.0	0.4	10.0
Garden trimmings	47.8	6.0	38.0	3.4	0.3	4.5
Wood	49.5	6.0	42.7	0.2	0.1	1.5
Misc organics	48.5	6.5	37.5	2.2	0.3	5.0
Dirt, ashes, brick, etc	26.3	3.0	2.0	0.5	0.2	68.0

4. **Energy content:** The energy content of the organic components in municipal solid waste can be determined by:
   - Using a full scale boiler as a calorimeter.
   - Using a laboratory bomb calorimeter.
   - Calculation, if the elemental composition is known.

Calorific value of MSW Indicates its Suitability for Incineration

Typical data on inert residue and energy content of MSW is tabulated below.

Component	Inert residue (after complete combustion), %		Energy, KJ/kg (as discarded basis)	
	Range	Typical	Range	Typical
Food wastes	2-8	5	3,5000-7,000	4,650
Paper	4-8	6	11,600-18,600	16,750

Cardboard	3-6	5	13,950–17,450	16,300
Plastics	6-20	10	27,900–37,200	32,600
Textiles	2-4	2.5	15,100–18,600	17,450
Rubber	8-20	10	20,900–27,900	23, 250
Leather	8–20	10	15,100–19,800	17,450
Garden trimmings	2-6	4.5	2,300–18,600	6,500
Wood	0.6-2	1.5	17,450–19,800	18,600
Misc. organics	2-8	6	11,000–26,000	18,000
Glass	96-99	98	100–250	150
Tin cans	96-99	98	250–1,200	700
Non–ferrous metals	90-99	96	-	-
Ferrous metals	94-99	98	250–1,200	700
Dirt, ashes, bricks, etc	60-80	70	2,300–11,650	7,000
MSW	-	-	9,300–12,800	10,500

Comparison of wet solid waste characterisation worldwide (% by weight) is tabulated below.

Location	Putrescibles	Paper	Metals	Glass	Plastics, Rubber, Leather	Textiles	Ceramics, Dust, Stones	Wt (g) cap/ day
Bangalore, India	75.2	1.5	0.1	0.2	0.9	3.1	19.0	400
Manila, Philippines	45.5	14.5	4.9	2.7	8.6	1.3	27.5	400
Asunción, Paraguay	60.8	12.2	2.3	4.6	4.4	2.5	13.2	460
Seoul, Korea	22.3	16.2	4.1	10.6	9.6	3.8	33.4[a]	2,000[a]
Vienna, Austria	23.3	33.6	3.7	10.4	7.0	3.1	18.9[b]	1,180
Mexico City, Mexico	59.8[c]	11.9	1.1	3.3	3.5	0.4	20.0	680
Paris, France	16.3	40.9	3.2	9.4	8.4	4.4	17.4	1,430
Australia	23.6	39.1	6.6	10.2	9.9		9.0	1,870
Sunnyvale, California, USA	39.4[d]	40.8	3.5	4.4	9.6	1.0	1.3	2,000
Bexar County, Texas, USA	43.8[d]	34.0	4.3	5.5	7.5	2.0	2.9	1,816

[a] Includes briquette ash (average). [b] Includes "all others". [c] Includes small amounts of wood, hay, and straw. [d] Includes garden waste.

Wastes generated in countries located in humid, tropical, and semitropical areas usually are characterised by a high concentration of plant debris; whereas those generated in areas subject to seasonal changes in temperature or those in which coal or wood are used for cooking and heating may contain an abundance of ash. The concentration of ash may be substantially higher during winter. Regardless of climatic differences, the wastes usually are more or less contaminated with nightsoil. These differences prevail even in wastes generated in large metropolitan areas of a developing country.

Ideally, solid waste should not contain faecal matter or urine, and the mixing of these materials with household waste should be prohibited by law. Handling of pathological wastes, abattoir wastes, industrial wastes, and similar materials, in association with household wastes, also should not be permitted. Nevertheless, it is important to keep in mind that despite all precautions, some pathogens and chemical residues inevitably will be present in the waste.

The Functional Elements of Solid Waste

Waste generation: It encompasses activities in which materials are identified as no longer being of value and are either thrown out or gathered together for disposal. Waste generation is, at present, an activity that is not very controllable. In future, however, more control is likely to be exercised over the generation of wastes. Reduction of waste at source, although not controlled by solid waste managers, is now included in system evaluations as a method of limiting the quantity of waste generated. It is estimated that solid waste generated in small, medium and large cities and towns is about 0.1 kg, 0.3 – 0.4 kg and 0.5 kg per capita per day respectively.

Waste Collection: The functional element of collection includes not only the gathering of solid waste and recyclable materials, but also the transport of these materials, after collection, to the location where the collection vehicle is emptied. This location may be a materials processing facility, a transfer station or a landfill disposal site. Collection and storage of MSW is an important issue which has great impact on the overall solid waste management. Community / municipal storage based system was mostly used in our cities. Lately, there is increased stress on door-step collection for better service delivery and controlling littering as well as unauthorized dumping of municipal garbage.

Current practices of waste collection in residential areas differ from city to city. Door-to-door collection is not widely practiced. Door-to-door (or house-to-house collection is the responsibility of the urban local bodies.The local authorities should arrange for primary collection of waste from sources of waste generation. Door-to-door collection of waste can be carried out with handcarts, tricycles or any small motorized vehicles having bell or horns as a means of announcing the arrival of collection staff with active public participation. Wastes from private societies, multistoried buildings, commercial complexes, *etc*. are collected through community bins. Lane wise or door step or community bin waste collection can be followed for slum areas. Based on the density of population in the area, work can be assigned either to the sweeper or tricycle staff for collecting wastes. Local authorities are responsible for planning the collection of waste in a productive manner.

Waste handling & separation, storage and processing at the source: It involves activities associated with waste management until the waste is placed in storage containers for collection. Handling also encompasses the movement of loaded containers to the point of collection. Separating different types of waste components is an important step in the handling and storage of solid waste at the source.

Waste segregation is the first step towards waste diversion and reduction. In order that the MSW management systems and waste treatment facilities work efficiently and for extending the life of the waste disposal facilities, it is imperative that waste is properly segregated early in the systems management. .

- Segregation at the collection point/source reduces the cost of processing and disposal.
- Separation at site by rag-pickers for recycling.
- Incentives for segregation otherwise punitive action.

Separation and processing & transformation of solid wastes: The types of means and facilities that are now used for the recovery of waste materials that have been separated at the source include curbside collection, drop off and buy back centers. The separation and processing of wastes that have been separated at the source and the separation of commingled wastes usually occur at a Materials Recovery Facility (MRF), transfer stations, combustion facilities and disposal sites.

The recovery of sorted materials, processing of solid waste and transformation of solid waste that occurs primarily in locations away from the source of waste generation are encompassed by this functional element. Sorting often includes the separation of bulky items, separation of waste components by size using screens, manual separation of waste components, and separation of ferrous and non-ferrous metals.

The recyclable wastes, if handled and managed properly, could form a major part of revenue resource. The municipal authorities should establish appropriate mechanisms for collection and sale of the recyclable materials without impacting the livelihood of the rag pickers community and the related industry.

Waste processing is undertaken to recover conversion of products and energy. The organic fraction of MSW can be transformed by a variety of biological and thermal processes.Waste transformation is undertaken to reduce the volume, weight, size or toxicity of waste without resource recovery. Transformation may be done by a variety of mechanical (*e.g.* shredding)/ thermal (*e.g.* incineration) / chemical (*e.g.* encapsulation) techniques.

Waste transfer and transport: The functional element of transfer and transport involves two steps:

- The transfer of wastes from the smaller collection vehicles such as tricycles to the larger transport equipment, usually at transfer station and
- The subsequent transportation of wastes from transfer station to the processing or disposal site.

A transfer station is a solid waste processing site where solid waste is transferred from one vehicle to another vehicle or to storage device for temporary storage until transferred to a permanent disposal site approved or permitted by the appropriate authority. Location of transfer stations should be well identified after examining traffic routes for the transportation of wastes for smooth traffic movement and safety of the local community. To know the waste generation rates and waste characterization regular field investigations and inspections can be carried out at these transfer stations. The transfer stations could be designed in a manner that recyclable wastes that are not picked at the primary collection points are segregated, stored and sold or transported to relevant processing facilities. Transfer stations shall be well equipped with appropriate facilities and equipments to handle these activities and to avoid pollution.

Waste disposal: Today, the disposal of wastes by land filling or land spreading is the most common ultimate fate of all solid wastes, whether they are residential wastes collected and transported directly to a landfill site, residual materials from material recovery facilities, residue from the combustion of solid waste, compost, or other substances from various solid waste processing facilities.

A modern sanitary landfill is not a dump; it is an engineered facility used for disposing of solid wastes on land without creating nuisances or hazards to public health or safety, such as the breeding of insects and the contamination of ground water.

Energy generation: Municipal solid waste can be used to generate energy. Several technologies have been developed that make the processing for energy generation cleaner and more economical than ever before, including landfill gas capture, combustion, pyrolysis, gasification.

In order to mitigate potential impacts of waste disposal, a landfill is to be designed as an engineered facility used for disposing solid wastes on land without creating nuisance or hazard to public health or safety, such as breeding of rodents, insects and contamination of surrounding natural environment, including groundwater & surface water resources and air quality.

There are number of solid waste disposal options (refer Figure further), each has its distinct merits and demerits, which guide us to choose appropriate technology for a given local condition.

Despite the best efforts to reduce, reuse and recycle, there will always be residual waste requiring disposal.

Source Reduction/Recycling/Reuse

Source reduction: Source reduction, also known as waste prevention or pollution prevention, is the elimination or reduction of waste before it is created. It involves the design, manufacture, purchase or use of materials and products to reduce the amount or toxicity of what is thrown away.

The need of source reduction

- Shortage of suitable landfill space: In many areas, no suitable land is available for landfills development.

- The development of new landfill site is expensive: New landfills often resisted due to public concerns over groundwater contamination, odors, and truck traffic. The most effective way to solve the problem is by reducing waste in the first place, *i.e.* Stopping waste before it happens.
- The amount of waste each person creates has almost doubled. MSW generation Source reduction first, recycling and composting second, and disposal in landfills or waste combustors should be the last option.
- The number of landfill site has decreased.

The practice in source reduction

- Purchasing long-lasting goods;
- Seeking products and packaging that are as free of toxics as possible;
- Redesigning products to use less raw material in production, have a longer life, or be used again after its original use;
- Reusing items is another way to stop waste at the source; Saving natural resources; Reducing toxicity of waste; Reducing costs.

Benefits of source reduction and reuse

Many communities have instituted "pay-as-you-throw" programs where citizens pay for each can or bag of trash they set out for disposal; When businesses manufacture their products with less packaging, they are buying less raw material; Buying products with less packaging, or that are reusable (not single-use) frequently means a cost savings.

Recycling

Recycling refers to the collection, separation, processing, or use of materials that would otherwise become solid waste. The activities included under recycling include the initial collection of materials; marketing those raw materials; producing products from those materials; and use of those products in the marketplace.

Some of the materials from MSW that would be recycled are plastics, metals, paper, glass, rubber, rags, leather, etc. The recovery of the materials will reduce the need to use natural resources directly and may reduce emissions from extraction and processing of raw materials. On the other hand, there could be environmental or health effects from reprocessing materials which have been taken out of the waste stream.

Recycling process

Step 1. **Collection and Processing:** The recyclable materials are collected at the curb or from a dropoff centre, than transported into a recovery facility where they are cleaned, separated, and baled.

Step 2. **Manufacturing Recyclables** are processed into new products.

Step 3. **Purchasing Recycled Products:** Purchasing recycled products completes the recycling loop.

Benefits of Recycling

(1) Conserves resources for our children's future; (2) Prevents emissions of many greenhouse gases and water pollutants; (3) Supplies valuable raw materials to industry; (4) Creates jobs; (5) Stimulates the development of greener technologies; (6) Reduces the need for new landfills and incinerators (about 30% of the MSW is disposed through recycling); (7) Saves energy;

Recycling is an excellent way of saving energy and conserving the environment. We should know that: 1 recycled tin can would save enough energy to power a television for 3 hours; 1 recycled glass bottle would save enough energy to power a computer for 25 minutes; 1 recycled plastic bottle would save enough energy to power a 60-watt lights for 3 hours; 70% less energy is required to recycle paper compared with making it from raw materials.

Prices for recycled material can vary widely from year to year, depending on demand; The demand for recycled products doesn't keep pace with the growing supply.

The alternative treatment and disposal technologies for solid wastes are:

- Composting
- Anaerobic digestion / Biomethanation
- Pelletisation / Refuse Derived Fuel (RDF)
- Pyrolysis and Gasification
- Incineration
- Landfills: Sanitary Landfill / Bioreactor landfill / Secured landfill (for inert waste)

Among the various waste treatment and disposal options as mentioned above, MoEF (Ministry of Environment & Forest) has notified composting (windrow composting, vermi composting), anaerobic digestion, incineration, pelletization and landfill technologies and has given relevant standards for compost quality, leachate disposal, incineration operations & emissions and landfill specifications.

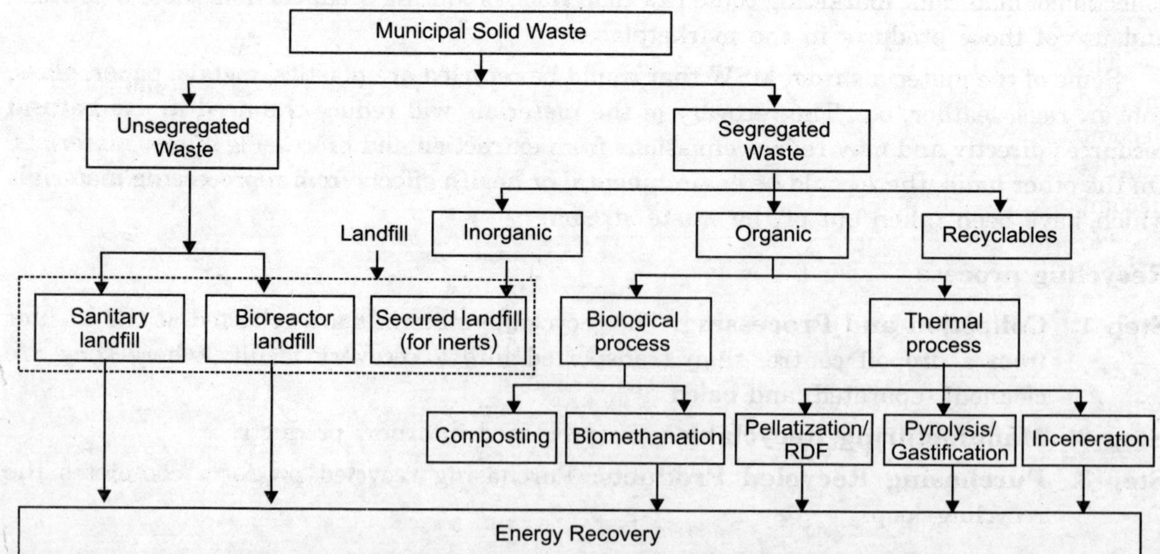

Figure 1.1: Technological Options for MSW Management

Composting

Composting is an organic method of producing compost manure by decomposition and stabilization of organic matter present in solid waste. Composting process (refer the figure below) results in the production of stable compost product reduced in size and free from offensive odors. Compost is useful as organic manure which contains plant nutrients (nitrogen, phosphorous and potassium) as well as micro nutrients which can be utilized for the growth of plants. Composting can be carried out in two ways — aerobically (with the presence of oxygen) or anaerobically (without the presence of oxygen) or vermi-composting or by any other biological mechanism.

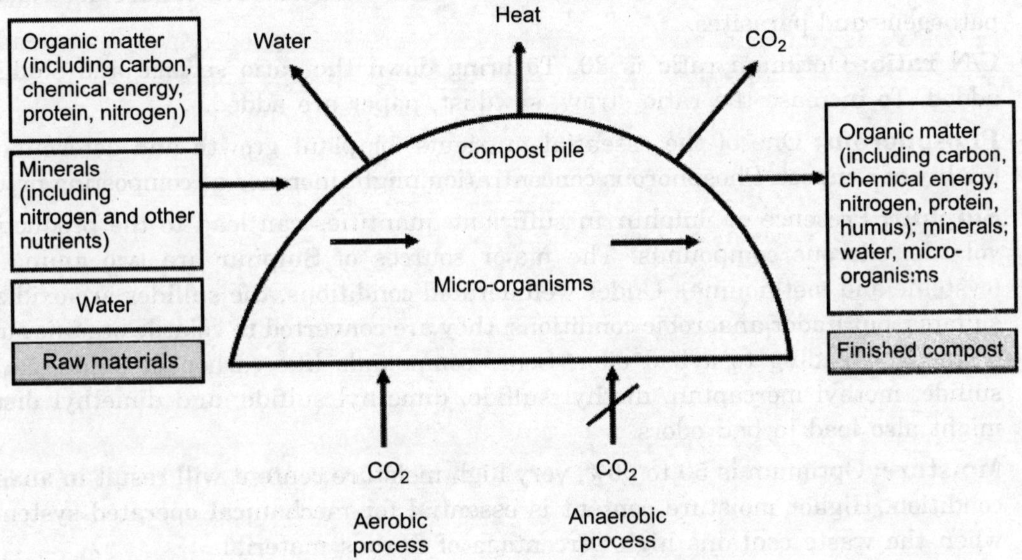

Figure 1.2: Schematic Diagram of Composting Process

There are various methods of composting and the approach in selecting the appropriate method of composting depends on time to complete composting, the material & volume to be decomposed, space available, the availability of resources (labour, finances, etc.) and the quality of finished product required. In general composting process consists of four decomposition phases:

- **Mesophilic phase (I):** In this phase slightly rotted material exists, in which mainly bacterial degradation of easily degradable substances takes place. The temperature rises up to 42°C.
- **Thermophilic phase (II):** In this phase fresh compost is produced where further degradation of easily degradable materials as well as degradation of cellulose, caused by thermophilic fungi and bacteria. The temperature in this phase rises up to 65°C which causes self limitation or decrease in reproduction of micro organisms.
- **Cooling phase (III):** Finished compost is produced in this phase, where degradation of cellulose by fungi and bacteria, and formation of humus substances takes place. A decrease in microbial activity and temperature occur in this phase.

- **Maturing phase (IV):** Matured compost is produced in this phase, with further decrease of temperature to the surrounding temperature. Very low microbial activity with further formation of humus substances and stabilization take place.

By controlling some of the composting influencing factors, natural composting process could be accelerated. These influencing factors also have impact on quality of compost produced. Some of the important factors in the composting process are temperature, C/N ratio, phosphorous, sulphur, moisture, particle size, oxygen flow, *etc*.

- **Temperature:** Optimum temperature for aerobic composting is 70ºC. High temperature results in increased rate of biological activity and faster stabilization of the material.Very high temperature results in Nitrogen loss. High temperatures ensure destruction of pathogens and parasites.
- **C/N ratio:** Optimum ratio is 30. To bring down the ratio sewage and sludge are added. To increase the ratio straw, sawdust, paper are added.
- **Phosphorous:** One of the essential nutrients for plant growth and determines the quality of compost. Phosphorous concentration might increase as composting proceeds.
- **Sulphur:** Presence of Sulphur in sufficient quantities can lead to the production of volatile, odorous compounds. The major sources of Sulphur are two amino acids (cysteine and methionine). Under well-aerated conditions, the sulfides are oxidized to sulfates, but under anaerobic conditions, they are converted to volatile organic sulfides or to H_2S, leading to a bad odor. Some compounds like carbon disulfide, carbonyl sulfide, methyl mercaptan, diethyl sulfide, dimethyl sulfide, and dimethyl disulfide might also lead to bad odors.
- **Moisture:** Optimum is 50 to 60%, very high moisture content will result in anaerobic condition. Higher moisture content is essential for mechanical operated system and when the waste contains high percentage of fibrous material.
- **Oxygen and aeration:** In case of aerobic process, it helps to decompose the organic matter at a faster rate. However, care must be taken not to provide more oxygen which might dry the system and slow down the composting process.
- **Particle size:** Smaller particles produce homogenous particle size which helps to maintain optimum temperatures. But too fine particle may not allow air to flow into the piles.

Physical and Chemical Properties of High Quality Compost are given below.

Physical Properties

Density: 500-800 g/L

Water content: 30-45%

Foreign substances: < 0.5%

stones: < 5%

Granulation size: Fine grained 4-12 m, coarse grained 12-40 mm.

Chemical Properties

Nutrient content should be within the following values (% TS / % Dry Matter):

N: 0.5 to 1.8

P_2O_5: 0.4 to 1.0
K_2O: 0.6 to 1.8
MgO: 0.7 to 3.0
CaO: 3.0 to 12.0
Salinity: 1.0-8.0 g kCl/L
pH: 7–8
Content of organic matter:
Measured as ignition loss – 20-50%
Matured compost – 20% organic matter
Raw compost -> 40% organic matter
Low content of heavy metals:
Lead: 50 to 100
Cadmium: 0.1 to 1.0
Chromium: 26 to 60
Copper: 30 to 50
Nickel: 10 to 30
Mercury: 0.1 to 0.5
Zinc: 150 to 350

Aerobic Composting

In aerobic process, aerobic micro-organisms oxidize organic compounds to carbon dioxide, nitrite and nitrate. This carbon is used as a source of energy while nitrogen is recycled (high nitrogen waste will grow bacteria). Due to this exothermic reaction the temperature of the mass rises and thus the organic waste will break down quickly and is free from odour. Some of the basic aerobic composting techniques are Indore method composting, windrow composting, vermi composting, in-vessel composting, *etc*. Aerobic composting of MSW is commonly carried out in windrows.

Indore Method of Composting

In this method composting is done in pits which involves filling of alternate layers of Solid Waste and night soil. The pit will be completely filled and a final soil layer is laid to prevent fly breeding, entry of rain water and for conservation of released energy.To ensure aerobic condition the material is turned at specific intervals for which a 60 cm strip on the longitudinal side of the pit is kept vacant. The first turn is manually given using long handled rakes 4 to 7 days after filling. The second turn is given after 5 to 10 more days. Further turning is normally not required and the compost is ready in 2 to 4 weeks. This method stabilizes the material in shorter time and needs lesser space. As no odorous gases are generated in this process, it is environment friendly & hence commonly preferred. While the organic matter is stabilized during the composting process, the moisture content also changes. The non-decomposable materials are rejected. Hence the quantity of compost is much lesser than the input and is normally around 50% and the exact value depends upon the characteristics of the input material.

Windrow Composting

Windrow composting is widely used in India at a large scale as the climatic condition is arid. Therefore, in areas where higher ambient temperatures are available, composting in open triangular or trapezoidal windrows is preferred. Windrow composting is the process of decomposing organic materials to form stabilized organic material. Compost is used in agriculture, horticulture, home gardening, land reclamation, wetland mitigation, and erosion prevention to help rebuild soil organic matter and to provide a good medium for plant growth. The limitation to this technology is the limited markets for compost used and environmental concerns about industrial or toxic wastes that may enter the waste stream and end up in the compost.

Windrow area should be with an impermeable base made from concrete of compacted clay of 40 to 50 cm thick. A slope of 1-2 % should be maintained in the base. The base should be circled with a lined drain for collection of leachate or surface runoff. Windrow composting is a two phase process.

Phase I: Rotting

- This phase starts with transferring the mechanically treated waste to a specific area designed especially for windrows. A coarse material such as wood chips is spread over that area to enhance ventilation and drainage at the bottom of the windrow, and to prevent saturation that might cause anaerobic conditions.
- Triangular or trapezoidal windrows are made parallel to each other with enough distance in between. The length and the number of windrows would depend on the quantity of organic waste that the plant is receiving. However, the following dimensions should be maintained.
  - Length of windrow = 100–130 m
  - Width of windrow = 3 m (base)
  - Height of windrow = 1.5 m
- Turning of waste and addition of water by special machine provides the oxygen and water necessary for aerobic decomposition. Air can be pumped into the waste for good ventilation (forced aeration). The waste remains in windrows for 12 weeks to decompose with turning and addition of water twice a week during the first three weeks and once a week for the remaining period. Windrows should be covered with special cover to prevent evaporation but without preventing air intrusion.

Phase II: Rotting

- In this phase, the fresh compost produced in the first phase is transferred to another area & piled up and kept to mature for a period of four weeks, without turning & water addition. Matured and dry compost (water content = 25 - 30%) is produced.
- The matured compost is separated into two fractions, fine and coarse by sieving. The fine fraction is packed in suitable quantities according to it purpose of used. The coarse fraction is sold without packaging.

Steps in windrow composting and windrow composting procedure is shown below in figure.

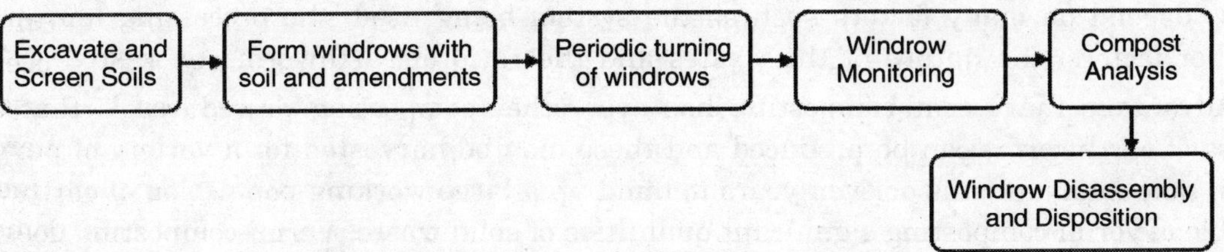

Figure 1.3: Steps in Windrow Composting

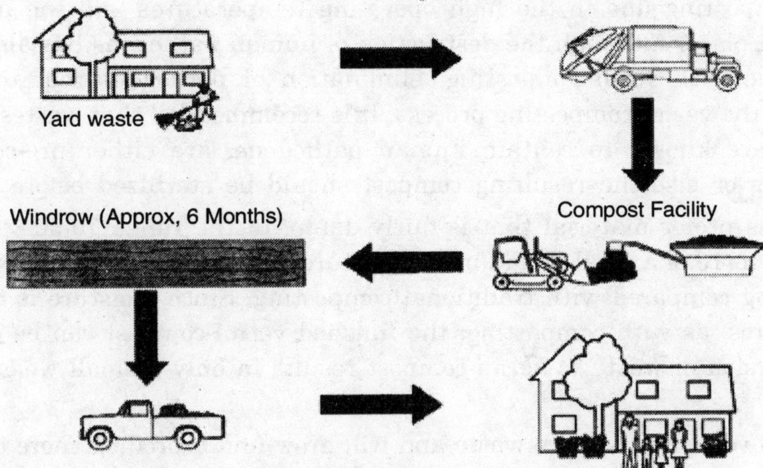

Figure 1.4: Windrow Composting Procedure

Vermi-composting

In vermi-composting, the aerobic decomposition of organic matter present in solid waste is by using microorganisms/earthworms to help decompose and transform organic wastes into useful compost. In this method, earthworms play important role in fragmenting, mixing and aerating the waste.

Vermi-composting is carried out at relatively low temperatures (under 25°C), compared with composting, where pile temperatures can exceed 70°C. With vermi-composting it is vitally important to keep low temperature; otherwise the earthworms will be killed. It is the joint action between earthworms and the aerobic microorganisms that thrive in these lower temperatures (mesophilic) that breaks down the waste. Hence it is common with vermi-composting systems to apply waste frequently in thin layers, a few centimeters thick, to beds or boxes containing earthworms in order to prevent overheating and to help the waste aerobic.In vermi composting, waste particles spend only a few hours inside the earthworm's gut and most the decomposition is actually carried out by microorganisms either before or after passing through the earthworm. Hence, earthworms accelerate waste decomposition rather than being the direct agent.

With in-vessel and windrow composting it usually takes at least six to twelve weeks to produce stable compost and vermi-composting takes around the same time. However, processing rates depend on many factors such as the system being used, the processing temperature & other factors, the nature of the wastes and the ratio of earthworms to waste.

Advantage that vermi-composting has over other composting procedures is that a net excess of earthworms can be produced and these may be harvested for a variety of purposes. It can take many months or even years to build up a large working population of earthworms capable of vermi-composting significant quantities of solid waste. Vermi-composting does have one serious disadvantage and this relates to the destruction of human and plant pathogens that can be present in some wastes. Destruction of most pathogens is more easily achieved in windrow composting due to the high operating temperatures and the intense microbial reactions taking place. Although the destruction of human pathogens has also been shown to be very effective with vermicomposting, elimination of pathogens requires very effective management of the vermi-composting process. It is recommended that wastes, such as sewage sludge, which are known to contain human pathogens, are either pre-composted before vermicomposting or else the resulting compost should be sterilized before use.

Earthworms prefer material that is fairly damp, in the range 70-90% moisture. Hence there is usually more of a need to add more moisture to the waste material before and during vermi-composting compared with traditional composting. Since moisture is not driven off by high temperatures, as with composting, the finished vermi-compost can be quite moist, and often the conversion of waste to vermi-compost results in only a small weight loss, typically around 10%.

Earthworms will process more waste and will grow and reproduce more quickly when fed with some wastes. Sewage sludge, animal manures, paper pulps, processed food slurries, brewery waste, mixed household waste, garden and vegetable wastes and many other biodegradable materials are used on a large scale to produce vermi-compost and to breed earthworms. Vermi-composting is similar to traditional composting in the sense that materials with carbon:nitrogen (C: N) ratios in the range 15–35:1 are considered suitable.Generally, fresh, finely shredded organic materials which, decompose easily will sustain the greatest numbers and diversity of microorganisms and this in turn will result in rapid decomposition and produce the highest earthworm growth and reproduction. The density of earthworms in any vermi-composting system is related to the rate of waste processing and if vermi-compost production is the main aim then it is advisable to maintain a high density of mature earthworms. However, high earthworm densities will eventually reduce the number of earthworms produced, by regulating growth and reproduction. Hence, if the main aim is to produce a net surplus of earthworms, comparatively low densities of immature earthworms should be used.

Rapid Composting Methods

Traditional composting methods take as long as 4 to 8 months to produce finished compost, while rapid composting process offer possibilities for reducing the processing period up to three weeks. A variety of approaches are used to hasten the composting process, which include active windrows, passive windrows, aerated static windrow, in-vessel composting, vermin-composting, *etc*. Most of these methods are based on aerobic process:

(a) Active windrows: Organic waste is placed in long windrows and turned manually or mechanically by front end loaders or turners. The optimum height and width of the windrows depends on the type of equipment used to turn them. The mechanical equipment is so selected to compact the composting material and results in less composting periods and good consistent quality product. Frequency of turning can be determined by knowing the temperature within the windrows.

(b) Passive windrows: Compost in windrows is produced by natural aeration over long periods of time. Porosity of the initial mix, uniform product mixing and particle size greatly improve the speed of the process and product quality. This method eliminates turning by supplying air to the composting materials through perforated pipes (with pipe ends open) embedded in each windrow. Air flows into the pipes and through the windrow because of the chimney effect created as the hot gases rise upward out of the windrow. The windrow should be well insulated with covering material. As the composting material is not turned after the windrows are formed, they must be thoroughly mixed before they are placed in the windrow. During construction of windrow, compaction should be avoided while mixing of materials. Aeration pipes are placed on top of the compost base. When the composting period is completed, the pipes are simply pulled out, and the base material is mixed with the compost.

(c) Aerated static windrows: Compost is produced in windrows with mechanical aeration and air is supplied through perforated plastic pipes, aeration cones or a perforated floor. Aeration is accomplished either by forcing or drawing air through the compost pile. Aeration systems can be relatively simple using electrical motors, fans and ducting, or they can be more sophisticated using sensors and alarms. This system of aeration requires electricity at the site and appropriate ventilation fans, ducts and monitoring equipment which determines the timing, duration & direction of airflow. The pile should be placed after the floors are first covered with a layer of a bulking agent, such as wood chips or finished compost. The material to be composted is then added and a topping layer of finished compost applied to provide insulation.

(d) In-vessel composting: In-vessel composting refers to a group of methods which confine the composting materials within a building, container, or vessel. In-vessel methods rely on a variety of forced aeration and mechanical turning techniques to speed up the composting process.

There are a variety of in-vessel methods with different combinations of vessels, aeration devices, and turning mechanisms. Some of the in-vessel methods are bin/box, channels, rotating drums, *etc.*

Aeration of the material is accomplished by continuous agitation using aerating machines which operate in concrete bays or by fans providing air flow from ducts built into concrete floors. The main advantages of the in-vessel system over other methods are; more efficient composting process and a decreased number of pathogens resulting in a safer and more valuable end product. In-vessel composting can maintain a rapid decomposition process year-round regardless of external ambient conditions.

Disadvantages of the enclosed vessel method include high capital and operational costs due to the use of computerized equipment and skilled labour. In-vessel composters are generally more automated than active or static pile systems and can produce a top quality finished product on a consistent basis.

Anaerobic Composting

Anaerobic composting is also called anaerobic digestion or bio-gasification. This technology is the biological conversion of biodegradable organic materials in the absence of oxygen at temperatures lower than 93°C. Therefore very slow working bacteria will be growing which does not require any air and the compost may take long period to break down. This breakdown process is carried out by anaerobic micro-organisms that convert carbon-containing compounds to a biogas (primarily methane and carbon dioxide). A very small quantity of energy is released during this process and the temperature of the composting mass does not raise much. This is a reduction process and final product is subjected to minor oxidation when applied on land. The residue is a stabilized organic material that can be used as a soil amendment. Anaerobic composts may have awful smell. Anaerobic digestion is suitable for the bio-degradables, including food wastes, yard waste, animal wastes, and some paper fibers. Bangalore method is an example of anaerobic composting

Bangalore Method of Composting

This is an anaerobic method conventionally carried out in pits. Formerly the waste was anaerobically stabilized in pits where alternate layers of Solid Waste and night soil were laid.

The pit is completely filled and a final soil layer is laid to prevent fly breeding, entry of rain water into the pit and for conservation of the released energy. The material is allowed to decompose for 4 to 6 months after which the stabilized material is taken out and used as compost. The Bangalore method requires longer time for stabilization of the material and hence needs larger land space. The gases generated in this anaerobic process also pose smell & odour problems.

Biomethanation/Anaerobic Digestion

Biomethanation is the process of conversion of organic matter in the waste (liquid or solid) to biomethane ("biogas") and manure by microbial action in the absence of air, known as "anaerobic digestion".

The solid waste and the slaughterhouse waste is first mixed with raw sewage and conveyed to the primary digester. Effluent from the primary digester is sent to the secondary digester after stabilization. The raw gas generated from the primary and the secondary digester is then sent to the gas holders for storage purpose. The excess effluent from the secondary digester will be re-circulated back to the primary digester for further generation of gas. The gas thus stored in the gas holder is passed through a scrubber where gases like H_2S, SO_2 and moisture are removed from the gas. This clean gas is conveyed under pressure to the Power Generating Engine to produce power supply. The excess sludge from the secondary digester is conveyed to the centrifuge to separate the liquid and solids for further disposal.

Production of Methane from MSW by this process involves three basic steps:

- First step involves preparation of organic fraction of MSW, which includes receiving, sorting, separation and size reduction.
- Second step involves addition of moisture & nutrients (*e.g.*, sewage sludge), blending, pH adjustment to about 6.7, heating of the slurry to between 55 to 60^0C, and anaerobic digestion in a reactor with continuous flow, in which the contents are well mixed for a period of time varying from 5 to 10 days.
- Third step involves capture, storage and if necessary, separation of gas components evolved during digestion process.

Pelletization and Refuse Derived Fuel (RDF)

Pellets are formed from the combustible portion of MSW. Pelletization initially involves segregation of waste into high and low calorific value materials and then shredded and compacted into pellets with the required bulk density and later can be dried to get the appropriate heat value. These pellets so produced have a calorific value of 4000 kcal/kg of the product which is quite close to that of coal and therefore is a good substitute for coal, wood, *etc.* to RDF plant. Comparatively, pellets have advantages over coal and are clean, energy efficient, eco-friendly fuel for coal based industries and power generating industries. Additional advantage of Pellets is easy storage and transportation. RDF can be produced from MSW through a sequence of processes consisting of:

- Separation at source
- Sorting or mechanical separation
- Size reduction (shredding, chipping and milling)
- Blending
- Drying and pelletizing
- Packaging
- Storage

The MSW is initially dried to reduce its moisture content. It is then screened to remove inerts such as sand, silt and soil. It is then processed to remove and separate incombustible materials such as glass, metal etc. and wet organic matter such as garden & food waste containing high moisture and high ash material. Sometimes the waste is further subjected to air separation and then shredded. The reduced size material can be directly used in boilers on site. If the material is to be used offsite, it is usually densified into pellets and then transported to the place where it is to be used.

RDF can be burned for fuel by itself or co-fired with other fuels. Previously, few RDF plants were setup with coal fired boilers when RDF was used along with coal but now due to strict emission standards it is burnt in dedicated boilers designed and built specifically for RDF.

Some of the options of using RDF from MSW to energy include:

- Co-combustion in coal fired boilers
- Co-incineration in cement kilns
- Co-gasification with coal or biomass

Incineration

Incineration is a process of controlled combustion for burning of wastes and residue containing combustible material. Carbon-dioxide, water vapor, ash and non-combustible materials are end products. The heat generated during incineration is recovered and utilized for production of steam, heating water and generating electricity. Incineration is highly exothermic. Incineration is used to achieve maximum volume reduction of solid waste and when there is shortage of landfilling facilities.

The emissions from incineration of solid waste are of health concern. Incineration should meet the operating and emission standards. In order to achieve the emission standards, suitable pollution control devices should be installed or retrofitted with the incinerator. Chlorinated plastics should not be taken for incineration and also low sulphur fuel or diesel should be used as fuel in the incinerator.

It is unlikely that specialized high temperature incineration or waste to energy plant would be economic for the small refuse volumes. More basic methods of incineration such as pit incinerators may be appropriate for burning selected waste materials in order to reduce volumes to landfill.

Advantages and Disadvantages of Incineration

Advantages: The amount and volume of the MSW can be reduced significantly (up to 90% by volume and 75% by weight);

Disadvantages: Not all waste can be burned (There will still be landfills).

Waste-to-energy; Release hundreds of toxic chemicals into the atmosphere; Disposal of the ash (The toxic substance are more concentrated in the ash); Highly related to the economic condition; A classic short-term solution (it destroys potentially useful recyclable or compostable material by turning it into toxic ash); The cost of disposing waste by incineration is greater than that of putting it in a landfill.

Pyrolysis

Pyrolysis is a thermal process where organic materials present in the waste are broken down under pressure and at temperatures >500°C in the absence of oxygen to become gas comprising smaller molecules (Syngas). Along with syngas, char and oil are also produced. The gases produced comprise carbon monoxide (25%), hydrogen & hydrocarbons (15%) and carbon dioxide & nitrogen (60%). Then, syngas is cleaned and burned in internal combustion (IC) engine generator sets or turbines to produce electricity.

The syngas produced can be utilized in boilers, gas turbines, or internal-combustion engines to generate electricity or be further processed into organic chemicals.

Thermal cracking and condensation reactions produce gaseous, liquid and solid fractions.

Three major component fractions resulting from Pyrolysis are:

(i) Gas Stream: Syngas comprising of H_2, CH_4, CO

(ii) Tar and/or oil stream: Liquid at room temperature containing chemicals such as acetic acid, acetone and methanol

(iii) A char consists of almost pure carbon plus any inert material that may have entered the process.

Out of the heat contained in the waste, 67-75% is recovered. However, when the heat recovered is compared to that provided as input, there is a heat loss due to endothermic nature of reaction.

The main advantages of pyrolysis in comparison to incineration are:

- The decomposition temperature is lower than the incineration temperature, so the thermal distress of the whole facility is less intense than in incineration.
- The decomposition takes place in reducing atmosphere and not in oxidizing like in incineration. The demand for less oxygen is also the reason for less air emissions in the case of pyrolysis.
- The ash content in carbon is much higher than in the case of incineration.
- The metals that are included in waste are not oxidized during pyrolysis and have higher commercial value.
- The produced gas is at different hearth and probably other site from the pyrolytic reactor.
- No ash is produced from the combustion of the pyrolysis gas and the cleaning of the off-gas is a simpler process.
- The initial waste volume is reduced at higher level in comparison with the incineration.

The main disadvantages of pyrolysis include:

- The big problem of this technique is that pre-treatment is required including cutting and separation of waste prior to pyrolysis which can increase the cost for the installation and operation of such units substantially.
- The pyrolysis products cannot be disposed without further treatment.
- The facilities for cleaning the gases and wastewater require extremely high cost.
- At present, the application of the method at large scale is limited. Nevertheless, the prospects for reactors of average temperature with the form of rotary drum or fluidized bed seem to be better.

Gasification

Gasification is the partial combustion of organic matter in the presence of restricted quantity of oxygen or air at high temperatures (than Pyrolysis). The gas so produced is producer gas. The producer gas is cleaned and burned in internal combustion (IC) engine generator sets or turbines to produce electricity.

The processes are carried out at a temperature between 500-1000°C to produce three component streams:

(i) Gas: Producer gas which is a mixture of combustible gases such as H_2, CO, CO_2, CH_4 and some hydrocarbons.

(ii) Liquid: It contains tar, pitch, light oil and low boiling organic chemicals like acetic acid, acetone, methanol *etc*.

(iii) Char: It consists of elemental carbon along with the inert materials in the incoming waste.

Landfills

Landfills are vital components of any well-designed Solid Waste management system. The afe and effective operation of landfills depends on sound planning, administration, and management of the entire MSW management system. Unscientific landfilling/dumping of solid waste pose problems of:

- Pollution in surface run-off during rainfall and leachate discharges to surface water channels.
- Pollution of soil/groundwater/down stream aquifers.
- Unhygienic/unsanitary condition in surrounding area.

Landfill can be of the following types:

- Sanitary landfill/bioreactor landfill/engineered sanitary landfill: Mixed waste with landfill gas recovery, leachate collection system and storm water management system.
- Secured MSW landfill: Inert waste without landfill gas recovery.
- Monofills: Only one kind of waste is used.

Sanitary Landfill

Sanitary landfill is the process of dumping of solid waste in a scientifically designed land area spreading waste in thin layers, compacting to the smallest volume and covering with soil on daily basis. Sanitary landfill would be good option for disposal of existing/mixed waste which cannot be segregated. Landfill gas such as methane from the anaerobic conditions prevailing in the landfill due to the presence of organic material in mixed waste can be recovered. The facilities at the sanitary landfill include leachate collection & treatment system, storm water management system avoiding ground & surface water pollution.

The overall approach to the development of any sanitary or engineered landfill is formulated to satisfy the regulatory requirement of Environmental protection and cost effectiveness.

The landfill so designed should be aimed to minimize the following:

- The ingress of water into the landfill.
- The production of leachate, its subsequent outflow and uncontrolled dispersions into surrounding aquatic environment.
- The accumulation, migration and uncontrolled release of landfill gas into the atmosphere.

Landfill Design Concepts and Considerations

- Collection of Baseline data such as temperature, rainfall, population, socio-economic status, terrain features, soil characteristics, geological parameters, ground water table, flood plains, transportation, etc.
- Waste management studies generated within the locality: Waste composition, chemical and physical characteristics, etc.

- Field investigations on handling, collection, transportation and disposal of waste.
- Pre-feasibility studies on availability of methane gases from the proposed landfill.
- Selection of landfill method based on design life and other baseline factors.
  - Landfill above ground level, landfill below ground level, slope landfill, valley landfills, combination of slope with others.
- Estimates on quantity and quality of leachate generated based on precipitation
- Defining the landfill foot print area based on the quantity/volume of existing and new waste and preparing a layout plan.
  - The layout plan may include access roads, Weighbridge, leachate collection system, waste processing area, storm water management system, administrative office building, temporary storage and transfer area for waste, drainage facilities, landfill gas collection and management facilities, safety provisions, etc.
- Developing operating methodology: Cell or phase wise operation for progressive use of landfill.
- Selection of base liners: It is recommended that for all MSW landfills the following single liner system be adopted as a minimum requirement.
- Leachate drainage layer of 30 cm thick made of granular soil having permeability greater than 10^{-2} cm/sec.
  - Protection layer of silty soil of 20 to 30 cm thick.
  - Geomembrane of thickness 1.5 mm or more.
  - Compacted clay barrier of 1 m thickness having permeability of less than 10^{-7} cm/sec.
- Selection of final covers: Vegetative cover, gas venting layer, drainage layer with appropriate thicknesses.
- Final cover should be provided a slope of 3 to 5 % for proper surface water drainage.
- Designing leachate collection system including perforated HDPE pipes, drainage layer, leachate collection sumps, leachate trenches, located with appropriate slopes to maximize the leachate flow in the pipes.
  - Leachate drainage layer is usually 30 cm thick with slope of 2% or higher.
  - The pipe spacing is governed by the requirement that the leachate head should not be greater than drainage layer thickness.
  - Design of wells/side slopes risers for leachate removal.
  - Design of holding tank.
  - Estimating size of pipes, sumps and pumps.
  - Deciding the leachate management option: Leachate discharge to waste water treatment system, recirculation within the landfill for faster decomposition of biodegradable waste, evaporation of leachate, treatment of leachate based on its characteristics.
- Landfill gas collection and management system with a safe gas venting system to collect the gas consisting of HDPE pipes.

The gas control system involves the following features:

– A containment system which encloses the gas within the site and prevents migration outside the landfill.

– A system for collecting and removing landfill gas from within the landfill and in particular from the perimeter of the landfill.

– A system for flaring or utilizing the collected gas with adequate back up facilities.

– Gas vents will be placed 30 to 75 m on the landfill cover and level of methane will be monitored regularly.

- Designing storm water management system for the maximum rainfall intensity to avoid surface water pollution and include storm water ponds, swales, etc based the annual rainfall, slope of the area,
- Stability of the landfill: stability analysis shall be conducted for the following cases:
  – Stability of excavated slopes.
  – Stability of liner system along excavated slopes.
  – Stability of temporary waste slopes constructed to their full height.
  – Stability of slopes of above ground portion of completed landfills.
  – Stability of cover systems in above ground landfills.
- Equipments for landfill site operations: Weighbridge, tipper, Compactor, JCB, etc. their number would depend on the quantity of waste to be handled.
- Site infrastructure: Administrative office, storeroom, parking area, weighbridge, access roads, waste segregation area, vehicle cleaning area, waste inspection and transfer, site fencing, green belt, lighting, etc.
- Environmental monitoring plan to ensure optimal performance of the landfill: Monitoring of environmental parameters like – surface water quality, ground water quality, leachate quality, ambient air quality during the active and post closure period.
- Location criteria for landfills as per environmental regulation guidelines:
  – No landfill within 200 m of a lake or pond.
  – No landfill within 100 m from river.
  – No landfill within flood prone areas.
  – No landfill within 200 m of right of way of any state or National Highway.
  – No landfill within 500 m from a notified habitant area.
  – No landfill within 300 m of public park.
  – No landfills within wetlands.
  – No landfill within 20 km of an airport or airbase.
  – No landfill in a coastal regulation zone.
  – No landfill in potentially unstable zones.
  – Landfill should have a buffer zone around it up to a distance prescribed by the regulatory agencies.

- Exclude the areas with unstable geological features such as weak soils (organic soils or soft clay or clay-sand mixtures or soils that lose strength with compaction or with wetting, *etc.*)
- Exclude the areas with high population, unique archaeological, historical, paleontogical and religious interests.
- Exclude areas of ground water recharge and extremely high water table zone.
- Exclude areas prone to natural hazards (such as volcanic activity, seismic disturbance and landslides).
- Exclude areas with subsidence (such as owing to subsurface mines; water, oil or gas withdrawal; or solution-prone subsurface).
- Exclude agricultural/forest areas.

In exceptional cases, the committee may consider certain sites if it has reasons to believe that the proposed mitigation measures can ensure anticipated impacts within the acceptable limits.

Bioreactor Landfill

A bioreactor landfill is a sanitary landfill that uses enhanced microbiological processes to transform and stabilize the readily and moderately decomposable organic solid waste constituents within 5 to 10 years of bioreactor process implementation. The bioreactor landfill significantly increases the extent of organic waste decomposition, conversion rates and process effectiveness over what would otherwise occur within the landfill. The "bioreactor landfill" provides control and process optimization, primarily through the addition of leachate or other liquid amendments, the addition of sewage sludge or other amendments, temperature control, and nutrient supplementation. Beyond that, bioreactor landfill operation may involve the addition of air. Based on waste biodegradation mechanisms, different kinds of "bioreactor landfills" including anaerobic bioreactors, aerobic bioreactors, and aerobic-anaerobic (hybrid) bioreactors have been constructed and operated worldwide.

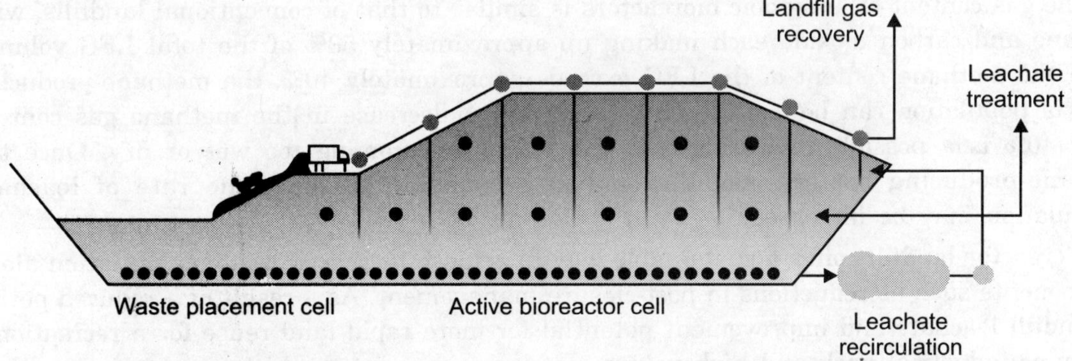

Figure 1.6: Schematic Diagram of Bioreactor Landfill

Aerobic landfill processes are analogous to wet composting operations in which biodegradable materials are rapidly biodegraded using air, moisture, and increased temperatures created by biodegradation. First liquid is pumped under pressure into the waste mass through injection wells in order to maintain moisture content between 50 to 70% by weight. Once optimal moisture conditions have been reached, air injection commences. Blowers are used to force air into the waste mass through a network of perforated wells that have been installed in the landfill. The rates of injection of air and leachate into the landfill are similar to the air and moisture application rates used in many composting systems. The aerobic process continues until most of the easily and moderately degradable compounds have been degraded and the compost temperature gradually decreases during the final phase of "curing" or maturation of the remaining organic matter.

Aerobic bioreactor landfills are operationally more intense than anaerobic bioreactor landfills; however, post closure costs would be substantially lower due to reductions in landfill gas (LFG) generation and cover settlement.

Anaerobic bioreactor landfills tend to stabilize the landfilled waste rapidly by the addition of moisture (through recirculation of leachate) to uniformly wet the waste mass. Landfill degradation of MSW frequently is rate-limited by insufficient moisture. The maximum methane production in landfills occurs at moisture content of 60-80% wet weight, for which reason, most landfills are well below the optimum moisture content for methane production. In addition, the liquid absorptive capacity of the waste, in general, is about 16-29% or about 150-300 litres/m^3 of waste which represents a large potential capacity for leachate storage.

Leachate can be injected into the waste via horizontal trenches, vertical wells, surface infiltration ponds, spraying, and pre wetting of waste. Anaerobic bioreactor landfills initially should be carefully monitored. If the waste is wetted too rapidly, a buildup of volatile organic acids might lower the leachate pH, inhibiting the methane-producing bacteria population and reducing the rate of biodegradation. Leachate parameters (such as pH, volatile organic acids, and alkalinity) and LFG parameters (such as methane content) are direct indicators of an established methane-producing bacteria population. Optimal conditions for methane-producing bacteria are a pH of greater than 6.5. A high volatile organic acids-to-alkalinity ratio (>0.25) indicates that the leachate might have a low buffering capacity and conditions could soon inhibit methane generation.

The gas content of anaerobic bioreactors is similar to that of conventional landfills, with methane and carbon dioxide each making up approximately 50% of the total LFG volume. When the methane content of the LFG exceeds approximately 40%, the methane-producing bacteria population can be considered established. A decrease in the methane gas content below 40% is a possible indication that the waste is becoming too wet or dry. Once the methane-producing bacteria population has become established, the rate of leachate recirculation may be increased.

Bioreactor landfills offer a sustainable way to achieve increased waste degradation along with benefits such as reductions in post-closure management. As a result of a reduced period for landfill leachate and improvement potential for more rapid land reuse for a recreational facility or industrial park and high volumes of gas is generated which can be recovered as a potential source of energy. Bioreactor landfills have advantages over traditional landfills. They reduce the cost of removing and disposing leachate, which is used on site. Anaerobic bioreactors begin producing methane much more quickly than landfills designed to inhibit degradation. Bioreactors also gain space as the waste degrades, meaning more waste can be added.

Secured MSW Landfill for Inerts

A secured landfill is a carefully engineered depression in the ground (or built on top of the ground) into which wastes are dumped to avoid pollution to the surrounding environment. Secured MSW landfill should be restricted to non-biodegradable, inert waste and other waste not suitable for recycling or for biological processing.

The important features that should be considered before designing a landfill include:

- Site Selection
- Facilities at the site
- Specifications for land filling
- Pollution prevention
- Water quality monitoring
- Plantation at landfill site
- Closure of landfill site and post care
- Special provisions for hilly areas

Environmental and Health risk concerns of improper solid waste management.

Potential hazards of solid wastes are numerous to the living community when it is improperly managed. Solid wastes have the potential to pollute all the vital components of living environment (*i.e.*, air, land and water). Some of the hazards caused by solid wastes are listed below;

- Uncollected wastes often end up in drains, causing blockages that result in flooding and unsanitary conditions.
- Open and overflowing bins attract stray dogs, which has been a major cause of the pread of rabies.
- Open waste bins also attract stray and domestic cattle. Cattle in the city causes nuisance by blocking the traffic on the roads. Cattle that graze on the waste from bins end up eating the plastic along with the vegetable matter, which proves to be fatal for them. The milk obtained from the cattle that feed on waste can be contaminated and can prove to be unsafe for human health.
- Flies breed in some constituents of solid wastes, and flies are very effective vectors that spread disease.
- Mosquitoes breed in blocked drains and in rainwater that is retained in discarded cans, tire and other objects. Mosquitoes spread disease, including malaria and dengue.
- Rats find shelter and food in waste dumps. Rats consume and spoil food, spread disease, damage electrical cables and other materials and inflict unpleasant bites.
- The open burning of waste causes air pollution; the products of combustion include dioxins that are particularly hazardous.

- Aerosols and dusts can spread fungi and pathogens from uncollected and decomposing wastes.
- Uncollected waste degrades the urban environment, discouraging efforts to keep streets and open spaces in a clean and hygienic condition. Plastic bags are in particular an aesthetic nuisance.
- Waste collection workers face particular occupational hazards, including strains from lifting, injuries from sharp objects and contact with pathogens when manually handling the waste.
- Dangerous items (such as broken glass, razor blades, hypodermic needles and other healthcare wastes, aerosol cans and potentially explosive containers and chemicals from industries) may pose risks of injury or poisoning, particularly to children and people who sort through the waste.
- Heavy refuse collection trucks can cause significant damage to the surfaces of roads that were not designed for such weights.
- Waste items that are reused without being cleaned effectively or sterilized can transmit infection to later users. (Examples are bottles and medical supplies.)
- Polluted water (leachate) flowing from waste dumps and disposal sites can cause serious pollution of water supplies, ponds and lakes. Chemical wastes (especially persistent organics) may be fatal or have serious effects if ingested, inhaled or touched and can cause widespread pollution of water supplies.
- Waste that is treated or disposed of in unsatisfactory ways can cause a severe aesthetic nuisance in terms of smell and appearance.
- Liquids and fumes, escaping from deposits of wastes (perhaps formed as a result of chemical reactions between components in the wastes), can have fatal or other serious effects.
- Methane (one of the main components of landfill gas) is much more effective than carbon dioxide as a greenhouse gas, leading to climate change.
- Fires on disposal sites can cause major air pollution, causing illness and reducing visibility, making disposal sites dangerously unstable, causing explosions of cans, and possibly spreading to adjacent property.
- Former disposal sites provide very poor foundation support for large buildings, so buildings constructed on former sites are prone to collapse.
- Rag pickers working on landfill are prone to many diseases like respiratory infections such as lung impairment. In a study carried out in Delhi slum, nearly 75 rag pickers from the sample group of 98 had higher frequency of upper respiratory symptoms (sinusitis, running or stuffy nose, sore throat, common cold, fever) and 81.6 % showed lower respiratory symptoms (dry cough, cough with phlegm, wheezing, and chest discomfort) and breathing problem.

CHAPTER 2

Municipal Solid Waste (MSW) Management

SECTION-A: SOURCES AND TYPES OF MUNICIPAL SOLID WASTES

Due to rapid increase in the production and consumption processes, societies generate as well as reject solid materials regularly from various sectors—agricultural, commercial, domestic, industrial and institutional. The considerable volume of wastes thus generated and rejected is called solid wastes. In other words, solid wastes are the wastes arising from human and animal activities that are normally solid and are discarded as useless or unwanted.

Solid Waste

Solid waste refers to non-soluble material such as agricultural refuse, industrial waste, mining residues, demolition waste, municipal garbage or even sewage sludge. Most of these kinds of wastes cannot be recycled or rehabilitated for further use.

Solid Waste Management

Solid waste management (SWM) is associated with the control of waste generation, its storage, collection, transfer & transport, processing and disposal in a manner that is in accordance with the best principles of public health, economics, engineering, conservation, aesthetics, public attitude and other environmental considerations.

SWM processes differ depending on factors such as economic status (*e.g.*, the ratio of wealth created by the production of primary products to that derived from manufactured goods, per capita income, etc.), degree of industrialisation, social development (*e.g.*, education, literacy, healthcare, etc.) and quality of life of a location. In addition, regional, seasonal and economic differences influence the SWM processes.

CLASSIFICATION OF SOLID WASTES

Solid wastes are the organic and inorganic waste materials such as product packaging, grass clippings, furniture, clothing, bottles, kitchen refuse, paper, appliances, paint cans, batteries, etc., produced in a society, which do not generally carry any value to the first user(s). Solid wastes, thus, encompass both a heterogeneous mass of wastes from the urban community as well as a more homogeneous accumulation of agricultural, industrial and mineral wastes. While wastes have little or no value in one setting or to the one who wants to dispose them, the discharged wastes may gain significant value in another setting. Knowledge of the sources and types of solid wastes as well as the information on composition and the rate at which wastes are generated/ disposed is, therefore, essential for the design and operation of the functional elements associated with the management of solid wastes.

Source-based classification

(i) **Residential:** This refers to wastes from dwellings, apartments, etc., and consists of leftover food, vegetable peels, plastic, clothes, ashes, etc.

(ii) **Commercial**: This refers to wastes consisting of leftover food, glasses, metals, ashes, etc., generated from stores, restaurants, markets, hotels, motels, auto-repair shops, medical facilities, etc.

(iii) **Institutional:** This mainly consists of paper, plastic, glasses, etc., generated from educational, administrative and public buildings such as schools, colleges, offices, prisons, etc.

(iv) **Municipal:** This includes dust, leafy matter, building debris, treatment plant residual sludge, etc., generated from various municipal activities like construction and demolition, street cleaning, landscaping, etc.

(v) **Industrial**: This mainly consists of process wastes, ashes, demolition and construction wastes, hazardous wastes, etc., due to industrial activities.

(vi) **Agricultural:** This mainly consists of spoiled food grains and vegetables, agricultural remains, litter, etc., generated from fields, orchards, vineyards, farms, etc.

(vii) **Open areas:** This includes wastes from areas such as streets, alleys, parks, vacant lots, playgrounds, beaches, highways, recreational areas, etc.

Type-based Classification

Classification of wastes based on types, *i.e.*, physical, chemical, and biological characteristics of wastes, is as follows:

(i) **Garbage:** This refers to animal and vegetable wastes resulting from the handling, sale, storage, preparation, cooking and serving of food. Garbage comprising these wastes contains putrescible (rotting) organic matter, which produces an obnoxious odour and attracts rats and other vermin. It, therefore, requires special attention in storage, handling and disposal.

(ii) **Ashes and residues:** These are substances remaining from the burning of wood, coal, charcoal, coke and other combustible materials for cooking and heating in houses, institutions and small industrial establishments. When produced in large quantities, as in power-generation plants and factories, these are classified as industrial wastes. Ashes consist of fine powdery residue, cinders and clinker often mixed with small pieces of metal and glass. Since ashes and residues are almost entirely inorganic, they are valuable in landfills.

(iii) Combustible and non-combustible wastes: These consist of wastes generated from households, institutions, commercial activities, etc., excluding food wastes and other highly putrescible material. Typically, while combustible material consists of paper, cardboard, textile, rubber, garden trimmings, etc., non-combustible material consists of such items as glass, crockery, tin and aluminium cans, ferrous and non-ferrous material and dirt.

(iv) Bulky wastes: These include large household appliances such as refrigerators, washing machines, furniture, crates, vehicle parts, tyres, wood, trees and branches. Since these household wastes cannot be accommodated in normal storage containers, they require a special collection mechanism.

(v) Street wastes: These refer to wastes that are collected from streets, walkways, alleys, parks and vacant plots, and include paper, cardboard, plastics, dirt, leaves and other vegetable matter. Littering in public places is indeed a widespread and acute problem in many countries including India, and a solid waste management system must address this menace appropriately.

(vi) Biodegradable and non-biodegradable wastes: Biodegradable wastes mainly refer to substances consisting of organic matter such as leftover food, vegetable and fruit peels, paper, textile, wood, etc., generated from various household and industrial activities. Because of the action of micro-organisms, these wastes are degraded from complex to simpler compounds. Non-biodegradable wastes consist of inorganic and recyclable materials such as plastic, glass, cans, metals, etc.

(vii) Dead animals: With regard to municipal wastes, dead animals are those that die naturally or are accidentally killed on the road. Note that this category does not include carcasses and animal parts from slaughter-houses, which are regarded as industrial wastes. Dead animals are divided into two groups – large and small. Among the large animals are horses, cows, goats, sheep, pigs, etc., and among the small ones are dogs, cats, rabbits, rats, etc.The reason for this differentiation is that large animals require special equipment for lifting and handling when they are removed. If not collected promptly, dead animals pose a threat to public health since they attract flies and other vermin as they decay. Their presence in public places is particularly offensive from the aesthetic point of view as well.

(viii) Abandoned vehicles: This category includes automobiles, trucks and trailers that are abandoned on streetsand other public places. However, abandoned vehicles have significant scrap value for their metal, and their value to collectors is highly variable.

(ix) Construction and demolition(C&D) wastes: These are wastes generated as a result of construction, refurbishment, repair and demolition of houses, commercial buildings and other structures. They consist mainly of earth, stones, concrete, bricks, lumber, roofing and plumbing materials, heating systems and electrical wires and parts of the general municipal waste stream.

(x) **Farm Wastes:** These wastes result from diverse agricultural activities such as planting, harvesting, production of milk, rearing of animals for slaughter and the operation of feedlots. In many areas, the disposal of animal waste has become a critical problem, especially from feedlots, poultry farms and dairies.

(xi) **Hazardous wastes:** Hazardous wastes are those defined as wastes of industrial, institutional or consumer origin that are potentially dangerous either immediately or over a period of time to human beings and the environment. This is due to their physical, chemical and biological or radioactive characteristics like ignitability, corrosivity, reactivity and toxicity. Note that in some cases, the active agents may be liquid or gaseous hazardous wastes. These are, nevertheless, classified as solid wastes as they are confined in solid containers. Typical examples of hazardous wastes are empty containers of solvents, paints and pesticides, which are frequently mixed with municipal wastes and become part of the urban waste stream. Certain hazardous wastes may cause explosions in incinerators and fires at landfill sites. Others such as pathological wastes from hospitals and radioactive wastes also require special handling. Effective management practices should ensure that hazardous wastes are stored, collected, transported and disposedof separately, preferably after suitable treatment to render them harmless.

(xii) **Sewage wastes:** The solid by-products of sewage treatment are classified as sewage wastes. They are mostly organic and derived from the treatment of organic sludge separated from both raw and treated sewages. The inorganic fraction of raw sewage such as grit and eggshells is separated at the preliminary stage of treatment, as it may entrain putrescible organic matter with pathogens and must be buried without delay.The bulk of treated, dewatered sludge is useful as a soil conditioner but is invariably uneconomical.Solid sludge, therefore, enters the stream of municipal wastes, unlessspecial arrangements are made for its disposal.

SWM (SOLID WASTE MANAGEMENT) SYSTEM

A SWM system refers to a combination of various functional elements associated with the management of solid wastes. The system, when put in place, facilitates the collection and disposal of solid wastes in the community at minimal costs, while preserving public health and ensuring little or minimal adverse impact on the environment. The functional elements that constitute the system are:

(i) **Waste generation:** Wastes are generated at the start of any process, and thereafter, at every stage as raw materials are converted into goods for consumption. For example, wastes are generated from households, commercial areas, industries, institutions, street cleaning and other municipal services. The most important aspect of this part of the SWM system is the identification of waste.

(ii) **Waste storage:** Storage is a key functional element because collection of wastes never takes place at the source or at the time of their generation. The heterogeneous wastes generated in residential areas must be removed within 8 days due to shortage of storage space and presence of biodegradable material. Onsite storage is of primary importance due to aesthetic consideration, public health and economics involved. Some of the options for storage are plastic containers, conventional dustbins (of households), used oil drums, large storage bins (for institutions and commercial areas or servicing depots), etc.

(iii) Waste collection: This includes gathering of wastes and hauling them to the location, where the collection vehicle is emptied, which may be a transfer station (*i.e.*, intermediate station where wastes from smaller vehicles are transferred to larger ones and also segregated), a processing plant or a disposal site. Collection depends on the number of containers, frequency of collection, types of collection services and routes. Typically, collection is provided under various management arrangements, ranging from municipal servicesto franchised services, and under various forms of contracts.

(iv) Transfer and transport: This functional element involves:

The transfer of wastes from smaller collection vehicles, where necessary to overcome the problem of narrow access lanes, to larger ones at transfer stations.

The subsequent transport of the wastes, usually over long distances, to disposal sites. The factors that contribute to the designing of a transfer station include the type of transfer operation, capacity, equipment, accessories and environmental requirements.

(v) Processing: Processing is required to alter the physical and chemical characteristics of wastes for energy and resource recovery and recycling. The important processing techniques include compaction, thermal volume reduction, manual separation of waste components, incineration and composting.

(vi) Recovery and recycling: This includes various techniques, equipment and facilities used to improve both the efficiency of disposal system and recovery of usable material and energy. Recovery involves the separation of valuable resources from the mixed solid wastes, delivered at transfer stations or processing plants. It also involves size reduction and density separation by air classifier, magnetic device for iron and screens for glass. The selection of any recovery process is a function of economics, *i.e.*, costs of separation versus the recovered-material products. Certain recovered materials like glass, plastics, paper, etc., can be recycled as they have economic value.

(vii) Waste disposal: Disposal is the ultimate fate of all solid wastes, be they residential wastes, semi-solid wastes from municipal and industrial treatment plants, incinerator residues, composts or other substances that have no further use to the society. Thus, land use planning becomes a primary determinant in the selection, design and operation of landfill operations. A modern sanitary landfill is a method of disposing solid waste without creating a nuisance and hazard to public health. Generally, engineering principles are followed to confine the wastes to the smallest possible area, reduce them to the lowest particle volume by compaction at the site and cover them after each day's operation to reduce exposure to vermin. One of the most important functional elements of SWM, therefore, relates to the final use of the reclaimed land.

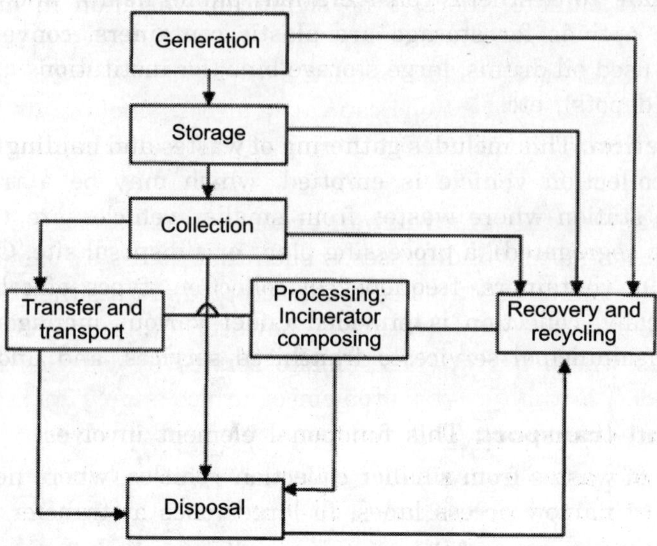

Figure 2.1: Typical SWM System: Functional Elements

Factors Affecting SWM System

(i) Quantities and characteristics of wastes: The quantities of wastes generated generally depend on the income level of a family, as higher income category tends to generate larger quantity of wastes, compared to low-income category. The quantity ranges from about 0.25 to about 2.3 kg per person per day, indicating a strong correlation between waste production and per capita income. One of the measures of waste composition (and characteristics) is density, which ranges from 150 kg/m^3 to 600 kg/m^3. Proportion of paper and packaging materials in the waste largely account for the differences. When this proportion is high, the density is low and vice versa. The wastes of high density reflect a relatively high proportion of organic matter and moisture and lower levels of recycling.

(ii) Climate and seasonal variations: There are regions in extreme north (> 70 N Latitude) and south (> 60 S Latitude), where temperatures are very low for much of the year. In cold climates, drifting snow and frozen ground interfere with landfill operations, and therefore, trenches must be dug in summer and cover material stockpiled for winter use. Tropical climates, on the other hand, are subject to sharp seasonalvariations from wet to dry season, which cause significant changes in the moisture content of solid waste, varying from less than 50% in dry season to greater than 65% in wet months. Collection and disposal of wastes in the wet months are often problematic.

High temperatures and humidity cause solid wastes to decompose far more rapidly than they do in colder climates. The frequency of waste collection in high temperature and humid climates should, therefore, be higher than that in cold climates. In sub-tropical or desert climate, there is no significant variation in moisture content of wastes (due to low rainfall) and low production of leachate from sanitary landfill. High winds and wind blown sand and dust, however, cause special problems at landfill sites. While temperature inversions can cause airborne pollutants to be trapped near ground level, landfill sites can affect groundwater by altering the thermal properties of the soil.

(iii) **Physical characteristics of an urban area:** In urban areas (*i.e.*, towns and cities), where the layout of streets and houses is such that access by vehicles is possible and door-to-door collection of solid wastes is the accepted norm either by large compaction vehicle or smaller vehicle. The picture is, however, quite different in the inner and older city areas where narrow lanes make service by vehicles difficult and often impossible. Added to this is the problem of urban sprawl in the outskirts (of the cities) where population is growing at an alarming rate. Access ways are narrow, unpaved and tortuous, and therefore, not accessible to collection vehicles. Problems of solid waste storage and collection are most acute in such areas.

(iv) **Financial and foreign exchange constraints:** Solid waste management accounts for sizeable proportions of the budgets of municipal corporations. This is allocated for capital resources, which go towards the purchase of equipments, vehicles, and fuel and labour costs. Typically, 10% to 40% of the revenues of municipalities are allocated to solid waste management. In regions where wage rates are low, the aim is to optimize vehicle productivity. The unfavourable financial situation of some countries hinders purchase of equipment and vehicles, and this situation is further worsened by the acute shortage of foreign exchange. This means that the balance between the degree of mechanisation and the size of the labour force becomes a critical issue in arriving at the most cost-effective solution.

(v) **Cultural constraints:** In some regions, long-standing traditions preclude the intrusion of waste collection on the precincts of households, and therefore, influence the collection system. In others, where the tradition of caste persists, recruits to the labour force for street cleaning and handling of waste must be drawn from certain sections of the population, while others will not consent to placing storage bins in their immediate vicinity. Social norms of a community more often than not over-ride what many may consider rational solutions. Waste management should, therefore, be sensitive to such local patterns of living and consider these factors in planning, design and operation.

(vi) **Management and technical resources**: Solid waste management, to be successful, requires a wide spectrum of workforce in keeping with the demands of the system.

PHYSICAL CHARACTERISTICS OF SOLID WASTE

Density

It is expressed as mass per unit volume (kg/m^3). This parameter is required for designing a solid waste management program. A reduction in volume by 75% is achieved through normal compaction equipment, so that an initial density of 100 kg/m^3 may readily be increased to 400 kg/m^3. Significant changes in the density occur as waste moves from sources to disposal site, as a result of scavenging, handling, wetting, and drying by the weather and vibration during transport. Density is critical in the design of sanitary landfill as well as for storage, collection and transport of wastes. Efficient operation of landfill requires compaction of wastes to optimum density.

Moisture Content

Moisture increases the weight of the solid wastes and therefore the cost of collection and transport increases. Consequently waste should be insulated from rain or other extraneous water source. Moisture content is critical determinant in the economic feasibility of waste treatment by incineration. During incineration energy must be supplied for evaporation of water and raising the temperature of vapour. Values greater than 40% are not common.

CHEMICAL CHARACTERISTICS OF SOLID WASTE

Information of chemical characteristics is important in evaluating alternative processing and recovery options. Typically waste is considered as combination of combustible and noncombustible components. If solid waste is to be used as a fuel or for any other use we should know its chemical components.

Lipids

These are included in the class of fats, oils and grease. The principal sources of lipids in the garbage are cooking oil and fats. Lipids have high heating values about 38,000 kJ/kg (kilo joules/kilograms), which makes the waste with high lipid content suitable for energy recovery. Since lipids become liquids at temperature slightly above ambient they add to the liquid content during waste decomposition. They are biodegradable, but they have low solubility in water and hence the rate of biodegradation is slow.

Carbohydrates

These are primarily originated from the food sources rich in starch and celluloses. These readily biodegrade into carbon dioxide, water and methane. Decomposition of carbohydrates attracts the flies and rats and hence should not be left exposed for long duration.

Proteins

These are the compounds containing carbon, hydrogen, nitrogen and oxygen and organic acid with amino groups. They are primarily found in food and garden wastes, but their partial decomposition result in the production of amines, which impart unpleasant odors.

Natural Fibers

These are the natural products contain cellulose and lignins that are relatively resistant to biodegradation. These are found in paper products, food and yard wastes. Paper is almost 100% cellulose, cotton over 95% and wood products over 40-50%. These are highly combustible products most suitable for incineration. The calorific value of oven dried paper products are in the range 12000-18000 kJ/kg.

Synthetic Organic Materials

In the recent years plastics have become a significant components of solid waste, accounting for 1-10%. They are highly resistant to the biodegradation; hence their presence in the waste is objectionable. Currently much attention is given to reduce this component at disposal sites. Plastics have a high heating value, about 32000 kJ/kg, which makes them very suitable for incineration. However, among the plastics Polyvinyl chloride (PVC) when burnt produces dioxin and acid gas. The trace gases produced during the burning of plastic are proved to be carcinogenic.

SECTION-B: ONSITE STORAGE & PROCESSING OF SOLID WASTE

Hauled and Stationary Containers

The design of an efficient waste collection system requires careful consideration of the type, size and location of containers at the point of generation for storage of wastes until they are collected. While single-family households generally use small containers, residential units, commercial units, institutions and industries require large containers. Smaller containers are usually handled manually whereas the larger, heavier ones require mechanical handling. The containers may fall under either of the following two categories:

(i) Stationary containers: These are used for contents to be transferred to collection vehicles at the site of storage.

(ii) Hauled containers: These are used for contents to be directly transferred to a processing plant, transfer station or disposal site for emptying before being returned to the storage site. The desirable characteristics of a well-designed container are low cost, size, weight, shape, resistance to corrosion, water tightness, strength and durability. For example, a container for manual handling by one person should not weigh more than 20 kg, lest it may lead to occupational health hazards such as muscular strain, etc. Containers that weigh more than 20 kg, when full, require two or more crew members to manually load and unload the wastes, and which result in low collection efficiency.

Containers should not have rough or sharp edges, and preferably have a handle and a wheel to facilitate mobility. They should be covered to prevent rainwater from entering (which increases the weight and rate of decomposition of organic materials) into the solid wastes. The container body must be strong enough to resist and discourage stray animals and scavengers from ripping it as well as withstand rough handling by the collection crew and mechanical loading equipment.

Containers should be provided with a lifting bar, compatible with the hoisting mechanism of the vehicle. The material used should be light, recyclable, easily moulded and the surface must be smooth and resistant to corrosion. On the one hand, steel and ferrous containers are heavy and subject to corrosion; the rust peels off exposing sharp edges, which could be hazardous to the collection crew. On the other, wooden containers (*e.g.*, bamboo, rattan and wooden baskets) readily absorb and retain moisture and their surfaces are generally rough, irregular and difficult to clean.

Waste Processing Technique: The processing of wastes helps in achieving the best possible benefit from every functional element of the solid waste management (SWM) system and, therefore, requires proper selection of techniques and equipment for every element. Accordingly, the wastes that are considered suitable for further use need to be paid special attention in terms of processing, in order that we could derive maximum economical value from them.

(iii) **Improving efficiency of SWM system:** Various processing techniques are available to improve the efficiency of SWM system. For example, before waste papers are reused, they are usually baled to reduce transporting and storage volume requirements. In some cases, wastes are baled to reduce the haul costs at disposal site, where solid wastes are compacted to use the available land effectively. If solid wastes are to be transported hydraulically and pneumatically, some form of shredding is also required. Shredding is also used to improve the efficiency of the disposal site.

(iv) **Recovering material for reuse:** Usually, materials having a market, when present in wastes in sufficient quantity to justify their separation are most amenable to recovery and recycling. Materials that can be recovered from solid wastes include paper, cardboard, plastic, glass, ferrous metal, aluminium and other residual metals.

(v) **Recovering conversion products and energy:** Combustible organic materials can be converted to intermediate products and ultimately to usable energy. This can be done either through incineration, pyrolysis, composting or bio-digestion. Initially, the combustible organic matter is separated from the other solid waste components. Once separated, further processing like shredding and drying is necessary before the waste material can be used for power generation.

Waste Evaluation Options in India

The problem of municipal solid waste management has acquired alarming dimensions in India especially over the last decade, before which waste management was hardly considered an issue of concern as the waste could be easily disposed of in an environmentally safe manner.

The physical and chemical characteristics of Indian city refuse, nonetheless, show that about 80% of it is compostable and ideal for biogas generation due to adequate nutrients (NPK), moisture content of 50-55% and a carbon-to-nitrogen ratio of 25-40:1. Therefore, the development of appropriate technologies for utilisation of wastes is essential to minimise adverse health and environmental consequences.

Against this backdrop, let us discuss below the quantum of wastes generated in India, their composition, disposal methods, recycling aspects, and health and environment impacts:

(i) **Waste quantum:** The per capita waste generation rate is about 500 g/day. This along with increased population has contributed to higher total waste generation quantum.

(ii) Waste composition: Studies reveal that the percentage of the organic matter has remained almost static at 41% in the past 3 decades, but the recyclables have increased from 9.56% to 17.18%.

Garbage in Indian cities is estimated to contain about 45-75% biodegradable waste (as against 25% of US city-garbage) with 50-55% moisture; 35-45% being fruits, vegetable and food biomass; and 8-15% non organic materials like plastic, metal, glass, stones, etc. Refuse from Indian cities also contains high organic and low combustible matter, if the studies carried out in six cities are of any indication.

(iii) Waste disposal methods: Waste disposal is the final stage of the waste management cycle. About 90% of the municipal waste collected by the civic authorities in India is dumped in low-lying areas outside the city/town limits, which have no provision of leachate collection and treatment, and landfill gas collection and use.

(iv) Recycling: This involves collection of recyclables from various sources, which ultimately reach recycling units. It is estimated that about 40-80% of plastic waste gets recycled in India, as compared to 10-15% in the developed nations of the world. However, due to lack of suitable government policies, incentives, subsidies, regulations, standards, etc., related to recycling, this industry is still far behind its western counterparts in terms of technology and quality of manufactured goods. Nevertheless, recycling in India is a highly organised and profit-making venture, though informal in nature.

(v) Health impacts: Due to the absence of standards and norms for handling municipal wastes, municipal workers suffer occupational health hazards of waste handling. At the dumpsites in the city of Mumbai, for example, 95 workers were examined and it was found that about 80% of them had eye problems, 73% respiratory ailments, 51% gastro intestinal ailments and 27% skin lesions. Also, municipal workers and rag pickers who operate informally for long hours rummaging through waste also suffer from similar occupational health diseases ranging from respiratory illnesses (from ingesting particulates and bio-aerosols), infections (direct contact with contaminated material), puncture wounds (leading to tetanus, hepatitis and HIV infection) to headaches and nausea, etc. Studies among the 180 rag pickers at open dumps of Kolkata city reveal that average quarterly incidence of diarrhoea was 85%, fever 72% and cough and cold 63%.

(vi) Environmental impacts: In addition to occupational health, injury issues and environmental health also need to be mentioned in the context of waste management. Contaminated leachate and surface run-off from land disposal facilities affects ground and surface water quality. Volatile organic compounds and dioxins in air-emissions are attributed to increasing cancer incidence and psychological stress for those living near incinerators or land disposal facilities. Drain clogging due to uncollected wastes leading to stagnant waters and subsequent mosquito vector breeding is a few of the environmental health issues, which affect the waste workers as well as the public.

Vehicle Storage Method

Waste Collection Vehicles

Almost all collections are based on collector and collection crew, which move through the collection service area with a vehicle for collecting the waste material. The collection vehicle selected must be appropriate to the terrain, type and density of waste generation points, the way it travels and type and kind of material. It also depends upon strength, stature and capability of the crew that will work with it. The collection vehicle may be small and simple (*e.g.*, two-wheeled cart pulled by an individual) or large, complex and energy intensive (*e.g.*, rear loading compactor truck). The most commonly used collection vehicle is the dump truck fitted with a hydraulic lifting mechanism. A description of some vehicle types follows:

(i) **Small-scale collection and muscle-powered vehicles:** These are common vehicles used for waste collection in many countries and are generally used in rural hilly areas. As Figure below illustrates, these can be small rickshaws, carts or wagons pulled by people or animals, and are less expensive, easier to build and maintain compared to other vehicles.

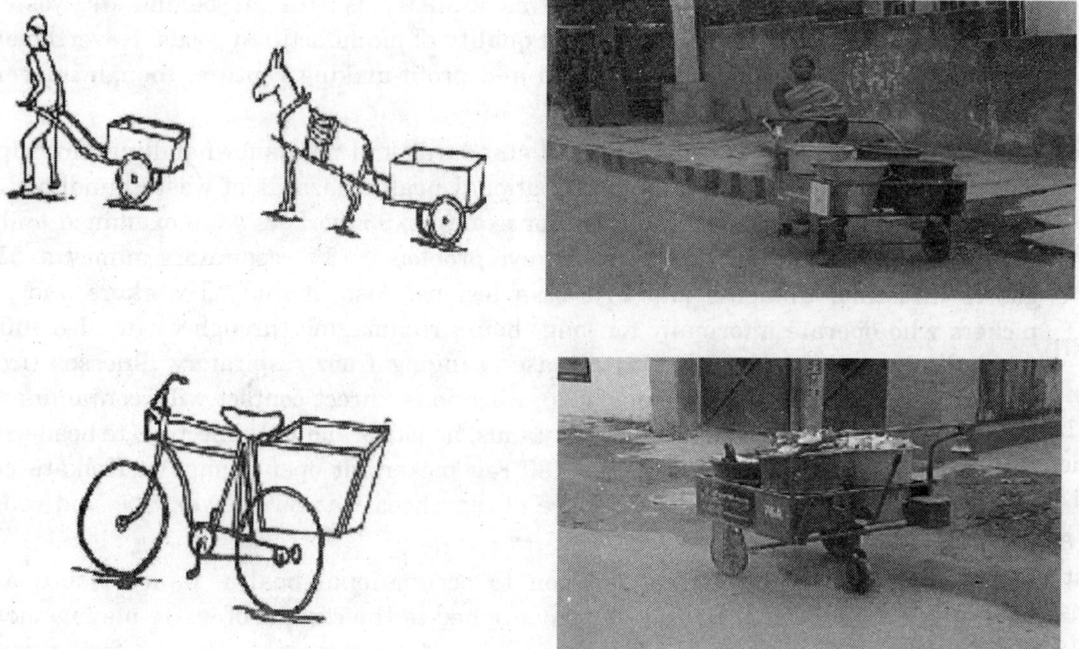

Figure 2.2: Small-scale Collection Vehicles: An Illustration

They are suitable for densely populated areas with narrow lanes, and squatter settlements, where there is relatively low volume of waste generated. Some drawbacks of these collection vehicles include limited travel range of the vehicles and weather exposure that affect humans and animals.

(ii) Non-compactor trucks: Non-compactor trucks are efficient and cost effective in small cities and in areas where wastes tend to be very dense and have little potential for compaction.

Figure 2.3. Non-compactor Trucks

When these trucks are used for waste collection, they need a dumping system to easily discharge the waste. It is generally required to cover the trucks in order to prevent residue flying off or rain soaking the wastes. Trucks with capacities of 10–12 m^3 are effective, if the distance between the disposal site and the collection area is less than 15 km. If the distance is longer, a potential transfer station closer than 10 km from the collection area is required. Non-compact trucks are generally used, when labour cost is high. Controlling and operating cost is a deciding factor, when collection routes are long and relatively sparsely populated.

Compactor Truck

Compaction vehicles are more common these days, generally having capacities of 12–15 m^3 due to limitations imposed by narrow roads. Although the capacity of a compaction vehicle is similar to that of a dump truck, the weight of solid wastes collected per trip is 2 to 2.5 times larger since the wastes are hydraulically compacted .

A compactor truck allows waste containers to be emptied into the vehicle from the rear, front or sides and inhibits vectors (of disease) from reaching the waste during collection and transport. It works poorly when waste stream is very dense, wet, collected materials are gritty or abrasive, or when the roads are dusty. The advantages of the compactor collection vehicle include the following:

- Containers are uniform, large, covered and relatively visually inoffensive;
- Waste is set out in containers so that the crew can pick them up quickly;
- Health risk to the collectors and odour on the streets are minimized, waste is relatively inaccessible to the waste pickers.

The success of waste management depends on the level of segregation at source.

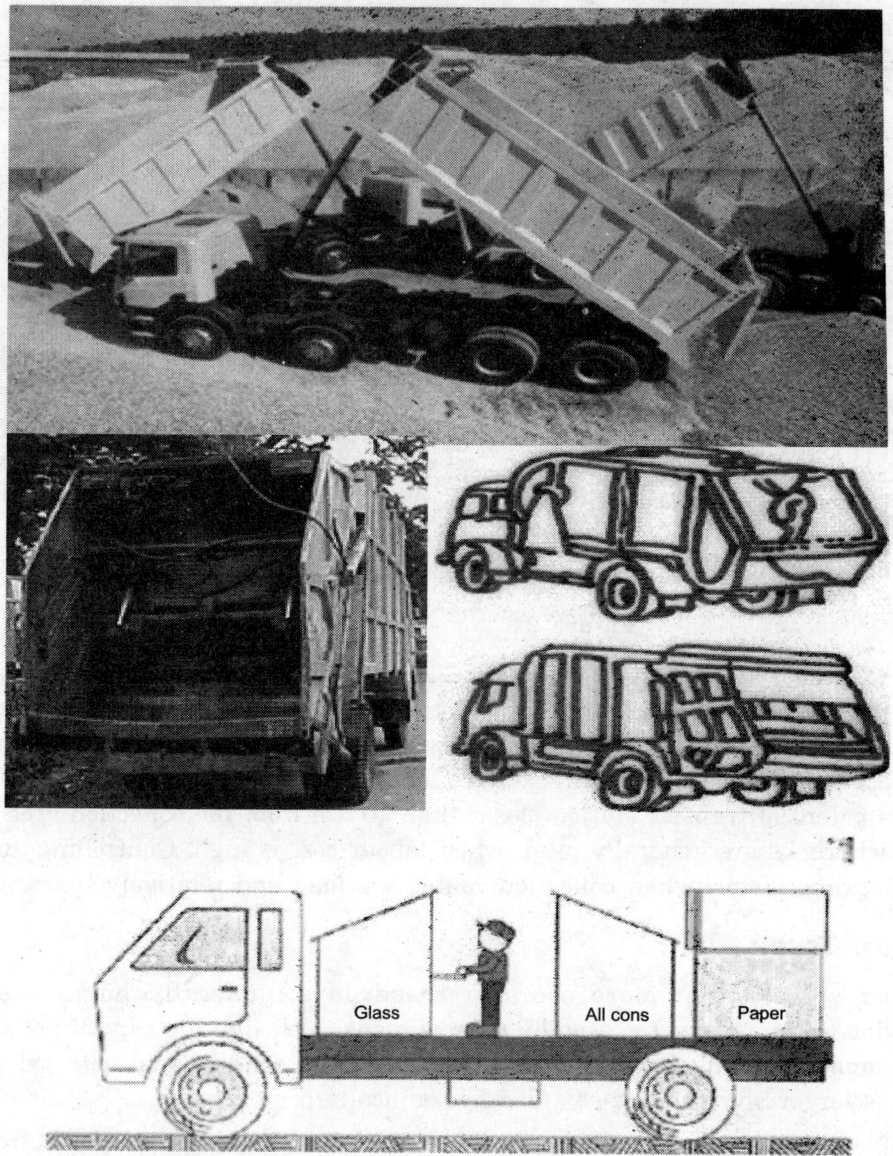

Figure 2.4: Compactor Truck

Factors affecting the waste collection

(i) **Finalising and implementing the system management plan:** For proper implementation of collection and transfer system, it is necessary to have clear organisational structures and management plans. The organisational structure should be simple, with a minimum of administrative and management layers between collection crews andtop management. All workers in the department should clearly understand the department's mission and their roles. Through training, incentives and reinforcement by management, workers should be encouraged to be customer-oriented and team contributors. Feedback mechanisms must be introduced to help the crew review their performance and help managers monitoring the performance of crews, equipment, etc. It is also important to periodically review the management plans and structures, as implementation services continues.

(ii) **Purchasing and managing equipment:** For purchasing equipment, most municipalities issue bid specifications. Detailed specifications include exact requirements for equipment sizes and capacities, power ratings, etc. Performance specifications often request that equipment be equivalent to certain available models and meet standards for capacity, speed, etc. Municipalities may either perform equipment maintenance themselves; contract with a local garage, or in some cases, contract with the vehicle vendor at the time of purchase. As part of the preventive maintenance programme, the collection crew should check the vehicle chassis, tyres and body daily and report any problems to maintenance managers. In addition, each vehicle should have an individual maintenance record that includes the following items:

- Preventive maintenance schedule;
- Current list of specific engine;
- A description of repairs and a list containing information on the repair date, mechanic, cost, type and manufacturer of repair parts;
- The length of time the truck was out of service, for each maintenance event.

(iii) **Hiring and training personnel:** As in all organisations, good personnel management is essential to an efficient, high-quality waste collection system. Authorities responsible for SWM should, therefore, strive to hire and keep well-qualified personnel. The recruitment programme should assess applicants' abilities to perform the types of physical labour required for the collection, equipment and methods used. To retain employees, management should provide a safe working environment that emphasises career advancement, participatory problem solving and worker incentives. Worker incentives should be developed to recognise and reward outstanding performance by employees. Ways to accomplish motivation include merit-based compensation, awards programme and a work structure. Feedback on employee performance should be regular and frequent.

Safety is especially important because waste collection employees encounter many hazards during each workday. As a result of poor safety records, insurance costs for many collection services are high. To minimise injuries, haulers should have an ongoing safety programme. This programme should outline safety procedures and ensure that all personnel are properly trained on safety issues. Haulers should develop an employee-training programme that helps employees improve and broaden the range of their job-related skills. Education should address such subjects as driving skills, first aid, safe lifting methods, identification of household hazardous wastes, avoidance of substance abuse and stress management.

(iv) **Providing public information:** Maintaining good communication with the public is important to a well-run collection system. Residents can greatly influence the performance of the collection system by co-operating in separation requirements, and by keeping undesirable materials from entering the collected waste stream. Commonly used methods of communicating information include brochures, articles in community newsletters, newspaper articles, announcements, and advertisements on radio and television, information attachments to utility bills (either printed or given separately) and school handouts. Communication materials should be used to help residents understand the community waste management challenges and the progress in meeting them. Residents should also be kept informed about issues such as the availability and costs of landfill capacity so that they develop an understanding of the issues and a desire to help meet their waste management needs.

(v) **Monitoring system cost and performance:** Collection and transfer facilities should develop and maintain an effective system for cost and performance reporting. Each collection crew should complete a daily report containing the following information:

- Total quantity hauled.
- Total distance and travel times to and from the disposal site.
- Amounts delivered to each disposal, transfer, or processing facility. Waiting time at sites.
- Number of loads hauled.
- Vehicle or operational problems needing attention.

Collected data should be used to forecast workloads, truck costs, identify changes in the generation of wastes and recyclables, trace the origin of problematic waste materials and evaluate crew performance. Just as the goals of a collection programme set its overall directions, a monitoring system provides the short-term feedback necessary to identify the corrections needed to achieve those goals.

SECTION-C: COLLECTION AND TRANSFER OF SOLID WASTE

WASTE COLLECTION COMPONENTS

(i) **Collection points:** These affect such collection system components as crew size and storage, which ultimately control the cost of collection. Note that the collection points depend on locality and may be residential, commercial or industrial.

(ii) **Collection frequency:** Climatic conditions and requirements of a locality as well as containers and costs determine the collection frequency. In hot and humid climates, for example, solid wastes must be collected at least twice a week, as the decomposing solid wastes produce bad odour and leachate. And, as residential wastes usually contain food wastes and other putrescible (rotting) material, frequent collection is desirable for health and aesthetic reasons. Besides climates, the quality of solid waste containers on site also determines the collection frequency. For instance, while sealed or closed containers allow collection frequency up to three days, open and unsealed containers may require daily collection. Collection efficiency largely depends on the demography of the area (such as income groups, community, etc.), where collection takes place, cost, *e.g.*, optimal collection frequency reduces the cost as it involves fewer trucks, employees and reduction in total route distance; storage space, *e.g.*, less frequent collection may require more storage space in the locality; sanitation, *e.g.*, frequent collection reduces concerns about health, safety and nuisance associated with stored refuse.

(iii) **Storage containers:** Proper container selection can save collection energy, increase the speed of collection and reduce crew size. Most importantly, containers should be functional for the amount and type of materials and collection vehicles used. Containers should also be durable, easy to handle, and economical, as well as resistant to corrosion, weather and animals. In residential areas, where refuse is collected manually, standardised metal or plastic containers are typically required for waste storage. When mechanised collection systems are used, containers are specifically designed to fit the truck-mounted loading mechanisms efficiency, *i.e.*, the containers should help maximise the overall collection efficiency.

- Convenience, *i.e.*, the containers must be easily manageable both for residents and collection crew.
- Compatibility, *i.e.*, the containers must be compatible with collection equipment.
- Public health and safety, *i.e.*, the containers should be securely covered and stored.
- Ownership, *i.e.*, the municipal ownership must guarantee compatibility with collection equipment.

(iv) **Collection crew:** The optimum crew size for a community depends on labour and equipment costs, collection methods and route characteristics. The size of the collection crew also depends on the size and type of collection vehicle used, space between the houses, waste generation rate and collection frequency. For example, increase in waste generation rate and quantity of wastes collected per stop due to less frequent collection result in a bigger crew size. Note also that the collection vehicle could be a motorised vehicle, a pushcart or a trailer towed by a suitable prime mover (tractor, etc.). It is possible to adjust the ratio of collectors to collection vehicles such that the crew idle time is minimised. However, it is not easy to implement this measure, as it may result in an overlap in the crew collection and truck idle time. An effective collection crew size and proper workforce management can influence the productivity of the collection system. The crew size, in essence, can have a great effect on overall collection costs. However, with increase in collection costs, the trend in recent years is towards:

- Decrease in the frequency of collection;
- Increase in the dependence on residents to sort waste materials;
- This trend has, in fact, contributed to smaller crews in municipalities.

(v) **Collection route:** The collection programme must consider the route that is efficient for collection. An efficient routing of collection vehicles helps decrease costs by reducing the labour expended for collection. Proper planning of collection route also helps conserve energy and minimise working hours and vehicle fuel consumption. It is necessary therefore to develop detailed route configurations and collection schedules for the selected collection system. The size of each route, however, depends on the amount of waste collected per stop, distance between stops, loading time and traffic conditions. Barriers, such as railroad, embankments, rivers and roads with heavy traffic, can be considered to divide route territories. Routing (network) analyses and planning can:

- Increase the likelihood of all streets being serviced equally and consistently;
- Help supervisors locate or track crews quickly;
- Provide optimal routes that can be tested against driver judgement and experience.

(vi) **Transfer station:** A transfer station is an intermediate station between final disposal option and collection point in order to increase the efficiency of the system, as collection vehicles and crew remain closer to routes. If the disposal site is far from the collection area, it is justifiable to have a transfer station, where smaller collection vehicles transfer their loads to larger vehicles, which then haul the waste long distances. In some instances, the transfer station serves as a pre-processing point, where wastes are dewatered, scooped or compressed. A centralised sorting and recovery of recyclable materials are also carried out at transfer stations (EPA, 1989). The unit cost of hauling solid wastes from a collection area to a transfer station and then to a disposal site decreases, as the size of the collection vehicle increases.

STORAGE: CONTAINERS/COLLECTION VEHICLES

Containers/Storage Bins

The design of an efficient waste collection system requires careful consideration of the type, size and location of containers at the point of generation for storage of wastes until they are collected. While single-family households generally use small containers, residential units, commercial units, institutio and industries require large containers. Smaller containers are usually handled manually whereas the larger, heavier ones require mechanical handling. The containers may fall under either of the following two categories:

(i) Stationary containers: These are used for contents to be transferred to collection vehicles at the site of storage.

(ii) Hauled containers: These are used for contents to be directly transferred to a processing plant, transfer station or disposal site for emptying before being returned to the storage site.

The desirable characteristics of a well-designed container are low cost, size, weight, shape, resistance to corrosion, water tightness, strength and durability. For example, a container for manual handling by one person should not weigh more than 20 kg, lest it may lead to occupational health hazards such as muscular strain, etc. Containers that weigh more than 20 kg, when full, require two or more crew members to manually load and unload the wastes, and which result in low collection efficiency.

Containers should not have rough or sharp edges, and preferably have a handle and a wheel to facilitate mobility. They should be covered to prevent rainwater from entering (which increases the weight and rate of decomposition of organic materials) into the solid wastes. The container body must be strong enough to resist and discourage stray animals and scavengers from ripping it as well as withstand rough handling by the collection crew and mechanical loading equipment. Containers should be provided with a lifting bar, compatible with the hoisting mechanism of the vehicle. The material used should be light, recyclable, easily moulded and the surface must be smooth and resistant to corrosion. On the one hand, steel and ferrous containers are heavy and subject to corrosion; the rust peels off exposing sharp edges, which could be hazardous to the collection crew.

Communal Containers

The use of communal containers is largely dependent on local culture, tradition and attitudes towards waste. Communal containers may be fixed on the ground (stationary) or movable (hauled). Movable containers are provided with hoists and tails compatible with lifting mechanism of collection vehicles and such containers have capacities of 1–4 m^3. The waste management authority must monitor, maintain and upgrade the communal containers. Note that in residential and commercial areas in India, the communal containers are often made of concrete.

In areas with very high waste generation rates, *i.e.*, rates exceeding two truckloads daily, such as wet markets, large commercial centres and large business establishments, roll-on-roll or hoisted communal containers with capacities of 12–20 m^3 and a strong superstructure with wheels are used.

Normally, the collection vehicle keeps an empty container as a replacement before it hauls the filled container. When a truck is used as a collection vehicle, the use of communal containers may be appropriate.

Figure 2.5: Typical Communal Container

This means that the farthest distance the householder will have to walk is 50 meters. However, in narrow streets with low traffic, where the house owner can readily cross the street, a longer distance is advisable. If the collection vehic le has to stop frequently, say, at every 50 m or so, fuel consumption increases, and this must be avoided.

Disadvantages of Communal Containers

The major disadvantage of communal containers is the potential lack of maintenance and upgrading. The residuals and scattered solid wastes emit foul odours, which discourage residents from using the containers properly. In addition, if fixed containers are built below the vehicle level, the collection crew may be held responsible for sweeping and loading the solid wastes into transfer containers before being loaded into the collection vehicle. Sweeping and cleaning the communal containers of residuals obviously impinge on the time of the crew members and take a longer time than if the wastes are placed in smaller containers. As fixed communal containers have higher rates of failure, their use is not advisable.

To overcome the problem of maintaining communal containers, individual residents should maintain their own containers and locate them in designated areas. The communal area must have water and drains to facilitate the cleaning of the containers. This practice has the advantage of reducing the number of collection stops and at the same time maintaining the householder's responsibility for cleaning them. The residents must also be properly educated on the importance of good housekeeping as the containers in the communal area are subject to vandalism. In the main, if communal containers are to be successful, the design of the containers, loading and unloading areas, and collection vehicle accessories should be coordinated.

WASTE COLLECTION OPERATION

Movement of Collection Crew

In cultures such as India, Bangladesh, etc., solid waste collection is assigned to the lowest social group. More often, the collection crew member accepts the job as a temporary position or stopgap arrangement, while looking for other jobs that are considered more respectable.

Apart from this cultural problem, the attitude of some SWM authorities affects collection operation. For example, some authorities still think that the collection of solid waste is mechanical, and therefore, the collection crew does not need any training to acquire special skills. As a result, when a new waste collector starts working, he or she is sent to the field without firm instruction concerning his or her duties, responsibilities and required skills. For an effective collection operation, the collection team must properly be trained. The collection crew and the driver of the collection vehicle must, for example, work as a team, and this is important to maintain the team morale and a sense of social responsibility among these workers.

The difference may be one or two minutes per collection stop, but it matters with the number of stops the crew will take in a working shift. Multiplying the minutes by the total number of crew working and labour cost depicts the amount of labour hours lost in terms of monetary value.

Generally, familiarity of the crew with the collection area improves efficiency. For example, the driver becomes familiar with the traffic jams, potholes and other obstructions that he or she must avoid. The crew is aware of the location of the containers and the vehicle stops. It is, therefore, important to assign each crew specific areas of responsibility. Working together also establishes an understanding of the strong and weak points of the team members and efficient work sequences. The collection operation must also observe a strict time schedule. Testing of new routes, new gadgets and vehicles is best carried out first in the laboratory and later in a pilot area. Testing of a new sequence using the whole service area could result in disorder and breakdown of the solid waste collection system. Studies show that it takes two hours to recover for every hour of a failed system.

Collection Vehicle Routing

Efficient routing and re-routing of solid waste collection vehicles can help decrease costs by reducing the labour expended for collection. Routing procedures usually consist of the following two separate components:

(i) **Macro-routing:** Macro-routing, also referred to as route-balancing, consists of dividing the total collection area into routes, sized in such a way as to represent a day's collection for each crew. The size of each route depends on the amount of waste collected per stop, distance between stops, loading time and traffic conditions. Barriers, such as railroad embankments, rivers and roads with heavy competing traffic, can be used to divide route territories. As much as possible, the size and shape of route areas should be balanced within the limits imposed by such barriers.

(ii) **Micro-routing:** Using the results of the macro-routing analysis, micro- routing can define the specific path that each crew and collection vehicle will take each collection day. Results of micro-routing analyses can then be used to readjust macro- routing decisions. Micro-routing analyses should also include input and review from experienced collection drivers.

WASTE TRANSFER STATION

The transfer of waste is frequently accompanied by removal, separation or handling of waste. In areas, where wastes are not already dense, they may be compacted at a transfer station. The technical limitations of smaller collection vehicles and the low hauling cost of solid waste, using larger vehicles, make a transfer station viable. Also, the use of transfer station proves reasonable, when there is a need for vehicles servicing a collection route to travel shorter distances, unload and return quickly to their primary task of collecting the waste.

Limitations in hauling solid wastes are the main factors to be considered, while evaluating the use of transfer stations. These include the additional capital costs of purchasing trailers, building transfer stations and the extra time, labour and energy required for transferring wastes from collection truck to transfer trailer.

Types of transfer stations. Depending on the size, transfer stations can be either of the following two types:

(i) **Small to medium transfer stations:** These are direct-discharge stations that provide no intermediate waste storage area. The capacities are generally small (less than 100 tonnes/day) and medium (100 to 500 tonnes/day). Depending on weather, site aesthetics and environmental concerns, transfer operations of this size may be located either indoor or outdoor. More complex small transfer stations are usually attended during hours of operation and may include some simple waste and materials processing facilities. For example, it includes a recyclable material separation and processing centre. The required overall station capacity (*i.e.*, the number and size of containers) depends on the size and population density of the area served and the frequency of collection.

(ii) **Large transfer stations:** These are designed for heavy commercial use by private and municipal collection vehicles. The typical operational procedure for a larger station is as follows:

- When collection vehicles arrive at the site, they are checked in for billing, weighed and directed to the appropriate dumping area;
- Collection vehicles travel to the dumping area and empty the wastes into a waiting trailer, a pit or a platform;
- After unloading, the collection vehicle leaves the site, and there is no need to weigh the departing vehicle, if its weight (empty) is known;
- Transfer vehicles are weighed either during or after loading. If weighed during loading, trailers can be more consistently loaded to just under maximum legal weights and this maximises payloads and minimises weight violations.

Transfer

Figure 2.6: Waste Transfer Station

SECTION-D: OFFSITE PROCESSING & STORAGE OF SOLID WASTE

PROCESS OF SOURCE SEPERATION

(i) **Product reuse:** Using reusable products, instead of their disposal equivalents, reduce the amount of materials that are to be managed as wastes. An example of product reuse is the reusable shopping bag.

(ii) **Material volume reduction:** Reducing the volume of material used changes the amount of waste entering the waste stream. This helps in controlling the waste generated and its disposal. For example, buying in bulk or using large food containers reduces the amount of packaging waste generated.

(iii) **Toxicity reduction:** Source reduction reduces the amount of toxic constituents in products entering the waste stream and reduces the adverse environmental impacts of recycling or other waste management activities. For example, substitution of lead and cadmium in inks (solvent-based to water- based) and paints is a source reduction activity.

(iv) **Increased product lifetime:** Source reduction facilitates the use of products with longer lifetime over short-lived alternatives that are designed to be discarded at the end of their useful lives. Put differently, it encourages a product design that allows for repair and continued use rather than disposal. Manufacturing long-life tyres is a good example of increasing product lifetime.

(v) **Decreased consumption:** This refers to the reduced consumption of materials that are not reusable (*e.g.*, using a reusable shopping bag instead of picking up plastic bags from the store). Consumer education about the materials that are difficult to dispose of or are harmful to the environment is essential. Buying practices can thus be altered (*e.g.*, buying in bulk)to reflect environmental consciousness.

FULL STREAM PROCESSING TECHNIQUE

This is a high technology separation technique, which processes all components of municipal waste. The materials recovered by this process tend to be of lower quality than those recovered or source separated in MRF because the former is a mix of various types of wastes. To achieve a better quality, the materials obtained through the full stream processing must be cleaned, which is a costly process. However, this technique remains attractive because it does not require source separation, and it isused in the following applications:

(i) **Refuse derived fuel (RDF) preparation:** In this application, it is used to extract the combustible portion of municipal waste.

(ii) **Municipal waste composting:** In this application, it is used to concentrate the compostable portion of municipal solid waste. Note that this is sometimes performed as part of RDF preparation.

(iii) **Material recovery:** In this application, it is used to recover and resell certain materials, and thereby making material recovery a recycling technology as well. In full stream processing, depending on the facility design, the materials are separated either mechanically or by hand, and size and weight are the main characteristics used to separate the materials.

- When the material is dumped, oversized materials such as furniture, etc., are removed;
- Rotating screens are used to separate materials of different sizes (small and large);
- Ferrous material is extracted using a magnet system;
- Air classifier is used to separate the lighter material;
- Light materials including plastic and paper are further processed into RDF; heavy fraction is mechanically or manually sorted to recover saleable materials such as cardboard, etc.

Recovery of wastes

Recycling is perhaps the most widely recognised form of source reduction involving the process of separating, collecting, processing, marketing and ultimately using a material that would have otherwise been discarded. This form of source reduction, *i.e.*, recycling, is similar to other forms, in that it:

- Lessens reliance on landfills and incinerators;
- Protects human health and the environment by removing harmful substances from the waste stream;
- Conserves natural resources by reducing the demand for raw materials.

Recycling is one of the fundamental parts of the waste management plan. Although it alone cannot solve a community's municipal SWM problem, it can divert a significant portion of waste stream from disposal in landfill and combustion facilities. Recycling has a lot of direct and indirect significance for the society, and this can be grouped under the following three broad areas.

(i) Economic significance: Economic assessment of waste recycling is a difficult task as many of the beneficial environmental and social impacts of recycling are long-term and are intangible, and, therefore, are difficult to quantify.

Some of the short- and long-term economic benefits are:

Cost reduction: Resource recovery through recycling of solid waste could be of interest to waste management authorities as a means of reducing the waste disposal cost. Any saving in waste management cost could be a significant incentive to the authorities to increase the coverage of service areas and improve the service level. They can save cost from fuel for transportation, operation and maintenance, and generate revenue by sale of recyclables, etc.

Employment: Recycling of waste is a labour intensive activity, and its potential to ease the unemployment problem is high. Enhanced recycling activities, for example, can create an additional job market for skilled and unskilled workforce, and they can adapt to any of the occupations such as a labourer in recycling business or industry or a dealership.

Energy saving: Use of recyclablesin some industrial processes that consume less energy than the use of any other raw material. The reduction in energy consumption in one industry could mean its availability for some other industry in need.

Reduced health care costs: Improved health and sanitary conditions in urban areas resulting from indirect benefits of waste recycling can reduce the investment in public health programme.

Saving costs for other public utilities: Enhanced solid waste recycling practices can reduce the frequency of sewer clogging, blocking of natural watercourses and pollution of water bodies. This will benefit the concerned public utilities through reduced cost in cleaning sewers and improved public safety due to blocked sewers and narrowing of natural watercourses.

(ii) Environmentaland health significance: The volume of waste is increasing rapidly because of population growth and economic development. The composition of waste is also changing, leading to waste production with more recyclables. At the same time, polluted waste fractions are increasing because of increasing complex processes being used in industries, and these contribute increasingly to environmental degradation. This notwithstanding, recycling helps, among others, in the following ways, to facilitate effective waste management:

Improved environment: The environmental pollution may be due to inadequate SWM as well as due to its effect on other urban infrastructure. Recycling reduces the volume of waste that has to be finally dumped, and thereby causing reduction in pollution at the waste disposal sites. When there is reduction in volume of waste because of its increased reuse, different types of pollution (*e.g.*, water, air and land) will get abated.

Natural resource conservation: Industries with natural products as their raw material for production recyclable solid wastes pressure on these precious are depleting natural resources. Use of more and more in industrial production will relieve the tremendous resources. For example, recycling of waste paper means a lower demand for wood, which means less cutting of trees and an enhanced possibility for sustainable use of the forest. Using recyclable items in the production process would reduce the demand for energy as well.

(iii) Social significance: People engaged in waste collection activities are normally of low social and economic standing. This is especially true with scavengers, which is evident from persisting poor quality of their living and working conditions. Different groups of people engaged in waste recycling have a hierarchical social and economic status, in which, processors are at the top of the hierarchy followed by waste dealers and wholesalers, waste buyers and waste collectors in that very order, while scavengers are at the bottom. Although there is this social and economic hierarchy within the waste recycling business, the overall social esteem of waste recycling operators is low.

A formal recycling arrangement will help promote the social esteem of waste workers and facilitate their upward social mobility due to increased earning. In addition, the improved recycling activity will increase the economic value of the waste and will reduce waste scavenging activity providing opportunity for scavengers to switch to a more socially acceptable occupation. In short, institutionalised recycling programmes will help remove the stigma associated with waste scavenging and transform it to an economic enterprise.

Waste Recycling Programme

Numerous recycling options are available, and recycling programme development requires strategic planning. Planning for recycling involves understanding markets, assessing local expertise, setting goals and fostering public participation. An efficient recycling programme requires a systematic approach to all programme components, which are interrelated, and therefore, decisions about one must be made taking into consideration other components. As a successful recycling requires public participation, programmes must be designed keeping in view public convenience and support.

(i) **Build local expertise:** Small projects help build local expertise in recycling and minimise the problems associated with poor planning. With small-scale projects, it is easy to compare and evaluate the programmes and techniques that are considered most successful within the community. When the time comes to develop a large-scale programme, there will be practical experience and an established decision-making framework, which will enhance the programme's success.

(ii) **Understand and develop a recycling market:** While planning for a recycling programme, it is important to find an outlet for the recyclable material. Market analysisis both a planning and ongoing activity, as even the most successful recycling programme can be severely affected by market fluctuations. Recycling programmes must, therefore, be designed with the flexibility to handle fluctuating and uncertain outlets for material.

(iii) **Foster public education and involvement:** Public participation is one of the most important factors deciding a programme's success. The public has a right and a responsibility to understand the full costs and liabilities of managing the waste they produce. A well-planned public education and involvement programme will foster public interest in recycling.

(iv) **Assess local waste stream:** Planning any recycling programme requires the knowledge of the local waste stream. Choosing the right material to recycle and designing the logistics of the programme are the important parts of the planning process.

(v) **Augment existing programme:** Recycling should augment the success that has been attained by other groups operating recycling programmes. This is very important for planning and success. Other programmes may be run by local volunteer organisations to raise funds or as a community service.

(vi) **Set goals and objectives:** Part of the planning process involves setting goals and objectives. The preliminary assessment of waste stream helps in deciding long-term goals for a community. Planning objectives may include determining the type of waste stream component that should be programmed, investigating the feasibility of the curbside (kerbside) programme, public outreach avenues, etc. The community will benefit from carefully developed achievable goals and objectives, and from an integrated approach to waste management (see Unit 10 for a detailed discussion of the integrated approach to waste management).

(vii) **Coordinate the programme:** Recycling programme is considered a public service. Therefore, local governments are required to ensure that all services are provided properly. Like any other public service, recycling programmes should be consistent, predictable, equitable and efficient.

(viii) **Evaluate the programme:** New programmes and technologies are evolving continuously, which make the planning for recycling an ongoing process. This requires experiment and evaluation. Eventhe best recycling programmes experiment with new techniques to improve on their current efforts.

Processing Equipments for Recycling

Recycling involves a number of processing techniques and these processes require different equipments. However, some of the special equipments used in recycling are:

Balers: Balers can be used to densify many types of materials including paper, cardboard, plastics and cans. Balers can improve space utilisation and reduce material transportation costs.

Can densifiers: Can crushers are used to densify aluminium and steel cans prior to transport.

Glass crushers: These are used to process glass fraction separated by colo break it into **small** pieces. This crushed material is then called cullet, and can be repro into new glass products.

Magnetic separators: These are used to remove ferrous material from a mixt materials.

Wood grinders: These are chippers and are used to shred large pieces of woo chips that can be used as much or as fuel.

Scales: These are used to measure the quantity of materials recovered or sold.

Material recovery facilities (MRF)

MRF is a centralised facility that receives, separates, processes and markets recyclable material. It can be operated with both drop off and curbside programmes. The primary advantage of MRF is that it allows materials directly from the municipalities and processes them uniformly. It is generally designed to handle all type of recyclables. Implementation of MRF in a municipality depends upon a number of factors as follows:

Market demand: When additional processing is required, MRF is more useful as buyers may have certain material specifications.

Separate collection: In systems that require residents to separate their recyclables, intermediate separation and processing is required.

Number of different recyclables: In general, a MRF will be more beneficial when a large number of different recyclables are collected.

Quantities of materials: Because MRF involves substantial capital and operating costs (*e.g.*, buildings, equipment and labour), it is expected to handle a significant amount of materials to justify its operation.

Motion Time Measurement (MTM) Technique

Motion time measurement (MTM) studies are now an integral part of the standard procedure in the development of solid waste collection systems. MTM is a technique to observe and estimate the movement of the collection crew with the help of stopwatches. Sophisticated MTM studies involve hidden or open video cameras at different collection stops to record, replay and study the operation sequence of the collection crew. If the crew is conscious of being observed, they tend to work faster and reduce time wastage in unauthorised salvaging and other non-scheduled activities. Once the crew is familiar with the person(s) observing them, it begins to perform more credibly. In studies involving video cameras, therefore, the first two or three hours of observation are often neglected.

SECTION-E: WASTE DISPOSAL SYSTEM

PROPER WASTE DISPOSAL SYSTEM

(i) **Municipal capacities:** With the increasing volume of waste generation, collection of wastes gets more attention than disposal. Furthermore, in India, only a few municipalities seem to have the required experience or capacity for controlled disposal. Some municipalities may have identified disposal sites but still only few may actively manage them. In some places, contracting out waste disposal is seen as a solution. But, municipalities are not equipped to deal with the problems associated with it, such as issues of privatisation and monitoring of the contract.

(ii) **Political commitment:** SWM is more than a technical issue, as any successful programme needs effective political and governmental support. This is rarely a priority of government authorities, unless there is a strong and active public interest as well as international interventions.

(iii) **Finance and cost recovery:** Development of a sanitary landfill site represents a major investment and it generally receives less priority over other resource demands. And, even when establishment costs are secured for a disposal site, recurrent costs to maintain it always pose problems.

(iv) **Technical guidelines:** Standards established for waste disposal in one country need not necessarily be appropriate for another, due to reasons such as climatic conditions, resources availability, institutional infrastructure, socio-cultural values, etc. In the absence of adequate data and/or the means of collecting/acquiring it, officials often struggle to plan a safe and economically viable disposal option.

(v) **Institutional role and responsibility:** A disposal site may be located outside the boundary of a town and may serve more than one town. This necessitates the coordination of all authorities concerned, and the roles and responsibilities of different departments need to be clearly defined and accepted by all concerned.

(vi) Location: The accessibility of a disposal site, especially its distance from town, is an important factor in site selection, especially when staff and public do not have a strong incentive to use it, when compared to indiscriminate dumping. Site selection is perhaps the most difficult stage in the development of suitable disposal option.

DISPOSAL OPTIONS AND SELECTION CRITERIA

The most common disposal option practised currently in many countries is either uncontrolled dumping or dumping with moderate control. The environmental costs of uncontrolled dumping include breeding of disease causing vectors (*e.g.*, flies, mosquitoes and rodents), pollution, odour and smoke.

Disposal Options

(i) Uncontrolled dumping or non-engineered disposal: As mentioned, this is the most common method being practised in many parts of the world, and India is no exception. In this method, wastes are dumped at a designated site without any environmental control. They tend to remain there for a long period of time, pose health risks and cause environmental degradation. Due to the adverse health and environmental impact associated with it, the non-engineered disposal is not considered a viable and safe option.

(ii) Sanitary landfill: Unlike the non-engineered disposal, sanitary landfill is a fully engineered disposal option in that the selected location or wasteland is carefully engineered in advance before it is pressed into service. Operators of sanitary landfills can minimise the effects of leachate (*i.e.*, polluted water which flows from a landfill) and gas production through proper site selection, preparation and management. This particular option of waste disposal is suitable when the land is available at an affordable price, and adequate workforce and technical resources are available to operate and manage the site.

(iii) Composting: This is a biological process of decomposition in which organisms, under controlled conditions of ventilation, temperature and moisture, convert the organic portion of solid waste into humus-like material. If this process is carried out effectively, what we get as the final product is a stable, odour-free soil conditioner. Generally, the option of composting is considered, when a considerable amount of biodegradable waste is available in the waste stream and there is use or market for composts.

(iv) **Incineration:** This refers to the controlled burning of wastes, at a high temperature (roughly 1200–500°C), which sterilises and stabilises the waste in addition to reducing its volume. In the process, most of the combustible m aterials (*i.e.*, self-sustaining combustible matter, which saves the energy needed to maintain the combustion) such as paper or plastics get converted into carbon dioxide and ash. Incineration may be used as a disposal option, when land filling is not possible and the waste composition is highly combustible. An appropriate technology, infrastructure and skilled workforce are required to operate and maintain the plant.

(v) Gasification: This is the partial combustion of carbonaceous material (through combustion) at high temperature (roughly 1000 °C) forming a gas, comprising mainly carbon dioxide, carbon monoxide, nitrogen, hydrogen, water vapour and methane, which can be used as fuel.

(vi) Refuse-derived fuel (RDF): This is the combustible part of raw waste, separated for burning as fuel. Various physical processes such as screening, size reduction, magnetic separation, etc., are used to separate the combustibles.

(vii) Pyrolysis: This is the thermal degradation of carbonaceous material to gaseous, liquid and solid fraction in the absence of oxygen. This occurs at a temperature between 200 and 900 °C.

Selection criteria for waste disposal options

With the help of proper frameworks and sub-frameworks, we can assess the effectiveness of each of the waste disposal options. While a framework represents an aid to decision-making and helps to ensure the key issues are considered, a sub-framework explains how and why the necessary information should be obtained. A framework contains a list of issues and questions pertaining to the technical, institutional, financial, social and environmental features of a waste disposal system to assess the capacity of a disposal option to meet the requirements. For example, an appraisal of waste disposal option must include the following:

(i) Technical: This feature, involving efficient and effective operation of the technology being used, evaluates the following components of a SWM system:

- Composition of wastes, *e.g.*, type, characteristics and quantity.
- Existing practices, *e.g.*, collection, transport, and recycling process.
- Siting, *e.g.*, location of disposal site, engineering material, etc.
- Technology, *e.g.*, operation, maintenance, technical support, etc.
- Impact, *e.g.*, anticipated by-product, requirement for their treatment and disposal, etc.

(ii) Institutional: This involves the ability and willingness of responsible agencies to operate and manage the system by evaluating the following:

- Structures, roles and responsibilities, *e.g.*, current institutional frameworks.
- Operational capacity, *e.g.*, municipal capacities, local experience and staff training.
- Incentives, *e.g.*, management improvement and waste disposal practices.
- Innovation and partnership.

(iii) Financial: This assesses the ability to finance the implementation, operation and maintenance of the system by evaluating the following:

- Financing and cost recovery, *e.g.*, willingness to raise finance for waste management.
- Current revenue and expenditure on waste management.
- Potential need for external finance for capital cost.

(iv) Social: This helps in avoiding adverse social impact by evaluating the following:

- Health and income implication.
- Public opinions on the existing and proposed system.

SANITARY LANDFILL

The term landfill generally refers to an engineered deposit of wastes either in pits/trenches or on the surface. And, a sanitary landfill is essentially a landfill, where proper mechanisms are available to control the environmental risks associated with the disposal of wastes and to make available the land, subsequent to disposal, for other purposes. However, you must note that a landfill need not necessarily be an engineered site, when the waste is largely inert at final disposal, as in rural areas, where wastes contain a large proportion of soil and dirt. This practice is generally designated as non-engineered disposal method. When compared to uncontrolled dumping, engineered landfills are more likely to have pre-planned installations, environmental monitoring, and organised and trained workforce. Sanitary landfill implementation, therefore, requires careful site selection, preparation and management.

The four minimum requirements we need to consider for a sanitary landfill are:

(i) Full or partial hydrological isolation;

(ii) Formal engineering preparation;

(iii) Permanent control;

(iv) Planned waste emplacement and covering.

Principle of Landfilling

The purpose of landfilling is to bury or alter the chemical composition of the wastes so that they do not pose any threat to the environment or public health. Landfills are not homogeneous and are usually made up of cells in which a discrete volume of waste is kept isolated from adjacent waste cells by a suitable barrier. The barriers between cells generally consist of a layer of natural soil (*i.e.*, clay), which restricts downward or lateral escape of the waste constituents or leachate.

Land filling relies on containment rather than treatment (for control) of wastes.

If properly executed, it is a safer and cheaper method than incineration. An environmentally sound sanitary landfill comprises appropriate liners for protection of the groundwater (from contaminated leachate), run-off controls, leachate collection and treatment, monitoring wells and appropriate final cover design.

Landfill Processes

Site selection process and considerations: This requires the development of a working plan – a plan, or a series of plans, outlining the development and descriptions of site location, operation, engineering and site restoration. Considerations for site include public opinion, traffic patterns and congestion, climate, zoning requirements, availability of cover material and liner as well, high trees or buffer in the site perimeter, historic buildings, and endangered species, wetlands, and site land environmental factors, speed limits, underpass limitations, load limits on roadways, bridge capacities, and proximity of major roadways, haul distance, hydrology and detours.

Settling process: The waste body of a landfill undergoes different stages of settling or deformation.

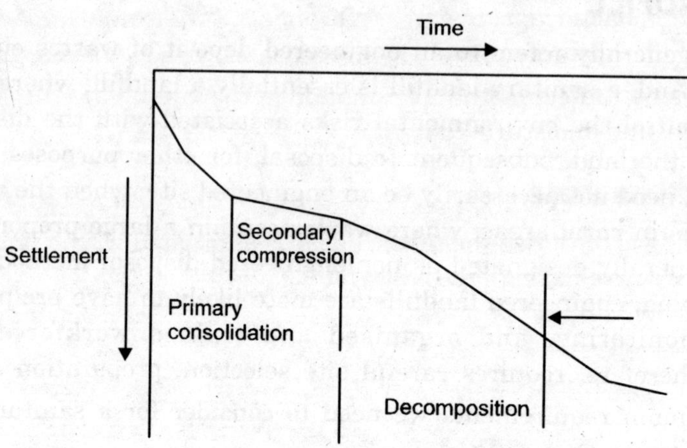

Figure 2.7: Settling Processes in Landfill

The three stages shown in the figure above are described below:

Primary consolidation: During this stage, a substantial amount of settling occurs. This settlement is caused by the weight of the waste layers. The movement of trucks, bulldozers or mechanical compactors will also enhance this process. After this primary consolidation, or short-term deformation stage, *aerobic degradation* processes occur.

Secondary compression: During this stage, the rate of settling is much lower than that in the primary consolidation stage, as the settling occurs through compression, which cannot be enhanced.

Decomposition: During the degradation processes, organic material is converted into gas and leachate. The settling rate during this stage increases compared to the secondary compression stage, and continues until all decomposable organic matter is degraded. The settling rate, however, gradually decreases with the passage of time. To appropriately design protective liners, and gas and leachate collection systems, it is, therefore, necessary to have a proper knowledge of the settling process of wastes.

Microbial degradation process: The microbial degradation process is the most important biological process occurring in a landfill. These processes induce changes in the chemical and physical environment within the waste body, which determine the quality of leachate and both the quality and quantity of landfill gas. Assuming that landfills mostly receive organic wastes, microbial processes will dominate the stabilisation of the waste and therefore govern landfill gas generation and leachate composition. Soon after disposal, the predominant part of the wastes becomes *anaerobic*, and the bacteria will start degrading the solid organic carbon, eventually to produce carbon dioxide and methane. The *anaerobic degradation* process undergoes the following stages:

- Solid and complex dissolved organic compounds are hydrolysed and fermented by the fermenters primarily to volatile fatty acids, alcohols, hydrogen and carbon dioxide.
- An acidogenic group of bacteria converts the products of the first stage to acetic acid, hydrogen and carbon dioxide.
- Methanogenic bacteria convert acetic acid to methane and carbon dioxide and hydrogenophilic bacteria convert hydrogen and carbon dioxide to methane.

The biotic factors that affect methane formation in the landfill are pH, alkalinity, nutrients, temperature, oxygen and moisture content.

Landfill Gas and Leachate

Leachate and landfill gas comprise the major hazards associated with a landfill. While leachate may contaminate the surrounding land and water, landfill gas can be toxic and lead to global warming and explosion leading to human catastrophe. (Note that global warming, also known as greenhouse effect, refers to the warming of the earth's atmosphere by the accumulation of gases (*e.g.*, methane, carbon dioxide and chlorofluorocarbons) that absorbs reflected solar radiation.

- **Nature of waste:** The deposition of waste containing biodegradable matter invariably leads to the production of gas and leachate, and the amount depends on the content of biodegradable material in the waste.
- **Moisture content:** Most micro-organisms require a minimum of approximately 12% (by weight) moisture for growth, and thus the moisture content of landfill waste is an important factor in determining the amount and extent of leachate and gas production.
- **pH:** The methanogenic bacteria within a landfill produce methane gas, which will grow only at low pH range around neutrality.
- **Particle size and density:** The size of waste particle affects the density that can be achieved upon compaction and affects the surface area and hence volume. Both affect moisture absorption and therefore are potential for biological degradation.
- **Temperature:** An increase in temperature tends to increase gas production. The temperature affects the microbial activity to the extent that it is possible to segregate bacteria, according to their optimum temperature operating conditions.

LANDFILL GAS EMISSION

Landfill gas contains a high percentage of methane due to the anaerobic decomposition of organic matter, which can be utilised as a source of energy.

Composition and Properties of Landfill Gases

Climatic and environmental conditions also influence gas composition. Due to the heterogeneous nature of the landfill, some acid-phase anaerobic decomposition occurs along with the methanogenic decomposition. Since aerobic and acid-phase degradation give rise to carbon dioxide and not methane, there may be a higher carbon dioxide content in the gas generated than what would otherwise be expected. Furthermore, depending on the moisture distribution, some carbon dioxide goes into solution. This may appear to increase (artificially) the methane content of the gas measured in the landfill. A typical landfill gas contains a number of components such as the following, which tend to occur within a characteristic range:

- **Methane:** This is a colourless, odourless and flammable gas with a density lighter than air, typically making up 50–60% of the landfill gas.
- **Carbon dioxide:** This is a colourless, odourless and non-inflammable gas that is denser than air, typically accounting for 30–40%.
- **Oxygen:** The flammability of methane depends on the percentage of oxygen. It is, therefore, important to control oxygen levels, where gas abstraction is undertaken.
- **Nitrogen:** This is essentially inert and will have little effect, except to modify the explosive range of methane.

Hazards of Landfill Gases

Landfill gas consists of a mixture of flammable, asphyxiating and noxious gases and may be hazardous to health and safety, and hence the need for precautions.

Some of the major hazards are listed below:

- **Explosion and fire:** Methane is flammable in air within the range of 5–15% by volume, while hydrogen is flammable within the range of 4.1–7.5% (in the presence of oxygen) and potentially explosive. Fire, occurring within the waste, can be difficult to extinguish and can lead to unpredictable and uncontrolled subsidence as well as production of smoke and toxic fumes.
- **Trace components:** These comprise mostly alkanes and alkenes, and their oxidation products such as aldehydes, alcohols and esters. Many of them are recognised as toxicants, when present in air at concentrations above occupational exposure standards.
- **Global warming:** Known also as greenhouse effect, it is the warming of the earth's atmosphere by the accumulation of gases (methane, carbon dioxide and chlorofluorocarbons) that absorbs reflected solar radiation.

Migration of Landfill Gases

During landfill development, most of the gas produced is vented to the atmosphere, provided the permeable oxidation, which converts methane to carbon dioxide, physical factors affect gas migration. The physical factors that affect gas migration include:

- **Environmental conditions:** These affect the rate of degradation and gas pressure build up.
- **Geophysical conditions:** These affect migration pathways. In the presence of fractured geological strata or a mineshaft, the gas may travel large distances, unless restricted by the water table.
- **Climatic conditions:** Falling atmosphericpressure, rainfall and water infiltration rate affect landfill gas migration.

The proportion of void space in the ground, rather than permeability, determines the variability of gas emission. If the landfill gas is controlled and proper extraction system is designed, this gas can be utilised as a source of energy. If landfill gas is not utilised, it should be burnt by means of flaring. However, landfill gas utilisation can save on the use of fossil fuels since its heating value is approximately 6 kWh/m^3 and can be utilised in internal combustion engines for production of electricity and heat.

It is important that landfill gas is extracted during the operation phase. It is extracted out of the landfill by means of gas wells, which are normally drilled by auger and are driven into the landfill at a spacing of 40–70 m. In addition, horizontal systems can be installed during operation of the landfill. The gas wells consist mainly of perforated plastic pipes surrounded by coarse gravel and are connected with the gas transportation pipe with flexible tubing. The vacuum necessary for gas extraction and transportation is created by means of a blower. The most important factors influencing planning and construction of landfill gas extraction systems are settling of waste, water tables in landfills and gas quality.

LEACHATE FORMATION

Leachate can pollute both groundwater and surface water supplies. The degree of pollution will depend on local geology and hydrogeology, nature of waste and the proximity of susceptible receptors. Once groundwater is contaminated, it is very costly to clean it up. Landfills, therefore, undergo siting, design and construction procedures that control leachate migration.

Composition and Properties of Leachate

Leachate comprises soluble components of waste and its degradation products enter water, as it percolates through the landfill. The amount of leachate generated depends on:

- Water availability;
- Landfill surface condition;
- Refuse state;
- Condition of surrounding strata.

The major factor, *i.e.*, water availability, is affected by precipitation, surface runoff, waste decomposition and liquid waste disposal.

Control of Leachate

The best way to control leachate is through prevention, which should be integral to the site design. In most cases, it is necessary to control liquid access, collection and treatment, all of which can be done using the following landfill liners:

- **Natural liners:** These refer to compacted clay or shale, bitumen or soil sealants, etc., and are generally less permeable, resistant to chemical attack and have good sorption properties. They generally do not act as true containment barriers, because sometimes leachate migrates through them.
- **Synthetic (geo-membrane) liners:** These are typically made up of high or medium density polyethylene and are generally less permeable, easy to install, relatively strong and have good deformation characteristics. They sometimes expand or shrink according to temperature and age.

Treatment of Leachate

Concentrations of various substances occurring in leachate are too high to be discharged to surface water or into a sewer system. These concentrations, therefore, have to be reduced by removal, treatment or both. The various treatments of leachate include:

- **Leachate recirculation:** It is one of the simplest forms of treatment. Recirculation of leachate reduces the hazardous nature of leachate and helps wet the waste, increasing its potential for biological degradation.
- **Biological treatment:** This removes BOD, ammonia and suspended solids. Leachate from land filled waste can be readily degraded by biological means, due to high content of volatile fatty acids (VFAs). The common methods are aerated lagoons (*i.e.*, special devices which enhance the aerobic process es of degradation of organic substances over the entire depth of the tank) and activated sludge process, which differs from aerated lagoons in that discharged sludge is recirculated and is often used for BOD and ammonia removal. While under conditions of low COD, rotating biological contactors (*i.e.*, biomass is brought into contact with circular blades fixed to a common axle which is rotated) are very effective in removing ammonia. In an anaerobic treatment system, complex organic molecules are fermented in filter. The common types are anaerobic filters, anaerobic lagoon and digesters.
- **Physico chemical treatment:** After biological degradation, effluents still contain significant concentrations of different substances. Physicochemical treatment processes could be installed to improve the leachate effluent quality. Some of these processes are flocculation-precipitation. (Note that addition of chemicals to the water attracts the metal by floc formation). Separation of the floc from water takes place by sedimentation, adsorption and reverse osmosis.

ENVIRONMENTAL EFFECTS OF LANDFILL

The environmental effects of a landfill include wind-blown litter and dust, noise, obnoxious odour, vermin and insects attracted by the waste, surface runoff and inaesthetic conditions.

(i) Wind-blown litter and dust are continuous problems of the ongoing landfill operation and a nuisance to the neighbourhood. Covering the waste cells with soil and spraying water on dirt roads and waste in dry periods, in combination with fencing and movable screens, may minimise the problem of wind-blown litter and dust. However, note that the problem will remain at the tipping front of the landfill.

(ii) Movement of waste collection vehicles, emptying of wastes from them, compactors, earthmoving equipment, etc., produce noise. Improving the technical capability of the equipment, surrounding the fill area with soil embankments and plantations, limiting the working hours and appropriately training the workforce will help minimise noise pollution.

(iii) Birds (*e.g.*, scavengers), vermin, insects and animals are attracted to the landfill for feeding and breeding. Since many of these may act as disease vectors, their presence is a potential health problem.

(iv) Surface run-off, which has been in contact with the land filled waste, may be a problem in areas of intense rainfall. If not controlled, heavily polluted run-off may enter directly into creeks and streams.

(v) An operating landfill, where equipment and waste are exposed, appears inaesthetic. This problem may be reduced by careful design of screening soil embankments, plantings, rapid covering and re-vegetation of filled sections.

(vi) Gas released, as a result of degradation or volatilisation of waste components, causes odour, flammability, health problems and damage of the vegetation (due to oxygen depletion in the root zone). The measures to control this include liners, soil covers, passive venting or active extraction of gas for treatment before discharge into the atmosphere.

(vii) Polluted leachate appears shortly after disposal of the waste. This may cause groundwater pollution and pollution of stream s through sub-surface migration. Liners, drainage collection, treatment of leachate, and groundwater and downstream water quality monitoring are necessary to control this problem.

LANDFILL OPERATIONAL ISSUES

(i) Site infrastructure: The size, type and number of buildings required at a landfill depend on factors such as the level of waste input, the expected life of the site and environmental factors. Depending on the size and complexity of the landfill, buildings range from single portable cabins to big complexes.

- Need to comply with planning, building, fire, health and safety regulations and controls;
- Security and resistance to vandalism;
- Durability of service and the possible need to relocate accommodation during the lifetime of the site operations;
- Ease of cleaning and maintenance;
- Availability of services such as electricity, water, drainage and telecommunication. Paying some attention to the appearance of the site entrance is necessary, as it influences the perception of the public about the landfill site. All landfill sites need to control and keep records of vehicles entering and leaving the site, and have a weighbridge to record waste input data, which can be analysed by a site control office. Note that at small sites, the site control office can be accommodated at the site itself.

(ii) Earthworks: Various features of landfill operations may require substantial earthworks, and therefore, the working plan must include earthworks to be carried out before wastes can be deposited. Details about earthworks gain significance, if artificial liners are to be installed, which involves grading the base and sides of the site (including construction of 25 slopes to drain leachate to the collection areas) and the formation of embankments. Material may also have to be placed in stockpiles for later use at the site. The cell method of operation requires the construction of cell walls. At some sites, it may be necessary to construct earth banks around the site perimeter to screen the landfill operations from the public. Trees or shrubs may then be planted on the banks to enhance the screening effect. The construction of roads leading to disposal sites also involves earthworks.

(iii) **Lining landfill sites:** Where the use of a liner is envisaged, the suitability of a site for lining should be evaluated at the site investigation stage. However, they should not be installed, unt il the site has been properly prepared. The area to be lined should be free of objects likely to cause physical damage to the liner, such as vegetation and hard rocks. If synthetic liner materials are used, a binding layer of suitable fine-grained material should be laid to support the liner. However, if the supporting layer consists of low permeable material (*e.g.*, clay), the synthetic liner must be placed on top of this layer.

(iv) **Leachate and landfill gas management:** The basic elements of the leachate collection system (*i.e.*, drain pipes, drainage layers, collection pipes, sumps, etc.) must be installed immediately above the liner, before any waste is deposited. Particular care must also be taken to prevent the drain and collection pipes from settling. During landfill operations, waste cells are covered with soil to avoid additional contact between waste and the environment. The soil layers have to be sufficiently permeable to allow downward leachate transport. Landfill gas is not extracted before completion, which includes construction of final cover, of the waste body. Extraction wells (diameter 0.3 to 1.0 m) may be constructed during or after operation.

(v) **Landfill capping:** Capping is required to control and minimise leachate generation (by minimising water ingress into the landfill) and facilitate landfill gas control or collection (by installing a low permeability cap over the whole site). A cap may consist of natural (*e.g.*, clay) or synthetic (*e.g.*, poly-ethylene) material with thickness of at least 1 m. An uneven settlement of the waste may be a major cause of cap failure. Designs for capping should, therefore, include consideration of leachate and landfill gas collection wells or vents. For the cap to remain effective, it must be protected from agricultural machinery, drying and cracking, plant root penetration, burrowing animals and erosion.

CHAPTER 3

INDUSTRIAL SOLID WASTE MANAGEMENT

In addition to domestic wastes industrial solid wastes also pose a grave problem. The generation of industrial solid waste is highly variable and the composition depends on the type of industries. The wastes may be inert, biodegradable, toxic and even hazardous. In general the solid waste generating industries are:

(a) **Extractive industries:** Minning, bulk is inert material and is piled up. Quarrying, 5% of minning is solid waste material. Agriculture, produce large amount wastes crop residues, straw, stubbles, leaves, hulls

(b) **Process industries:** Metallurgical, active material is extracted and the rests is left as solid wastes. Chemical processing—slurries, sludges or solid cakes. Paper—paper boards, boiler cinder, chip screen dust, lime, sludges from bleach plants. Plastics—wastes emanate from trimmings and processing. Textiles—cotton fibers, cotton seeds, comber wastes, lime, flax polyesters. Thermal Power Plants—fly ash.

(c) **Fabricating industries:** Packaging—aluminium sheets, steel, glass, plastic card boards, corrugated paper boards, plastic and paper laminates. Automobile—Shipping and packaging materials, components of tyres, batteries, generators, carburetors, wheels, bumpers etc. Electronics—Though small but produces plastic, broken glass, wire, bakelite sheets. Construction—residues of building materials, cement, sand, bricks, lime, gravel. Food Processing—moderate quantities of biodegradeable wastes as seed, peelings and pulp, milk and dairy products, slaughter house wastes, hides, skin, blood, cartillage, bones, offals.

(d) **Hospital Wastes:** Most dangerous. At most places, these wastes are piled up outside the municipal limits. On decay they produce acids and when it rains soluble chemicals leach into soil and create nuisance conditions. Leachates even reach ground waters. Sanitary landfills also contribute to pollution of land but substantially smaller than open dumps. Medical wastes even transmit pathogens in underground layers.

Some of the industries generating solid waste include steel industry, leather industry, sugar industry, textile industry and dyeing industry. Integrated steel plants usually consist of five main units, viz., coal washery, coke oven, blast furnace, steel melting, and rolling mills (hot and cold). In addition to the above the plants may have auxiliary units like oxygen plant and captive thermal power plant for their own uses.

The major solid wastes generated in steel plantsare, blast furnace slag, steel making slag, fly ash from the captive power plants, blast furnace clarifier sludges, blast furnace flue dusts, steel making dust, mill scales, waste refractories, coke breeze etc. Generation of such products depends on the quality and quantity of raw materials used in the process.

Leather industry has been categorized as one of the highly polluting industries and there are concerns that leather making activity can have adverse impact on the environment. So many chemicals are used in leather processing. The tannery effluents are characterized by high contents of dissolved suspended organic & inorganic solids giving rise to high oxygen demand and potential toxic metal salts &chromium metal ion. The odor emitted from decomposition of waste material and the presence of sulphide, ammonia and other volatile organic compounds are also associated with tanning activities.Solid waste generated in leather industries contribute mainly skin trimming, fleshing waste and buffing wastes. It constitutes protein as the main component and other chemicals. It will pose hazardous pollution problem to the environment.

Sugar is produced from sugarcane. While in many other places beetroot are used as the raw material for the sugar production. In India most of the sugar mills are situated in the country side and operated for about 4 to 8 months just after the harvesting of the sugarcane. A large volume of waste of organic nature is produced during the period of productions. The solid waste of sugar industry includes Bagasse, Molasses and Waste fiber.

Textile manufacturing is a major industry. It is based on the conversion of three types of fiber into yarn, then fabric, and then textiles. These are then fabricated into clothes or other artifacts. Cotton remains the most important natural fiber. There are many variable processes available at the spinning and fabric-forming stages coupled with the complexities of the finishing and coloration processes to the production of wide ranges of products. The solid waste of textile industry is fabric waste.

With increases in demand for milk products, many dairies of different sizes have come up in different places. These dairies collect the milk from the producers, and then either simply bottle it for marketing, or produce different milk products according to their capacities. The solid waste of Dairy industry is Fat, Plastics.

The most satisfactory approaches to manage solid wastes are those which help to minimize the quantity of waste requiring disposal. These methods are beginning to be more widely used. By modifying production processes, the volumes of wastes generated can often be reduced. Many wastes contain useful materials which can be reclaimed and reused. In certain cases, the amount of hazardous wastes for disposal can be reduced by transferring some to another industry which can use them as raw materials. However, opportunities for this approach may be limited as a result of mismatches between waste stream composition and process specifications. These approaches can be justified because of savings in raw materials and energy inputs, as well as reductions in the costs of disposal.

The major generators of industrial solid wastes are the thermal power plants producing coal ash, the integrated iron and steel mills producing blast furnace slag & steel melting slag, non-ferrous industries like aluminum, zinc and copper producing red mud & tailings, sugar industries generating press mud, pulp and paper industries producing lime & fertilizer and allied industries producing gypsum.

DESCRIPTION OF IMPORTANT INDUSTRIAL SOLID WASTE

Coal Ash

In general, a 1,000 MW station using coal middling of CV-3, 500 kcal/kg and ash content of 40-50% would need about 500 hectares for disposal of fly ash for about 30 years' operation. It is, therefore, necessary that flyash should be utilised wherever possible to minimize environmental degradation. The thermal power plant should take into account the capital and operation/maintenance cost of fly ash disposal system as well as the associated environmental protection cost, vis-a-vis dry system of collection and its utilisation by the thermal power plant or other industry, in evaluating the feasibility of such system.

Fly ash can be successfully utilised for production of bricks, cement and other building materials. Indigenous technology for construction of building materials utilising fly ash is available and are being practised in a few industries. However, large scale utilisation is yet to take off. Even if the full potential of fly ash utilisation through manufacture of fly ash bricks and blocks is explored, the quantity of fly ash produced by the thermal power plants are so huge that major portion of it will still remain unutilised. Hence, there is a need to evolve strategies and plans for safe and environmentally sound method of disposal.

Integrated Iron & Steel Plant Slag

The Blast Furnace (BF) and Steel Melting Shop (SMS) slags in integrated iron and steel plants are at present dumped in the surrounding areas of the steel plants making hillocks encroaching on the agricultural land. Although, the BF slaghas potential for conversion into granulated slag, which is a useful raw material in cement manufacturing, it is yet to be practised in a big way. Even the use of slag as road subgrade or land-filling is also very limited.

Phosphogypsum

Phosphogypsum is the waste generated from the phosphoric acid, ammonium phospate and hydrofluoric acid plants. This is very useful as a building material. At present very little attention has been paid to its utilisation in making cement, gypsum board, partition panel, ceiling tiles, artificial marble, fiber boards etc.

Red Mud

Red mud as solid waste is generated in non-ferrous metal extraction industries like aluminum and copper. The red mud at present is disposed in tailing ponds for settling, which more often than not finds its course into the rivers, especially during monsoon. However, red mud has recently been successfully tried and a plant has been set up in the country for making corrugated sheets. Demand for such sheet should be popularised and encouraged for use. This may replace asbestos which is imported and also banned in developed countries for its hazardous effect. Attempts are also made to manufacture polymer and natural fibres composite panel doors from red mud.

Lime Mud

Lime sludge, also known as lime mud, is generated in pulp & paper mills which is not recovered for reclamation of calcium oxide for use except in the large mills. The lime mud disposal by dumping into low-lying areas or into water courses directly or as run-off during monsoon is not only creating serious pollution problem but also wasting the valuable non-renewable resources. The reasons for not reclaiming the calcium oxide in the sludge after recalcination is that it contains high amount of silica. Although a few technologies have been developed to desilicate black liquor before burning, none of the mills in the country are adopting desilication technology.

Waste Sludge and Residues

Treatment of industrial wastes/effluents results in generation of waste sludge/residues which, is not properly disposed, may cause ground and surface water pollution. The aforesaid solid wastes has a very good potential to be utilised in the manufacture of various building materials.

IMPACT OF SOLID WASTE

The infiltration of rainfall into landfill, together with the biochemical and chemical breakdown of the wastes, produces a leachate which is high in suspended solids and of varying organic & inorganic content. All household and most industrial wastes will produce leachate. If the leachate enters surface or groundwater before sufficient dilution has occurred, serious pollution incidents can occur. In surface waters, leachate high in organic material and reduced metals will cause severe oxygen depletion and result in fish-kills. Leachate high in non biodegradable synthetic organic compounds is a particular threat, through bioaccumulation, concentrations of these substances may increase to toxic levels and endanger animal & human life. The decomposition of solid wastes in landfill results in the production of carbon dioxide and methane (landfill gas), both important greenhouse gases. 7% of methane generated by man's activities is estimated to be coming from landfill. Operation of incinerators can cause nuisance and atmospheric pollution from the emission of particulates, acidic gases, unburnt waste material, heavy metals, and trace quantities of organic compounds.

HEALTH CONSEQUENCES OF POOR INDUSTRIAL WASTE DISPOSAL

The solid waste generated from industrial sources contains a large number of chemicals, some of which are toxic. The waste is considered toxic, if the concentration of the ingredients exceeds a specified value. Although the levels of some ingredients may occasionally exceed the permissible level, the waste as such is considered to be toxic only if the average value of ingredients exceeds the toxicity level. Various criteria and tests have been devised by different agencies to determine the toxicity of a given substance. It is necessary to know the properties of the waste so as to assess whether its uncontrolled release to the environment would lead to toxic effects on humans or other living organism in ecosystem. This evaluation is carried out using criteria such as toxicity, phytotoxicity, genetic activity and bio-concentration. The potential toxic effects also depend on quantity of the toxic constituents. Substances are classified as hazardous or otherwise depending on the dose, exposure, and duration of exposure. For a chemical to affect human health it must come in contact with or enter the human body. There areseveral ways in which this can happen.

Skin contact: Chemicals that cause dermatitis usually do so through direct contact with skin. Some chemicals like corrosive acids can damage the skin by a single contact while others, like organic solvent, may cause damage by repeated exposure.

Inhalation: Inhalation is the most common source of workplace exposure to chemicals and the most difficult to control. Air pollutants can directly damage respiratory tract or gets absorbed through lung and cause system/systemic effects.

Ingestion: Groundwater and sub soil water contamination from leachates from refuse dumps and poorly managed landfill sites can result in ingestion of toxic chemicals by population groups who live far away from the factory sites and decades after the garbage has been dumped.

There are very few studies conducted in India on specific health problems resulting from accidental exposure to toxic industrial solid waste. There had been reports that sacks, cardboard cartons and paper envelopes contaminated with chemicals packed in them were burnt and the irritating fumes from these caused respiratory problems. There had also been reports of skin or respiratory irritation following exposure to corrosives chemicals.

Wastes from slaughterhouse is potentially infectious. All precautions to ensure that potential pathogens to not gain a foot hold in the workers in the slaughterhouse and in the general population, have to be taken during collection, storage and disposal of the slaughter-house waste.

Wastes from non hazardous industries can at times produce health problems, not only among the workers and handlers of waste, but also among general population. One example of this category is the cotton dust. Cotton wasteare generally non-hazardous; however they may, in susceptible individuals provoke respiratory allergic reactions; allergy may be due to inhalation of dust containing cotton wastes or fungus or other contaminants in the waste dust.

Effective Management of Solid Waste

Effective solid management systems are needed to ensure better human health and safety. They must be safe for workers and safeguard public health by preventing the spread of disease. Besides, an effective system of solid waste management must be both environmentally and economically sustainable.

- **Environmentally sustainable:** It must reduce, as much as possible, the environmental impacts of waste management.
- **Economically sustainable:** It must operate at a cost acceptable to community.

It is difficult to minimise these two variables, cost and environmental impact, simultaneously. There will always be a trade off. The balance that needs to be struck is to reduce the overall environmental impacts of the waste management system as far as possible, within an acceptable level of cost.

An economically and environmentally sustainable solid waste management system is effective if it follows an integrated approach *i.e.* it deals with all types of solid waste materials and all sources of solid waste. A multi-material, multi-source management approach is usually effective in environmental & economic terms than a material specific and source specific approach. Specific wastes should be dealt within such a system but in separate streams. An effective waste management system includes one or more of the following options:

(a) Waste collection and transportation.
(b) Resource recovery through sorting and recycling *i.e.* recovery of materials (such as paper, glass, metals) etc. through separation.
(c) Resource recovery through waste processing *i.e.* recovery of materials (such as compost) or recovery of energy through biological, thermal or other processes.
(d) Waste transformation (without recovery of resources) *i.e.* reduction of volume, toxicity or other physical/chemical properties of waste to make it suitable for final disposal.
(e) Disposal on land *i.e.* environmentally safe and sustainable disposal in landfills.

WASTE MANAGEMENT APPROACH

A two-tier approach should be thought of for waste management, *e.g.*, (a) prevention & (b) control of environmental pollution. Prevention aims at minimisation of industrial wastes at source, while the latter stresses on treatment & disposal of wastes.

Prevention—A Waste Minimisation Approach

Reduction and recycling of wastes are inevitably site/plant specific. Generally, waste minimisation techniques can be grouped into four major categories which are applicable for hazardous as well as non-hazardous wastes.These groupsare as follows:

Inventory Management and Improved Operations

- Inventorisation and tracing of all raw materials;
- Purchasing of fewer toxic and more non-toxic production materials, and
- Improving material receiving, storage, and handling practices.

Modification of Equipment

- Installation of equipment that produce minimal or no wastes;
- Modification of equipment to enhance recovery or recycling options;
- Redesigning of equipment or production lines to produce less waste;
- Improving operating efficiency of equipment; and
- Maintaining strict preventive maintenance programme.

Production Process Changes

- Substitution of non-hazardous for hazardous raw materials;
- Segregation of wastes by type for recovery;
- Elimination of sources of leaks and spills;
- Separation of hazardous wastes from non-hazardous wastes;
- Redesigning or reformulation for products to be less hazardous; and
- Optimisation of reactions and raw material use.

Recyclingand Reuse

- Installation of closed-loop systems;
- Recycling off site for use; and
- Exchange of wastes.

Waste minimisation at source may be achieved within the industry through application of various approaches described above.

Waste Management at Source

A specific example is removal of fly ash through coal beneficiation process at the mine head in view of high ash content. It is evident that the larger the volume of waste and the longer the distance of transportation of raw material (coal), the bigger will be the economic benefit infavour of coal beneficiation instead of carrying the filthy fly ash. However, benefit-cost analyses have to be made before taking appropriate decision. It is possible to cut down waste generation at source by simple, in expensive measures, modifying production processes, through change of raw materials/product design and by employing recovery/recycling and reuse techniques.

To avoid treatment through utilisation of waste, it is important from the environmental pollution view point as well as for the benefit of entrepreneurs to recycle and reuse the wastes generated by adoption of certain process change or by use of low/no-waste generation technology.

Waste minimisation can be practised at various places in the industrial processes. Waste minimisation requires careful planning, creative problem evolving, changing in attitude, sometimes capital investment, and most important a real commitment. Investment on waste minimisation and recovery pays off tangibly within a short time.

CURRENT PRACTICE OF INDUSTRIAL SOLID WASTE MANAGEMENT

Collection of Wastes

Manual handling of industrial waste is the usual practice in developing countries . Wastes are shovelled by hand into storage containers and loaded manually into lorries. Although there may not be a health risk in handling clean waste paper, people handling or salvaging waste without protective clothing are atrisk when waste is mixed with chemicals. Apart from the likelihood of cuts caused by broken glass or sharp metals, sorting through waste contaminated with hazardous chemical materials could cause skin burns, excessive lacrimation, or even loss of consciousness; chronic hazards include respiratory problems from dust inhalation, and potential carcinogenicity from toxic chemicals present in discarded containers or surface deposits in other waste. Personnel handling waste from tanneries or hide processors may also be exposed to such diseases as anthrax. Necessary precautions will reduce and minimise hazards associated with manual handling of industrial wastes. Personnel handling hazardous wastes should wear appropriate protective clothing. Mechanical methods for handling waste should be adopted wherever possible, and people should be educated about the dangers of manual handling of hazardous waste.

Storage & Transportation

The storage of industrial solid waste is often one of the most neglected areas of operation of a firm. Very little attention is paid to proper storage and heaps of mixed waste piled against a wall or on open ground are a common sight in many factories. Concrete bays or disused drums are also often used for storage. Whereas the sludges originating from holding tanks or interceptors do not present storage problems as no separate sludge storage is required, because the sludge is retained in the tank until sufficient quantities are collected.

Waste is rarely covered, protected from vermin or pretreated in any manner. There are no restrictions on access and employees are often encouraged to sort out through such wastes and take away any useful material or articles they find. Waste is regarded as an unwanted product by firms and no person is assigned for its control.

Transportation of industrial waste in metropolitan areas of developing countries is generally not by purpose-built vehicles such as skip-carrying lorries, but by open trucks. The wastes are not covered during transportation. It is rare for special arrangements to be made for hazardous wastes; they are usually collected together with the other wastes. Contractors who carry hazardous waste do not need to be licensed, and consequently, there is little control over either the types of firms engaged in carrying hazardous waste or the vehicles used. Drivers are not given a list of precautions to be taken; there is no manifest or labeling system of wastes during transport. Fly-tipping is prevalent and wastes are often taken to disposal sites in appropriate for the type of waste concerned.

Disposal of Industrial Solid Waste

Industrial waste, whilst presenting the same disposal problems as domestic waste, also contains hazardous waste, thereby exacerbating the difficulties of disposal. Fortunately, the types of industrial wastes generated in a municipal area of a developing country are such that there are not usually large quantities of particularly hazardous wastes for disposal. In the past there has been little control over the disposal of industrial wastes; indeed, it has only been during the last decade that even developed countries have brought in legislation to curb the uncontrolled and environmentally unacceptable practices that were widespread. Without such legislation disposal is almost always by uncontrolled landfill at sites which often pose a threat of water pollution due to leachates.

CHAPTER

4

Hazardous Waste Management

Hazardous wastes refer to wastes that, cause adverse effects on the ecosystem and human beings. These wastes pose risks to human health or living organisms, due to the fact that they:

- are non-degradable;
- can be biologically magnified;
- are highly toxic & lethal at very low concentrations.

The criteria used to determine the nature of hazard include toxicity, phytotoxicity, genetic activity and bio-concentration.

The Definition of "Hazardous Waste"

Thus, a waste is hazardous if it exhibits whether alone or when in contact with other wastes or substances, any of the characteristics identified below:

- Corrosivity
- Ignitability
- Explosive
- Infectious property
- Reactivity
- Toxicity
- Acute toxicity

Examples of Hazardous Waste

Furnace residue and debris, drilling mud and other drilling wastes, used or spent oil.

Examples of characteristics that would make waste hazardous

- Explosive
- Flammable
- Sulphides ≥ 20,000 mg/kg Toxic
- Toxic
- Benzene concentration ≥ 50 mg/kg
- Lead concentration ≤ 5000 mg/kg
- Corrosive
- Reactive

CHARACTERIZATION OF HAZARDOUS WASTE

Corrosivity

Waste exhibits characteristics of corrosivity if a of waste has either of the following properties:

- Any liquid which has a pH less than or equal to 2 or greater than or equal to 12.5.
- Waste, which can corrode steel at a rate greater than 6.35 mm per year at a test temperature of 55°C.

Reactivity

Waste exhibits the characteristics of reactivity, if the waste has any of the following properties:

- Normally unstable and readily undergoes violent change without detonating.
- Reacts violently with water.
- Forms potentially explosive mixture with water.
- Cyanide or sulphide bearing waste which when exposed to pH conditions between 2 and 12.5 can generate toxic gases, vapours or fumes in a quantity sufficient to pose danger to human health or environment .

Ignitability

Waste exhibits the characteristics of ignitability if a waste has any of the following properties:

- It is a liquid other than an aqueous solution containing less than 24% organic solvents by volume and has flash point less than 60°C as determined by a Pensky Martins closed cup tester .
- It is not a liquid and is capable under standard temperature and pressure, of causing fire through friction, absorption of moisture or spontaneous chemical changes, and when ignited burns so vigorously and persistently that it creates a hazard.
- Any oxidizing substance, when in contact with moisture or other materials/wastes, results in spontaneous fire or combustion.

Toxicity

A solid waste exhibits the characteristics of toxicity if leachate from the representative sample by Toxicity Characteristics Leaching Procedure (TCLP) test method (as followed by USEPA, vide No: S.W 46, till Indian standards are notified by MoEF/CPCB) contains any of the contaminants listed in Table below in excess of the concentration limits mentioned there upon.

Table 4.1: TCLP Test Limits

S. No.	*Contaminant*	*TCLP Limit (mg/L)*
01.	Arsenic	5.0
02.	Barium	100
03.	Benzene	0.5
04.	Cadmium	1.0
05.	Carbon tetrachloride	0.5
06.	Chlordane	0.03
07.	Chlorobenzene	100.0
08.	Chloroform	6.0
09.	Chromium	5.0
10.	o-Cresol	200.0a
11.	m-Cresol	200.0a
12.	p-Cresol	200.0a
13.	Cresol	200.0a
14.	2,4-D	10.0
15.	1,4-Dichlorobenzene	7.5
16.	1,2-Dichloroethane	0.5
17.	1,1-Dichloroethylene	0.7
18.	2,4-Dinitrotoluene	0.13
19.	Endrin	0.02
20.	Heptachlor (and its epaoxide)	0.008
21.	Hexachlorobenzene	0.1b
22.	Hexachlorobutadiene	0.5
23.	Hexachloroethane	3.0
24.	Lead	5.0
25.	Lindane	0.4
26.	Mercury	0.2
27.	Methoxychlor	10.0
28.	Methyl ethyl ketone	200.0
29.	Nitrobenzene	2.0
30.	Pentachlorophenol	100.0

31.	Pyridine	5.0
32.	Selenium	1.0
33.	Silver	5.0
34.	Tetrachloroethylene	0.7
35.	Toxaphene	0.5
36.	Trichloroethylene	0.5
37.	2,4,5-Trichlorophenol	400.0
38.	2,4,6-Trichlorophenol	2.0
39.	2,4,5-TP (Silvex)	1.0
40.	Vinyl chloride	0.2

Notes:

a. If o, m, p cresols concentration cannot be differentiated, the total cresol concentration is used.

   Total cresol concentration regulatory level: 200 mg/L

b. If the quantification limit is greater than calculated regulatory level, quantification limit becomes the regulatory limit:

   1. These limits shall be applicable till the notification of leachate standards (including test method) under the E (P) Act, 1986
   2. Best Demonstrated Available Technology (BDAT) standards shall be employed for parameters not mentioned.
   3. Leachate collected shall be treated and disposed as liquid effluent in compliance of the standards notified under the E (P) Act, 1986.

Explosive

Solid waste exhibits the characteristics of sudden, almost instantaneous release of gas, heat, and pressure, accompanied by loud noise when subjected to a certain amount of shock, pressure, or temperature.

Acute Toxicity

Waste exhibits the characteristics of being acutely hazardous, if a representative sample contains any of the following:

- Wastes generated in the manufacturing process of halogenated phenols and other halogenated compounds.
- Wastes generated in the manufacturing/formulating process of pesticides or pesticide derivatives.
- Wastes generated during the manufacturing process of halogenated benzene under alkaline conditions.

- Off-specification or discarded products generated from the above processes.
- Containers used for handling hazardous/toxic substances/wastes.

Infectious property

Wastes containing viable micro-organisms or their toxins which are known or suspected to cause disease in animal or humans fall under this category.

IDENTIFICATION OF HAZARDOUS WASTE

By using either or both of the following criteria, we can identify as to whether or not a waste is hazardous:

(i) The list provided by government agencies declaring that substance as hazardous.

(ii) Characteristics such as ignitibility, corrosivity, reactivity and toxicity of the substance.

(i) Listed Hazardous Wastes

Any waste that fits the definition of a listed waste is considered a hazardous waste. Four separate lists cover wastes from generic industrial processes, specific industrial sectors, unused pure chemical products and formulations that are either acutely toxic or toxic, and all hazardous waste regulations apply to these lists of wastes. These wastes, classified in the F, K, P, and U industrial waste codes respectively, as described below:

- **F-list:** The F-list contains hazardous wastes from non-specific sources, i.e, various industrial processes that may have generated the waste. The list consists of solvents commonly used in degreasing, metal treatment baths & sludges, wastewaters from metal plating operations and dioxin containing chemicals or their precursors. Examples of solvents that are F-listed hazardous wastes, along with their code numbers, include benzene (F005), carbon tetrachloride (F001), cresylic acid (F004), methyl ethyl ketone (F005), methylene chloride (F001), 1,1,1, trichloroethane (F001), toluene (F005) and trichloroethylene (F001). Solvent mixtures or blends, which contain greater than 10% of one or more of the solvents listed in F001, F002, F003, F004 and F005 are also considered F-listed wastes.
- **K-list:** The K-list contains hazardous wastes generated by specific industrial processes. Examples of industries, which generate K-listed wastes include wood preservation, pigment production, chemical production, petroleum refining, iron & steel production, explosive manufacturing and pesticide production.
- **P and U lists:** The P and U lists contain discarded commercial chemical products, off-specification chemicals, container residues and residues from the spillage of materials. These two lists include commercial pure grades of the chemical, any technical grades of the chemical that are produced or marketed, and all formulations in which the chemical is the sole active ingredient. An example of a P or U listed hazardous waste is a pesticide, which is not used during its shelf-life and requires to be disposed in bulk. The primary distinction between the two lists is the quantity at

which the chemical is regulated. The P-list consists of acutely toxic wastes that are regulated when the quantity generated per month, or accumulated at any time, exceeds one kilogram, while U-listed hazardous wastes are regulated when the quantity generated per month exceeds 25 kilograms . Examples of businesses that typically generate P or U listed wastes include pesticide applicators, laboratories and chemical formulators.

(ii) Characteristics of Hazardous Wastes

The regulations define characteristic hazardous wastes as wastes that exhibit measurable properties posing sufficient threats to warrant regulation. For a waste to be deemed a characteristic hazardous waste, it must cause, or significantly contribute to, an increased mortality or an increase in serious irreversible or incapacitating reversible illness, or pose a substantial hazard or threat of a hazard to human health or the environment, when it is improperly treated, stored, transported, disposed of, or otherwise mismanaged.

If the wastes generated at a facility are not listed in the F, K, P, or U lists, the final step to determine whether a waste is hazardous is to evaluate it against the following 4 hazardous characteristics:

(i) **Ignitability** (EPA Waste Identification Number D001): A waste is an ignitable hazardous waste, if it has a flash point of less than 60 C; readily catches fire and burns so vigorously as to create a hazard; or is an ignitable compressed gas or an oxidiser. Naphtha, lacquer thinner, epoxy resins, adhesives and oil based paints are all examples of ignitable hazardous wastes.

(ii) **Corrosivity** (EPA Waste Identification Number D002): A liquid waste which has a pH of less than or equal to 2 or greater than or equal to 12.5 is considered to be a corrosive hazardous waste. Sodium hydroxide, a caustic solution with a high pH, is often used by many industries to clean or degrease metal parts. Hydrochloric acid, a solution with a low pH, is used by many industries to clean metal parts prior to painting. When these caustic or acid solutions are disposed of, the waste is a corrosive hazardous waste.

(iii) **Reactivity** (EPA Waste Identification Number D003): A material is considered a reactive hazardous waste, if it is unstable, reacts violently with water, generates toxic gases when exposed to water or corrosive materials, or if it is capable of detonation or explosion when exposed to heat or a flame. Examples of reactive wastes would be waste gunpowder, sodium metal or wastes containing cyanides or sulphides.

(iv) **Toxicity** (EPA Waste Identification Number D004): To determine if a waste is a toxic hazardous waste, a representative sample of the material must be subjected to a test conducted in a certified laboratory. The toxic characteristic identifies wastes that are likely to leach dangerous concentrations of toxic chemicals into ground water.

Classification of hazardous waste: From a practical standpoint, there are far too many compounds, products and product combinations that fit within the broad definition of hazardous waste. For this reason, groups of waste are considered in the following five general categories:

(i) Radioactive substance: Substances that emit ionising radiation are radioactive. Such substances are hazardous because prolonged exposure to radiation often results in damage to living organisms. Radioactive substances are of special concern because they persist for a long period. The period in which radiation occurs is commonly measured and expressed as *half-life*, *i.e.*, the time required for the radioactivity of a given amount of the substance to decay to half its initial value. For example, uranium compounds have half-lives that range from 72 years for U232 to 23,420,000 years for U236. The management of radioactive wastes is highly controlled by national and state regulatory agencies. Disposal sites that are used for the long-term storage of radioactive wastes are not used for the disposal of any other solid waste.

(ii) Chemicals: Most hazardous chemical wastes can be classified into four groups: synthetic organics, inorganic metals, salts, acids and bases, and flammables and explosives. Some of the chemicals are hazardous because they are highly toxic to most life forms. When such hazardous compounds are present in a waste stream at levels equal to, or greater than, their threshold levels, the entire waste stream is identified as hazardous.

(iii) Biomedical wastes: The principal sources of hazardous biological wastes are hospitals and biological research facilities. The ability to infect other living organisms and the ability to produce toxins are the most significant characteristics of hazardous biological wastes. This group mainly includes malignant tissues discarded during surgical procedures and contaminated materials, such as hypodermic needles, bandages and outdated drugs. This waste can also be generated as a by-product of industrial biological conversion processes.

(iv) Flammable wastes: Most flammable wastes are also identified as hazardous chemical wastes. This dual grouping is necessary because of the high potential hazard in storing, collecting and disposing of flammable wastes. These wastes may be liquid, gaseous or solid, but most often they are liquids. Typical examples include organic solvents, oils, plasticisers and organic sludges.

(v) Explosives: Explosive hazardous wastes are mainly ordnance (artillery) materials, *i.e.*, the wastes resulting from ordnance manufacturing and some industrial gases. Similar to flammables, these wastes also have a high potential for hazard in storage, collection and disposal, and therefore, they should be considered separately in addition to being listed as hazardous chemicals. These wastes may exist in solid, liquid or gaseous form.

(vi) Household hazardous wastes: Household wastes such as cleaning chemicals, batteries, nail polish etc. in MSW constitute hazardous waste. Especially batteries contain mercury which are alkaline which is dangerous enough to kill people. Generic household hazardous material include non chlorinated organic, chlorinated organic, pesticides, latex paint, oil based paints, waste oil, automobile battery and household battery.

Most hazardous wastes in India are generated by highly polluting industries that fall into 17 major categories. These categories are listed below in Table along with the main hazardous wastes they produce:

Table 4.2: Categories of highly polluting industries, with the main hazardous wastes they produce.

Industry	Main Hazardous Wastes Produced
• Aluminum smelter	• Sludges from off-gas treatment; cathode residues including pot-lining wastes; tar containing wastes; flue gas and other particulates; wastes from the treatment of salt slags and black drosses
• Caustic soda	• Mercury bearing sludge; residues/sludges and filter cakes/ brine sludge containing mercury
• Cement	• Wastes/residues; metal compound emissions from cement kilns and use of waste materials as fuel 8
• Copper smelter	• Flue gas dust from roasting; process residues; arsenic-bearing sludge; non-ferrous metal bearing sludge and residue; sludge from scrubbers; spent electrolytic solutions; sludges and filter cakes
• Distilleries	• Sludge from wet scrubbers; ash from incineration of hazardous waste; flue gas cleaning residues; spent acid from batteries; distillation residues from contaminated organic solvents
• Drugs and pharmaceuticals	• Process residues and wastes; spent catalyst/spent carbon; off specification products; date-expired, discarded and off-specification drugs/medicines; spent organic solvents
• Dyes and dye intermediates	• Process waste sludge/residues containing acid or other toxic metals or organic complexes; dust from air filtration system
• Fertilizer	• Spent catalyst; spent carbon; sludge/residue containing arsenic; chromium sludge from water cooling tower
• Integrated iron and steel plant	• Sludge from acid recovery unit; benzol acid sludge; decanter tank tar sludge; tar storage tank residue
• Leather processing including tanneries	• Chromium bearing residues and sludges

• Oil refineries	• Oily sludge/emulsion; spent catalyst; slop oil; organic residues from process; spent clay containing oil
• Pesticides	• Process wastes/residues; chemical sludge containing residue pesticides; date-expired and off- specification pesticides
• Petrochemicals	• Furnace/reactor residue and debris; tarry residues; oily sludge emulsion; organic residues; residues from alkali wash of fuels; still bottoms from distillation process; spent catalyst and molecular sieves; slop oil from wastewater; drill cuttings containing oil; sludge containing oil ; drilling mud and other drilling wastes; oil-containing cargo residue; washing water and sludge; chemical-containing cargo residue and sludge; ballast water containing oil from ships; oily sludge/ emulsion; spent catalyst; slop oil; spent clay containing oil
• Pulp and paper	• Spent chemicals, corrosive wastes arising from use of strong acid and bases; process sludge containing adsorbable organic halides (AOx)
• Sugar	• Sugar processing wastewater with a high content of organic material and high biochemical oxygen demand (BOD)
• Thermal power plants	• Condenser cooling waters, chlorine, boil blowdowns (oil and grease copper, iron), cooling tower blowdown (chlorine, zinc, chromium, phosphate, corrosion inhibiting materials), ash pond effluent (pH), suspended solids, oil and grease
• Zinc smelter	• Sludge and filter press cake arising out of production of zinc sulphate and other zinc compounds; zinc fines/ dust/ash/skimmings (dispersible form); other residues from processing of zinc ash/skimmings; flue gas and other particulates

Health Effects for Certain Hazardous Wastes are tabulated below.

Substance	Potential Health Effects
Arsenic	Carcinogenic to humans (skin, lung, bladder, liver) – stomach and intestinal irritation, nausea, vomiting – decreased production of red and white blood cells – damage to blood vessels – skin changes – abnormal heart rhythm

Benzene	Carcinogenic to humans (leukemia) – harmful to bone marrow, decreased red blood cells, anemia – vomiting, stomach irritation – drowsiness dizziness, rapid heart rate, headaches, tremors, convulsions, unconsciousness
Cadmium	Likely to be carcinogenic to humans – kidney, bone, and lung damage – stomach irritation, vomiting, diarrhea – birth defects in some animal studies
Chloroform	Likely to be carcinogenic to humans – liver and kidney
Lead	Likely to be carcinogenic to humans – damage to the brain and nervous system (adults, children, unborn children) – miscarriage, premature births, neonatal mortality due to decreased birth weight, decreased male fertility – diminished learning abilities in children – increased blood pressure – kidney damage
Mercury	Brain, kidney, and lung damage – serious harm to neural development of fetuses and young children – chest pains, nausea, vomiting, diarrhea – skin rashes and eye irritation – increased blood pressure and heart rate – irritability, sleep disturbances, tremors, coordination problems, changes in vision and hearing, memory problems
Perchlorate	Inhibition of iodine uptake – hypothyroidism, which may adversely affect the skin, heart, lungs, kidneys, gastrointestinal tract, liver, blood, neuromuscular system, nervous system, skeleton, reproductive system, and numerous endocrine organs
Polychlorinated Biphenyls	Likely to be carcinogenic to humans – liver damage – skin rashes and acne – decreased birth weight – short-term behavioral and immune system impacts in children exposed via breast milk
Polycyclic aromatic Hydrocarbons	Likely to be carcinogenic to humans – irritation of skin, lungs, and stomach – reproductive and birth defects in animal studies
Tetrachloroethylene	Likely to be carcinogenic to humans – dizziness, headaches, sleepiness, confusion, nausea, difficulty speaking and walking, unconsciousness
Trichloroethylene	Carcinogenic to humans – liver, kidney, and nervous system damage – impaired immune system and heart function – impaired fetal development – skin rashes, lung irritation, headaches, dizziness, nausea, unconsciousness

Sources & Health effects of some more hazardous wastes are tabulated below.

Hazardous waste	Source	Health effects
Heavy metals		
Arsenic	Mining, non anthropogenic geo-chemical formation	Carcinogenic, cardiac disorders, anemia,
Cadmium	Mining, fertilizer industry, battery waste	Carcinogenic, damage to livers and kidneys, chronic obstructive pulmonary diseases, cardiovascular and skeletal disorders.
Chromium	Mining areas, tanneries	Hidney damage, skin disease, acute tubular damage.
Lead	Lead acid battery smelters	Lead poisoning, neurotoxic, mental impairment in children, damage to brain, kidney and liver
Manganese	Mining areas	Respiratory disease, neuropsychiatric disorder
Mercury	Chlor-alkali industries, health care institutes	Hg poisoning affects human brain, central nervous system, kidneys and liver. High Hg exposure causes vision, speech and hearing impairment. May lead to death
Nickel	Mining, metal refining	Lung and nasal cancer, damage to gastrointestinal system, cerebral edema, respiratory failure
Hydrocarbons		
Benzene	Petrochemical industries, solvents	Headaches, nausea, leukemia, damage to bone marrow
Vinyl chloride	Plastics	Carcinogenic (liver and lung cancer), depression of central nervous system, embryotoxic
Pesticides	Insecticides	Cancers, genetic damage, stillbirths, immune system disturbances, embryo damage
Organic chemicals		
Dioxins	Waste incineration, herbicides	Cancer, birth defects, skin disease
PCBs	Fluorescent lights, E-waste, Hydraulic fluid	Skin damage, possibly carcinogenic, gastrointestinal damage

Hazards of solid wastes having different hazardous characteristics are tabulated below.

S.N.	Hazardous characteristics	Potential hazards on living animals/environment
1	Flammable/explosive	This type of waste may cause damage to the surroundings by producing harmful gases at high temperature and pressure or by causing fire hazards.
2	Oxidizing	Type of wastes that may yield oxygen and thereby cause or contribute to the combustion of other materials.
3	Poisonous (acute)	These wastes have high potential to cause death, serious injury or to harm health if swallowed, inhaled or by skin contact.
4	Infectious substances	Hazardous wastes containing micro-organisms and their toxins, and responsible for diseases in animals or humans.
5	Corrosives	These wastes are chemically active and may cause severe damage to the flora and fauna, or to the other materials by direct contact with them.
6	Eco-toxic	These wastes may present immediate or delayed adverse impacts to the environment by means of bioaccumulation and/or toxic effects upon biotic systems.
7	Toxic (delayed or chronic)	These wastes, if inhaled or ingested or if they penetrate the skin, may cause delayed or chronic effects, including carcinogenicity.
8	Organic peroxides	These are organic waste containing bivalent-O-O-structure and may undergo exothermic self-accelerating decomposition.

Schedule I

[See rules 3 (l)]

List of processes generating hazardous wastes

S.No.	Processes	Hazardous Waste *
1.	Petrochemical processes and pyrolytic operations	Furnace/reactor residue and debris Tarry residues Oily sludge emulsion

		Organic residues Residues from alkali wash of fuels Still bottoms from distillation process Spent catalyst and molecular sieves Slop oil from wastewater
2.	Drilling operation for oil and gas production	Drill cuttings containing oil Sludge containing oil Drilling mud and other drilling wastes
3.	Cleaning, emptying and maintenance of petroleum oil storage tanks including ships	Oil-containing cargo residue, washing water and sludge Chemical-containing cargo residue and sludge Sludge and filters contaminated with oil Ballast water containing oil from ships.
4.	Petroleum refining/re-processing of used oil/recycling of waste oil	Oily sludge/emulsion Spent catalyst Slop oil Organic residues from process Spent clay containing oil
5.	Industrial operations using mineral/ synthetic oil as lubricant in hydraulic systems or other applications	Used/spent oil Wastes/residues containing oil
6.	Secondary production and/or industrial use of zinc	Sludge and filter press cake arising out of production of zinc sulphate and other zinc compounds. Zinc fines/dust/ash/skimmings (dispersible form) Other residues from processing of zinc ash/ skimmings Flue gas dust and other particulates
7.	Primary production of zinc/lead/copper and other non-ferrous metals except aluminium	Flue gas dust from roasting Process residues Arsenic-bearing sludge Non ferrous metal bearing sludge and residue. Sludge from scrubbers

8.	Secondary production of copper	Spent electrolytic solutions Sludges and filter cakes Flue gas dust and other particulates
9.	Secondary production of lead	Lead bearing residues Lead ash/particulate from flue gas
10.	Production and/or industrial use of cadmium and arsenic and their compounds	Residues containing cadmium and arsenic
11.	Production of primary and secondary aluminium	Sludges from off-gas treatment Cathode residues including pot lining wastes Tar containing wastes Flue gas dust and other particulates Wastes from treatment of salt slags and black drosses
12.	Metal surface treatment, such as etching, staining, polishing, galvanising, cleaning, degreasing, plating, etc.	Acid residues Alkali residues Spent bath/sludge containing sulphide, cyanide and toxic metals Sludge from bath containing organic solvents Phosphate sludge Sludge from staining bath Copper etching residues Plating metal sludge
13.	Production of iron and steel including other ferrous alloys (electric furnaces; steel rolling and finishing mills; Coke oven and by product plant)	Sludge from acid recovery unit Benzol acid sludge Decanter tank tar sludge Tar storage tank residue
14.	Hardening of steel	Cyanide-, nitrate-, or nitrite-containing sludge Spent hardening salt
15.	Production of asbestos or asbestos-containing materials	Asbestos-containing residues Discarded asbestos Dust/particulates from exhaust gas treatment.

16.	Production of caustic soda and chlorine	Mercury bearing sludge Residue/sludges and filter cakes Brine sludge containing mercury
17.	Production of mineral acids	Residues, dusts or filter cakes Spent catalyst
18.	Production of nitrogenous and complex fertilizers	Spent catalyst Spent carbon Sludge/residue containing arsenic Chromium sludge from water cooling tower
19.	Production of phenol	Residue/sludge containing phenol
20.	Production and/or industrial use of solvents	Contaminated aromatic, aliphatic or napthenic solvents may or may not be fit for reuse. Spent solvents Distillation residues
21.	Production and/or industrial use of paints, pigments, lacquers, varnishes, plastics and inks	Process wastes, residues & sludges Fillers residues
22.	Production of plastic raw materials	Residues of additives used in plastics manufacture like dyestuffs, stabilizers, flame retardants, etc. Residues and waste of platicisers Residues from vinyl chloride monomer production Residues from acrylonitrile production Non-polymerised residues
23.	Production and/or industrial use of glues, cements, adhesive and resins	Wastes/residues (not made with vegetable or animal materials)
24.	Production of canvas and textiles	Chemical residues
25.	Industrial production and formulation of wood preservatives	Chemical residues Residues from wood alkali bath
26.	Production or industrial use of synthetic dyes, dye-intermediates and pigments	Process waste sludge/residues containing acid or other toxic metals or organic complexes Dust from air filtration system

27.	Production compounds of organo-silicone	process residues
28.	Production/formulation of drugs/ pharmaceuticals & health care product	Process Residues and wastes Spent catalyst/spent carbon Off specification products Date-expired, discarded and off-specification drugs/medicines Spent organic solvents
29.	Production and formulation of pesticides including stock-piles	Process wastes/residues Chemical sludge containing residue pesticides Date-expired and off-specification pesticides
30.	Leather tanneries	Chromium bearing residues and sludges
31.	Electronic industry	Process residues and wastes Spent etching chemicals and solvents
32.	Pulp and paper industry	Spent chemicals Corrosive wastes arising from use of strong acid and bases Process sludge containing adsorbable organic halides [AOx]
33.	Disposal of barrels/containers used for handling of hazardous wastes/ chemicals	Chemical-containing residue arising from decontamination. Sludge from treatment of wastewater arising out of cleaning / disposal of barrels / containers discarded containers / barrels / liners contaminated with hazardous wastes/chemicals
34.	Purification and treatment of exhaust air, water and wastewater from the processes in this schedule and common industrial effluent treatment plants (CETP's)	Flue gas cleaning residue Spent ion exchange resin containing toxic metals Chemical sludge from waste water treatment Oil and grease skimming residues Chromium sludge from cooling water

35.	Purification process for organic compounds/solvents	Filters and filter material which have organic liquids in them, *e.g.* mineral oil, synthetic oil and organic chlorine compounds Spent catalyst Spent carbon
36.	Hazardous waste treatment processes, *e.g.* incineration, distillation, separation and concentration techniques	Sludge from wet scrubbers Ash from incineration of hazardous waste, flue gas cleaning residues Spent acid from batteries Distillation residues from contaminated organic solvents

*** The inclusion of wastes contained in this Schedule does not preclude the use of Schedule 2 to demonstrate that the waste is not hazardous. In case of dispute, the matter would be referred to the Technical Review Committee constituted by MoEF.**

Note: *The high volume low effect wastes such as fly ash, phosphogypsum, red mud, slags from pyrometallurgical operations, mine tailings and ore beneficiation rejects are excluded from the category of hazardous wastes. Separate guidelines on the management of these wastes shall be issued by CPCB.*

(iii) List of Hazardous Characteristics

Code	Characteristic
H 1	**Explosive** An explosive substance or waste is a solid or liquid substance or waste (or mixture of substances or wastes) which is in itself capable by chemical reaction of producing gas at such a temperature and pressure and at such speed as to cause damage to the surroundings (UN Class 1; HI)
H 3	**Flammable liquids** The word "flammable" has the same meaning as "inflammable". Flammable liquids are liquids, or mixtures of liquids, or liquids containing solids in solution or suspension (for example, paints, varnishes, lacquers, etc. but not including substances or wastes otherwise classified on account of their dangerous characteristics) which give off a flammable vapour at temperatures of not more than 60.5°C, closed-cup test, or not more than 65.5°C, open-cup

test. (Since the results of open-cup tests and of closed- cup tests are not strictly comparable and even individual results by the same test are often variable, regulations varying from the above figures to make allowance for such differences would be within the spirit of this definition).

H 4.1 Flammable solids

Solids, or waste solids, other than those classed as explosives, which under conditions encountered in transport are readily combustible, or may cause or contribute to fire through friction.

H 4.2 Substances or wastes liable to spontaneous combustion

Substances or wastes which are liable to spontaneous heating under normal conditions encountered in transport, or to heating up on contact with air, and being then liable to catch fire.

H 4.3 Substances or wastes which, in contact with water emit flammable gases

Substances or wastes which, by interaction with water, are liable to become spontaneously flammable or to give off flammable gases in dangerous quantities.

H 5.1 Oxidizing

Substances or wastes which, while in themselves not necessarily combustible, may, generally by yielding oxygen cause, or contribute to, the combustion of other materials.

H 5.2 Organic peroxides

Organic substances or wastes which contain the bivalent-O-O- structure are thermally unstable substances which may undergo exothermic self-accelerating decomposition.

H 6.1 Poisons (acute)

Substances or wastes liable either to cause death or serious injury or to harm health if swallowed or inhaled or by skin contact.

H 6.2 Infectious substances

Substances or wastes containing viable micro organisms or their toxins which are known or suspected to cause disease in animals or humans.

H 8 Corrosives

Substances or wastes which, by chemical action, will cause severe damage when in contact with living tissue, or, in the case of leakage, will materially damage, or even destroy, other goods or the means of transport; they may also cause other hazards.

H 10 **Liberation of toxic gases in contact with air or water**

Substances or wastes which, by interaction with air or water, are liable to give off toxic gases in dangerous quantities.

H 11 **Toxic (delayed or chronic)**

Substances or wastes which, if they are inhaled or ingested or if they penetrate the skin, may involve delayed or chronic effects, including carcinogenicity).

H 12 **Ecotoxic**

Substances or wastes which if released present or may present immediate or delayed adverse impacts to the environment by means of bioaccumulation and/or toxic effects upon biotic systems.

CHAPTER 5

RADIOACTIVE WASTE MANAGEMENT

Radioactive wastes are the leftovers from the use of nuclear materials for the production of electricity, diagnosis & treatment of disease, and other purposes.

The spontaneous emission of particles and rays by an unstable nucleus is called radioactivity and such substances are called radioactive substances *e.g.* radium, uranium, thorium. Radioactive pollution can be defined as the release of radioactive substances or high-energy particles into the air water, or earth as a result of human activity, either by accident or by design. Sometimes natural sources of radioactivity, such as radon gas emitted from beneath the ground, are considered pollutants when they become a threat to human health. The sources of radioactive wastes are:

- **Natural sources**: Solar radiation, radionuclides in the earth crust, human internal radiation, environmental radiations.
- **Anthropogenic sources**: The sources of such waste include: (1) nuclear weapon testing or detonation; (2) the *nuclear fuel cycle,* including the mining, separation, and production of nuclear materials for use in nuclear power plants or nuclear bombs; (3) accidental release of radioactive material from nuclear power plants..

Radioactive waste is material that is radioactive that is no longer needed at the plant and can be disposed of. The following are some examples of the sources of radioactive waste.

After a fuel assembly has been used in the reactor core to generate power, there is a large inventory of fission products held inside the cladding of the fuel. Since the processing of spent fuel is not done for commercial power plants, the fuel must be disposed of in some safe fashion.

The activation products that are carried by the reactor coolant system are collected by the filters and demineralizers in the cleanup systems. When the filters and demineralizer resins are full, they must be disposed of as radioactive waste.

A paper towel or rag used to wipe up radioactive water must be disposed of as radioactive waste.

A contaminated piece of equipment that is no longer useable must be disposed of as radioactive waste.

Since even a small amount of radiation exposure can have serious (and cumulative) biological consequences, and since many radioactive wastes remain toxic for centuries, radioactive pollution in a serious environmental concern even though natural sources of radioactivity far exceed artificial ones are present. The faster a radioisotope is decaying, the more radioactive it will be. Another factor in deciding how dangerous a pure radioactive substance will be is the energy of the radiation. Some decays yield more energy than others. This is further complicated by the fact that few radioisotopes decay immediately to a stable state, but rather to a radioactive decay product leading to decay chains.

Radioactive pollution that is spread through the earth's atmosphere is termed *fallout*. Such pollution was most common in the two decades following World War II, when the United States, the Soviet Union, and Great Britain conducted hundreds of nuclear weapons tests in the atmosphere.

Three types of fallout result from nuclear detonations: local, tropospheric and stratospheric.

- Local fallout is quite intense but short-lived.
- Tropospheric fallout (in the lower atmosphere) is deposited at a later time and covers a larger area, depending on meteorological conditions.
- Stratospheric fallout, which release extremely fine particles into the upper atmosphere, may continue for years after an explosion and attain a worldwide distribution.

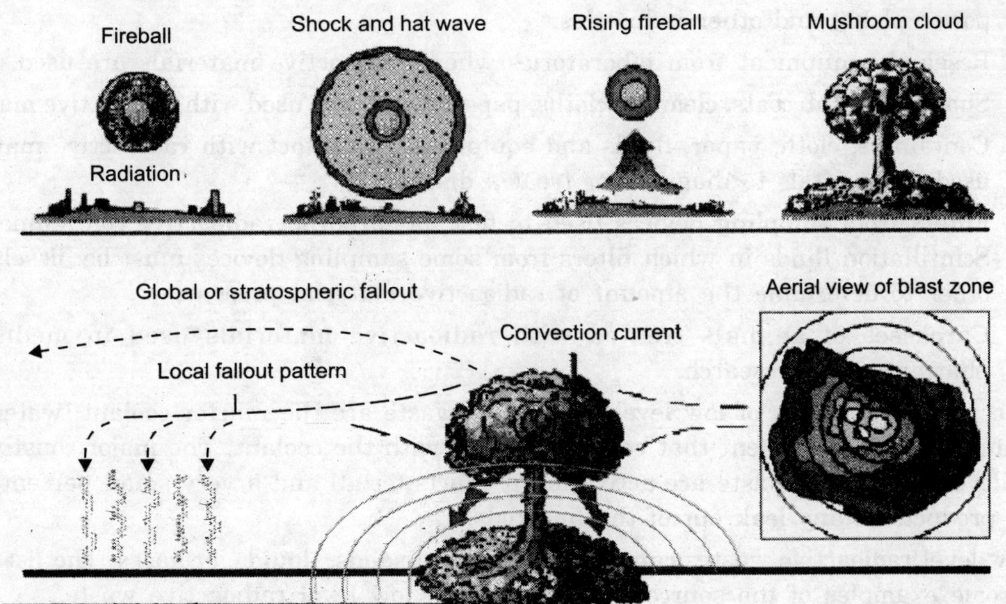

Types of Radioactive Waste

Low level Waste (LLW) is generated from hospitals and industry, as well as the nuclear fuel cycle. It comprises paper, rags, tools, clothing, filters etc which contain small amounts of mostly short-lived radioactivity. It does not require shielding during handling and transport and is suitable for shallow land burial. To reduce its volume, it is often compacted or incinerated before disposal.

LLW includes items that have become contaminated with radioactive material or have become radioactive through exposure to neutron or gamma radiation. Low-level wastes are not spent fuel, milling tailings, reprocessed materials, or transuranic materials. However, "low level" does not mean "not dangerous". The level of radioactivity and the half life of the radioactive isotopes in LLW are relatively less. This type of waste is generated from hospitals, laboratories and industry as well as in every stage of the nuclear fuel cycle. LLW which come from reactors can be divided into two categories: (i) fuel wastes which are fission products that leak out of fuel rods into cooling water and (ii) non-fuel wastes result when stray neutrons bombard any material in the core other than the fuel such as the reactor vessel itself and cause them to become radioactive. LLW contains virtually no alpha emitters, and is comparatively easy to dispose. Storing the waste for a period of about 10 to 50 years will allow most of the radioactive isotopes in LLW to decay, at which point the waste can be disposed off as normal waste. LLW is generally buried in shallow landfill sites. Examples of low-level wastes are:

- Ion exchange resins and filter materials used to clean water at a nuclear power plant.
- Contaminated hand tools, components, piping and other equipment from nuclear power plants and other industries.
- Research equipment from laboratories where radioactive materials are used.
- Shoe covers, lab coats, cleaning cloths, paper towels etc., used with radioactive material.
- Containers, cloth, paper, fluids and equipment in contact with radioactive materials used in hospitals to diagnose or treat a disease.
- Filters from sampling devices used to test for airborne radioactive contamination.ü Scintillation fluids in which filters from some sampling devices must be dissolved in order to determine the amount of radioactive material present.
- Carcasses of animals treated with radioactive materials used in medical or pharmaceutical research.

The principal sources of low level radioactive waste are the reactor coolant (water) and the components & equipment that come in contact with the coolant. The major constituents of low level radioactive waste are activation products (crud) and a very small percentage of fission products (if any leak out of the fuel rods).

Low level radioactive wastes can be in the form of solids, liquids, or gases. The list below gives some examples of the sources of each form of low level radioactive waste.

Solid radioactive waste: Contaminated rags, tools, clothing, etc., spent filter cartridges, spent demineralizer resins.

Liquid radioactive waste:Equipment leakoff points, Equipment vents and drains, Floor drain system

Gaseous radioactive waste: Equipment vents , Liquid waste system (evaporator gas stripper)

Low Level Radioactive Waste Handling

Because of the different characteristics of solids, liquids, and gases, each must be processed differently. The waste must also be processed in such a manner as to minimize the risk of exposure to the public.

Liquids are processed to remove the radioactive impurities. These processes might include:

- Filtering,
- Routing through demineralizers,
- Boiling off the water (evaporation) and leaving the solid impurities (which are then processed as solid radioactive waste), and/or
- Storing the liquid for a time period to allow the radioactive material to decay.

After processing, the water will be sampled. If samples show the water meets the required standards, the water can be placed in the storage tanks for use in the plant or be released to the environment. If the samples show the water does not meet the standards, it will be reprocessed.

Some materials, such as the evaporator bottoms (solids that remain after the water is evaporated off), will be mixed with some material to form a solid (such as concrete). This is also sometimes done with spent demineralizer resins. After mixing with a hardener, the material is processed as solid radioactive waste.

Gaseous wastes are filtered, compressed to take up less space, and then allowed to decay for some time period. After the required time has passed, the gases will be sampled. If the required limits are met, the gases will be released to the atmosphere, or sometimes the gases will be reused in specific areas of the plant.

Solid wastes are packaged as required and shipped to a burial site for disposal .

Intermediate Level Waste (ILW) contains higher amounts of radioactivity and some requires shielding. It typically comprises resins, chemical sludges and metal fuel cladding, as well as contaminated materials from reactor decommissioning. It may be solidified in concrete or bitumen for disposal. Generally short lived waste (mainly from reactors) is buried in a shallow repository, while long lived waste (from fuel reprocessing) will be disposed of deep underground.

ILW contains higher amount of radioactivity and in some cases it requires shielding for handling. This waste includes ion exchange resins used to purify the water circulating through the reactor, chemical sludge and fuel cladding material as well as contaminated materials from reactor decommissioning. It may be solidified in concrete or bitumen for disposal. The short-lived radioactive waste other than fuel materials from reactors is buried in shallow repositories, while the long-lived waste which are generated from fuel fabrication and fuel-reprocessing operations is deposited in deep underground facilities.

Transuranic Waste arises mainly from weapons production, and consists of clothing, tools, rags, residues, debris and other such items contaminated with small amounts of radioactive elements — mostly plutonium. These elements have an atomic number greater than uranium — thus called transuranic (beyond uranium). Because of the long half-lives of these elements, this waste is not disposed of either as low level or intermediate level waste. It does not have the very high radioactivity of high level waste, nor its high heat generation. The United States currently permanently disposes off transuranic waste at the Waste Isolation Pilot Plant.

High Level Waste (HLW) arises from the use of uranium fuel in a nuclear reactor and nuclear weapons processing. It contains the fission products and transuranic elements generated in the reactor core. It is highly radioactive and hot. It can be considered the "ash" from "burning" uranium. HLW accounts for over 95% of the total radioactivity produced in the process of nuclear electricity generation.

HLW is the first cycle raffinate generated from the aqueous reprocessing of spent nuclear fuel and it consists of unrecovered uranium and plutonium, fission product elements and other corrosion products leached out from clad. The yield of fission products depends on the type of fissile atom loaded in the reactor, burn-up and the neutron energy. Most of the radioactive isotopes in HLW emit large amount of radiation. Some of them have extremely long half-lives requiring longer time periods before the waste settles to safe levels of radioactivity. While it is only 3% by volume of total waste, it holds 95% of the radioactivity. It generates considerable amount of heat and requires cooling as well as special shielding during handling and transport. The HLW is vitrified by incorporating it into borosilicate glass and is sealed inside canisters for eventual disposal into deep underground.

The constituents of HLW are:

(a) Corrosion products: Depending on the burn-up, the stainless steel clad tubes used to contain the fuel, corrode in boiling nitric acid during the dissolution of spent fuel. The reprocessing plant components for spent nuclear fuels are normally constructed from stainless steel. As corrosion of the clad tubes and of vessels inner surfaces takes place because of the use of boiling nitric acid, the solution will contain primarily iron, chromium, nickel and manganese.

(b) Fission products: Depending on the composition of the fuel and burn-up, the fission products Cs, Rb, Sr, Ba, Ru, Mo, Zr, Pd, Tc, Rh, Te, Sb and rare earths have been observed to be present in HLW after reprocessing.

(c) Unextracted uranium and plutonium: Although the basic objective of the reprocessing plant is to separate uranium and plutonium from the dissolved fuel solution for subsequent reuse, the separation can never be perfect and traces of uranium and plutonium will end up along with the fission products in the waste solution.

(d) ***TRU elements:*** The trans-uranium elements neptunium, americium and curium are formed from uranium and plutonium by neutron capture followed by β-decay. These elements are α-active and are of particular concern in long-term waste management because their half-lives are very long.

(e) ***Chemical additives:*** Variety of chemicals like HNO_3, Al, Na^+, PO_4, SO_4, Cl, F etc. introduced at various stages of reprocessing are present in HLW.

(f) ***Organic impurities:*** Organic materials like dibutyl phosphoric acid and mono butyl phosphoric acid, which are the degraded products of tributyl phosphate dissolve in nitric acid, and the degraded product of the diluents (*n*-dodecane/NPH) and tributyl phosphate form emulsions. These components, if present in significant amounts, could cause difficulties during the waste treatment steps.

Disposal of High Level Nuclear Waste

The procedure for the disposal of high level nuclear waste is complex, unlike the LLW and ILW. Methods for the disposal of nuclear waste include:

(a) ***Short term storage:*** Short term storage will reduce the radioactivity of the HLW (raffinate) significantly. The reduction in radioactivity during short term storage facilitates handling and shipment of the waste much easier. After short term storage, the waste will be sent for transmutation or long term storage.

(b) ***Long term storage:*** Long term refers to a period of thousands of years. The waste must not be allowed to escape into the outside environment by anyway, which includes accidental uncovering, leaching of the waste into the water resources and exposure due to earthquake or other geological activities.

(c) ***Transmutation:*** Transmutation is the transformation of one element into another. The goal of transmutation in radioactive waste disposal is to transmute long half-life, highly radioactive elements into shorter half life and low radioactive waste elements.

(d) ***HLW management in India:*** HLW generated during reprocessing of spent nuclear fuels is concentrated by evaporation and stored in stainless steel tanks with the capacity of 250-500 m^3 each. These storage tanks require cooling and continuous surveillance. Liquid storage in stainless steel tanks is at best an interim step and a three-step strategy for the management of HLW has been adopted in India :

Step 1: Immobilization of HLW by converting it into inert and stable vitreous matrices.

Step 2: Interim storage under surveillance and cooling.

Step 3: Ultimate disposal of solidified HLW.

The vitrification facilities are co-located near the reprocessing plants to avoid long-term transportation of HLW. HLW is transferred from the reprocessing plant to vitrification plant through underground piping. India is having operating vitrification plants at Tarapur & Trombay and Kalpakkam. A solid storage and surveillance facility (SSSF) has been set up at Tarapur for interim storage of vitrified HLW. An elaborate programme on deep geological disposal is being pursued to realize the third stage of the programme.

The long term strategy for the treatment of HLW would involve its partitioning that would not only result in the reduction of radioactivity but could also have resource advantage. The final utilization/transmutation of the partitioned long lived radionuclides would be evolved based on the available technological options involving FBRs and Accelerator Driven Systems. Development of ceramic waste forms like synroc, NZP and metal waste forms etc. is also being pursued to address specific waste streams on account of partitioning leading to waste volume reduction and enhanced long term safety.

The procedure adopted for radioactive waste management in India is summarized in Figure below.

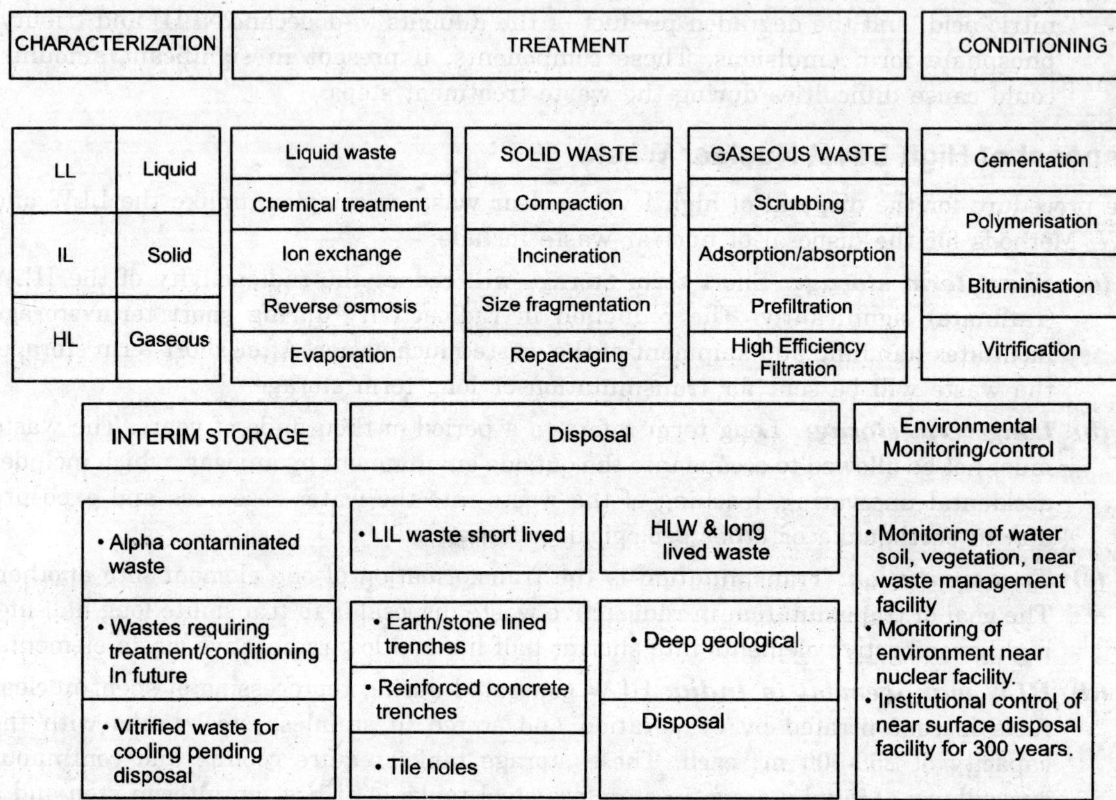

Figure 5.1: Procedure adopted for radioactive waste management in India

CLASSIFICATION OF RADIOACTIVE WASTE

Both the qualitative and quantitative modes of classifying the radioactive wastes essentially lead to 3 classes of wastes:

(i) High level waste (HLW);

(ii) Intermediate level waste (ILW); and

(iii) Low level waste (LLW).

These three classes are primarily organised to include appropriate disposal safety. The radioactivity levels of wastes range from negligible to very high concentration of radionuclides; with decay periods varying from tens of years to few million years. There is an increased need to isolate them from reaching biosphere through suitable disposal options that may range from simple earth trench to deep underground geological repository. This is mainly aimed at, where suitable. The waste may be either stored for decay and then exempted, disposed off in near surface disposal facility, or isolated from biosphere in deep geological formations.

High Level Waste (HLW)

The highly radioactive liquid arising from chemical processing of irradiated fuels falls in this category and this liquid contains predominantly fission and activation products along with some actinides. These wastes contain radioactivity levels intense to generate significant quantities of decay heat for several years. Spent fuel, if it is declared as waste, will also fall in this category. Specific activities of these wastes depend on many parameters such as decay periods, and conditioning techniques. They are in the range of 5.5 × 10" TBq/m^3 and a decay heat generation of about 2–20 kW/m^3 is considered adequate to distinguish HLW from other wastes. The relevance of heat generation derives importance in relation to heat removal situations (like storage geometry, ventilation, thermal conductivity) envisaged in storage or disposal options.

Intermediate Level Waste (ILW)

The radioactivity waste which because of its radionuclide content requires shielding but need little or no provision for heat dissipation during handling and transportation falls in this category. A contract dose rate of 2 mGy/hr has been used to distinguish this class from LLW, however, this distinction becomes relatively of secondary importance in terms of migration behaviour.

Low Level Waste (LLW)

This class of wastes contain low radionuclide content and do not require shielding during handling and transportation.

Short-lived Low and Intermediate Level Waste (LIL W-SL)

A differentiation has also been made within LLW classification based on half-lives and a bearing waste as presented in Table below. For example, short-lived low and intermediate level waste contain high concentrations of short-lived radionuelides but very low concentrations of long-lived radionuelides. The term short-lived indicates that the waste will decay to acceptably low value from radiological considerations in a time period of about 300 years during which administrative controls are expected to last. Since LILW-SL is generated with a wide range of radionuelides with varying concentrations, the disposal modes are also adopted appropriately for the management of this waste. The disposal options vary from simple earth trench to engineered facilities constructed above ground or underground at depths of few metres below the grade level. On an average, the gross b, g activity range of 1 × 10^{-1} × 10^4 TBq/m^3 is adopted for this class of waste.

Long-lived Low and Intermediate Level Waste (LILW-LL)

LILW-LL contain long-lived a emitters in significant quantities and require high degree of isolation from the biosphere. This is envisaged in deep geological formations. The boundary line of radioactive waste disposal between LILW-SL and LILW-LL cannot be specified in a universal manner with respect to concentration levels, as they depend on actual waste management option and the properties of individual radionuelides. The specific activity of wastes having transuranic radionuclides is limited to 400 Bq/g averaged over the site and 4000 Bq/g per package for near-surface disposal facility in our country and this is in conformity with international practice. The waste packages whose activity exceed 4000 Bq/g are stored in retrievable form pending ultimate disposal.

Exempt Waste (EW)

The exempt waste contains so little radioactive material that cannot be considered as radioactive and is exempted from regulatory control. The exempt levels for solid radioactive materials are based on limited the annual doses to members of public to 0.01 mSv. Since the individual radiation doses are limited to deminimus level, no specific attention is made for the unrestrictive release of radionuclides below the exempt concentration levels. For example, the exempt level for gross b, g activity is considered as 10 Bq/g while the same for a nuclides is adopted as 1 Bq/g. It is realised that exempt levels and derived limits for routine releases are distinctly different. For example, the mining and milling wastes, though they generate long-lived a radionuclides like U, Th and Ra at sufficiently low concentrations, are not treated as exempt wastes but are subjected to disposal options similar to the short-lived radioactive waste.

Table 5.1. New classification of solid and solidified radioactive waste by International Atomic Energy Agency

	Waste classes	Typical characteristics	Disposal options
1.	Exempt waste (EW)	Activity at or below clearance levels, which are based on an annual close to members of the public of less than 0.01 mSv.	No radiological restrictions
2.	Low and intermediate level waste (LILW)	Activity levels above clearance levels and thermal power below about 2 k\Wm^3.	
2.1	Short-lived waste (LILW-SL)	Limitation of long-lived alpha emitting radionuclides 4000 Bq/kg in individual waste packages and to an overall average of 400 Bq/kg per waste package.	Near surface or geological disposal facility
2.2	Long-lived waste (LILW-LL)	Long-lived radionuclide concentration exceeding limitations for short-lived waste.	Geological disposal facility

3.	High level waste (HLW)	Thermal power above $2kW/m^3$ and long-lived radionuclide concentration exceeding limitations for short-lived waste.	Geological disposal facility

ORIGIN OF RADIOACTIVE WASTE

Radioactive wastes arise at every stage of nuclear fuel cycle. The quantities mentioned are normalised to the production of 1 GWa of electricity, *i.e.* for output of 1 GW (e) reactor producing electricity continuously for 1 year assuming a net efficiency of 32.5 percent. The radioactive wastes produced at each stage of the nuclear fuel cycle are almost entirely different in terms of activity content and waste volume.

Uranium Mining and Milling Waste

The uranium mill at Jaduguda operates with a processing rate of about 1000 tons/day for extraction of uranium from the ore containing uranium in the range of 0.04-0.06 percent. The product is a semi-refined uranium compound (U_3O_8) called yellow cake which is the feed material for the production of uranium hexafluoride (UF_6), The yellow cake is produced by sulphuric acid leach process.

Large amounts of solid waste tailings are generated following the removal of uranium. The mill generates 1000 tons/day of tailing solids slurred in 3500 tons of waste milling solutions. The failing piles could have a radiological impact on environment through atmospheric pathway by continuous discharge of radon and its daughter products. Finally, ^{226}Ru and ^{230}Th can be blown off the pile by wind into the atmosphere and can be leached from the pile into the surface water.

The liquid effluent from the mill consists of waste solutions from leaching, grinding, extraction and washing circuits of the mill. The solutions which have pH between 1.5 and 2.0 contain unreacted portions of sulphuric acid used as the leaching agent in mill process, and sulphates and silica as the primary dissolved solids with trace quantities of soluble metals and organic solvents. The liquid is discharged into the tailing pond after neutralisation with lime and precipitation with pyrolusite. This method reduces the levels of many potential contaminants in seepage from the tailings impoundment.

The mining and milling of uranium ore produces large volumes of both solid and liquid wastes and they are characterised by significant content of naturally occurring radionuclidcs. The tailings contain most of decay products of uranium notably ^{226}Ra which decays to radon and its progeny.

Fuel Fabrication

The uranium concentrate (yellow cake) is converted into UO_2 powder after dewatering and calcination. The power is then pressed into fuel pellets that are sintered to optimum density and chemical stoichiometry. The waste arising from, fuel fabrication operations include HEPA filters and other dry trash contaminated with UO_2. The liquid waste stream of oil, water and traces of UO_2 powder is also produced when the pallets are grounded to size before they are inserted in the fuel cladding.

Nuclear Reactor Operations

The total thermal output of 3.1 GW of energy during one year operation requires about 3 × 10^{27} fission events. A variety of radionuclides arise from the fission process itself and the neutron capture reactions in the nuclear fuel lead to the production of isotopes of actinide series. The neutron activation of the metallic materials used as the fuel cladding and other components produce short-lived neutron activation products which contaminate the primary cooling circuits. The highest concentration of radioactivity arises from reactions in the fuel by fission and neutron capture reactions. Though the detailed inventory of radionuclides in the spent fuel depends on the isotopic composition of the fuel, neutron spectrum in the reactor and the duration of irradiation; the differences are relatively small. The inventory of fission products and actinides in natural fuelled PHWR after irradiation to 6400 MWd/ton at full power of 1 GW (c) will be about 4 × 10^6 TBq, This reduces after 100 years of storage to about 4 × 10^4 TBq because of the decay of short-lived fission products such as ^{89}Sr, 95Zr, ^{131}I and some of the neutron activation products such as ^{65}Co, ^{59}Fe and 6^{5}Ni formed on the structural components. The total radioactivity content of spent fuel decreases with time, as one after the other, the various constituent radionuclides decay.

Most of the fission products and actinides along with some activation products formed in the fuel cladding material are contained in the fuel matrix only. The main activation products formed in PHWR moderator and coolant systems are ^{3}H and ^{14}C along with traces of ^{41}A (especially in recent designs of PHWR). The gaseous radionuclides are released into the atmosphere through filters. The solid waste stream consists of spent ion-exchange resin from primary heat transport system, moderator loop and spent fuel storage hay. Other minor sources of waste include filter sludge, filter catridgcs, evaporator bottoms and compactible and non-compactible trash. The compactible trash consists of contaminated clothes, mops, bags and gloves while the non-compactible trash includes contaminated conduits, instruments and some reactor components. The liquid waste stream from reactors consists of washings, leakage and solutions used for decontamination processes. The liquid concentrates originate from evaporative volume reduction of contaminated water from regeneration of resins, decontamination procedures and active chemical waste. The magnitude of radioactivity contained in reactor wastes is presented in Table.

Waste Arising from Fuel Reprocessing

The liquid waste from fuel reprocessing (first cycle raffinate) is highly radioactive and contains almost all the fission products having $T_{1/2} > 5y$ (if the storage period is only 10 y). This solution is pumped into underground stainless steel storage tanks for final vitrification. The secondary stream of less radioactive liquid originates from further treatment of the organic solvent and this treatment is continued until almost all the fission products are removed from the solvent (second and third cycle raffinate).

The fuel cladding becomes radioactive from irradiation during nuclear operations. Some quantities of fission products and actinides adhere to the cladding even after strong acid treatment during reprocessing. Significant amounts of noble gas fission products such as ^{85}Kr, ^{129}I and minor quantities of ^{3}H and ^{14}C are released into the atmosphere during reprocessing.

Decommissioning of Reactors

After an expected operating life time, nuclear reactors will be shut down and dismantled after removing the fuel core and residual radioactivity. This procedure is called decommissioning and decontamination. The world-wide experience has been limited to the decommissioning of a few small research reactors. Dismantling requires removal of materials including soil having radioactivity above the regulatory limits from the site to facilitate unrestricted use of the site. The expected volume of waste and radioactivity from decommissioning process would be about 104 m/GWa and 10^6 Bq/GWa respectively.

Other Sources

Other sources of radioactive wastes originates from medical, agricultural and industrial applications of radionuclides. Sealed radioactive sources are used in many industrial applications like portable radiographic devices used for inspection of welds and instruments for well-logging. Sealed sources are also used in consumer products such as smoke alarms and luminous watches. The radionuclides used in sealed source applications are characterised by relatively long-half lives such as ^{117}Cs ($T_{1/2}$ = 30y), ^{92}Ir (73.8 y) and ^{60}Co (5.2 y). The spent sealed sources and contaminated materials like dry trash, sweeping, tools and glassware are the revsulting radioactive wastes.

The pharmaceutical industry converts radioactive chemicals into forms that are useful to the medical community. The radionuclides used to label the pharmaceutical materials are produced in research reactors and the typical radionuclides used by these industries are ^{32}P (14.3d), ^{35}S (88 d), ^{3}H (12.3 y) and ^{14}C (5630y). Most of the radioisotopes used for clinical applications have relatively short half-lives. Typical radionuclides used for imaging are $^{99m}T_c$ (6 hr), ^{67}Ga (3.3 d), ^{201}TI (3.1 d) and ^{131}I (8.3 d). Comparatively long-lived isotopes used basically for radioimmunosassy tests include ^{3}H, ^{125}I (60 d) and ^{57}Co (271 d). The wastes generated from clinical applications arc spent sources, contaminated items of glassware and biological wastes.

NATURALLY OCCURRING RADIOACTIVE MATERIAL (NORM)

Substances containing natural radioactivity are known as **NORM**. After human processing that exposes or concentrates this natural radioactivity (such as mining bringing coal to the surface or burning it to produce concentrated ash), it becomes tech ologically enhanced naturally occurring radioactive material (TENORM). A lot of this waste is **alpha particle-** emitting matter from the decay chains of **uranium** and **thorium.**

TENORM is not regulated as restrictively as nuclear reactor waste, though there are no significant differences in the radiological risks of these materials.

Coal

Coal contains a small amount of radioactive uranium, barium, thorium and potassium, but, in the case of pure coal, this is significantly less than the average concentration of those elements in the Earth's crust. The surrounding strata, if shale or mudstone, often contain slightly more than average and this may also be reflected in the ash content of 'dirty' coals. The more active ash minerals become concentrated in the fly ash precisely because they do not burn well. The radioactivity of fly ash is about the same as black shale and is less than phosphate rocks, but is more of a concern because a small amount of the fly ash ends up in the atmosphere where it can be inhaled.

Oil and Gas

Residues from the oil and gas industry often contain radium and its decay products. The sulfate scale from an oil well can be very radium rich, while the water, oil and gas from a well often contain radon. The radon decays to form solid radioisotopes which form coatings on the inside of pipework. In an oil processing plant the area of the plant where propane is processed is often one of the more contaminated areas of the plant as radon has a similar boiling point to propane.

Effect of Radioactive Wastes

Radioactive waste causes:

- Soil pollution
- Water pollution

In these two pollutions, pollution hazards finally enter into the food chain the human who is the final victim of radioactive pollution as he is at the end of all reactions and interactions.

The effect of radioactive pollution depends upon:

- Half-life
- Energy releasing capacity
- Rate of diffusion
- Rate of deposition of the contaminant.
- Various atmospheric and climatic conditions such as wind, temperature, rainfall also determine their effects.

The possible general effects of radioactive wastes are categorised into;

- Somatic effect
- Genetic effect
- Biomagnification

Somatic effect: Affects somatic cells. It appears within individual and disappears with the death of the individual.

Immediate effects: Anaemia, Reduced immune response, haemorrhage, skin burn, mouth ulcers, CNS damage.

Delayed effects: Eye cataract, leukemia, cardiovascular disease, premature ageing, reduced life span, reduction of fertility.

Genetic Effects: The radiation affects the genes of the gamete cells. The changes are not apparent in the individual. The effects are exhibited by offspring and in the subsequent generations. They affect the DNA, RNA replication and chromosome. It causes:

- Mutation
- Chromosomal aberration
- Chromosomal fragmentation
- Inhibition of RNA, DNA synthesis

Radioactive Pollution Incidents

The two best known examples illustrating the effect of fallout contamination are the bombing of Hiroshima and Nagasaki, Japan in 1945, and the Chernobyl Nuclear Power Station disaster in April 1986. Within five years of the American bombing of Japan, as many as 225,000 people had died as a result of long-term exposure to radiation from the bomb blast, chiefly in the form of fallout.

The disaster at the Chernobyl Nuclear Power Station in Ukraine on April 26, 1986 produced a staggering release of radioactivity. In ten days at least 36 million curies spewed across the world. The fallout contaminated approximately 1,000 square mites (2,590 sq. km) of farmland and villages in the Soviet Union. In addition to the hundreds killed at the time of the explosion, scientists predict the eventual Soviet death toll from the Chernobyl accident is around 200,000; the estimated mortality in western Europe may be around 40,000.

Control of Radioactive pollution

The main objective in managing and disposing of radioactive (or other) waste is to protect people and the environment. This means isolating or diluting the waste so that the rate or concentration of any radionuclides returned to the biosphere is harmless. To achieve this for the more dangerous wastes, the preferred technology to date has been deep and secure burial. Transmutation, long-term retrievable storage, and removal to space have also been suggested.

- Nuclear devices should never be exploded in air. If these activities are extremely necessary they should be exploded underground.
- In nuclear reactions, closed-cycle coolant system with gaseous coolants of very high purity may be used to prevent extraneous activation products.
- In nuclear and chemical industries, the use of radio-isotopes may be carried under a set of soil or water instead of power or gaseous forms.
- In Nuclear mines, wet drilling may be employed along the underground drainage.
- Nuclear reactors must be enclosed in broad concrete walls to prevent the radiations that emerge out.
- Workers should wear protective garments and glass spectacles should be screened from radiation.

- Extreme care should be exercised in the disposal of industrial waste contaminated with radionuclides. The spend rods are very radioactive containing about 1% U-235 and 1% plutonim.

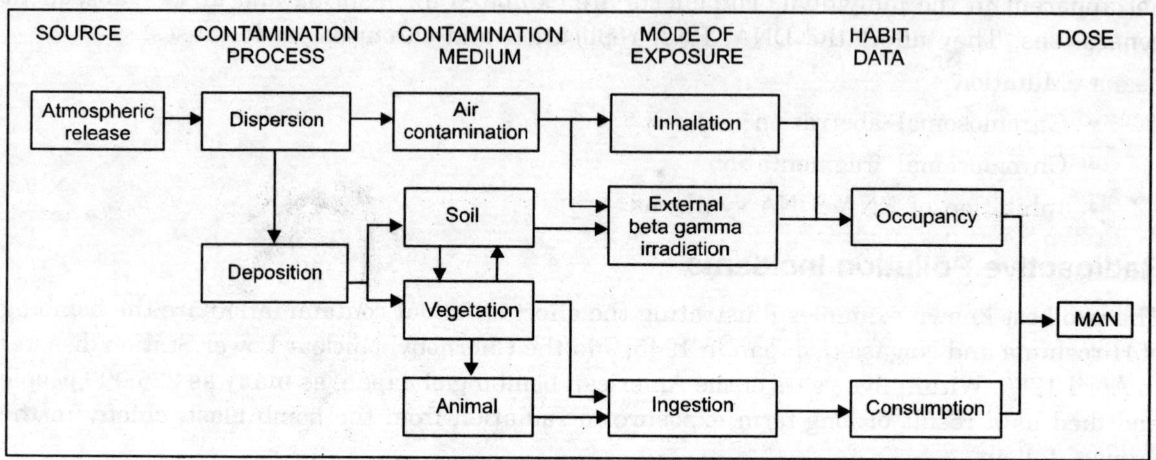

Possible paths of human exposure in the environment for gaseous effluents is shown above.

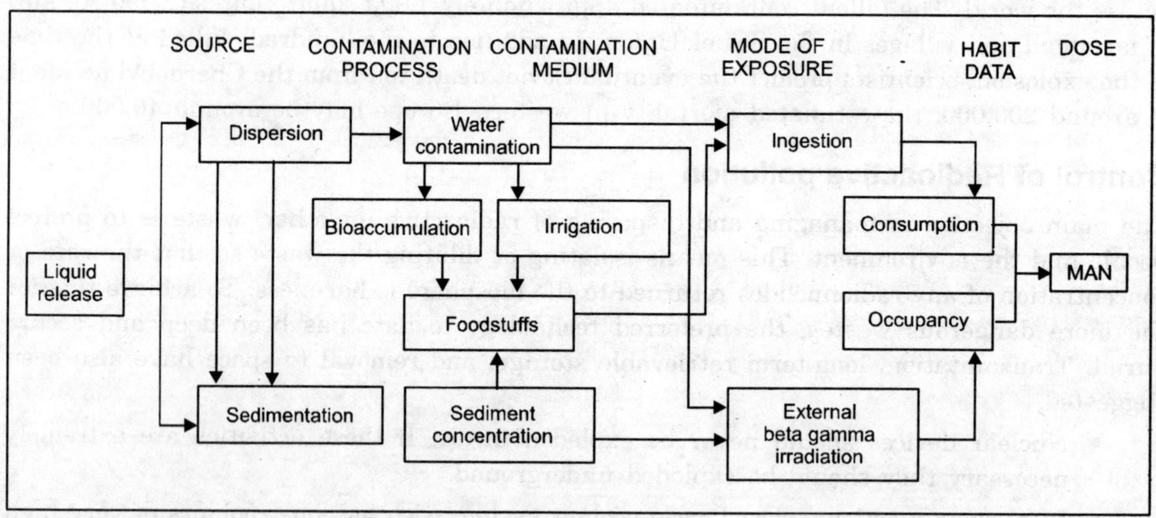

Possible paths of human exposure in the environment for liquid effluents is shown above.

MANAGEMENT OF RADIOACTIVE WASTE

Three general principles employed in the management of radioactive waste are:

(a) ***Dilute and disperse:*** A method followed when the radioactivity in the effluent can be reduced to levels acceptable for discharge into the environment.

(b) ***Concentrate and contain:*** A method adopted for liquid waste with a high level of radioactivity and toxic materials. The radioactive materials are concentrated by volume reduction and the waste stored in special tanks until further treatment.

(c) ***Delay and decay:*** In this method, the waste containing short half life elements are held in a suitable container over a certain period, until the radioactivity is reduced to a level acceptable for discharge or for further treatment.

Out of these three methods, the first two are also used in the management of non-radioactive wastes. However, delay and decay is unique to radioactive waste management; it means that the waste is stored and its radioactivity is allowed to decrease naturally through decay of the radioisotopes present in it.

Once created, radioactive waste will undergo some of the following stages depending on the type of waste and the strategy for its management:

Pretreatment is the initial step that occurs just after waste generation. It may involve collection, segregation, chemical adjustment and decontamination and may also include a period of interim storage. The aim of this step is to segregate waste into streams that will be managed in similar ways, and to isolate non-radioactive wastes or those materials that can be recycled.

Treatment involves changing the characteristics of the waste by volume reduction, radionuclide removal or change of composition. Typical treatment operations include:

- Compaction of dry solid waste or incineration of solid or organic liquid wastes (volume reduction);
- Filtration or ion exchange of liquid waste (radionuclide removal); and
- Precipitation or flocculation of chemical species (change of composition).
- Conditioning involves transforming radioactive waste into a form that is suitable for handling, transportation, storage and disposal. This might involve immobilisation of radioactive waste, placing waste into containers or providing additional packaging. Common immobilisation methods include solidification of LLW and ILW liquid radioactive waste in cement, and vitrification of HLW in a glass matrix. Immobilised waste may be placed in steel drums or other engineered containers to create a waste package.
- Storage of radioactive waste may take place at any stage in the radioactive waste management process and aims to isolate the radioactive waste, help protect the environment and make it easier to control its disposal. Storage may be used to make the next step in the management process more straightforward or to act as a buffer between or within steps. Waste might be stored for many years before it undergoes further processing and disposal. Some storage facilities are located within a nuclear power plant or a licensed disposal facility, others are separate facilities.
- Retrieval involves recovering waste packages from storage either for inspection, for disposal or for further storage in new facilities. Some storage facilities are designed so the equipment that deposits waste can be operated in reverse to retrieve waste packages. Others may need retrieval equipment to be installed.
- Disposal occurs when packages of radioactive waste are deposited in a disposal facility with no intention of retrieval. Disposal may also include discharging radioactive wastes such as liquid and gaseous effluent into the environment and transfer of wastes from one site to another.

- Which steps are employed in a particular situation depends on the types of radioactive waste and the methods of radioactive waste management that are to be used. In some cases individual steps may be closely linked or carried out together. The whole process needs to take place so that the way wastes are managed at each step is compatible with the subsequent steps.

Initial treatment of radioactive waste

Vitrification

Long-term storage of radioactive waste requires the stabilization of the waste into a form which will neither react nor degrade for extended periods of time. One way to do this might be through vitrification. Currently, the high-level waste is mixed with sugar and then calcined. Calcination involves passing the waste through a heated, rotating tube. The purposes of calcination are to evaporate the water from the waste, and de-nitrate the fission products to assist the stability of the glass produced.

The 'calcine' generated is fed continuously into an induction heated furnace with fragmented glass. The resulting glass is a new substance in which the waste products are bonded into the glass matrix when it solidifies. As a melt, this product is poured into stainless steel cylindrical containers ("cylinders") in a batch process. When cooled, the fluid solidifies ("vitrifies") into the glass. After being formed, the glass is highly resistant to water.

After filling a cylinder, a seal is welded onto the cylinder head. The cylinder is then washed. After being inspected for external contamination, the steel cylinder is stored, usually in an underground repository. In this form, the waste products are expected to be immobilized for thousands of years.

Ion Exchange

It is common for medium active wastes in the nuclear industry to be treated with ion exchange or other means to concentrate the radioactivity into a small volume. The much less radioactive bulk (after treatment) is often then discharged. For instance, it is possible to use a ferric hydroxide floc to remove radioactive metals from aqueous mixtures. After the radioisotopes are absorbed onto the ferric hydroxide, the resulting sludge can be placed in a metal drum before being mixed with cement to form a solid waste form. In order to get better long-term performance (mechanical stability) from such forms, they may be made from a mixture of fly ash, or blast furnace slag, and Portland cement, instead of normal concrete (made with Portland cement, gravel and sand).

Synroc (Synthetic Rock)

The Australian Synroc (synthetic rock) is a more sophisticated way to immobilize such waste, and this process may eventually come into commercial use for civil wastes (it is currently being developed for US military wastes). The Synroc contains pyrochlore and cryptomelane type minerals. The original form of Synroc (Synroc C) was designed for the liquid high level waste from a light water reactor. The main minerals in this Synroc are hollandite ($BaAl_2Ti_6O_{16}$), zirconolite ($CaZrTi_2O_7$) and perovskite ($CaTiO_3$). The zirconolite and perovskite are hosts for the actinides. The strontium and barium will be fixed in the perovskite. The caesium will be fixed in the hollandite.

The following radioactive waste disposal options have been proposed sometime or the other:

- Deep geological repositories
- Ocean dumping
- Seabed burial
- Sub-seabed disposal
- Subductive waste disposal method
- Transforming radioactive waste to non-radioactive stable waste
- Dispatching the waste to the Sun.

Geologic disposal

Geologic disposal in deep geological formations – whether under continental crust or under seabed – as a means of radioactive waste disposal has been recognized since 1957, for handling long-lived waste.

The deep geological sites provide a natural isolation system that is stable over hundreds of thousands of years to contain long-lived radioactive waste. In practice it is noted that low-level radioactive waste is generally disposed in near-surface facilities or old mines. High-level radioactive waste is disposed in host rocks that are crystalline (granitic, gneiss) or argillaceous (clays) or salty or tuff. Since, in most of the countries, there is not a big backlog of high level radioactive waste urgently awaiting disposal, interim storage facilities, which allow cooling of the wastes over a few decades, are in place.

Ocean-dumping

For many years the industrialized countries of the world (*e.g.* USA, France, Great Britain, etc.) opted for the least expensive method for disposal of the wastes by dumping them into the oceans. Before 1982, when the United States Senate declared a moratorium on the dumping of radioactive wastes, the US dumped an estimated 112,000 drums at thirty different sites in the Atlantic and Pacific oceans.

Though this practice has been banned by most of the countries with nuclear programmes, the problem still persists. Russia, which currently controls sixty per cent of the world's nuclear reactors, continues to dispose of its nuclear wastes into the oceans.

Although radioactive waste has known negative effects on humans and other animals, no substantial scientific proof of bad effects on the ocean and marine life has been found. Hence some nations have argued that ocean-dumping should be continued. Others argue that the practice should be banned until further proof of no harm is available.

Oceanic Disposal Management Inc., a British Virgin Islands company, has also proposed disposing of nuclear and asbestos waste by means of Free-Fall Penetrators. Essentially, waste-filled missiles, which when dropped through 4000 m of water, will embed themselves 60–80 m into the seabed's clay sediments. These penetrators are expected to survive for 700 to 1500 years. Thereafter the waste will diffuse through the sediments.

Penetrator disposal is potentially both feasible and safe, its implementation would depend on international acceptance and the development of an appropriate international regulatory framework.

Sub-seabed Disposal

Seabed disposal is different from sea-dumping which does not involve isolation of low-level radioactive waste within a geological strata. The floor of deep oceans is a part of a large tectonic plate situated some 5 km below the sea surface, covered by hundreds of metres of thick sedimentary soft clay. These regions are desert-like, supporting virtually no life. The Seabed Burial Proposal envisages drilling these 'mud-flats' to depths of the order of hundreds of metres, such boreholes being spaced apart several hundreds of metres. The high-level radioactive waste contained in canisters, would be lowered into these holes and stacked vertically one above the other interspersed by 20 m or more of mud pumped in.

The proposal to use basement-rock in oceans for radioactive waste disposal is met with some problems: variability of the rock and high local permeability. Oceanic water has a mixing time of the order of a few thousand years which does not serve as a good barrier for long-lived radionuclides.these potential waste repositories are geologically stable over periods of the order of 10^7 years and are likely not to have human activities, as they are not resources of fishes or hydrocarbons or minerals.

Atlantic oceans have 'showed an uninterrupted history of geological tranquillity over the past 50–100 million years'.

However there are questions that remain to be answered:

- Whether migration of radioactive elements through the ocean floor is at the same rate as that already measured in the laboratories?
- What is the effect of nuclear heat on the deep oceanic-clays?
- What is the impact on the deep oceanic fauna and waters above?
- In case the waste reaches the seabed-surface, will the soluble species (for example, Cs, Tc, etc.) be diluted to natural background levels? If so, at what rate?
- What happens to insoluble species like plutonium?
- What is the likelihood of radioactivity reaching all the way to the sea surface?
- In problems of accidents in the process of seabed burial leading to, say, sinking ships, to loss of canisters, etc. how does one recover the waste-load under such scenarios?
- What is the likelihood that the waste is hijacked from its buried location?

Added to these technical problems are others:

International agreement to consider seabed-burial as distinct from 'ocean-dumping'.

This method would be expensive to implement, but its cost would be an impediment to any future plutonium-mining endeavour.

Subductive Waste Disposal Method

The principle involved is the removal of the material from the biosphere faster than it can return. It is considered that 'the safest, the most sensible, the most economical, the most stable long-term, the most environmentally benign, the most utterly obvious places to get rid of nuclear waste, high-level waste or low-level waste is in the deep oceans that cover 70% of the planet'.

Subduction is a process whereby one tectonic plate slides beneath another and is eventually reabsorbed into the mantle. The subductive waste disposal method forms a high-level radioactive waste repository in a subducting plate, so that the waste will be carried beneath the Earth's crust where it will be diluted and dispersed through the mantle. The rate of subduction of a plate in one of the world's slowest subduction zones is 2.1 cm annually. This is faster than the rate (1 mm annually) of diffusion of radionuclides through the turbidite sediments that would overlay a repository constructed in accordance with this method. The subducting plate is naturally predestined for consumption in the Earth's mantle. The subducting plate is constantly renewed at its originating oceanic ridge. The slow movement of the plate would seal any vertical fractures over a repository at the interface between the subducting plate and the overriding plate.

Transmutation of High-level Radioactive Waste

This route of high-level radioactive waste envisages that one may use transmutational devices, consisting of a hybrid of a subcritical nuclear reactor and an accelerator of charged particles to 'destroy' radioactivity by neutrons.The fission fragments can be transmuted by neutron capture and beta decay, to produce stable nuclides. Transmutation of actinides involves several competing processes, namely neutron-induced fission, neutron capture and radioactive decay. The large number of neutrons produced in the spallation reaction by the accelerator are used for 'destroying' the radioactive material kept in the subcritical reactor. The scheme has not yet been demonstrated to be practical and cost-effective.

Solar Option

It is proposed that 'surplus weapons' plutonium and other highly concentrated waste might be placed in the Earth orbit and then accelerated so that waste would drop into the Sun. Although theoretically possible, it involves vast technical development and extremely high cost compared to other means of waste disposal. Robust containment would be required to ensure that no waste would be released in the event of failure of the 'space transport system'.

Pros and Cons of Long Term Management of Radioactive Waste

The time frame in question when dealing with radioactive waste ranges from 10,000 to 1,000,000 years, according to studies based on the effect of estimated radiation doses. Practical studies only consider up to 100 years as far as effective planning and cost evaluations are concerned. Long term behavior of radioactive wastes remains a subject for ongoing research projects.

Above-ground Disposal

Dry cask storage typically involves taking waste from a spent fuel pool and sealing it (along with an inert gas) in a steel cylinder, which is placed in a concrete cylinder which acts as a radiation shield. It is a relatively inexpensive method which can be done at a central facility or adjacent to the source reactor. The waste can be easily retrieved for reprocessing.

Geologic Disposal

The process of selecting appropriate deep final repositories for high level waste and spent fuel is now under way in several countries with the first expected to be commissioned soon. The basic concept is to locate a large, stable geologic formation and use mining technology to excavate a tunnel, or large-bore tunnel boring machines (similar to those used to drill the Channel Tunnel from England to France) to drill a shaft 500 metres to 1,000 metres below the surface where rooms or vaults can be excavated for disposal of high-level radioactive waste. The goal is to permanently isolate nuclear waste from the human environment. Many people remain uncomfortable with the immediate stewardship cessation of this disposal system, suggesting perpetual management and monitoring would be more prudent.

Because some radioactive species have half-lives longer than one million years, even very low container leakage and radionuclide migration rates must be taken into account. Moreover, it may require more than one half-life until some nuclear materials lose enough radioactivity to cease being lethal to living things

Ocean floor disposal of radioactive waste has been suggested by the finding that deep waters in the North Atlantic Ocean do not present an exchange with shallow waters for about 140 years based on oxygen content data recorded over a period of 25 years. They include burial beneath a stable abyssal plain, burial in a subduction zone that would slowly carry the waste downward into the Earth's mantle,[and burial beneath a remote natural or human-made island. While these approaches all have merit and would facilitate an international solution to the problem of disposal of radioactive waste, they would require an amendment of the Law of the Sea.

The proposed land-based subductive waste disposal method disposes of nuclear waste in a subduction zone accessed from land and therefore is not prohibited by international agreement. Another approach termed Remix & Return would blend high-level waste with uranium mine and mill tailings down to the level of the original radioactivity of the uranium ore, then replace it in inactive uranium mines. This approach has the merits of providing jobs for miners who would double as disposal staff, and of facilitating a cradle-to-grave cycle for radioactive materials, but would be inappropriate for spent reactor fuel in the absence of reprocessing, due to the presence in it of highly toxic radioactive elements such as plutonium.

Deep borehole disposal is the concept of disposing off high-level radioactive waste from nuclear reactors in extremely deep boreholes. Deep borehole disposal seeks to place the waste as much as 5 kilometres beneath the surface of the Earth and relies primarily on the immense natural geological barrier to confine the waste safely and permanently so that it should never pose a threat to the environment. The Earth's crust contains 120 trillion tons of thorium and 40 trillion tons of uranium (primarily at relatively trace concentrations of parts per million each adding up over the crust's 3×10^{19} ton mass), among other natural radioisotopes. Since the fraction of nuclides decaying per unit of time is inversely proportional to an isotope's half-life, the relative radioactivity of the lesser amount of human-produced radioisotopes (thousands of tons instead of trillions of tons) would diminish once the isotopes with far shorter half-lives than the bulk of natural radioisotopes decayed.

Transmutation—There have been proposals for reactors that consume nuclear waste and transmute it to other, less-harmful nuclear waste. In particular, the Integral Fast Reactor was a proposed nuclear reactor with a nuclear fuel cycle that produced no transuranic waste and in fact, could consume transuranic waste. Another approach, considered safer but requiring more development, is to the transmutation of the left-over transuranic elements.

Re-use of Waste

Another option is to find applications for the isotopes in nuclear waste so as to re-use them. Already, caesium-137, strontium-90 and a few other isotopes are extracted for certain industrial applications such as food irradiation and radioisotope thermoelectric generators. While re-use does not eliminate the need to manage radioisotopes, it reduces the quantity of waste produced.

Space Disposal

Space disposal is attractive because it removes nuclear waste from the planet. It has significant disadvantages, such as the potential for catastrophic failure of a launch vehicle, which could spread radioactive material into the atmosphere and around the world. A high number of launches would be required because no individual rocket would be able to carry very much of the material relative to the total amount that needs to be disposed of. This makes the proposal impractical economically and it increases the risk of at least one or more launch failures.

In second half of 20th century, several methods of disposal of radioactive waste were investigated by nuclear nations, which are:

- "Long term above ground storage", not implemented.
- "Disposal in outer space" (for instance, inside the Sun), not implemented – as it would be currently too expensive.
- "Deep borehole disposal", not implemented.
- "Rock-melting", not implemented.
- "Disposal at subduction zones", not implemented.
- "**Ocean disposal**", done by the USSR, the United Kingdom, Switzerland, the United States, Belgium, France, The Netherlands, Japan, Sweden, Russia, Germany, Italy and South Korea. (during 1954–93) This is no longer permitted by international agreements.
- "Sub seabed disposal", not implemented, not permitted by international agreements.
- "Disposal in ice sheets", rejected in Antarctic Treaty
- "**Direct injection**", done by USSR and USA.

In the USA, waste management policy completely broke down with the ending of work on the incomplete Yucca Mountain Repository. At present there are 70 nuclear power plant sites where spent fuel is stored.

CHAPTER

6

BIOMEDICAL WASTE MANAGEMENT

Health care waste is a source of generation of biomedical waste. Of the total waste generated by healthcare activities, about 85% is general waste. The remaining 15% is considered hazardous that may be infectious, toxic or radioactive. Hospital waste refers to all waste generated, discarded and not intended for further use in the hospital.

BIOMEDICAL WASTE (BMW)

Any solid, fluid and/or liquid waste, including its container & any intermediate product, which is generated during the diagnosis, treatment or immunisation of human being or animals, in research pertaining thereto, or in the production or testing of biological and the animal waste from slaughter houses or any other similar establishment. All biomedical wastes are hazardous. In hospital it comprises of 15% of total hospital waste.

In other words, BMW includes the following:

- **Animal waste:** Carcasses, body parts, etc. that have been inoculated with microorganisms infectious to humans.
- **Human blood and blood products:** Waste blood and materials containing free-flowing blood.
- **Cultures and stocks:** Culture dishes, blood specimen tubes, devices used to transfer, inoculate, and mix cultures that are infectious to humans.
- **Pathological waste:** Tissue coming from biopsies, surgery, obstetrical procedures or autopsies.
- **Sharps waste:** All hypodermic needles, syringes & tubing with needles attached, scalpel blades and lancets.
- **Respiratory isolation waste:** Waste contaminated with blood or other potentially infectious bodily fluids from humans isolated for disease spread by respiratory or droplet transmission.

EFFECTS OF BIOMEDICAL WASTE

Biomedical waste poses health hazard due to two principal reasons – the first is infectivity and other toxicity. Besides, the improper management of bio-medical waste causes stern environmental problems that causes air, water and land pollution. The pollutants that cause damage can be classified into biological, chemical and radioactive. There are several legislations and guidelines in India concerning environmental problems, which can be addressed.

Air Pollution

Air pollution can be caused in both indoors and outdoors atmosphere. Biomedical waste that generated by air pollution are been classified in three types namely—biological, chemical and radioactive.

In-door Air Pollution

Pathogens present in the waste can enter and remain in the air for a long period in the form of spores or as pathogens .Segregation of waste, pre-treatment at source etc., can also reduce this problem to a great extent. Sterilizing the rooms will also help in checking the indoor air pollution due to biological. The indoor air pollution caused due to the chemicals from poor ventilation can cause diseases like Sick Building Syndrome (SBS). Proper building design and well-maintained air conditioners can reduce the SBS. Chemicals should be utilized as per prescribed norms. Over use of chemicals should be avoided.

Out-door Air Pollution

Outdoor air pollution can be caused by pathogens. The biomedical waste without pre-treatment if transported outside the institution, or if it is dumped in open areas, pathogens can enter into the atmosphere. Chemical pollutants that cause outdoor air pollution have two major sources-open burning and incinerators. Open burning of bio-medical waste is the most harmful practice. When inhaled can cause respiratory diseases. Certain organic gases such as dioxins and furans are carcinogenic . The design parameters and maintenance of such treatment and disposal technology should be as per the prescribed standards .

Water Pollution

The liquid waste generated when let into sewers can also lead to water pollution , if not treated properly. Water pollution can alter parameters such as pH, BOD, DO, COD, *etc.* There are instances where dioxins are reported from water bodies near incinerator plants. Dioxins enter the water body from the air.

Land Pollution

Soil pollution from bio-medical waste is caused due to infectious waste, discarded medicines, chemicals used in treatment and ash & other waste generated during treatment processes. Heavy metals such as cadmium, lead, mercury etc., which are present in the waste will get absorbed by plants and can then enter the food chain. Nitrates and phosphates present in leachates from landfills are also pollutants. Excessive amounts of trace nutrient elements and other elements including heavy metals in soil are harmful to crops and are also harmful to animals and human beings. Minimizing the waste and proper treatment before disposal on land are the only ways of reducing this kind of pollution.

Radioactive Emissions

Research and radio-immunoassay activities may generate small quantities of radioactive gas. Gaseous radioactive material should be evacuated directly to the outside. The use of such device requires maintenance of the trap and monitoring of the off-gas.

Radioactive waste in liquid form can come from chemical or biological research, from body organ imaging, from decontamination of radioactive spills, from patient's urine and from scintillation liquids used in radio immune assay. Under normal circumstances, urine and faeces can be handled as no radioactive waste so long as the patient's room is routinely monitored for radioactive contamination.

Biomedical waste consists of:

- Human anatomical waste like tissues, organs and body parts.
- Animal wastes generated during research from veterinary hospitals.
- Microbiology and biotechnology wastes.
- Waste sharps like hypodermic needles, syringes, scalpels and broken glass.
- Discarded medicines and cytotoxic drugs.
- Soiled waste such as dressing, bandages, plaster casts, material contaminated with blood, tubes and catheters.
- Liquid waste from any of the infected areas.
- Incineration ash and other chemical wastes.

Classification of Biomedical Waste

The World Health Organization (WHO) has classified medical waste into eight categories:

- General waste
- Radioactive
- Infectious to potentially infectious waste
- Pharmaceuticals
- Pathological
- Chemical
- Sharps
- Pressurized containers

Examples of Different Types of BMW according to WHO

The World Health Organisation (WHO) has classified medical wastes according to their weight, density and constituents into different categories. These are:

Infectious: Materials containing pathogens in sufficient concentrations or quantities that, if exposed, can cause diseases. This includes waste from surgery and autopsies on patients with infectious diseases, sharps, disposable needles, syringes, saws, blades, broken glasses, nails or any other item that could cause a cut.

Pathological: Tissues, organs, body parts, human flesh, foetuse, blood and body fluids, drugs and chemicals that are returned from wards, spilled, outdated, contaminated, or are no longer required.

Radioactive: Solids, liquids and gaseous waste contaminated with radioactive substances used in diagnosis and treatment of diseases like toxic goiter; and

Others: Waste from the offices, kitchens, rooms, including bed linen, utensils, paper, etc.

Sources of Biomedical Waste

Hospitals produce waste, which is increasing over the years in its amount and type. The hospital waste, in addition to the risk for patients and personnel who handle them also poses a threat to public health and environment.

Major Sources of BMW

- Govt. hospitals/private hospitals/nursing homes/dispensaries.
- Primary health centers.
- Medical colleges and research centers/paramedic services.
- Veterinary colleges and animal research centers.
- Blood banks/mortuaries/autopsy centers.
- Biotechnology institutions.
- Production units.

Minor Sources of BMW

- Physicians/dentists' clinics
- Blood donation camps.
- Acupuncturists/psychiatric clinics/cosmetic piercing.
- Funeral services.
- Animal houses/slaughter houses.
- Vaccination centers.
- Institutions for disabled persons

Major & minor sources of BMW are categorized below:

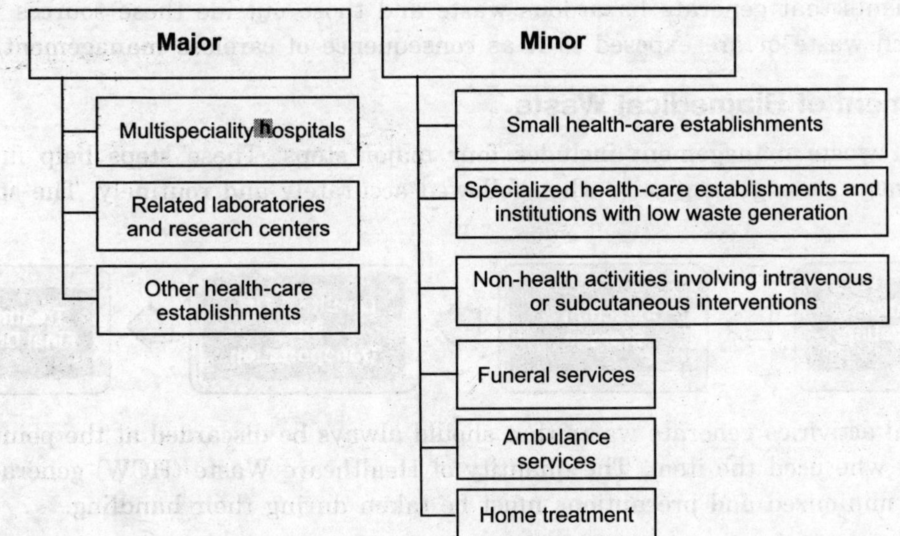

Amount and composition of hospital waste generated:

(a) Amount

Country	Quantity (kg/bed/day)
U.K.	2.5
U.S.A.	4.5
France	2.5
Spain	3.0
India	1.5

(b) Hazardous/non-hazardous

Hazardous	15%
(a) Hazardous but non-infective	5%
(b) Hazardous and infective	10%
Non-hazardous	85%

Hazardous Waste Related to Biomedical Waste

Healthcare waste includes a large component of general waste and smaller proportion of hazardous waste. Exposure to hazardous healthcare waste can result in disease or injury. The hazardous nature of healthcare waste may be due to one or more of the following characteristics: it contains infectious agent; it is genotoxic;it contains toxic or hazardous chemical or pharmaceuticals; it is radioactive; it contains sharps; All individual exposed to hazardous healthcare waste are potentially at risk, including those within healthcare establishments that generate hazardous waste and those outside these sources who either handle such waste or are exposed to it as consequence of careless management.

Management of Biomedical Waste

Biomedical waste management includes four major steps. These steps help in achieving effective waste management only when followed accurately and routinely. The steps are as follows:

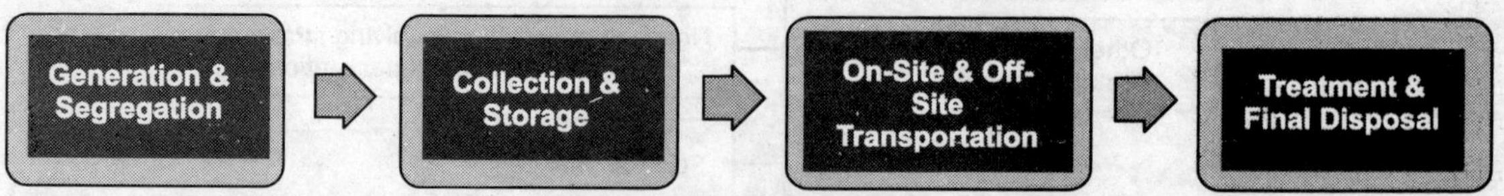

Medical activities generate waste that should always be discarded at the point of use by the person who used the item. The quantity of Healthcare Waste (HCW) generated should always be minimized and precautions must be taken during their handling.

Typical Composition and Characteristics of Infectious Waste.

Particulars	Percent
Composition:	
Celluloid material (paper & cloth)	50-70
Plastics	20-60
Glassware	10-20
Fluids	1-10
Typical Characteristics:	
Moisture	8.5-17 by weight
Incombustibles	8 by weight
Heating value	7,500 BTU/lb

Need of biomedical waste management in hospitals

The reasons due to which there is great need of management of hospitals waste are:

- Injuries from sharps leading to infection to all categories of hospital personnel and waste handler.
- Nosocomial infections in patients from poor infection control practices and poor waste management.
- Risk of infection outside hospital for waste handlers and scavengers and at time general public living in the vicinity of hospitals.
- Risk associated with hazardous chemicals, drugs to persons handling wastes at all levels.
- "Disposable" being repacked and sold by unscrupulous elements without even being washed.
- Drugs which have been disposed of, being repacked and sold off to unsuspecting buyers.
- Risk of air, water and soil pollution directly due to waste, or due to defective incineration emissions and ash.

Benefits of Biomedical Waste Management

- Cleaner and healthier surroundings.
- Reduction in the incidence of hospital acquired and general infections.
- Reduction in the cost of infection control within the hospital.
- Reduction in the possibility of disease and death due to reuse and repackaging of infectious disposables.
- Low incidence of community and occupational health hazards.

- Reduction in the cost of waste management and generation of revenue through appropriate treatment and disposal of waste.
- Improved image of the healthcare establishment and increase the quality of life.

The main aims of biomedical waste management are:

- Minimizing risk for personnel, general public and environment
- Minimizing the amounts of waste being generated
- Segregation and separation of wastes
- Designation of deposit areas in the wards
- Establishment of safe routes for the transportation of the waste
- Establishment of a safe and proper area for the temporary storage
- Proper waste treatment and disposal.

Biomedical Waste Management Process

Hospitals and other health care facilities generate lots of waste which can transmit infections, particularly HIV, Hepatitis B & C and Tetanus, to the people who handle it or come in contact with it.

Most countries of the world, especially the developing nations, are facing the grim situation arising out of environmental pollution due to pathological waste arising from increasing populations and the consequent rapid growth in the number of health care centres. India is no exception to this and it is estimated that there are more than 20,000 small and private hospitals and nursing homes in the country. This is apart from clinics and pathological labs, which also generate sizeable amounts of medical waste.

India generates around five million tonnes of medical wastes every year and the amount is expected to grow at ten per cent annually. Creating large dumping grounds and incinerators is the first step.

Barring a few large private hospitals in metros, none of the smaller hospitals and nursing homes have any effective system to safely dispose of their wastes. With no care or caution, these health establishments have been dumping waste in local municipal bins or even worse, out in the open. Such irresponsible dumping has been promoting unauthorized reuse of medical waste by the rag pickers for some years now.

After the notification of the Biomedical Waste (Handling and Management) Rules, 1998, these establishments are slowly streamlining the process of waste segregation, collection, treatment, and disposal. Many of the larger hospitals have either installed the treatment facilities or are in the process of doing so.

There is a big network of Health Care Institutions in India. The hospital waste like body parts, organs, tissues, blood and body fluids along with soiled linen, cotton, bandage and plaster casts from infected and contaminated areas are very essential to be properly collected, segregated, stored, transported, treated and disposed of in safe manner to prevent nosocomial or hospital acquired infection. BMW management process consists of following steps:

- Waste minimisation
- Waste collection
- Treatment and disposal
- Final disposal
- Segregation
- Transportation and storage
- Transport to final disposal site

The biomedical waste (BMW) management requires its categorisation as a first step. The BMW Rules classify the BMW into ten categories.

CATEGORIES OF BIOMEDICAL WASTE (SCHEDULE–I)

WASTE CATEGORY	TYPE OF WASTE	TREATMENT AND DISPOSAL OPTION
Category No. 1	Human Anatomical Waste (Human tissues, organs, body parts)	Incineration@/deep burial*
Category No. 2	Animal Waste (Animal tissues, organs, body parts, carcasses, bleeding parts, fluid, blood and experimental animals used in research, waste generated by veterinary hospitals and colleges, discharge from hospitals, animal houses)	Incineration@/deep burial*
Category No. 3	Microbiology & Biotechnology Waste (Wastes from laboratory cultures, stocks or specimen of live micro organisms or attenuated vaccines, human and animal cell cultures used in research and infectious agents from research and industrial laboratories, wastes from production of biologicals, toxins and devices used for transfer of cultures)	Local autoclaving/ microwaving/ incineration@
Category No. 4	Waste Sharps (Needles, syringes, scalpels, blades, glass, etc. that may cause puncture and cuts. This includes both used and unused sharps)	Disinfecting (chemical treatment@@ /autoclaving / microwaving and mutilation / shredding##
Category No. 5	Discarded Medicine and Cytotoxic drugs (Wastes comprising of outdated, contaminated and discarded medicines)	Incineration@/destruction and drugs disposal in secured landfills
Category No. 6	Soiled Waste (Items contaminated with body fluids including cotton, dressings, soiled plaster casts, lines, bedding and other materials contaminated with blood.)	Incineration@/ autoclaving/ microwaving

Category No. 7	Solid Waste (Waste generated from disposable items other than the waste sharps such as tubing, catheters, intravenous sets, etc.)	Disinfecting by chemical treatment@@/ auto-claving/microwaving and mutilation/ shredding##
Category No. 8	Liquid Waste (Waste generated from the laboratory and washing, cleaning, house keeping and disinfecting activities)	Disinfecting by chemical treatment@@ and discharge into drains
Category No. 9	Incineration Ash (Ash from incineration of any biomedical waste)	Disposal in municipal landfill
Category No.10	Chemical Waste (Chemicals used in production of biologicals, chemicals used in disinfecting, as insecticides, etc.)	Chemical treatment@@ and discharge into drains for liquids and secured landfill for solids.

@@ Chemical treatment using at least 1% hypochlorite solution or any other equivalent chemical reagent. It must be ensured that chemical treatment ensures disinfection.

** Mutilations/Shredding must be such as to prevent unauthorised reuse.

@ There will be no chemical pre-treatment before incineration. Chlorinated plastics shall not be incinerated.

* Deep burial shall be an option available only in towns with population less than five lakh and in rural areas.

Waste minimization: Waste minimization is an important first step in managing wastes safely, responsibly and in a cost effective manner. This management step makes use of reducing, reusing and recycling principles. There are many possible routes to minimize the amount of both general waste and biomedical wastes within the health care or related facility. Alternative technologies for biomedical waste minimization (*e.g.*, microwave treatment; hammer mill) have been investigated and are not considered to be practical. As far as possible, purchase of reusable items made of glass and metal should be encouraged. Select non-PVC plastic items. Adopt procedures and policies for proper management of waste generated, the mainstay of which is segregation to reduce the quantity of waste to be treated. Establish effective and sound recycling policy for plastic recycling and get in touch with authorised manufactures.

BMW Segregation

Segregation refers to the basic separation of different categories of waste generated at source and thereby reducing the risks as well as cost of handling and disposal. Segregation is the most crucial step in bio-medical waste management. Effective segregation alone can ensure effective biomedical waste management. The BMWs must be segregated in accordance to guidelines laid down under schedule 1 of BMW Rules, 1998.

Segregation of BMW helps in the following ways:

- Segregation reduces the amount of waste needs special handling and treatment.
- Effective segregation process prevents the mixture of medical waste like sharps with the general municipal waste.
- Prevents illegally reuse of certain components of medical waste like used syringes, needles and other plastics.
- Provides an opportunity for recycling certain components of medical waste like plastics after proper and thorough disinfection.
- Recycled plastic material can be used for non-food grade applications.
- Of the general waste, the biodegradable waste can be composted within the hospital premises and can be used for gardening purposes.
- Recycling is a good environmental practice, which can also double as a revenue generating activity.
- Reduces the cost of treatment and disposal (85% of a hospital's waste is general waste, which does not require special treatment, provided it is not contaminated with other infectious waste)

Proper Labelling of Bins

The bins and bags should carry the biohazard symbol indicating the nature of waste to the patients and public. Schedule III (Rule 6) of Biomedical Waste (Management and Handling) Rules, 1998 specifies the Label for Biomedical Waste Containers / Bags as:

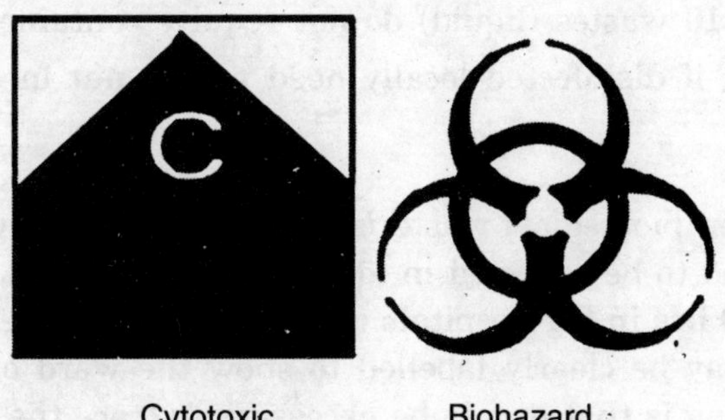

Cytotoxic Biohazard

Label shall be non-washable and prominently visible.

Collection

The collection of biomedical waste involves use of different types of container from various sources of biomedical wastes like Operation Theatre, laboratory, wards, kitchen, corridor etc. The containers/ bins should be placed in such a way that 100 % collection is achieved. Sharps must always be kept in puncture-proof containers to avoid injuries and infection to the workers handling them.

COLOUR CODING AND TYPE OF CONTAINER TO BE USED (SCHEDULE-II of BMW rules)

Colour coding	Type of container	Waste category	Treatment options as per Schedule I
Yellow	Plastic bag	Cat.1, Cat.2, Cat.3 and Cat.6	Incineration/deep burial
Red	Disinfected container/ plastic bag	Cat.3, Cat.6, and Cat.7	Autoclaving/microwaving/ chemical treatment
Blue/white Translucent	Plastic bag/puncture proof container	Cat.4 and Cat.7	Autoclaving/microwaving/ chemical treatment and destruction/ shredding
Black	Plastic bag	Cat.5, Cat.9, and Cat.10 (solid)	Disposal in secured landfill

Notes:

- Colour coding of waste categories with multiple treatment options as defined in Schedule I, shall be selected depending on treatment option chosen, which shall be specified in Schedule I.
- Waste collection bags for waste types needing incineration shall not be made of chlorinated plastics.
- Categories 8 and 10 wastes (liquid) do not require containers/bags.
- Category 3 waste, if disinfected locally need not be put in containers/bags.

Storage

Once collection occurs then biomedical waste is stored in a proper place. Segregated wastes of different categories need to be collected in identifiable containers. The duration of storage should not exceed for 8-10 hrs in big hospitals (more than 250 bedded) and 24 hrs in nursing homes. Each container may be clearly labelled to show the ward or room where it is kept. The reason for this labelling is that it may be necessary to trace the waste back to its source. Besides this, storage area should be marked with a caution sign.

Transportation

The waste should be transported for treatment either in trolleys or in covered wheelbarrow. Manual loading should be avoided as far as for as possible. The bags /Container containing BMWs should be tied/lidded before transportation. Before transporting the bag containing BMWs, it should be accompanied with a signed document by Nurse/ Doctor mentioning date, shift, quantity and destination.

Special vehicles must be used so as to prevent access to, and direct contact with, the waste by the transportation operators, the scavengers and the public. The transport containers should be properly enclosed. The effects of traffic accidents should be considered in the design, and the driver must be trained in the procedures he must follow in case of an accidental spillage. It should also be possible to wash the interior of the containers thoroughly.

Within hospital, waste routes must be designated to avoid the passage of waste through patient care areas. Separate time should be earmarked for transportation of biomedical waste to reduce chances of it's mixing with general waste. Dediccated wheeled containers, trolleys or carts should be used to transport the waste/plastic bags to the site of storage/ treatment.

Trolleys or carts should be thoroughly cleaned and disinfected in the event of any spillage. The wheeled containers should be so designed that the waste can be easily loaded, remains secured during transportation, does not have any sharp edges and is easy to clean and disinfect. Hazardous biomedical waste needing transport to a long distance should be kept in containers and should have proper labels. The transport is done through desiccated vehicles specially constructed for the purpose having fully enclosed body, lined internally with stainless steel or aluminium to provide smooth and impervious surface, which can be cleaned. The drivers compartment should be separated from the load compartment with a bulkhead. The load compartment should be provided with roof vents for ventilation.

Safety Measures

All the generators of biomedical waste should adopt universal precautions and appropriate safety measures while doing therapeutic and diagnostic activities and also while handling the biomedical waste.

It should be ensured that:

- Drivers, collectors and other handlers are aware of the nature and risk of the waste.
- Written instructions, provided regarding the procedures to be adopted in the event of spillage/accidents.
- Protective gears provided and instructions regarding their use are given.
- Workers are protected by vaccination against tetanus and hepatitis B.

Personnel Safety Devices

The use of protective gears should be made mandatory for all the personnel handling BMW.

Gloves: Heavy-duty rubber gloves should be used for waste handling by the waste retrievers. This should be bright yellow in colour. After handling the waste, the gloves should be washed twice. The gloves should be washed after every use with carbolic soap and a disinfectant. The size should fit the operator.

Aprons, gowns, suits or other apparels: Apparel is worn to prevent contamination of clothing and protect skin. It could be made of cloth or impermeable material such as plastic. People working in incinerator chambers should have gowns or suits made of non-inflammable material.

Masks: Various types of masks, goggles, and face shields are worn alone or in combination, to provide a protective barrier. It is mandatory for personnel working in the incinerator chamber to wear a mask covering both nose and mouth, preferably a gas mask with filters.

Boots: Leg coverings, boots or shoe-covers provide greater protection to the skin when splashes or large quantities of infected waste have to be handled. The boots should be rubber-soled and anti-skid type. They should cover the leg up to the ankle.

Cleaning Devices

Brooms: The broom shall be a minimum of 1.2 m long, such that the worker need not stoop to sweep. The diameter of the broom should be convenient to handle. The brush of the broom shall be soft or hard depending on the type of flooring.

Dustpans: The dustpans should be used to collect the dust from the sweeping operations. They may be either of plastic or enamelled metal. They should be free of ribs and should have smooth contours, to prevent dust from sticking to the surface. They should be washed with disinfectants and dried before every use.

Mops: Mops with long handles must be used for swabbing the floor. They shall be of either the cloth or the rubber variety. The mop has to be replaced depending on the wear and tear. The mechanical-screw type of mop is convenient for squeezing out the water.

Vacuum cleaners: Domestic vacuum cleaners or industrial vacuum cleaners can be used depending on the size of the rooms.

Storage Devices

Dustbins: It is very important to assess the quantity of waste generated at each point. Dustbins should be of such capacity that they do not overflow between each cycle of waste collection. Dustbins should be cleaned after every cycle of clearance of waste with disinfectants. Dustbins can be lined with plastic bags, which are chlorine-free, and colour coded as per the law.

Handling Devices for BMW

Trolleys: The use of trolleys will facilitate the removal of infectious waste at the source itself, instead of adding a new category of waste.

Wheelbarrows: Wheelbarrows are used to transfer the waste from the point source to the collection centres. There are two types of wheelbarrow – covered and open. Wheelbarrows are made of steel and provided with two wheels and a handle. Care should be taken not to directly dump waste into it. Only packed waste (in plastic bags) should be carried. Care should also be taken not to allow liquid waste from spilling into the wheelbarrow, as it will corrode. These are ideal for transferring debris within the institution. Wheelbarrows also come in various sizes depending on the utility.

Chutes: Chutes are vertical conduits provided for easy transportation of refuse vertically in case of institutions with more than two floors. Chutes should be fabricated from stainless steel. It should have a self-closing lid. These chutes should be fumigated everyday with formaldehyde vapours. The contaminated linen (contaminated with blood and or other body fluids) from each floor should be bundled in soiled linen or in plastic bags before ejecting into the chute.

Alternately, elevators with mechanical winches or electrical winches can be provided to bring down waste containers from each floor. Chutes are necessary to avoid horizontal transport of waste thereby minimizing the routing of the waste within the premises and hence reducing the risk of secondary contamination.

Treatment of Hospital Waste

Treatment of waste is required to:

- Disinfect the waste so that it is no longer the source of infection.
- Reduce the volume of the waste.
- Make waste unrecognizable for aesthetic reasons.
- Make recycled items unusable.

Technology Options for Treatment

There are mainly five technology options available for the treatment of Biomedical Waste which can be grouped as:

- Chemical processes
- Mechanical processes
- Biological processes
- Thermal processes
- Irradiation processes

Chemical Processes

These processes use chemical that act as disinfectants. Sodium hypochlorit, dissolved chlorine dioxide, peracetic acid, hydrogen peroxide, dry inorganic chemical and ozone are examples of such chemical. Most chemical processes are water-intensive and require neutralising agents.

Thermal Processes

These processes utilise heat to disinfect. Depending on the temperature they operate it is been grouped into two categories, which are Low-heat systems and High-heat systems. Low-heat systems (operates between 93-177°C) use steam, hot water, or electromagnetic radiation to heat and decontaminate the waste.

Autoclave & Microwave are low heat systems. Autoclaving is a low heat thermal process and it uses steam for disinfection of waste. Autoclaves are of two types depending on the method they use for removal of air pockets are gravity flow autoclave and vacuum autoclave.

Microwaving is a process which disinfect the waste by moist heat and steam generated by microwaveenergy. High-heat systems (operates between 540-8, 300°C) employ combustion and high temperature plasma to decontaminate and destroy the waste.

Incinerator & Hydroclaving are high heat systems. Hydroclaving - is steam treatment with fragmentation and drying of waste. Incineration is a burn technology.

Mechanical Processes

These processes are used to change the physical form or characteristics of the waste either to facilitate waste handling or to process the waste in conjunction with other treatment steps.

The two primary mechanical processes are:

Compaction – used to reduce the volume of the waste.

Shredding – used to destroy plastic and paper waste to prevent their reuse. Only the disinfected waste can be used in a shredder.

Irradiation Processes

It exposes wastes to ultraviolet or ionizing radiation in an enclosed chamber. These systems require post shredding to render the waste unrecognizable.

Biological Processes

It uses biological enzymes for treating medical waste. It is claimed that biological reactions will not only decontaminate the waste but also cause the destruction of all the organic constituents so that only plastics, glass, and other inert will remain in the residues.

POINTS TO PONDER IN PROCESSING THE WASTE

Incineration

- Incinerators should be suitably designed to achieve the emission limits.
- Wastes to be incinerated shall not be chemically treated with any chlorinated disinfectants.
- Toxic metals in the incineration ash shall be limited within the regulatory quantities.
- Only low sulphur fuel like Diesel shall be used as fuel in the incinerator.

Autoclaving

The autoclave should be dedicated for the purpose of disinfecting and treating biomedical waste.

1. When operating a gravity flow autoclave, medical waste shall be subjected to:
    - A temperature of not less than 121°C and pressure of about 15 pounds per square inch (psi) for an autoclave residence time of not less than 60 minutes; or
    - A temperature of not less than 135°C and a pressure of 31 psi for an autoclave residence time of not less than 45 minutes; or
    - A temperature of not less than 149°C and a pressure of 52 psi for an autoclave residence time of not less than 30 minutes.
2. When operating a vacuum autoclave, medical waste shall be subjected to a minimum of one per vacuum pulse to purge the autoclave of all air. The waste shall be subjected to the following:
    - A temperature of not less than 121°C and a pressure of 15 psi per an autoclave residence time of not less than 45 minutes; or
    - Temperature of not less than 135°C and a pressure of 31 psi for an autoclave residence time of not less than 30 minutes; or Medical waste shall not be considered properly treated unless the time, temperature and pressure indicate stipulated

limits. If for any reason, these were not reached, the entire load of medical waste must be autoclaved again until the proper temperature, pressure and residence time were achieved.

Microwaving

- Microwave treatment shall not be used for cytotoxic, hazardous or radioactive wastes, contaminated animal carcasses, body parts and large metal items.
- The microwave system shall comply with the efficacy tests/routine tests.
- The microwave should completely and consistently kill bacteria and other pathogenic organism that is ensured by the approved biological indicator at the maximum design capacity of each microwave unit.

Deep Burial

- A pit or trench should be dug about 2 m deep. It should be half filled with waste, and then covered with lime within 50 cm of the surface, before filling the rest of the pit with soil.
- It must be ensured that animals do not have access to burial sites.
- Covers of galvanised iron/wire meshes may be used.
- On each occasion, when wastes are added to the pit, a layer of 10cm of soil be added to cover the wastes.
- Burial must be performed under close and dedicated supervision.
- The site should be relatively impermeable and no shallow well should be close to the site.
- The pits should be distant from habitation, and sited so as to ensure that no contamination occurs of any surface water or groundwater.
- The area should not be prone to flooding or erosion.
- The location of the site will be authorized by the prescribed authority.
- The institution shall maintain a record of all pits for deep burial.

Disposal of Sharps

- Blades and needles waste after disinfection should be disposed in circular or rectangular pits.
- Such pits can be dug and lined with brick, masonry, or concrete rings.
- The pit should be covered with a heavy concrete slab, which is penetrated by a galvanized steel pipe projecting about 1.5 m above the slab, within internal diameter of upto 20 mm.
- When the pipe is full it can be sealed completely after another has been prepared.

Radioactive Waste from Medical Establishments

- It may be stored under carefully controlled conditions until the level of radioactivity is so low that they may be treated as other waste.
- Special care is needed when old equipment containing radioactive source is being discarded.
- Expert advice should be taken into account.

Mercury Control

Wastes containing Mercury due to breakage of thermometer and other measuring equipment need to be given:

- Proper attention should be given to the collection of the spilled mercury, its storage and sending of the same back to the manufacturers.
- Must take all measures to ensure that the spilled mercury does not become part of biomedical wastes.
- Waste containing equal to or more than 50 ppm of mercury is a hazardous waste and the concerned generators of the wastes including the health care units are required to dispose the waste as per the norms.

Standard For Liquid Waste

The effluent generated from the hospitals must confirm to the following:

Parameter	Permissible limit
pH	6.5 – 9.0
Suspended solids	100 mg/L
Oil and grease	10 mg/L
BOD	30 mg/L
COD	250 mg/L
Bioassay test	90% survival of fish after 96 hours in 100% effluent

These limits are applicable to those hospitals which are either connected with sewers that have no terminal sewage treatment plant or not connected to public sewers that have terminal facilities. In addition, the general standards as notified under the Environment (Protection) Act, 1986 shall be applicable..

Biomedical waste management is shown below diagrammatically.

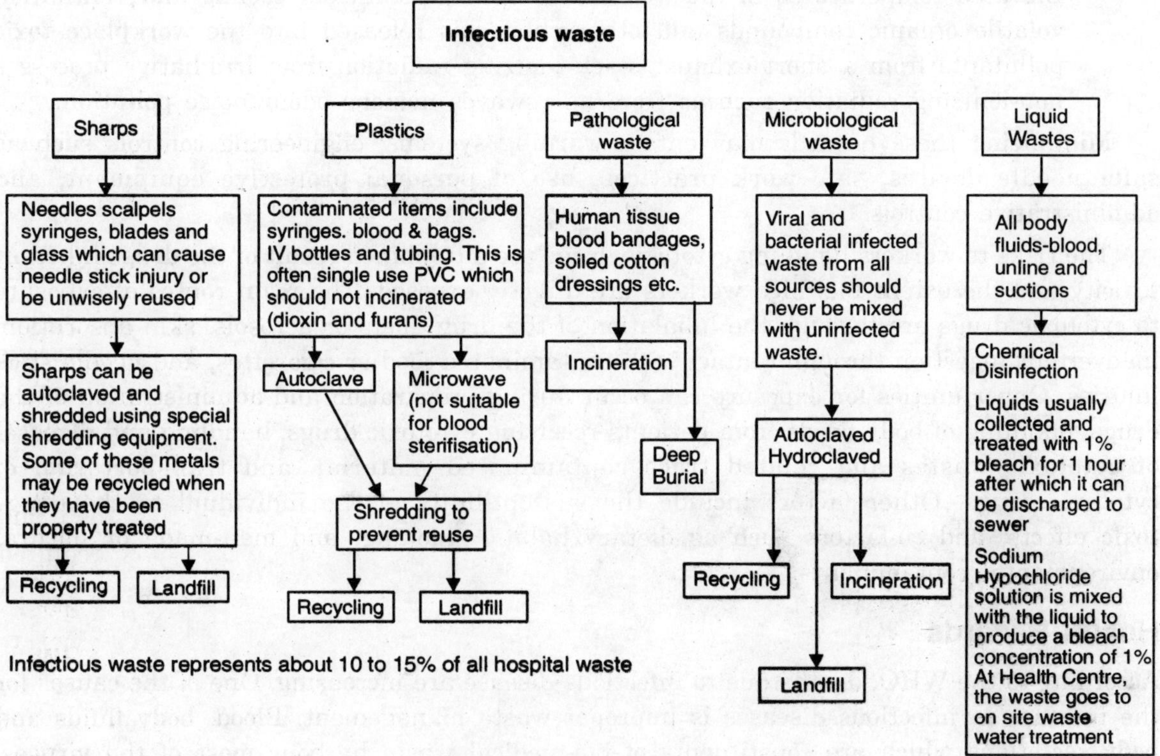

Figure 6.1: Biomedical waste management

Occupational Safety and Health Hazards

Personnel involved in the treatment of medical waste are exposed to infectious agents through several routes including skin penetration, skin contact, or by the aerogenic route. Exposure routes vary with the type of treatment used. Medical waste contains a variety of human pathogens including bacteria, fungi, viruses, and parasitic organisms as well as microbial toxins.

There are many potential hazards when dealing with medical waste. Some hazards are associated with handling and transport such as:

- Needle-stick.
- Injuries due to other sharps, such as broken glass ... ergonomic issues especially related to lifting blood splatter during waste handling aerosolized pathogens (disease causing microorganisms released as aerosols or tiny droplets suspended in air) during loading, compaction, or break up of untreated wastespillschemical and hazardous drug exposure.

Other hazards depend on which treatment technology is used *e.g.*:

- Hot surfaces that cause burns

- Steam from a treatment chamber
- Elevated temperatures in the work area due to insufficient cooling and ventilation volatile organic compounds and other chemicals released into the workplace toxic pollutants from a short exhaust stack ionizing radiation from irradiative processes non-ionizing radiation such as from microwaves noxious odoursnoise pollution.

Minimizing these hazards may entail: warning systems, engineering controls such as safer needle devices, safe work practices, use of personal protective equipment, and administrative controls.

The risks to workers handling cytotoxic drugs are a combined result of the drugs inherent toxicity and the extent to which workers are directly exposed. The main routes of exposure to cytotoxic drugs are through the inhalation of the drug dusts or aerosols, skin absorption, inadvertent ingestion through contact with contaminated food or cigarettes, and needle stick injuries. Opportunities for exposure can occur during preparation and administration of the drugs, handling of body fluids from patients receiving cytotoxic drugs, handling and disposal of cytotoxic wastes and related trace contaminated material, and transportation of cytotoxic drugs. Other factors include the susceptibility of the individual to the drugs toxic effects, and co-factors such as dietary habits, smoking, and man-made or natural environmental contaminants.

Health Hazards

According to the WHO, deaths due to infectious disease are increasing. One of the causes for the increase in infectious diseases is improper waste management. Blood, body fluids and body secretions which are constituents of bio-medical waste harbour most of the viruses, bacteria and parasites that cause infection.

This passes via a number of human contacts, all of whom are potential 'recipients' of the infection. Human Immunodeficiency Virus (HIV) and hepatitis viruses spearhead an extensive list of infections and diseases which spread through bio-medical waste. Tuberculosis, pneumonia, diarrhea diseases, tetanus, whooping cough etc., are other common diseases spread due to improper waste management.

The health hazards due to improper waste management can affect:

- The occupants in institutions and spread in the vicinity of the institutions.
- People happened to be in contact with the institution like laundry workers, nurses, emergency medical personnel, and refuse workers.
- Risks of infections outside hospital for waste handlers, scavengers and (eventually) the general public.
- Risks associated with hazardous chemicals, drugs, being handled by persons handling wastes at all levels.
- Injuries from sharps and exposure to harmful chemical waste and radioactive waste also cause health hazards to employees.

Health Hazards to General Public

The general public's health can also be adversely affected by bio-medical waste.

- Improper practices such as dumping of bio-medical waste in municipal dustbins, open spaces, water bodies etc., leads to the spread of diseases.
- Emissions from incinerators and open burning also lead to exposure to harmful gases which can cause cancer and respiratory diseases.
- Exposure to radioactive waste in the waste stream can also cause serious health hazards.
- An often-ignored area is the increase of in-home healthcare activities. An increase in the number of diabetics who inject themselves with insulin, home nurses taking care of terminally ill patients etc., all generate bio-medical waste, which can cause health hazards.

Biomedical waste can cause health hazards to animals and birds too

- Plastic waste can choke animals, which scavenge on open dumps.
- Injuries from sharps are common feature affecting animals.
- Harmful chemicals such as dioxins and furans can cause serious health hazards to animals and birds.
- Heavy metals can even affect the reproductive health of the animals.
- Change in microbial ecology, spread of antibiotic resistance.

What can we do for good BMW management?

- Use only disposable syringes. After use throw the syringes after breaking them.
- Bandages, cotton and other blood stained materials should not be thrown with general garbage.
- Use black plastic bags to dispose biomedical wastes.
- Keep trash out of reach of small children and infants.
- Diapers, sanitary napkins etc. should also be disposed separately.
- Drugs that are past date of expiry must never be used.

Legal aspect of BMW management

The Central Government, to perform its functions effectively as contemplated under sections 6, 8, and 25 of the Environment Protection Act, 1986, has made various Rules, Notifications and Orders including the Biomedical Wastes (Management & Handling) Rules, 1998.

A brief summary of the provisions in Biomedical Wastes (Management & Handling) Rules, 1998 is given below.

- Section 3 establishes the authority of the government to undertake various steps for protection and improvement of the environment.
- Section 5 provides for issuance of directions in writing.
- Section 6 empowers the government to make rules.

- Section 8 permits the education of individuals dealing with hazardous wastes regarding various safety measures.
- Section 10 bestows authority to enter the premises and inspect.
- Section 15 allows the government to take punitive steps against defaulters. This involves imprisonment up to five years or penalty of upto rupees one lakh or both. In case the default continues, it would then attract a penalty of rupees five thousand per day up to one year and thereafter imprisonment up to seven years.
- Section 17 provides for punishment in case of violations by government departments.

Even after the June, 2000 deadline most of the large hospitals have not complied with these Rules, as there is no specified authority to monitor the implementation of these Rules. But, the fact is that in most of the states, the pollution control boards that are connected with waste in general do not have adequate powers or commitment to enforce the Rules.

Applicability of BMW Rules, 1998

The BMW Rules are applicable to every occupier of an institution generating biomedical waste which includes a hospital, nursing homes, clinic, dispensary, veterinary institutions, animal houses, pathological lab, blood bank by whatever name called, the rules are applicable to even handlers.

Common Biomedical Wastes Treatment Facility [CBWTFs]

The Common Biomedical wastes treatment facility, (see rules 14, amended in June 2000, which cast the responsibilities on municipal bodies to collect biomedical wastes/treated biomedical wastes and also provide sites for setting up of incinerator.) The owner of CBWTFs are service providers, who are providing services to health care units for collection of BMWs for its final disposal to their site.

The components of a common biomedical waste treatment and disposal facility [CBWTFs] are autoclave, shredder, compactor, and incinerator for anatomical waste, secured landfill facility, laboratory and vehicles for transportation of wastes.

CHAPTER 7

E-WASTE MANAGEMENT

E-waste (Electronic Waste) comprises of wastes generated from used electronic devices and house hold appliances which are not fit for their original intended use and are destined for recovery, recycling or disposal. Such wastes includes electrical & electronic devices such as computers, cellular phones, personal stereos, including large household appliances such as refrigerators, air conditioners etc. E-wastes contain over 1000 different substances many of which are toxic & potentially hazardous to environment and human health, if these are not handled in an environmentally sound manner.

Electronic and electrical waste (e-waste), also referred to as waste electrical and electronic equipment (WEEE), is dened as any end-of-life "equipment, which is dependent on electrical currents or electromagnetic elds in order to work properly. E-waste now makes up to ve percent of all municipal solid waste worldwide, nearly the same amount as all plastic packaging, but it is much more hazardous.

E-waste consists of all waste from electrical and electronic equipments which have reached their end- of- life period or are not in useful condition and it should be either recycled or disposed. It includes computer and its accessories as monitors, printers, keyboards, central processing units; typewriters, mobile phones & chargers, remotes, compact discs, headphones, batteries, LCD/Plasma TVs, air conditioners, refrigerators and other household appliances. The e-waste consists of ferrous & non-ferrous metals, plastics, glass, wood & plywood, printed circuit boards, concrete, ceramics, rubber and other items. Iron and steel constitute about 50% of the waste, followed by plastics (21%), non- ferrous metals (13%) and other constituents. Non-ferrous metals consist of metals like copper, aluminium and precious metals like silver, gold, platinum, palladium and so on. Due to the presence of elements like lead, mercury, arsenic, cadmium, selenium, hexavalent chromium, and flame retardants beyond threshold quantities, e-waste become hazardous in nature. It contains over 1000 different substances, many of which are toxic, and creates serious pollution upon disposal. Obsolete computers pose the most significant environmental danger and threat to human health among the e-wastes.

The increase of electrical and electronic products, consumption rates and higher obsolescence rate leads to higher generation of e-waste. Electronic waste or e-waste is one of the rapidly growing problems of the world. E-waste comprises of a multitude of components, some containing toxic substances that can have an adverse impact on human health and the environment if not handled properly.

The electronic and electrical goods are largely classied under three major heads, as: 'white goods,' comprising of household appliances like air conditioners, dishwashers, refrigerators and washing machines; 'brown goods,' comprising of TVs, camcorders, cameras, etc.; 'grey goods,' like computers, printers, fax machines, scanners, etc. The grey goods are comparatively more complex to recycle due to their toxic composition.

E-waste is growing because the markets in which these products are produced are also growing rapidly. People are upgrading their mobile phones, computers, televisions, audio equipment and printers more frequently. Electronic waste, or E-Waste, the components of electronics that are discarded, is of growing concern worldwide, particularly as purchases of electronics increases and options for recycling remain limited. E-waste is often globally traded and discarded in unhealthy and environmentally toxic ways. Toxic corrosives are often used to treat metals, and improper disposal & handling have severe health and environmental consequences.

Discard Rate of Electronics

Item	Discard/replace rate
Mobile telephone	1 to 3 years
PC	Every 2 years
Camera	3 to 5 years
Television	10-15 years
Refrigerator	10-15 years
Washing Machine	10-15 years
IT accessories	Very fast

The composition of e-waste

Composition of e-waste is very diverse and differs in products across different categories. It contains more than 1000 different substances, which fall under "hazardous" & "non-hazardous" categories.

- Substances found in large quantities include epoxy resins, fiberglass, PCBs, PVC (polyvinyl chlorides), thermosetting plastics, lead, tin, copper, silicon, beryllium, carbon, iron and aluminium.
- Elements found in small amounts include cadmium, mercury, and thallium.
- Elements found in trace amounts include americium, antimony, arsenic, barium, bismuth, boron, cobalt, europium, gallium, germanium, gold, indium, lithium, manganese, nickel, niobium, palladium, platinum, rhodium, ruthenium, selenium, silver, tantalum, terbium, thorium, titanium, vanadium, and yttrium.

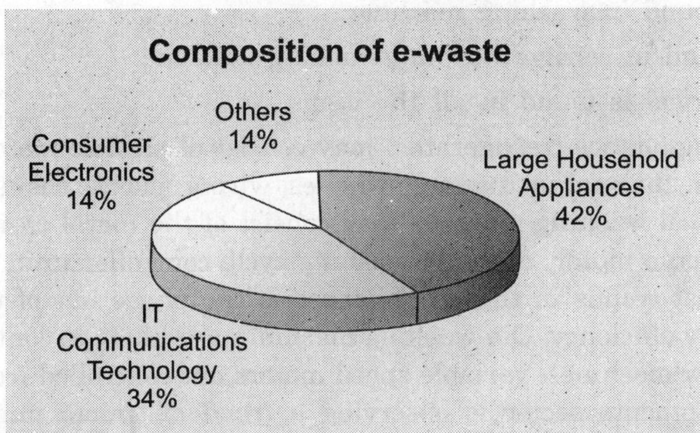

COMPONENTS OF E-WASTE

E-waste has been categorized into three main categories, Viz. Large Household Appliances, IT & Telecom and Consumer Equipments. Refrigerator and Washing Machine represent large household appliances, Personal Computer, Monitor and Laptop represent IT & Telecom, while Television represents Consumer Equipment. Each of these E-waste items has been classified with respect to twenty six common components, which could be found in them. These components form the "Building Blocks" of each item and therefore they are readily "identifiable" and "removable". These components are metal, motor/compressor, cooling, plastic, insulation, glass, LCD, rubber, wiring/ electrical, concrete, transformer, magnetron, textile, circuit board, fluorescent lamp, incandescent lamp, heating element, thermostat, BFR-containing plastic, batteries, CFC/HCFC/HFC/HC, external electric cables, refractory ceramic fibers, radio active substances and electrolyte capacitors (over L/D 25 mm).

The kinds of components, which are found in Refrigerator, Washing Machine, Personal Computers (PC) and TVs, are summarized below.

- Radioactive substances, refractory ceramic fibers, electrolyte capacitors (over L/D 25 mm), textile and magnetron are not present in any item.
- Plastic, circuit board and external electric cables are present in majority of items. BFR containing plastic is present in refrigerator, laptop and television.
- Refrigerators are unique items because of presence of CFC/HCFC/HFC/HC, cooling, insulation, incandescent lamp and compressor.
- Heating element is found in washing machine, while thermostat is found in both refrigerator and washing machine.
- Fluorescent lamp is found only in laptop.
- Metal and motor are found in majority of items except refrigerator.
- Transformer is not found in washing machine and refrigerator.
- CRT is found in personal computer and TV, while LCD is found in PC and TV.
- Batteries are found in PC and laptop.

- Concrete is found in washing machine.
- Rubber is found in refrigerator and washing machine.
- Wiring/ Electrical is found in all the items.

Large household appliance (refrigerator) may consist of electric motor, a circuit board, a transformer, capacitor, thermal insulation, switches, wiring, plastic casing that contain flame retardants etc. A typical washing machine may consist of the metal casing, concrete ballast, inner and outer drums, a motor, a pump, washing cycle controller unit, switches and other components. The latest trends in these appliances is the phase out of the use of ODS and improvement of energy efficiency. Old washing machines are likely to contain large capacitors, while in relatively new machines, variable speed motors are controlled from the circuit board. IT and Telecom equipments sector is observing a trend of "micro miniaturization", while CRTs are being replaced by LCD/LED screens.

Process used for processing various e-waste components is tabulated below.

E-waste components	Process used
Cathode Ray Tubes (CRTs)/ Picture tube	Breaking and removal of Copper yoke and dumping
PCB (Printed Circuit Board)	Desoldering and removing computer chips
Dismantled PCB Processing	Open burning of boards to remove metals
Chips and other gold plated components	Chemical stripping using nitric and sulphuric acid along river banks
Plastics	Shredding and low temperature melting to manufacture poor grade plastics
Wires	Open burning to recover copper
Miscellaneous parts	Open burning to recover steel and other metals
Toner cartridges	Use of paint brushes to recover toner without any protection
Secondary steel or copper or precious metals	Furnace recovery of steel or copper from waste
Aluminium	Used in PWB,CRT connectors
Selenium	Send picture signals over wire
Zinc	Picture tubes, glass plate of television cameras has coating of ZnS
Iron	Inductors in PCB
Copper	Conductors
Solder(Constituent in lead)	PCB, glass panel and gasket in monitor
Mother board(Constituent in Beryllium)	Removal of plastics and metal by breaking the parts
Lead	Soldering of PCB

THE HEALTH & ENVIRONMENTAL HAZARD OF E-WASTE

E-waste is going to be the biggest challenge for the industry in the future.

Workers are poorly-protected in an environment where e-waste from PC monitors, Printed Circuit Boards, CDs, motherboards, cables, toner cartridges, light bulbs and tube-lights are burned in the open, releasing lead, mercury and other toxins into the air. Working in poorly-ventilated enclosed areas, without masks and technical expertise, results in exposure to dangerous and slow-poisoning chemicals.

- When old electronics are thrown into a landûll, all the energy that directly or indirectly goes into making a product is lost. This means that more energy and water is needed to make new products, emitting more greenhouse gases and using more water. Thus land lling old electronics also wastes the natural resources used to make a product.
- Some of the materials used in electronic products are extremely rare and are running out.
- When disposed of in landlls, toxic chemicals from the e-waste seep into the ground. For people living in the vicinity of these landlls, it could mean permanent health damage to the central & peripheral nervous system, various health hazards such as seizures, retardation, kidney failures and even effect child development.
- Toxins generated from the open burning of Plastic shells, PCB boards and other non-ferrous materials contained in e-waste pollute the air, water & land and are a growing concern where such practices take place.
- Due to the presence of PVC and brominated ame- retardants in wires, the emissions contain high levels of both brominated and chlorinated dioxins & furans – two of the most deadly persistent organic pollutants (POPs).
- High traces of cancer causing polycyclic aromatic hydrocarbons (PAHs) are found in the emissions and the ash of E-waste.
- Lead-laden monitor glass, which is a hazardous waste is dumped in land or pushed into rivers after the copper laden yoke of CRT monitor is extracted.
- Change in thyroid function, changes in cellular expression & function, adverse neonatal outcomes, changes in temperament & behaviour, and decreased lung function.
- Increases in spontaneous abortions, stillbirths, & premature births, and reduced birth-weights & birth lengths associated with exposure to e-waste.
- People living in e-waste recycling towns or working in e-waste recycling has evidence of greater DNA damage than those living in control towns.
- Signicant negative correlations between blood chromium concentrations and forced vital capacity in children has been observed.

Environmental effects of processing of various e-waste components are tabulated below.

E-Waste Component	Process Used	Potential Environmental Effects
Cathode ray tubes (used in TVs, computer monitors, ATM, video cameras)	Breaking and removal of yoke, then dumping	Lead, barium and other heavy metals leaching into the ground water and release of toxic phosphorus
Printed circuit board (a thin plate on which chips and other electronic components are placed)	De-soldering and removal of computer chips; open burning and acid baths to remove nal metals after chips are removed.	Air emissions as well as discharge into rivers of glass dust, tin, lead, brominated dioxin, beryllium cadmium, and mercury
Chips and other gold plated components	Chemical stripping using nitric and hydrochloric acid and burning of chips	Hydrocarbons, heavy metals, brominated substances discharged directly into rivers acidifying fish and flora. Tin & lead contamination of surface and groundwater. Air emissions of brominated dioxins, heavy metals and hydrocarbons
Plastics from printers, keyboards, monitors, etc.	Shredding and low temp melting to be reused	Emissions of brominated dioxins, heavy metals and hydrocarbons
Computer wires	Open burning and stripping to remove copper	Hydrocarbon ashes released into air, water and soil.

Health Hazards of e-waste	Potential Environmental Hazards
• Silicosis • Cuts from CRT glass • Inhalation of Phosphor, Cadmium etc.	Lead, barium and other heavy metals leaching into groundwater, release of toxic phosphor
• Tin and lead inhalation. Possible brominated dioxins, beryllium, cadmium, mercury inhalation • Causes neural damage and accumulates in kidney and liver	Air emission of the same substances causes air pollution
• Toxicity to workers and nearby residents from tin, lead, beryllium, mercury inhalation	Surface and ground water pollution and air pollution

• Acid contact with eyes, skin may result impermanent injuries • Inhalation of fumes of acid can cause respiratory irritation like pulmonary edema, circulatory failure and death	Hydrocarbons, heavy metals discharged to river and bank, acidifies river destroying aquatic life
• Probable hydrocarbon, Brominated dioxins and heavy metals exposure Disrupts endocrine system functions	Air emission of brominated dioxins and heavy metals and hydrocarbons
• Aromatic hydrocarbons (carcinogenic) exposure to workers.	Aromatic hydrocarbon discharged to air, water and soil
• Aromatic hydrocarbons and potential dioxins exposure	Hydrocarbon ashes discharged to air, water and soil
• Respiratory tract irritation • Carbon black leads to possible human carcinogen	Cyan, tallow and magenta toners unknown toxicity
• Exposure to dioxins and heavy metals causes asthmatic bronchitis and DNA damage	Air emission of dioxins and heavy metals
• Alzheimer's disease and Parkinson's disease	Disposal leads to water pollution
• Nausea, diarrhea, fatigue, hair loss and diseased nails	Disposal causes environmental threat
• Vomiting diarrhea and damage to kidney	Disposal causes water pollution and disturbs aquatic environment
• Siderosis disease	Disposal in landfill causes water pollution
• Wilson's disease	Disposal in landfill causes water pollution
• Damage to central and peripheral nervous system • Kidney damage • Affects brain development of children	Leaching in soil and water causes pollution
• Beryllicosiss • Skin disease like warts	Disposal leads to environmental damage
• Negative effect on children's brain development	Acute and chronic toxic effects on plants, animals, and microorganisms

Health & environmental hazards of e-waste are tabulated above.

Most electronic goods contain significant quantities of toxic metals and chemicals like mercury, which is currently being phased out in the developed countries. Mercury is mobile and poisonous in any form—inorganic, organic or elemental. Its organic compound methyl mercury is a neuro-toxicant that damages the brain. It is geno-toxic too as it passes through the placental and the blood-brain barrier, putting the foetus at risk. Mercury causes severe & permanent damage to the central nervous system, lungs and kidneys. It can trigger depression and suicidal tendencies and cause paralysis, Alzheimer's disease, speech & vision impairment, allergies, hypospermia and impotence. Mercury bio-accumulates (builds up in organisms) and biomagnifies (moves up the food chain). Even minuscule increases in methyl mercury exposures can affect the cardiovascular system.

E-waste typically contains complex combinations of materials and components down to microscopic levels. The wastes are broken down in not just for recycling but for the recoverable materials such as plastic, iron, aluminium, copper and gold. However, since e-waste also contains significant concentration of substances that are hazardous to human health and the environment, even a small amount of e-waste entering the residual waste will introduce relatively high amount of heavy metals and halogenated substances. Such harmful substances leach into the surrounding soil, water and air during waste treatment or when they are dumped in landfills or left to lie around near it. Sooner or later they would adversely affect human health and ecology.

e-waste toxins and affected body parts are tabulated below.

e-Waste Toxins and affected body parts

Components	Constituents	Affected body parts
Printed circuit boards	Lead and cadmium	Nervous system, kidney, lever
Motherboards	Berillium	Lungs, skin
Cathode ray tubes (CRTs)	Lead oxide, barium and cadmium	Heart, lever, muscles
Switches and flat-screen monitors	Mercury	Brain, skin
Computer batteries	Cadmium	Kidney, lever
Capacitors and transformers	Polychlorinated biphenyls (PCBs)	
Printed circuit boards, plastic	Brominated flame-retardant casings cable	
Cable insulation/coating	Polyvinyl chloride (PVC)	Immune system
Plastic housing	Bromine	Endocrine

E-waste contents, its effect and sources are tabulated below.

Waste Element	Effect on Human Being	Sources of E-waste
Lead	Central and peripheral nervous system, Blood system, kidney and reproduction system	Glass panel, Gasket in computer monitors, solder in PCB and other component
Cadmium	Kidney	SMD chip registers, infra red detectors and semiconductor chips
Mercury	Brain, Kidney, Foetus	Electrical and electronic equipment thermostats, sensors, relays, switches, medical equipment, lamps, mobile phone, batteries, flat panel display
Barium	Brain swelling, muscle weaknesss, damage to heart, liver and spleen	Used in computer in front panel of a CRT
Beryllium	Lung cancer, skin diseases	Motherboard, finger clips
Toners	Respiratory treat irritation	Plastic printer cartridge
Hexavalent chromium	Damage to DNA	Untreated steel

Pollutants and their occurrence in e-waste is tabulated below.

Pollutant	Occurrence
Arsenic:	Semiconductors, diodes, microwaves, LEDs (Light-emitting diodes), solar cells
Barium:	Electron tubes, filler for plastic and rubber, lubricant additives
Brominated flame-proofing agent:	Casing, circuit boards (plastic), cables and PVC cables
Cadmium:	Batteries, pigments, solder, alloys, circuit boards, computer batteries, monitor cathode ray tubes (CRTs)
Chrome:	Dyes/pigments, switches, solar
Cobalt:	Insulators
Copper:	Conducted in cables, copper ribbons, coils, circuitry, pigments
Lead:	Lead rechargeable batteries, solar, transistors, lithium batteries, PVC (polyvinyl chloride stabilizers, lasers, Liquid crystal Displays
Lithium:	Mobile telephones, photographic equipment, video equipment (batteries)

Mercury:	Components in copper machines and steam irons; batteries in clocks and pocket calculators, switches, LCDs
Nickel:	Alloys, batteries, relays, semiconductors, pigments
PCBs (polychlorinated softening biphenyls):	Transformers, capacitors, agents for paint, glue, plastic
Selenium	Photoelectric cells, pigments, photocopiers, fax machines
Silver:	Capacitors, switches (contacts), batteries, resistors
Zinc:	Steel, brass, alloys, disposable and rechargeable batteries, luminous substances

Listed in the table below are the harmful elements in the compositions of electrical and electronic appliances that can be hazardous to health & environment:

Metal	Danger
Lead:	A neurotoxin that affects the kidneys and the reproductive system. High quantities can be fatal. It affects mental development in children. Mechanical breaking of CRTs (cathode ray tubes) and removing solder from microchips release lead as powder and fumes.
Plastics:	Found in circuit boards, cabinets and cables, they contain carcinogens. BFRs or brominated flame retardants give out carcinogenic brominated dioxins and furans. Dioxins can harm reproductive and immune systems. Burning PVC, a component of plastics, also produces dioxins. BFR can leach into landfills. Even the dust on computer cabinets contains BFR.
Chromium:	Used to protect metal housings and plates in a computer from corrosion. Inhaling hexavalent chromium or chromium 6 can damage liver and kidneys and cause bronchial maladies including asthmatic bronchitis and lung cancer.
Mercury:	Affects the central nervous system, kidneys and immune system. It impairs foetus growth and harms infants through mother's milk. It is released while breaking and burning of circuit boards and switches. Mercury in water bodies can form methylated mercury through microbial activity. Methylated mercury is toxic and can enter the human food chain through aquatic.
Beryllium:	Found in switch boards and printed circuit boards. It is carcinogenic and causes lung diseases.
Cadmium:	A carcinogen. Long-term exposure causes *Itai-itai* disease, which causes severe pain in the joints and spine. It affects the kidneys and softens

	bones. Cadmium is released into the environment as powder while crushing and milling of plastics, CRTs and circuit boards. Cadmium may be released with dust, entering surface water and groundwater.
Acid:	Sulphuric and hydrochloric acids are used to separate metals from circuit boards. Fumes contain chlorine and sulphur dioxide, which cause respiratory problems. They are corrosive to the eye and skin.

Indian e-waste scenerio

Sixty-five cities in India generate more than 60% of the total e-waste generated in India. Ten states generate 70% of the total e-waste generated in India. Maharashtra ranks first followed by Tamil Nadu, Andhra Pradesh, Uttar Pradesh, West Bengal, Delhi, Karnataka, Gujarat, Madhya Pradesh and Punjab in the list of e-waste generating states in India. Among top ten cities generating e-waste, Mumbai ranks first followed by Delhi, Bangalore, Chennai, Kolkata, Ahmedabad, Hyderabad, Pune, Surat and Nagpur.

In India, e-waste management assumes greater signiûcance not only due to the generation of its own e-waste but also because of the dumping of e-waste from developed countries. This is coupled with India's lack of appropriate infrastructure and procedures for its disposal and recycling.

Projected growth of e-waste in India is shown below.

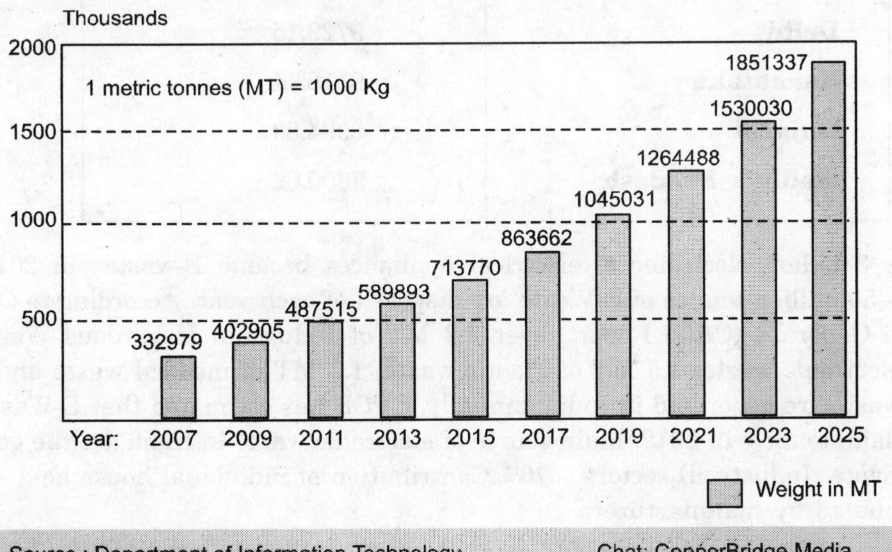

Source : Department of Information Technology Chat: CopperBridge Media

Of the total e-waste generated in the country, western India accounts for the largest population at 35%, while the southern, northern & eastern regions account for 30, 21 & 14%, respectively.

State	%
Maharashtra	19.8%
Taml Nadu	13.1%
Andhra Pradesh	12.5%
Uttar Pradesh	10.1%
West Bengal	9.8%
Delhi	9.5%
Karnataka	8.9%
Gujarat	8.8%
Madhya Pradesh	7.8%

State-wise E-waste Generation in India (Toones/year)

WEE Generating top ten state are listed below.

State	E–waste, Tonnes
Maharashtra	20270.59
Tamil Nadu	13486.24
Andhra Pradesh	12780.33
Utter Pradesh	10381.11
West Bengal	10059.36
Delhi	9729.15
Karnataka	9118.74
Gujarat	8994.33
Madhya Pradesh	7800.62

Globally 3 billion electronic & electrical appliances became E-waste in 2010.Globally about to 40- 50 million tonnes of E-Waste are disposed of each year. According to Comptroller and Auditor-General's (CAG) Report, over 7.2 MT of Industrial Hazardous Waste, 4 lakh Tonnes of electronic waste, 1.5 MT of Plastic waste, 1.7 MT of medical waste and 48 MT of municipal waste are generated in India annually. CPCB has estimated that E-Waste in India exceeded 8 lakh tonnes in 2012. Main source of electronic waste in India are the government, public & private (Industrial) sectors – 70%.Contribution of individual house hold – 15%.Rest being contributed by manufacturers.

Out of total e-waste volume in India:

Televisions—68%

Desktop, server—27%

Imports—2%

Mobiles—1%

A report of the United Nations predicted that by 2020, E-Waste from old computers would jump by 400% on 2007 levels in China and by 500% in India. Additionally E-Waste from discarded mobile phones would be about seven times higher than 2007 levels in China and in India 18 timers higher by 2020.

China already produces about 2.3 million tonnes of E-Waste domestically; second only to The USA with about 3 million Tonnes.

It is estimated that the total e-waste generated in the EU is about 14-15 kg per capita or 5 to 7 MT per annum. In countries like India and China, annual generation per capita is less than 1 kg. In Europe, e-waste contributes up to 6 million tonnes of solid waste per annum. The e-waste generation in the EU is expected to grow at a rate of 3 to 5 per cent per year. In the past, e-waste had increased by 16 to 28 per cent every five years which is three times faster than average annual municipal solid waste generation. In the U.S., e-waste accounts for 1 to 3 per cent of the total municipal waste generation.

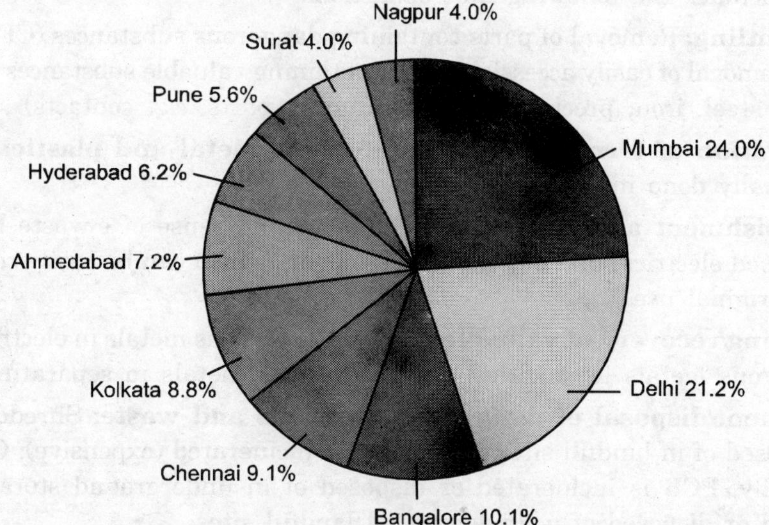

City-wise E-waste Generation In India (Tonnes/year)

Currently e-waste of Delhi is approximately 30,000 metric tonnes per annum and employs more than 1.5 lakh workers in city's various recycling units. Delhi alone gets around 85% of the electronic waste generated in the developed world. Though Mumbai and Chennai are the top importers of junk computers and electronic waste in India, Delhi has emerged as the main hub of e-waste recycling in India, and perhaps the world.

Tonnes of e-waste from Bangalore and across India are shipped to Singapore, Belgium and Japan. For India doesn't have a single full-fledged unit capable of extracting precious metals like gold, silver and platinum from it. Approximately 200 tonnes are sent annually to these three countries.

THE MANAGEMENT OF E-WASTE

It is estimated that only 15-20% of e-waste is recycled, the rest of these electronics go directly into landfills and incinerators causing health & environmental threat.

So, this e-waste needs to undergo treatment at three levels at the facility. The first level includes decontamination, dismantling and segregation of the waste. At the second level, materials such as plastics, cathode ray tubes (CRT), circuit boards and cables should be treated further by putting them through processes like electromagnetic separation, eddy-current separation and density separation. The third level should involve the recovery of metals, plastics and other items of economic value. For example, sorted plastics can be recycled into plastic products, lead can be recovered from batteries and CRTs can be converted into glass cullet.

Recycling, Reuse and Recovery Options for e-waste

The major approach to treat e-waste is to reduce the concentration of the hazardous chemicals & elements through recycle and recovery. In the process of recycling or recovery, certain e-waste fractions act as secondary raw material for recovery of valuable items. The recycle and recovery includes the following unit operations.

- **Dismantling:** Removal of parts containing dangerous substances (CFCs, Hg switches, PCB); removal of easily accessible parts containing valuable substances (cable containing copper, steel, iron, precious metal containing parts, *e.g.* contacts).
- **Segregation of ferrous metal, non-ferrous metal and plastic:** This separation is normally done in a shredder process.
- **Refurbishment and reuse:** Refurbishment and reuse of e-waste has potential for those used electrical and electronic equipments which can be easily refurbished to put to its original use.
- **Recycling/recovery of valuable materials:** Ferrous metals in electrical arc furnaces, non-ferrous metals in smelting plants, precious metals in separating works.
- **Treatment/disposal of dangerous materials and waste:** Shredder light fraction is disposed of in landfill sites or sometimes incinerated (expensive), CFCs are treated thermally, PCB is incinerated or disposed of in underground storages, Hg is often recycled or disposed of in underground landfill sites.

Treatment & Disposal Options for e-waste

Huge quantity of electronic waste presents an enormous environmental and health hazard to any community. This is best indicated by the table below which shows the amount of waste that 500 million computers can create.

How much waste is in 500 million computers?

Plastic	6.32 Billion Pounds
Lead	1.58 Billion Pounds
Cadmium	3 Million Pounds
Chromium	1.9 Million Pounds
Mercury	632,000 Pounds

There are basically four ways in which e-waste has been treated till date. But none has been found to be fully satisfactory. The most common one has been storing e-wastes in landfills, but it is replete with all the dangers of leaching. The hazardous effects are far worse in the older or less stringently maintained landfills or dumpsites. In the US, about 70% of heavy metals (including mercury and cadmium) found in landfills come from electronic discards. Because of its hazardous nature, dumping in landfills have been banned in most of the states in the US and European Union.

Another method commonly used has been to incinerate or burn the goods concerned, but this process releases heavy metals such as lead, cadmium and mercury into the atmosphere. Municipal incinerators have been some of the largest point sources for dioxins in the environments and of heavy metal contamination of the atmosphere.

Landfilling

The degradation processes of e-waste in landfills are very complicated and run over a wide time span. At present it is not possible to quantify environmental impacts from E-waste in landfills for the following reasons:

- Landfills contain mixtures of various waste streams;
- Emission of pollutants from landfills can be delayed for many years;
- According to climatic conditions and technologies applied in landfills (*e.g.* leachate collection & treatment, impermeable bottom layers, gas collection), data on the concentration of substances in leachate and landfill gas from municipal waste landfill sites differs with a factor 2-3.

The environmental risks from landfilling of e-waste cannot be neglected because the conditions in a landfill site are different from a native soil, particularly concerning the leaching behavior of metals. In addition it is known that cadmium and mercury are emitted in diffuse form or via the landfill gas combustion plant. Although the risks cannot be quantified and traced back to e-waste, landfilling is not an environmentally sound treatment method for substances, which are volatile and not biologically degradable (Cd, Hg, CFC), persistent (PCB) or with unknown behaviour in a landfill site (brominated flame retardants). As a consequence of the complex material mixture in e-waste, it is not possible to exclude environmental (long-term) risks even in secured landfilling.

Incineration

Advantage of incineration of e-waste is the reduction of waste volume and the utilization of the energy content of combustible materials. Some plants remove iron from the slag for recycling. By incineration some environmentally hazardous organic substances are converted into less hazardous compounds. Disadvantage of incineration are the emission to air of substances escaping, flue gas cleaning and the large amount of residues from gas cleaning & combustion.

There is no comparable data, which indicates the impact of e-waste emissions into the overall performance of municipal waste incineration plants. Waste incineration plants contribute significantly to the emissions of cadmium and mercury. In addition, heavy metals not emitted into the atmosphere are transferred to slag and exhaust gas residues and can re-enter the environment on disposal. Therefore, e-waste incineration will increase these emissions, if no reduction measures like removal of heavy metals form are taken.

Reusing and recycling are the other ways of dealing with e-wastes because they increase the lifespan of the products and therefore imply less waste over time. Re-use constitutes direct second hand use, or use after slight modifications are made to the original functioning equipment like memory upgrades, etc. However, they end up as waste eventually as they have limited life span. The reuse of second-hand electronic goods in the developing world including India falls in this category, where the waste ends up locally and where there is no adequate facility and competence to deal with them appropriately.

While recycling appears to be a safe method to utilize or dispose e-wastes, it can be a misleading characterization of disparate practices-including dismantling, shredding, burning, exporting, etc. which are mostly unregulated and often create additional hazards itself. "Recycling" of hazardous wastes, even under the best of circumstances, has little environment benefit as it simply moves the hazards into secondary products that eventually have to be disposed of. Recycling isn't just good for the environment but also good business practice. Recycling is therefore an important solution, especially if we consider that e-waste contains many valuable and rare materials.

E-WASTE LEGISLATION IN INDIA

The solid waste management process is defined in the Indian constitution under twelfth schedule and in municipal solid wastes (management & handling) rules, 2000 enacted by central government. These rule provide some guidelines for the management of the e-waste and can be used as a model in the e-waste recycling and disposal scheme such as house to house collection of waste, proper collection of waste from slums & squatters, hotels restaurants, office complexes and commercial areas, organizing awareness programmes for segregation of wastes; adopting suitable waste processing technologies; and restricting land filling of non-biodegradable inert waste. But there is no proper rule or regulation mainly for e-waste treatment. Some of the rules and regulation which are made related to e-waste are as follows:

A. The Hazardous Waste (management and handling) Rules, 2003

This rule categorized e-waste or its constituents under hazardous and non hazardous waste. As per the rules, "hazardous waste" is defined as any waste which by reason of any of its physical, chemical, reactive, toxic, flammable, explosive or corrosive characteristics causes danger or is likely to cause danger to health or environment, whether alone or when in contact with other wastes or substances.

B. The Hazardous Waste (Management. Handling and Transboundary Movement) Rules, 2008

These rules provide the registration process of hazardous waste recycler. According to these rules, every person desirous of recycling or reprocessing hazardous waste including electronic & electrical waste is required to register with the central pollution control board (CPCB). The e-waste handler is required to register with the CPCB. The authorized recycler or re-processer or re-user should have environmentally sound facilities for recovery of metal and plastic and the waste should be sent to them. Under these rule the ministry of environment and forest is the nodal ministry to deal with the transboundary movement of the hazardous wastes and to grant permission for transit of the hazardous wastes through any part of India.Part A of Schedule III (Basal No. 1180) consists of list of e-waste applicable for import with prior informed consent. Part B of schedule III (Basal No. 1110) deals with list of e-waste applicable for import and export not requiring prior informed consent.

C. Guideline for Environmentally Sound Management of e-waste, 2008

The guideline are given by the government of India and approved by ministry of environment and forest and central pollution control board. The objective of these guideline is to provide guidance for identification of various sources of e-waste and the approach & methodology for handling and disposal of e-waste in an environment friendly manner. These Guidelines include details such as e-waste composition and recycle potential of items of economic value, identification of possible hazardous contents in e-waste, the recycle, re-use & recovery options, treatment & disposal options and the environmentally sound e-waste treatment technologies. The guideline also covers the concept of Extended Producer Responsibility .

D. The e-waste (Management and Handling) Rules, 2011

The primary objective of these rules is to channelize the e-waste generated in the country to make the recycling of the e-waste in environmentally sound manner. The concept of extended producer responsibility is introduced in these rules by placing the main responsibility of e-waste management on the producer of the electrical and electronic equipment. These rules are applicable to every producer, consumer involved in the manufacture, sales purchase, and processing of electrical & electronic equipment or components, collection centres, dismantlers and recyclers of e-waste comes under this law. The is law is also applicable on the people involved in purchase and processing of electrical & electronic equipment or components.

Most of the Indian states have failed to implement e-waste rules in the country which came into being in 2011.

CHAPTER

8

INTEGRATED SOLID WASTE MANAGEMENT (ISWM)

Waste generation increases with population expansion and economic development. Improperly managed solid waste poses a risk to human health and the environment. Uncontrolled dumping and improper waste handling causes a variety of problems, including contaminating water, attracting insects & rodents, and increasing flooding due to blocked drainage canals or gullies. In addition, it may result in safety hazards from fires or explosions. Improper waste management also increases greenhouse gas (GHG) emissions, which contribute to climate change.

Integrated Solid Waste Management (ISWM) is a comprehensive waste prevention, recycling, composting, and disposal program. An effective ISWM system considers how to prevent, recycle, and manage solid waste in ways that most effectively protect human health & the environment. ISWM involves evaluating local needs & conditions, and then selecting & combining the most appropriate waste management activities for those conditions. The major ISWM activities are waste prevention, recycling & composting, and combustion & disposal in properly designed, constructed, and managed landfills. Each of these activities requires careful planning, financing, collection, and transport.

- **Waste Prevention.** Waste prevention—also called "source reduction" —seeks to prevent waste from being generated. Waste prevention strategies include using less packaging, designing products to last longer, and reusing products and materials. Waste prevention helps reduce handling, treatment, & disposal costs and ultimately reduces the generation of methane.
- **Waste Recycling and Composting.** Recycling is a process that involves collecting, reprocessing, and/or recovering certain waste materials (*e.g.*, glass, metal, plastics, paper) to make new materials or products. Some recycled organic materials are rich in nutrients and can be used to improve soils. The conversion of waste materials into soil additives is called composting. Recycling and composting generate many environmental & economic benefits. For example, they create jobs & income, supply

valuable raw materials to industry, produce soil-enhancing compost, and reduce greenhouse gas emissions and the number of landfills & combustion facilities.

- **Waste Disposal (landfilling and combustion).** These activities are used to manage waste that cannot be prevented or recycled. One way to dispose of waste is to place it in properly designed, constructed, and managed landfills, where it is safely contained. Another way to handle this waste is through combustion. Combustion is the controlled burning of waste, which helps reduce its volume. If the technology is available, properly designed, constructed, and managed landfills can be used to generate energy by recovering methane. Similarly, combustion facilities produce steam and water as a byproduct that can be used to generate energy.

Need for ISWM

- Cities are facing an increasing growth in population, and shares in GDP growth, resulting in – among other things – increasing quantities of waste being generated.
- Due to changing lifestyles and consumption patterns, the quantity of waste generated has increased with quality and composition of waste becoming more varied and changing.
- Industrialization and economic growth has produced more amounts of waste, including hazardous and toxic wastes.
- There is a growing realization of the negative impacts that wastes have had on the local environment (air, water, land, human health etc.)
- Complexity, costs and coordination of waste management has necessitated multi-stakeholder involvement in every stage of the waste stream. This calls for an integrated approach to waste management.
- Local Governments are now looking at waste as a *business opportunity*, (a) to extract valuable resources contained within it that can still be used and (b) to safely process and dispose wastes with a minimum impact on the environment.

An integrated approach to solid waste management can deliver both environmental and economic sustainability. An integrated system would include an optimised waste collection system and efficient sorting followed by options such as material recycling, biological treatment, thermal treatment and landfill.

Developing a Plan for Integrated Solid Waste Management

Planning is the first step in designing or improving a waste management system. Waste management planners should, take into consideration institutional, social, financial, economic, technical, and environmental factors which may vary from place to place.

Based on these factors, each community has the challenge of selecting the combination of waste management activities that best suits its needs.

Elements of ISWM Plan

(i) Baseline data on waste characterization and quantification with future trends and baseline data on prevailing waste management systems and gaps there in.

(ii) A list of targets to be achieved through the ISWM System.

(iii) A Plan with details of the Management System covering policies, technologies and voluntary measures.

(iv) Implementation Aspects such as time schedules, costs, institutional requirements etc.

(v) Monitoring and feedback mechanism.

An ISWM Plan is a package consisting of a Management System including:

- Policies (regulatory, fiscal, etc.).
- Technologies (basic equipment and operational aspects) & Voluntary measures (awareness raising, self regulations)
- A management System covers all aspects of waste management; from waste generation through collection, transfer, transportation, sorting, treatment and disposal.
- Data and information on waste characterization and quantification (including future trends),
- and assessment of current solid waste management system for operational stages provide the basis for developing a concrete and locality-specific management system.

Because integrated solid waste management involves both short- and long-term choices, it is critical to set achievable goals. While developing your ISWM plan, one should identify goals or objectives (*e.g.*, protect human health, protect water supplies, eliminate open dumping, increase recycling or composting). The ISWM plan helps guide through the implementation process.

Important Questions to Consider and Steps to Take When Developing an Integrated Solid Waste Management (I SWM) Plan is tabulated below.

Factors	**Questions to Consider**	**Steps to Take**
Institutional (laws and processes)	Are existing laws and policies adequate to allow the government to properly implement ISWM?	• Establish a national policy and pass laws on solid waste management standards and practices. • Identify the roles and responsibilities of each level of government • Ensure the local government has the authority and resources to implement an ISWM plan.
Social (local customs and religious practices, public education)	What types of waste does your community generate and how it is managed?	• Encourage citizen participation in all phases of waste management planning to help gain community awareness, input, and acceptance.

Financial (funding)	Where will you go to get funds for creating a solid waste management system?	• Identify sources that can provide funding for solid waste management, including general revenues or user fees, the private sector, and government or international agency grants and loans.
Economic (costs and job creation)	What will it cost to implement various waste management activities?	• Calculate the initial capital investment requirements and long-term operating and maintenance costs associated with the various waste management activities. • Evaluate the public's ability and willingness to pay. • Evaluate activities based on effectiveness in handling waste and potential for job creation.
Technical (location and equipment)	Where will you build collection and disposal facilities and what equipment will you need?	• Include geological factors, transport distances, and projected waste generation in siting and design considerations. • Determine what equipment and training will be necessary to perform the waste management tasks. (See *How To Establish Recycling and Composting Programs, What Are the Components of Waste Collection and Transport?*, and *What Are the Options for Waste Disposal?*
Environmental (natural resources and human health)	Will solid waste management activities (*e.g.*, landfilling or combustion) affect the environment?	• Establish procedures to verify the protection of groundwater and drinking water. • Monitor compliance with the national standards to ensure human health risks are minimized.

Implementing an Integrated Solid Waste Management Plan

Implementing an ISWM plan is an ongoing process, so expect to make adjustments to the plan along the way. Always evaluate system inefficiencies and make adjustments to improve or expand solid waste management services . Equally important, it emphasizes the need to provide public education and keep the community involved in every step of the process.Be flexible and creative when implementing your plan keeping in mind the ultimate goal of ISWM: to improve human health and protect the environment.

The steps involved in implementing ISWM are planning, price, publicity, political support and perseverance. A well-devised and comprehensive plan is necessary to implement a successful programme. Planning should involve political bodies, waste generators, haulers, construction contractors, etc., as each group has the potential to strengthen or derail a project. Sound economic analysis that considers the resources of the community and adverse impacts on the environment is necessary to adopt alternative strategies for managing waste. A plan for informing the public about the programme's progress should be developed and implemented as the programme succeeds. The support for a programme can erode quickly, unless attention is paid to keeping the programme on the public agenda and maintaining strong and positive public support. Political support is often crucial to obtaining finance and ensuring that the programme gets the resources needed to construct facilities and operate them efficiently. A community waste management programme must be prepared for the long term. The ultimate key to success is the political and public will to persevere until the programme is in place.

Elements of ISWM is shown below in figure.

Comprehensive ISWM planning process is shown below.

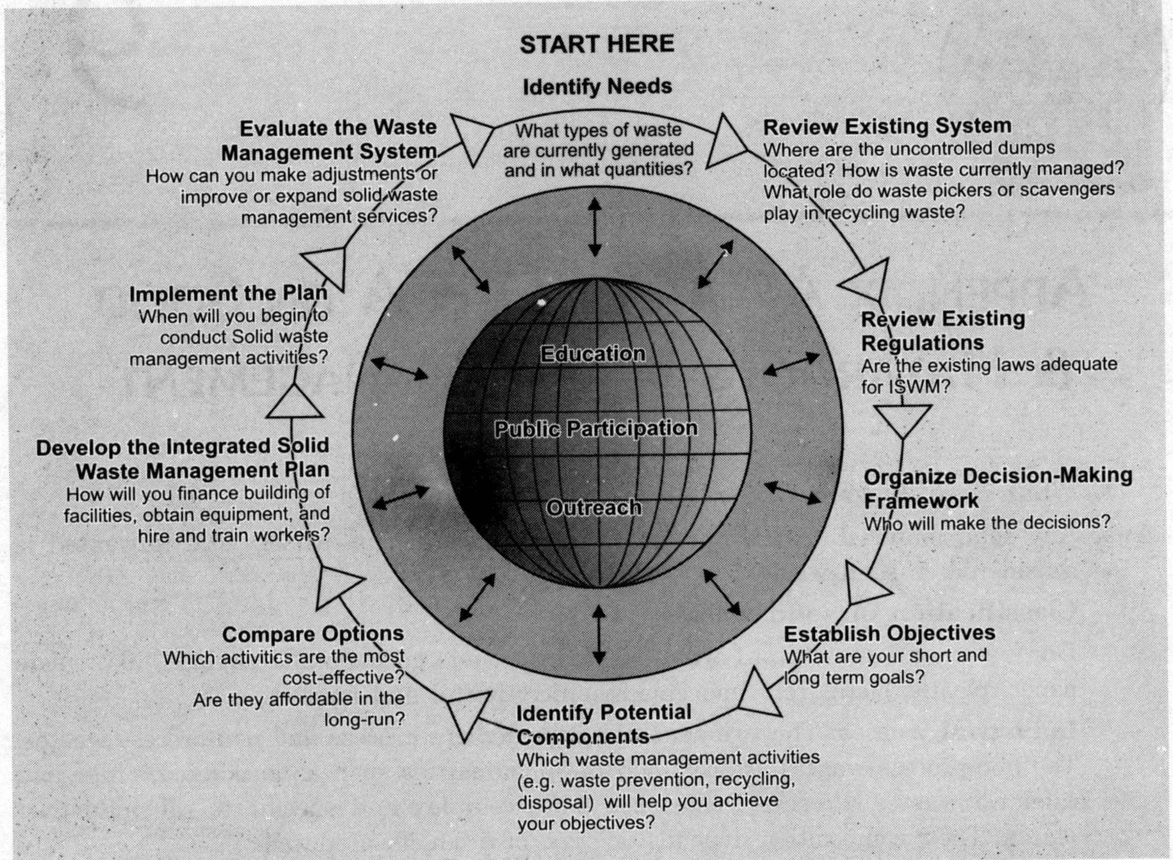

Benefits of ISWM

- Cleaner and safe neighborhoods
- Higher resource use efficiency
- Resource augmentation
- Savings in waste management costs due to reduced levels of final waste for disposal
- Better business opportunities and economic growth
- Local ownership & responsibilities/participation
- Turning vicious circle into virtuous circle

CHAPTER

9

APPENDIX A: SHORT Q & A ON SOLID & HAZARDOUS WASTE MANAGEMENT

1. What is solid waste? How do we classify it?

Ans. Any solid material that is thrown away or discarded as useless and unwanted is considered as solid waste.

Classification of solid wastes

Domestic and municipal wastes: These include garbage and rubbish, like waste paper, plastic, cloth from households, office, hostel and market.

Industrial wastes: The two general categories are process and non-process wastes. The non-process wastes are common to all industries such as packaging, office and cafeteria wastes. Process wastes are more complex and specific to the industrial plants. Their composition depends on type of products produced.

Agricultural wastes: These include cereal and millet straw, paddy husk, sugarcane trash and other crop residues.

Special wastes: The waste materials which endanger public health & welfare and seriously affect environment are:

(a) Radioactive wastes from atomic power stations, labs and hospitals

(b) Toxic wastes such as pesticides, heavy metals, pharmaceuticals

(c) Biomedical waste products such as antibiotics, enzymes, pathogens,hospital waste etc.

(d) E-waste products such as electronics components, computer parts etc.

2. Describe the effects of solid waste, if not managed wisely/properly.

Ans. Effects of improper management of solid waste is listed below:

- Affects our health and our socio-economic conditions .
- Affects our coastal and marine environment.
- Affects our climate.

- Green House Gases (GHGs) accumulate in Earth's atmosphere as a result of human activities, causing global mean surface air temperature and subsurface ocean temperature to rise.
- Rising global temperatures are expected to raise sea levels and change precipitation and other local climate conditions.
- Changing regional climates could alter forests, crop yields, and water supplies.
- This could also affect human health, animals, and many types of ecosystems.
- Deserts might expand into existing range lands, and features of some national parks might be permanently altered.
  - ❑ Some countries are expected to become warmer, although sulfates might limit warming in some areas.
  - ❑ Scientists are unable to determine which parts of those countries will become wetter or drier, but there is likely to be an overall trend toward increased precipitation and evaporation, more intense rainstorms, and drier soils.
  - ❑ Whether rainfall increases or decreases cannot be reliably projected for specific areas.
- Activities that have altered the chemical composition of the atmosphere:
  - ❑ Buildup of GHGs primarily carbon dioxide (CO_2) methane (CH_4), and nitrous oxide (N_2O).
  - ❑ CO_2 is released to the atmosphere by the burning of fossil fuels, wood & wood products, and solid waste.
  - ❑ CH_4 is emitted from the decomposition of organic wastes in landfills, the raising of livestock, and the production & transport of coal, natural gas, & oil.
  - ❑ NO_2 is emitted during agricultural and industrial activities, as well as during combustion of solid waste & fossil fuels.

3. What are various types of litter we generate and time it takes to degenerate?

Ans. The type of litter we generate and the approximate time it takes to degenerate is given below:

- Organic waste such as vegetable and fruit peels, leftover foodstuff, etc.: A week or two
- Paper: 10-30 days
- Cotton cloth: 2-5 months
- Wood: 10-15 years
- Woolen items: 1 year
- Tin, aluminium, and other metal items such as cans: 100-500 years
- Plastic bags: One million years?
- Glass bottles: Undetermined

4. Describe the Health Effects of Open Dumping of solid Waste .

Ans. Health effects of open dumping of waste are listed below:

- The health risks associated with illegal dumping are significant for rag pickers and residents living nearby.
- Areas used for illegal dumping may be easily accessible to people, especially children, who are vulnerable to the physical (protruding nails or sharp edges) and chemical (harmful fluids or dust) hazards posed by wastes.
- Rodents, insects, and other vermin attracted to open dumpsites may also pose health risks.
- Dumpsites with scrap tires provide an ideal breeding ground for mosquitoes, which can multiply 100 times fasterthan normal in the warm stagnant water standing in scrap tire casings.
- Severe illnesses, including encephalitis and dengue fever, have been attributed to disease-carrying mosquitoes originating from scrap tire piles.
- In addition, countless neighborhoods have evacuated and property damage has been significant because ofdumpsites that caught fire, either by spontaneous combustion or, more commonly, by arson. Illegal dumping can impact proper drainage of runoff, making areas more susceptible to flooding when wastes block ravines, creeks, culverts, and drainage basins.
- In rural areas, open burning at dumpsites containing chemicals may contaminate wells and surface water used as sources of drinking water.
- Dioxin emissions from open burning of garbage in one day by four families could equal the emissions from amunicipal solid waste incinerator burning 200 tons per day. Dioxins are known to suppress the immune system, disrupt hormonal balances and cause cancer.
- Other emissions resulting from open burning and their associated health risks include:
  - ❑ Benzene (leukemia)
  - ❑ Toluene diisocyanate (asthma)
  - ❑ Nitrogen dioxides (lung damage)
  - ❑ Nitrile compounds (metabolic poisons and carcinogens)
  - ❑ Burning garbage can also produce emissions of formaldehyde, hydrochloric & sulphuric acid, hydrogen cyanide, polycyclic aromatic hydrocarbons (PAHs), cadmium, lead, mercury and chromium.

5. Describe in detail various types of solid wastes.

Ans. Solid waste includes domestic wastes, municipal wastes, commercial wastes, garbage, rubbish, ashes, construction & demolition wastes, industrial wastes, hazardous wastes, hospital wastes, plastics, e-waste and sewage.

Domestic wastes: These wastes are generated by household activities such as cooking, cleaning, repairs, redecoration, empty containers, packaging, clothing, old books, newspapers, old furnishings, etc.

Commercial wastes: Solid wastes generated in offices, wholesale stores, restaurants, hotels, markets, warehouses and other commercial establishments. These are further classified into garbage and rubbish.

Institutional wastes: Wastes generated from institutions such as schools, colleges, hospitals, research institutions. The waste includes garbage, rubbish and hazardous wastes.

Municipal wastes: Wastes generated due to municipal activities and services such as street waste, deadanimals, market waste and abandoned vehicles. Generally, the term is used in a wider sense to incorporate domestic wastes, institutional wastes and commercial wastes.

Garbage: It includes animal and vegetable wastes due to various activities like storage, preparation and sale, cooking and serving. These are biodegradable.

Ashes: Residues from the burning of wood, charcoal and coke for cooking and heating in houses, institutions and small industries. Ashes consist of a fine powdery residue, cinders and clinker often mixed with small pieces of metal and glass.

Rubbish: Apart from garbage and ashes, other solid wastes produced in households, commercial establishments, and institutions are termed as rubbish.

Bulky wastes: Bulky wastes are large household appliances such as cookers, refrigerators and washing machines as well as furniture, crates, vehicle parts, tyres, wood, trees and branches. The bulky metallic wastes are sold as scrap metal but some portion is disposed as sanitary landfills.

Street wastes: Street wastes include paper, cardboard, plastic, dirt, dust, leaves and other vegetable matter collected from streets, walkways, alleys, parks and vacant plots.

Dead animals: It includes animals that die naturally or accidentally killed. It does not include carcass and animal parts from slaughterhouses as these are considered as industrial wastes.

Construction & demolition wastes: Major components of the construction materials are cement, bricks, cement plaster, steel, rubble, stone, timber, plastic and iron pipes. About 50% of the wastes are not currently recycled in India.

Industrial wastes: These are discarded solid material of manufacturing processes & industrial operations and are considered separately from municipal wastes. However, solid wastes from small industries/plants and ash from power plants are frequently disposed of at municipal landfills. Major producers of industrial wastes are the thermal power plants producing coal ash, integrated iron & steel plants producing blast furnace slag & steel melting slag, non-ferrous industries like aluminium, zinc & copper producing red mud and tailings, sugar industries generating press mud, pulp & paper industries producing lime and fertilizer & allied industries producing gypsum. Management of industrial solid waste is not the responsibility of local bodies. Industries generating solid wastes have to manage by themselves and are required to obtain prior permission from the respective state pollution control boards under relevant rules.

Slaughterhouse Waste: India has the world's largest population of livestock. Slaughter houses slaughter cattle, buffaloes, sheep, goat, pigs and poultry for domestic consumption as well as for export purposes. The waste generated here are liquid and solid in nature. Slaughtering of animals generates waste consisting of non-edible organs, stomach contents, dung, bones and sludge from waste water treatment.

Hospital waste: Hospital waste is generated during the diagnosis, treatment or immunization of human beings or animals. It may include wastes like sharps, soiled waste, disposables, anatomical waste, cultures, discarded medicines, chemical wastes, etc. These are in the form of disposable syringes, swabs, bandages, body fluids, human excreta, etc. This waste is highly infectious and can be a serious threat to human health if not managed in a scientific manner.

Biomedical waste: Biomedical waste means "any solid and/or liquid waste including its container and any intermediate product, which is generated during the diagnosis, treatment or immunisation of human beings or animals or in research pertaining thereto or in the production or testing thereof."

Biomedical waste consists of human anatomical waste like tissues, organs, body parts, animal wastes generated during research, from veterinary hospitals, microbiology and biotechnology wastes, waste sharps, hypodermic needles, syringes, scalpels, broken glass, discarded medicines and cytotoxic drugs, soiled waste, such as dressing, bandages, plaster casts, material contaminated with blood, tubes, catheters, liquid waste from any of the infected areas, incineration ash and other chemical wastes.

PLASTICS: Plastic, with its exclusive qualities of being light yet strong and economical, has invaded every aspect of our day-to-day life. It has many advantages: it is durable, light, easy to mould and can be adapted to different user requirements. Plastic is now a serious worldwide environmental and health concern, essentially due to its non-biodegradable nature. More than 50% of the plastic waste generated in the country is recycled and used in the manufacture of various plastic products.

Dioxin is a highly carcinogenic and toxic by-product of the manufacturing process of plastics. Burning of plastics, especially PVC, releases this dioxin and also furan into the atmosphere.

Plastics are so versatile in use that their impact on the environment is extremely wide ranging. Careless disposal of plastic bags chokes drains, blocks the porosity of the soil and causes problems for groundwater recharge. Plastic disturbs the soil microbial activity. Plastic bags can also contaminate foodstuffs due to leaching of toxic dyes and transfer of pathogens. In fact, a major portion of the plastic bags *i.e.* approximately 60-80% of the plastic waste generated in India is collected and segregated for recycling. 20-40% remains strewn on the ground, littered around in open drains.

Designing eco-friendly, biodegradable plastics are the need of the hour. Though partially biodegradable plastics have been developed and used, completely biodegradable plastics based on renewable starch rather than petrochemicals have only recently been developed and are in the early stages of commercialization. The incentives provided for this is not adequate. For example it is both easy and economical to deliver milk in plastic bags rather than in bottles. Plastics used in various applications are listed below.

Household	**Health and Medicare**
• Carry bags • Pet bottles • Containers • Trash bags	• Disposable syringes • Glucose bottles • Blood and uro bags • Intravenous tubes • Catheters • Surgical gloves
Hotel and Catering • Packaging items • Mineral water bottles • Plastic plates, cups, spoons	**Air/Rail Travel** • Mineral water bottles • Plastic plates, cups, spoons • Plastic bags

6. What are the sources & effects of solid wastes?

Ans. Solid waste, arise from human activities and are discarded as useless or unwanted one.

The types are: Urban solid waste; Industrial solid waste

Urban solid wastes include Residential area wastes, commercial area wastes, open area waste, constructional waste, biomedical waste, e-wastes etc.

Industrial solid wastes include wastes from chemical industry, paint industry, petroleum refinery industry, paper industry, metal industry etc.

The effects of solid wastes include:

- Spreading of fungal diseases.
- Bad odours.
- Burning of waste produce chemicals which are harmful to human life.
- Contaminates water.
- Affects the characteristics of soil.

7. Give examples of various biodegradable & non-biodegradable solid wastes.

Ans. **Biodegradable waste** includes organic waste, *e.g.* kitchen waste, vegetables, fruits, flowers, leaves from the garden, and paper.

Nonbiodegradable waste can be further segregated into:

(a) **Recyclable waste** - plastics, paper, glass, metal, etc.

(b) **Toxic waste** - old medicines, paints, chemicals, bulbs, fertilizer, containers, batteries.

(c) **Soiled waste** - hospital waste such as cloth soiled with blood and other body fluids.

8. Describe Source based classification of solid waste.

Ans. Sources of solid wastes are consistent, dependent on sectors & activities and these include the following:

(i) **Residential wastes:** This refers to wastes from dwellings, apartments, etc., and consists of leftover food, vegetable peels, plastic, clothes, ashes, etc.

(ii) **Commercial wastes:** This refers to wastes consisting of leftover food, glasses, metals, ashes, etc., generated from stores, restaurants, markets, hotels, motels, auto-repair shops, medical facilities, etc.

(iii) **Institutional wastes:** This mainly consists of paper, plastic, glasses, etc., generated from educational, administrative and public buildings such as schools, colleges, offices, prisons, etc.

(iv) **Municipal wastes:** This includes dust, leafy matter, building debris, treatment plant residual sludge, etc., generated from various municipal activities like construction and demolition, street cleaning, landscaping, etc.

(v) **Industrial wastes:** This mainly consists of process wastes, ashes, demolition & construction wastes, hazardous wastes, etc., due to industrial activities.

(vi) **Agricultural wastes:** This mainly consists of spoiled food grains & vegetables, agricultural remains, litter, etc., generated from fields, orchards, vineyards, farms, etc.

(vii) **Open areas wastes:** this includes wastes from areas such as Streets, alleys, parks, vacant lots, playgrounds, beaches, highways, recreational areas, etc.

9. Describe the Type-based classification of solid wastes.

Ans. Classification of wastes based on types, *i.e.*, physical, chemical, and biological characteristics of wastes, is as follows:

(i) **Garbage:** This refers to animal & vegetable wastes resulting from the handling, sale, storage, preparation, cooking and serving of food. Garbage comprising these wastes contains putrescible (rotting) organic matter, which produces an obnoxious odour and attracts rats & other vermin. It, therefore, requires special attention in storage, handling and disposal.

(ii) **Ashes and residues:** These are substances remaining from the burning of wood, coal, charcoal, coke and other combustible materials for cooking & heating in houses, institutions and small industrial establishments. When produced in large quantities, as in power-generation plants & factories, these are classified as industrial wastes. Ashes consist of fine powdery residue, cinders and clinker often mixed with small pieces of metal & glass. Since ashes and residues are almost entirely inorganic, they are valuable in landfills.

(iii) **Combustible and non-combustible wastes:** These consist of wastes generated from households, institutions, commercial activities, etc., excluding food wastes and other highly putrescible material. Typically, while combustible material consists of paper, cardboard, textile, rubber, garden trimmings, etc., non-combustible material consists of such items as glass, crockery, tin and aluminium cans, ferrous and non-ferrous material and dirt.

(iv) **Bulky wastes:** These include large household appliances such as refrigerators, washing machines, furniture, crates, vehicle parts, tyres, wood, trees and branches. Since these household wastes cannot be accommodated in normal storage containers, they require a special collection mechanism.

(v) **Street wastes:** These refer to wastes that are collected from streets, walkways, alleys, parks and vacant plots, and include paper, cardboard, plastics, dirt, leaves and other vegetable matter. Littering in public places is indeed a widespread and acute problem in many countries including India, and a solid waste management system must address this menace appropriately.

(vi) **Biodegradable and non-biodegradable wastes:** Biodegradable wastes mainly refer to substances consisting of organic matter such as leftover food, vegetable & fruit peels, paper, textile, wood, etc., generated from various household and industrial activities. Because of the action of micro-organisms, these wastes are degraded from complex to simpler compounds. Non-biodegradable wastes consist of inorganic & recyclable materials such as plastic, glass, cans, metals, etc.

(vii) **Dead animals:** With regard to municipal wastes, dead animals are those that die naturally or are accidentally killed on the road. This category does not include carcasses and animal parts from slaughterhouses, which are regarded as industrial wastes. Dead animals are divided into two groups - large and small. Among the large animals are horses, cows, goats, sheep, pigs, etc., and among the small ones are dogs, cats, rabbits, rats, etc. The reason for this differentiation is that large animals require special equipment for lifting and handling when they are removed. If not collected promptly, dead animals pose a threat to public health since they attract flies and other vermin as they decay. Their presence in public places is particularly offensive from the aesthetic point of view as well.

(viii) **Abandoned vehicles:** This category includes automobiles, trucks & trailers that are abandoned on streets and other public places. However, abandoned vehicles have significant scrap value for their metal, and their value to collectors is highly variable.

(ix) **Construction and demolition wastes:** These are wastes generated as a result of construction, refurbishment, repair & demolition of houses, commercial buildings and other structures. They consist mainly of earth, stones, concrete, bricks, lumber, roofing & plumbing materials, heating systems & electrical wires and parts of the general municipal waste stream.

(x) **Farm wastes:** These wastes result from diverse agricultural activities such as planting, harvesting, production of milk, rearing of animals for slaughter and the operation of feedlots. In many areas, the disposal of animal waste has become a critical problem, especially from feedlots, poultry farms and dairies.

(xi) **Hazardous wastes:** Hazardous wastes are those defined as wastes of industrial, institutional or consumer origin that are potentially dangerous either immediately or over a period of time to human beings and the environment. This is due to their physical, chemical & biological or radioactive characteristics like ignitability, corrosivity, reactivity and toxicity. In some cases, the active agents may be liquid or gaseous hazardous wastes. These are, nevertheless, classified as solid wastes as they are confined in solid containers. Typical examples of hazardous wastes are empty containers of solvents, paints & pesticides, which are frequently mixed with municipal wastes and become part of the urban waste stream. Certain hazardous wastes may cause explosions in incinerators and fires at landfill sites. Others such as pathological wastes from hospitals and radioactive wastes also require special handling. Effective management practices should ensure that hazardous wastes are stored, collected, transported and disposed of separately, preferably after suitable treatment to render them harmless.

(xii) **Sewage wastes:** The solid by-products of sewage treatment are classified as sewage wastes. They are mostly organic and derived from the treatment of organic sludge separated from both raw & treated sewages. The inorganic fraction of raw sewage such as grit & eggshells is separated at the preliminary stage of treatment, as it may entrain putrescible organic matter with pathogens and must be buried without delay. The bulk of treated, dewatered sludge is useful as a soil conditioner but is invariably uneconomical. Solid sludge, hence , enters the stream of municipal wastes, unless special arrangements are made for its disposal.

10. Describe the essential features of a Solid Waste Management (SWM) system.

Ans. A SWM system refers to a combination of various functional elements associated with the management of solid wastes. The system, when put in place, facilitates the collection and disposal of solid wastes in the community at minimal costs, while preserving public health and ensuring little or minimal adverse impact on the environment.

The functional elements that constitute the solid waste management system are:

(i) **Waste generation:** Wastes are generated at the start of any process, and thereafter, at every stage as raw materials are converted into goods for consumption. The source of waste generation, as we touched upon earlier in Section 1.1, determines quantity, composition and waste characteristics (see Unit 2 for details). For example, wastes are generated from households, commercial areas, industries, institutions, street cleaning and other municipal services. The most important aspect of this part of the SWM system is the identification of waste.

(ii) **Waste storage:** Storage is a key functional element because collection of wastes never takes place at the source or at the time of their generation. The heterogeneous wastes generated in residential areas must be removed within 8 days due to shortage of storage space and presence of biodegradable material. Onsite storage is of primary importance due to aesthetic consideration, public health and economics involved. Some of the options for storage are plastic containers, conventional dustbins (of households), used oil drums, large storage bins (for institutions and commercial areas or servicing depots), etc. Obviously, these vary greatly in size, form and material. We shall discuss waste storage in detail in Unit 3.

(iii) **Waste collection:** This includes gathering of wastes and hauling them to the location, where the collection vehicle is emptied, which may be a transfer station (*i.e.*, intermediate station where wastes from smaller vehicles are transferred to larger ones and also segregated), a processing plant or a disposal site. Collection depends on the number of containers, frequency of collection, types of collection services and routes. Typically, collection is provided under various management arrangements, ranging from municipal services to franchised services, and under various forms of contracts.

Note that the solution to the problem of hauling is complicated. For instance, vehicles used for long distance hauling may not be suitable or particularly economic for house-to-house collection. Every SWM system, therefore, requires an individual solution to its waste collection problem .

(iv) **Transfer and transport:** This functional element involves: the transfer of wastes from smaller collection vehicles, where necessary to overcome the problem of narrow access lanes, to larger ones at transfer stations; the subsequent transport of the wastes, usually over long distances, to disposal sites.

The factors that contribute to the designing of a transfer station include the type of transfer operation, capacity, equipment, accessories and environmental requirements.

(v) **Processing:** Processing is required to alter the physical and chemical characteristics of wastes for energy and resource recovery and recycling. The important processing techniques include compaction, thermal volume reduction, manual separation of waste components, incineration and composting.

(vi) **Recovery and recycling:** This includes various techniques, equipment and facilities used to improve both the efficiency of disposal system and recovery of usable material and energy. Recovery involves the separation of valuable resources from the mixed solid wastes, delivered at transfer stations or processing plants. It also involves size reduction and density separation by air classifier, magnetic device for iron and screens for glass. The selection of any recovery process is a function of economics, *i.e.*, costs of separation versus the recovered-material products. Certain recovered materials like glass, plastics, paper, etc., can be recycled as they have economic value.

(vii) **Waste disposal:** Disposal is the ultimate fate of all solid wastes, be they residential wastes, semi-solid wastes from municipal and industrial treatment plants, incinerator residues, composts or other substances that have no further use to the society. Thus, land use planning becomes a primary determinant in the selection, design and operation of landfill operations. A modern sanitary landfill is a method of disposing solid waste without creating a nuisance and hazard to public health. Generally, engineering principles are followed to confine the wastes to the smallest possible area, reduce them to the lowest particle volume by compaction at the site and cover them after each day's operation to reduce exposure to vermin. One of the most important functional elements of SWM, therefore, relates to the final use of the reclaimed land.

A typical SWM system with its functional elements and linkages is shown below in figure.

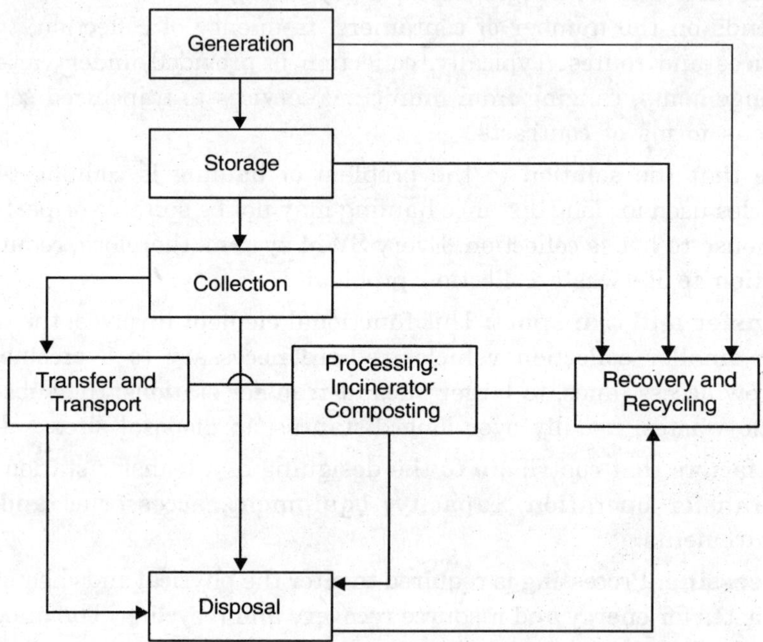

11. Describe the factors affecting Solid Waste Management (SWM) system.

Ans. The factors which influence the decision-making process in the implementation of a SWM system and need to be considered in developing a SWM system are listed below:

(i) **Quantities & characteristics of wastes:** The quantities of wastes generated generally depend on the income level of a family, as higher income category tends to generate larger quantity of wastes, compared to low-income category. One of the measures of waste composition (and characteristics) is density, which ranges from 150 to 600 kg/m^3 . Proportion of paper and packaging materials in the waste largely account for the differences. When this proportion is high, the density is low and vice versa. The wastes of high density reflect a relatively high proportion of organic matter & moisture and lower levels of recycling.

(ii) **Climate & seasonal variations:** There are regions where temperatures are very low for much of the year. In cold climates, drifting snow and frozen ground interfere with landfill operations, and therefore, trenches must be dug in summer and cover material stockpiled for winter use. Tropical climates, on the other hand, are subject to sharp seasonal variations from wet to dry season, which cause significant changes in the moisture content of solid waste, varying from less than 50% in dry season to greater than 65% in wet months. Collection and disposal of wastes in the wet months are often problematic. High temperatures and humidity cause solid wastes to decompose far more rapidly than they do in colder climates. The frequency of waste collection in high temperature and humid climates should, therefore, be higher than that in cold climates. In sub-tropical or desert climate, there is no significant variation in moisture content of wastes (due to low rainfall) and low production of leachate from sanitary landfill. High winds and wind blown sand & dust, however, cause special problems at landfill sites. While temperature inversions can cause airborne pollutants to be trapped near ground level, landfill sites can affect ground water by altering the thermal properties of the soil.

(iii) **Physical characteristics of an urban area:** In urban areas (*i.e.*, towns and cities), where the layout of streets and houses is such that access by vehicles is possible and door-to-door collection of solid wastes is the accepted norm either by large compaction vehicle or smaller vehicle. The picture is, however, quite different in the inner and older city areas where narrow lanes make service by vehicles difficult. Added to this is the problem of urban sprawl in the outskirts where population is growing at an alarming rate. Access ways are narrow, unpaved and tortuous, and therefore, not accessible to collection vehicles. Problems of solid waste storage and collection are most acute in such areas.

(iv) **Financial constraints:** Solid waste management accounts for sizeable proportions of the budgets of municipal corporations. This is allocated for capital resources, which go towards the purchase of equipments, vehicles, and fuel & labour costs. Typically, 10 to 40% of the revenues of municipalities are allocated to solid waste management. In regions where wage rates are low, the aim is to optimise vehicle productivity. The unfavourable financial situation of some countries hinders purchase of equipment & vehicles. This means that the balance between the degree of mechanisation and the size of the labour force becomes a critical issue in arriving at the most cost-effective solution.

(v) **Cultural constraints:** In some regions, traditions preclude the intrusion of waste collection on the precincts of households, and therefore, influence the collection system. In others, where the tradition of caste persists, recruits to the labour force for street cleaning and handling of waste must be drawn from certain sections of the population, while others will not consent to placing storage bins in their immediate vicinity. Social norms of a community more often than not over ride what many may consider rational solutions. Waste management should, therefore, be sensitive to such local patterns of living and consider these factors in planning, design & operation.

(vi) **Management and technical resources:** Solid waste management, to be successful, requires a wide spectrum of workforce in keeping with the demands of the system. The best system for a region is one which makes full use of indigenous crafts and professional skills and/or ensures that training programmes are in place to provide a self-sustaining supply of trained workforce.

12. What is Municipal Solid Waste and its management?

Ans. Municipal Solid Waste (MSW) is the trash or garbage that is discarded day to day in a human settlement. According to MSW Rules 2000 MSW includes commercial and residential wastes generated in a municipal or notified areas in either solid or semi-solid form excluding industrial hazardous wastes but including treated bio-medical wastes. Waste generation encompasses activities in which materials are identified as no longer being of value (being in the present form) and are either thrown away or gathered together for disposal. Municipal Solid Waste consists of the following kinds of waste:

Horticultural Waste, Construction & Demolition Waste, Road Sweeping Waste, General House Hold Waste (including Kitchen Waste), Drain Silt/Waste, Market & Commercial Waste, Institutional Waste, Slaughter House Waste & Dead Animals Sludge, Treated Biomedical Waste etc.

Municipal Solid Waste Management (MSWM) refers to a systematic process that comprises of waste segregation & storage at source, primary collection, secondary storage, transportation, secondary segregation, resource recovery, processing, treatment, and final disposal of solid waste.

13. What are the other kinds of waste found in urban settlements?

Ans. These include:

- Industrial or Hazardous Waste
- Bio-Medical or Hospital Waste
- E-Waste.

The Industrial hazardous waste is managed through Hazardous Waste (Management and Handling) Fourth Amendments Rules 2010. Hazardous waste is identified with properties of ignitability, corrosivity, reactivity and toxicity. Hence urban local bodies must ensure that industrial waste does not get mixed with the municipal solid waste stream, failing which will result in economic losses (as hazardous waste treatment costs much more higher than the municipal solid waste) and health & safety hazards (Contaminants like heavy metals, chromium, mercury, etc. when found in the municipal waste stream will contaminate the compost produced by the city. When farmers buy the compost it will indirectly affect the food chain.) while treating such wastes.

According to the Hazardous Waste Management Rules 2010, the onus of managing and treating hazardous waste lie with the waste generator, and the urban local body has to ensure that such waste does not contaminate municipal waste stream in their area of authority.

14. What is the Significance of Municipal Solid Waste Management?

Ans. Efficient municipal solid waste management benefits in maintaining hygienic conditions leading to lesser health issues, better living environment, improved economic prosperity in the area, aesthetically cleaner surroundings with cleaner drains for storm water flow, cleaner water sources and safer neighbourhoods. Some of the key benefits of solid waste management have been discussed below.

- **Environment, Health and Safety Benefits**

  Effective solid waste management helps preserve environment in the project area;

  - ❑ As it prevents waste to contamination of water (in drains) and soil in particular;
  - ❑ Reduces waste sent to the landfill, which may have negative impacts on ground water and air quality;
  - ❑ Reduce emissions from energy consumption—as waste when recycled requires less energy than making goods from virgin materials thereby reducing the energy demand and pressure on non renewable sources (oil, fossil fuels);
  - ❑ Contributes to Climate Change by reducing methane emissions from landfills. Waste prevention and recycling (including composting) divert organic wastes from landfills, reducing the methane released when these materials decompose. Thereby reducing the emission of greenhouse gases and climate change;
  - ❑ Improved waste management reduce chances of spread of diseases; and
  - ❑ Efficiently designed waste management reduces multiple handling of waste avoiding potentially injurious or dangerous practices.

- **Economic Benefits**

  - ❑ Reduction in quantum of waste by diverting it to recycling and other processing unit reduces the landfill costs;
  - ❑ Better managed waste management services indicate better value at same cost;
  - ❑ An effective waste management implies reducé, reuse and recycle waste matter leading to introduction of more and more of waste matter into the value chain leading to economic benefits; and
  - ❑ Waste management being a labour intensive activity, it helps in employment generation. Introduction of rag pickers into formalized waste collection and segregation process is a win win scenario for implementers.

15. Describe various physical characteristics of solid wastes.

Ans. Information on the physical characteristics of solid wastes are important for the selection & operation of equipment and for the analysis & design of disposal facilities.Important physical characteristics of solid wastes are described below:

(i) **Density:** Density of waste, *i.e.*, its mass per unit volume (kg/m^3), is a critical factor in the design of a SWM system, *e.g.*, the design of sanitary landfills, storage, types of collection & transport vehicles, etc. An efficient operation of a landfill demands compaction of wastes to optimum density. Any normal compaction equipment can achieve reduction in volume of wastes by 75%, which increases an initial density of 100 kg/m^3 to 400 kg/m^3. In other words, a waste collection vehicle can haul four times the weight of waste in its compacted state than when it is uncompacted. A high initial density of waste precludes the achievement of a high compaction ratio and the compaction ratio achieved is no greater than 1.5:1. Significant changes in density occur spontaneously as the waste moves from source to disposal, due to scavenging, handling, wetting & drying by the weather, vibration in the collection vehicle and decomposition. Effect of increasing the moisture content of the waste is detrimental in the sense that dry density decreases at higher moisture levels; soil-cover plays an important role in containing the waste; there is an upper limit to the density, and the conservative estimate of in-place density for waste in a sanitary landfill is about 600 kg/m^3.

(ii) **Moisture content:** Moisture content is defined as the ratio of the weight of water (wet weight - dry weight) to the total weight of the wet waste. Moisture increases the weight of solid wastes, and thereby, the cost of collection & transport. Besides, moisture content affects the economic feasibility of waste treatment by incineration, because wet waste consumes energy for evaporation of water and in raising the temperature of water vapour.Wastes should be insulated from rainfall or other extraneous water. A typical range of moisture content is 20 to 40%, representing the extremes of wastes in an arid climate and in the wet season of a region of high precipitation. However, values greater than 40% are not uncommon.

(iii) **Size:** Measurement of size distribution of particles in waste stream is important because of its significance in the design of mechanical separators and shredders. Generally, the results of size distribution analysis are expressed in the manner used for soil particle analysis. That is to say, they are expressed as a plot of particle size (mm) against percentage, less than a given value.

The physical properties that are essential to analyse wastes disposed at landfills are:

I. **Field capacity:** The field capacity of MSW is the total amount of moisture which can be retained in a waste sample subject to gravitational pull. It is a critical measure because water in excess of field capacity will form leachate, and leachate can be a major problem in landfills. Field capacity varies with the degree of applied pressure and the state of decomposition of the wastes.

II. **Permeability of compacted wastes:** The hydraulic conductivity of compacted wastes is an important physical property because it governs the movement of liquids and gases in a landfill. Permeability depends on the other properties of the solid material include pore size distribution, surface area and porosity.

Porosity: It represents the amount of voids per unit overall volume of material. The porosity of MSW varies typically from 0.40 to 0.67 depending on the compaction and composition of the waste. Porosity of solid waste, $n = e/(1+e)$ Where, e is void ratio of solid waste.

III. **Compressibility of MSW:** Degree of physical changes of the suspended solids or filter cake when subjected to pressure.

16. What are the chemical characteristics of solid wastes & its importance?

Ans. Knowledge of the chemical characteristics is essential for proper understanding of the behaviour of solid waste, as it moves through the waste management system. The products of decomposition and heating values are two examples of chemical characteristics. If solid wastes are to be used as fuel, or are used for any other purpose, we must know their chemical characteristics . Some of the important chemical characteristics include the following:

(i) **Lipids:** This class of compounds includes fats, oils & grease, and the principal sources of lipids are garbage, cooking oils & fats. Lipids have high heating values, about 38,000 kJ/kg, which makes waste with high lipid content suitable for energy recovery. Since lipids become liquid at temperatures slightly above ambient, they add to the liquid content during waste decomposition.Though they are biodegradable, the rate of biodegradation is relatively slow because lipids have a low solubility in water.

(ii) **Carbohydrates:** These are found primarily in food and yard wastes, which encompass sugar and polymer of sugars (*e.g.*, starch, cellulose, etc.) with general formula $(CH_2O)x$. Carbohydrates are readily biodegraded to products such as carbon dioxide, water and methane. Decomposing carbohydrates attract flies & rats, and therefore, should not be left exposed for long duration.

(iii) **Proteins:** These are compounds containing carbon, hydrogen, oxygen & nitrogen, and consist of an organic acid with a substituted amine group (NH2). They are mainly found in food and garden wastes. The partial decomposition of these compounds can result in the production of amines that have unpleasant odours.

(iv) **Natural fibres:** These are found in paper products, food & yard wastes and include the natural compounds, cellulose & lignin, that are resistant to biodegradation. (Note that paper is almost 100% cellulose, cotton over 95% and wood products over 40%.). Because they are a highly combustible solid waste, having a high proportion of paper and wood products, they are suitable for incineration. Calorific values of oven-dried paper products are in the range of 12,000 -18,000 kJ/kg and of wood about 20,000 kJ/kg, *i.e.*, about half that for fuel oil, which is 44,200 kJ/kg.

(v) **Synthetic organic material (Plastics):** Accounting for 1-10%, plastics have become a significant component of solid waste in recent years. They are highly resistant to biodegradation and, therefore, are objectionable and of special concern in SWM. Hence the increasing attention is being paid to the recycling of plastics to reduce the proportion of this waste component at disposal sites. Plastics have a high heating value, about 32,000 kJ/kg, which makes them very suitable for incineration. But, polyvinyl chloride (PVC), when burnt, produces dioxin and acid gas. The latter increases corrosion in the combustion system and is responsible for acid rain.

(vi) **Non-combustibles:** This includes glass, ceramics, metals, dust & ashes, and accounts for 12-25% of dry solids.

(vii) **Heating value:** An evaluation of potential of waste material for use as fuel for incineration requires a determination of its heating value. The heating value is determined experimentally using the Bomb calorimeter test, in which the heat generated, from the combustion of a dry sample is measured. Since the test temperature is below the boiling point of water (100°C), the combustion water remains in the liquid state. However, during combustion, the temperature of the combustion gases reaches above 100°C, and the resultant water is in the vapour form.

While evaluating incineration as a means of disposal or energy recovery, we need to consider the heating values of respective constituents. For example: Organic material yields energy only when dry. The moisture content in the waste reduces the dry organic material per kilogram of waste and requires a significant amount of energy for drying. Ash content of the waste reduces the proportion of dry organic material per kilogram of waste and retains some heat when removed from the furnace.

(viii) **Ultimate analysis:** This refers to an analysis of waste to determine the proportion of carbon, hydrogen, oxygen, nitrogen & sulphur, and the analysis is done to make mass balance calculation for a chemical or thermal process. Besides, it is necessary to determine ash fraction because of its potentially harmful environmental effects, brought about by the presence of toxic metals such as cadmium, chromium, mercury, nickel, lead, tin & zinc in it. Other metals (*e.g.*, iron, magnesium, etc.) may also be present but they are non-toxic. The result of ultimate analysis of a typical municipal solid waste (dry) is given below:

Elements	**Range, weight(%)**
Carbon	25-30
Hydrogen	2.5-6.0
Oxygen	15-30
Nitrogen	0.25-1.2
Sulphur	0.02-0.12
Ash	12-30

(ix) **Proximate analysis:** This is important in evaluating the combustion properties of wastes or refuse derived fuel. The fractions of interest are: moisture content, which adds weight to the waste without increasing its heating value, and the evaporation of water reduces the heat released from the fuel; ash, which adds weight without generating any heat during combustion; volatile matter, *i.e.*, that portion of the waste that is converted to gases before & during combustion; fixed carbon, which represents the carbon remaining on the surface grates as charcoal. A waste or fuel with a high proportion of fixed carbon requires a longer retention time on the furnace grates to achieve complete combustion than a waste or fuel with a low proportion of fixed carbon.

Components	Range	Value, percent Typical
Moisture	15-40	20
Volatile matter	40-60	53
Fixed carbon	5-12	7
Glass, metal, ash	15-30	20

17. What are the public health effect of improper handling & management of solid waste?

Ans. The volume of solid waste is increasing rapidly as a result of increasing population. This increased volume of wastes is posing serious problems due to insufficient workforce and other constraints in disposing of it properly. Public health consequences of improper management and handling of wastes are given below:

(i) **Disease vectors and pathways:** Wastes dumped indiscriminately provide the food & environment for thriving populations of vermin, which are the agents of various diseases. The pathways of pathogen transmission from wastes to humans are mostly indirect through insects - flies, mosquitoes & roaches and animals - rodents & pigs. Diseases become a public health problem when they are present in the human and animal population of surrounding communities, or if a carrier transmits the etiological agent from host to receptor.

(ii) **Flies:** Most common in this category is the housefly, which transmits typhoid, salmonellosis, gastro-enteritis and dysentery. Flies have a flight range of about 10 km, and therefore, they are able to spread their influence over a relatively wide area. The four stages in their life-cycle are egg, larva, pupa and adult. Eggs are deposited in the warm, moist environment of decomposing food wastes. When they hatch, the larvae feed on the organic material, until certain maturity is reached, at which time they migrate from the waste to the soil or other dry loose material before being transformed into pupae. The pupae are inactive until the adult fly emerges. The migration of larvae within 4 to 10 days provides the clue to an effective control measure, necessitating the removal of waste before migration of larvae. Consequently, in warm weather, municipal waste should be collected twice weekly for effective control. In addition, the quality of household and commercial storage containers is very significant. The guiding principle here is to restrict access to flies. Clearly, the use of suitable storage containers and general cleanliness at their location, as well as frequent collection of wastes, greatly reduces the population of flies. Control is also necessary at transfer stations, composting facilities and disposal sites to prevent them from becoming breeding grounds for flies. Covering solid wastes with a layer of earth at landfill sites at the end of every day arrests the problem of fly breeding at the final stage.

(iii) **Mosquitoes:** They transmit diseases such as malaria, filaria and dengue fever. Since they breed in stagnant water, control measures should centre on the elimination of breeding places such as tins, cans, tyres, etc. Proper sanitary practices and general cleanliness in the community help eliminate the mosquito problems caused by the mismanagement of solid waste.

(iv) **Roaches:** These cause infection by physical contact and can transmit typhoid, cholera & amoebiasis. The problems of roaches are associated with the poor storage of solid waste.

(v) **Rodents:** Rodents (rats) proliferate in uncontrolled deposits of solid wastes, which provide a source of food as well as shelter. They are responsible for the spread of diseases such as plague, murine typhus, leptospirosis, histoplasmosis, rat bite fever, dalmonelosis, trichinosis, etc. The fleas, which rats carry, also cause many diseases. This problem is associated not only with open dumping but also poor sanitation.

(vi) **Occupational hazards:** Workers handling wastes are at risk of accidents related to the nature of material and lack of safety precautions. The sharp edges of glass & metal and poorly constructed storage containers may inflict injuries to workers. It is, therefore, necessary for waste handlers to wear gloves, masks and be vaccinated. The infections associated with waste handling, include:

- Skin and blood infections resulting from direct contact with waste and from infected wounds;
- Eye and respiratory infections resulting from exposure to infected dust, especially during landfill operations;
- Diseases that result from the bites of animals feeding on the waste;
- Intestinal infections that are transmitted by flies feeding on the waste;
- Chronic respiratory diseases, including cancers resulting from exposure to dust and hazardous compounds.

In addition, the accidents associated with waste handling include: bone & muscle disorders resulting from the handling of heavy containers and the loading heights of vehicles; infecting wounds resulting from contact with sharp objects; reduced visibility, due to dust along the access routes, creates greater risk of accidents; poisoning & chemical burns resulting from contact with small amounts of hazardous chemical wastes mixed with general wastes such as pesticides, cleaning solutions & solvents in households and commercial establishments; burns & other injuries resulting from occupational accidents at waste disposal sites or from methane gas explosion at landfill sites; serious health hazards, particularly for children, due to careless dumping of lead-acid, nickel-cadmium & mercuric oxide batteries.

(vii) **Animals:** Apart from rodents, some animals (*e.g.*, dogs, cats, pigs, etc.) also act as carriers of disease. For example, pigs are involved in the spread of diseases like trichinosis, cysticerosis and toxoplasmosis, which are transmitted through infected pork, eaten either in raw state or improperly cooked. Solid wastes, when fed to pigs, should be properly treated (cooked at 1000C for at least 50 minutes) .

18. Describe in detail the environmental effects of improper solid waste handling & management.

Ans. Besides causing health disorders, inadequate and improper waste management causes adverse environmental effects such as the following:

(i) **Air pollution:** Burning of solid wastes in open dumps or in improperly designed incinerators emit pollutants (gaseous & particulate matters) to the atmosphere.The environmental consequences of open burning are greater than incinerators, especially with respect to aldehydes and particulates. Emissions from an uncontrolled incinerator system include particulate matter, sulphur oxides, nitrogen oxides, hydrogen chloride, carbon monoxide, lead and mercury. Discharge of arsenic, cadmium & selenium is to be controlled, since they are toxic at relatively low exposure levels. Polychlorinated dibenzofurans (PCDFs), commonly called dioxins and furans, are of concern because of their toxicity, carcinogenicity and possible mutagenicity.

(ii) **Water & land pollution:** Water pollution results from dumping in open areas& storm water drains, and improper design, construction and/or operation of a sanitary landfill. Control of infiltration from rainfall and surface runoff is essential in order to minimise the production of leachate. Pollution of groundwater can occur as a result of:

- the flow of groundwater through deposits of solid waste at landfill sites;
- percolation of rainfall or irrigation waters from solid wastes to the water table;
- diffusion and collection of gases generated by the decomposition of solid wastes.

The interaction between leachate contaminants and the soil depends on the characteristics of the soil. Soil bacteria stabilise biochemical oxygen demand (BOD), *i.e.*, the amount of oxygen required by micro-organisms to degrade organic matter, by anaerobic action, if toxic substances are in low concentration. The carbon dioxide produced keeps the pH level low, causing the water to dissolve minerals in the aquifers. Consequently, the change in groundwater quality may take place depending on the characteristics of the aquifer. Contamination can spread over considerable distances from the landfill, if the aquifers are of sand or gravel. In clayey soils, the rate of movement is greatly reduced. The capacity of clay to exchange ions restricts the movement of metal ions by capturing them in the soil matrix. Changes in its chemical characteristics are due to hardness, iron and manganese compounds.

(iii) **Visual pollution:** The aesthetic sensibility is offended by the unsightliness of piles of wastes on the roadside. The situation is made worse by the presence of scavengers rummaging in the waste. Waste carelessly discarded in public thoroughfares, along roads & highways and around communal bins (*i.e.*, makeshift containers, without lids, used for the storage of residential, commercial & institutional wastes) gives easy access to animals scavenging for food. The solution to this social problem undoubtedly lies in the implementation of public education at all levels - primary, secondary, tertiary and adult, both short- and long-term, and in raising the status of public health workers and managers in solid waste management.

(iv) **Noise pollution:** Undesirable noise is a nuisance associated with operations at landfills, incinerators, transfer stations and sites used for waste recycling. This is due to the movement of vehicles, the operation of large machines and the diverse operations at an incinerator site. The impacts of noise pollution may be reduced by careful siting of SWM operations and by the use of noise barriers.

(v) **Odour pollution:** Obnoxious odours due to the presence of decaying organic matter are characteristic of open dumps. They arise from anaerobic decomposition processes and their major constituents are particularly offensive. Proper landfill covering eliminates this nuisance.

(vi) **Explosion hazards:** Landfill gas, which is released during anaerobic decomposition processes, contains a high proportion of explosive methane (35-70%). It can migrate through the soil over a considerable distance, leaving the buildings in the vicinity of sanitary landfill sites at risk, even after the closure of landfills. Several methods are available for control of landfill gas, such as venting, flaring and the use of impermeable barriers.

19. What are the Occupational hazards associated with waste handling?

Ans. Occupational hazards associated with waste handling are listed below:

Infections.

- Skin and blood infections resulting from direct contact with waste, and from infected wounds.
- Eye and respiratory infections resulting from exposure to infected dust, especially during landfill operations.
- Different diseases that results from the bites of animals feeding on the waste.
- Intestinal infections that are transmitted by flies feeding on the waste.

Chronic diseases.

- Incineration operators are at risk of chronic respiratory diseases, including cancers resulting from exposure to dust and hazardous compounds.

Accidents.

- Bone and muscle disorders resulting from the handling of heavy containers.
- Infecting wounds resulting from contact with sharp objects.
- Poisoning and chemical burns resulting from contact with small amounts of hazardous chemical waste mixed with general waste.
- Burns and other injuries resulting from occupational accidents at waste disposal sites or from methane gas explosion at landfill sites.

20. Describe the health impacts of different types of solid waste.

Ans. With increase in the global population and the rising demand for food and other essentials, there has been a rise in the amount of waste being generated daily by each household. This waste is ultimately thrown into municipal waste collection centres from where it is collected by the area municipalities to be further thrown into the landfills and dumps. However, either due to resource crunch or inefficient infrastructure, not all of this waste gets collected and transported to the final dump sites. If at this stage the management & disposal is improperly done, it can cause serious impacts on health and problems to the surrounding environment.

Waste that is not properly managed, especially excreta and other liquid & solid waste from households and the community, are a serious health hazard and lead to the spread of infectious diseases. Unattended waste lying around attracts flies, rats, and other creatures that in turn spread disease. Normally it is the wet waste that decomposes and releases a bad odour. This leads to unhygienic conditions and thereby to a rise in the health problems. The plague outbreak in Surat is good example.

Plastic waste is another cause for ill health. Thus excessive solid waste that is generated should be controlled by taking certain preventive measures.The group at risk from the unscientific disposal of solid waste include - the population in areas where there is no proper waste disposal method, especially the pre-school children; waste workers; and workers in facilities producing toxic and infectious material. Other high-risk group includes population living close to a waste dump and those, whose water supply has become contaminated either due to waste dumping or leakage from landfill sites. Uncollected solid waste also increases risk of injury, and infection.

In particular, *organic domestic* waste poses a serious threat, since they ferment, creating conditions favourable to the survival and growth of microbial pathogens. Direct handling of solid waste can result in various types of infectious and chronic diseases with the waste workers and the rag pickers being the most vulnerable.

Exposure to hazardous waste can affect human health, children being more vulnerable to these pollutants. In fact, direct exposure can lead to diseases through chemical exposure as the release of chemical waste into the environment leads to chemical poisoning.

Waste from agriculture and industries can also cause serious health risks. Other than this, co-disposal of industrial hazardous waste with municipal waste can expose people to chemical and radioactive hazards.

Uncollected solid waste can also obstruct storm water runoff, resulting in the forming of stagnant water bodies that become the breeding ground of disease. Waste dumped near a water source also causes contamination of the water body or the ground water source. Direct dumping of untreated waste in rivers, seas, and lakes results in the accumulation of toxic substances in the food chain, through the plants and animals that feed on it directly or indirectly.

Disposal of hospital and other medical waste requires special attention since this can create major health hazards. This waste generated from the hospitals, health care centres, medical laboratories, and research centres such as discarded syringe needles, bandages, swabs, plasters, and other types of infectious waste are often disposed with the regular non-infectious waste.

Waste treatment & disposal sites can create health hazards for the neighbourhood. Improperly operated incineration plants cause air pollution and improperly managed & designed landfills attract all types of insects and rodents that spread disease. Ideally these sites should be located at a safe distance from all human settlement. Landfill sites should be well lined and walled to ensure that there is no leakage into the nearby ground water sources.

Recycling too carries health risks if proper precautions are not taken. Workers working with waste containing chemical and metals may experience toxic exposure.

Disposal of health-care wastes require special attention since it can create major health hazards, such as Hepatitis B and C, through wounds caused by discarded syringes. Rag pickers and others who are involved in scavenging in the waste dumps for items that can be recycled, may sustain injuries and come into direct contact with these infectious items.

21. How can we Produce Less Waste by Practicing the 3 R's *i.e.*, Reduce, Reuse, and Recycle?

Ans. **Reduce** the amount and toxicity of trash we discard. Source reduction can be a successful method of reducing waste generation. Source reduction has many environmental benefits. It prevents emissions of many greenhouse gases, reduces pollutants, saves energy, conserves resources, and reduces the need for new landfills & combustors.

Reuse containers and products; repair what is broken or give it to someone who can repair it. Reusing items by repairing them, donating them to charity & community groups, or selling them also reduces waste. Use a product more than once, either for the same purpose or for a different purpose.

Recycle as much as possible, which includes buying products with recycled content. Recycling involves the collection of used and discarded materials, processing these materials and making them into new products. Studies have revealed that only 10 to 15% of the waste is recycled. It is being used for composting, making pellets to be used in gasifiers, etc. Plastics are sold to the factories that reuse them.

22. What are the Environmental Impact of Solid Waste Disposal on Land?

Ans. When solid waste is disposed off on land in open dumps or in improperly designed landfills (*e.g.* in low lying areas), it causes the following impact on the environment;

(a) Groundwater contamination by the leachate generated by the waste dump.

(b) Surface water contamination by the run-off from the waste dump.

(c) Bad odour, pests, rodents and wind-blown litter in and around the waste dump.

(d) Generation of inflammable gas (*e.g.* methane) within the waste dump.

(e) Bird menace above the waste dump which affects flight of aircraft.

(f) Fires within the waste dump.

(g) Erosion and stability problems relating to slopes of the waste dump.

(h) Epidemics through stray animals.

(i) Acidity to surrounding soil.

(j) Release of green house gas.

23. What are the Most Common Recycled & reuse Materials?

Ans. Recyclable materials are as follows:

Paper: Newspaper is almost always recovered in community recycling programs.

Plastics: Most communities recycle plastic items such as detergent bottles, beverage containers (*e.g.*, soda, milk, and juice), and containers for various household products, from shampoo, lotion, & mouth wash containers to plastic peanut butter containers.

Aluminum: Almost all recycling programs include aluminum beverage can aluminum cans are made into new cans.

Steel: Many steel products manufactured contain a high percentage of recycled steel. Some are even made from 100 percent recycled steel.

Glass: Glass food containers, such as jars and bottles for pickles, juice, jam, or wine.

Reuse items: Reusing items by repairing them, donating them to charity & community groups, or selling them also reduces waste. Use a product more than once, either for the same purpose or for a different purpose. Ways to Reuse include:

- Refilling bottles &Reusing boxes.
- Turning empty jars into containers for leftover food.
- Purchasing refillable pens and pencils.

24. What are the benefits of recycling of materials?

Ans. There are several key benefits to recycling such as:

- Reduces the need for landfilling and incineration.
- Saves energy and prevents pollution caused by the extraction& processing of raw materials and the manufacture of products using raw materials.
- Decreases emissions of greenhouse gases that contribute to global climate change.
- Conserves natural resources such as timber, water, and minerals.
- Helps sustain the environment for future generations.
- **Reduces emissions from incinerators.** Recycling & waste prevention divert materials from incinerators and thus reduce greenhouse gas emissions from waste combustion.
- **Reduces methane emissions from landfills.** Waste prevention & recycling (including composting) divert organic wastes from landfills, reducing the methane that would be released if these materials decomposed in a landfill.

25. List out Some items that can be recycled or reused.

Ans. Recyclable items are listed below:

Paper

- Old copies
- Old books
- Paper bags
- Newspapers
- Old greeting cards
- Cardboard box

Plastic

- Containers
- Bags
- Sheets

Glass and ceramics

- Bottles
- Plates
- Cups
- Bowls

Miscellaneous

- Old cans
- Utensils
- Clothes
- Furniture

26. Mention the various activities involved in municipal solid waste (MSW) management.

Ans. Various activities involved are listed below.

- Waste generation.
- Onsite waste handling, storage & processing.
- Waste collection.
- Waste transfer & transport.
- Waste processing and recovery & disposal.

27. What are the auxiliary operations needed for solid waste treatment?

Ans. Auxiliary operations needed for solid waste treatment are as follows:

(i) Transport and handling (ii) Pulverization

(iii) Compaction

Transport and handling: Solid wastes are collected from source, transported in trucks with hydraulic and pneumatic system to a central place and to compact the waste to a high density, for disposal.

Pulverization: Pulverization of solid wastes is carried out prior to loading, land filling, compacting or incineration to facilitate these processes. Taw roll, impact and gyratory crushers and hammer mills are used for pulverization. It makes the solid waste homogenous and helps in greater initial settlement. The land can be more easily reclaimed and built on.

Compaction: Compaction and balling of solid wastes using hydraulic or pneumatic processes lead to reduction in refuse volume, reduction in collection and transport time & cost, lesser storage area & safety hazards and cleaner storage area.

The most effective way to ameliorate the solid waste disposal problem is to reduce the generation and toxicity of waste. But, as people search for better life and higher standard of living they tend to consume more goods and generate more wastes. Consequently society is searching for improved methods of waste management and ways to reduce the amount of waste management system. This consists of reducing the amount of toxicity of the wastes at the source, recycling, reusing or composting as much of the waste as is economically reasonable. Burning the waste that cannot be economically recycled to generate heat reduces the need for fossils and nuclear fuels.

28. Describe various components of solid waste collection.

Ans. Waste collection does not mean merely the gathering of wastes, but also includes the transporting of wastes to transfer stations and/or disposal sites. The factors & components that influence the waste collection system include the following:

(i) **Waste Collection points:** These affect such collection system components as crew size and storage, which ultimately control the cost of waste collection. The collection points depend on locality and may be residential, commercial or industrial.

(ii) **Waste Collection frequency:** Climatic conditions and requirements of a locality as well as containers and costs determine the collection frequency. In hot and humid climates, for example, solid wastes must be collected at least twice a week, as the decomposing solid wastes produce bad odour & leachate. And, as residential wastes usually contain food wastes & other putrescible (rotting) material, frequent collection is desirable for health & aesthetic reasons. Besides climates, the quality of solid waste containers on site also determines the collection frequency. For instance, while sealed or closed containers allow collection frequency up to three days, open & unsealed containers may require daily collection. Collection efficiency largely depends on the demography of the area (such as income groups, community, etc.), where collection takes place. While deciding collection frequency, therefore, we must consider the following:

- Cost, *e.g.*, optimal collection frequency reduces the cost as it involves fewer trucks, employees & reduction in total route distance;
- Storage space, *e.g.*, less frequent collection may require more storage space in the locality;
- Sanitation, *e.g.*, frequent collection reduces concerns about health, safety and nuisance associated with stored refuse.

(iii) **Waste Storage containers:** Proper container selection can save collection energy, increase the speed of collection and reduce crew size. Containers should be functional for the amount & type of materials and collection vehicles used. Containers should also be durable, easy to handle, & economical, as well as resistant to corrosion, weather & animals. In residential areas, where refuse is collected manually, standardised metal or plastic containers are typically required for waste storage. When mechanised collection systems are used, containers are specifically designed to fit the truck mounted loading mechanisms. While evaluating residential waste containers, consider the following:

- Efficiency, *i.e.*, the containers should help maximise the overall collection efficiency.
- Convenience, *i.e.*, the containers must be easily manageable both for residents and collection crew.

- Compatibility, *i.e.*, the containers must be compatible with collection equipment.
- Public health and safety, *i.e.*, the containers should be securely covered and stored.
- Ownership, *i.e.*, the municipal ownership must guarantee compatibility with collection equipment.

(iv) **Waste Collection crew:** The optimum crew size for a community depends on labour & equipment costs, collection methods and route characteristics. The size of the collection crew also depends on the size & type of collection vehicle used, space between the houses, waste generation rate and collection frequency. For example, increase in waste generation rate and quantity of wastes collected per stop due to less frequent collection result in a bigger crew size. The collection vehicle could be a motorised vehicle, a pushcart or a trailer towed by a suitable prime mover (tractor, etc.). It is possible to adjust the ratio of collectors to collection vehicles such that the crew idle time is minimised. However, it is not easy to implement this measure, as it may result in an overlap in the crew collection and truck idle time. An effective collection crew size and proper workforce management can influence the productivity of the collection system. The crew size, in essence, can have a great effect on overall collection costs. However, with increase in collection costs, the trend in recent years is towards:

- Decrease in the frequency of collection;
- Increase in the dependence on residents to sort waste materials;
- Increase in the degree of automation used in collection.

This trend has, in fact, contributed to smaller crews in municipalities.

(v) **Waste Collection route:** The collection programme must consider the route that is efficient for waste collection. An efficient routing of collection vehicles helps decrease costs by reducing the labour expended for collection. Proper planning of collection route also helps conserve energy and minimise working hours & vehicle fuel consumption. It is necessary therefore to develop detailed route configurations and collection schedules for the selected collection system. The size of each route, however, depends on the amount of waste collected per stop, distance between stops, loading time and traffic conditions. Barriers, such as railroad, embankments, rivers and roads with heavy traffic, can be considered to divide route territories. Routing (network) analyses and planning can:

- Increase the likelihood of all streets being serviced equally and consistently;
- Help supervisors locate or track crews quickly;
- Provide optimal routes that can be tested against driver judgement and experience.

(vi) **Waste Transfer station:** A transfer station is an intermediate station between final disposal option and collection point in order to increase the efficiency of the system, as collection vehicles & crew remain closer to routes. If the disposal site is far from the collection area, it is justifiable to have a transfer station, where smaller collection vehicles transfer their loads to larger vehicles, which then haul the waste long distances. In some instances, the transfer station serves as a pre-processing point, where wastes are dewatered, scooped or compressed. A centralised sorting and recovery of recyclable materials are also carried out at transfer stations. The unit cost of hauling solid wastes from a collection area to a transfer station and then to a disposal site decreases, as the size of the collection vehicle increases. This is due to various reasons such as the following:

- Labour costs remain constant;
- The ratio of payload to vehicle load increases with vehicle size;
- The waiting time, unloading time, idle time at traffic lights and driver rest period are constant, regardless of the collection vehicle size.

29. Describe various waste storage containers and waste collection vehicles.

Ans. Waste storage is an important component of a waste management system. Waste storage encompasses proper containers to store wastes and efficient transport of wastes without any spillage to transfer stations/disposal sites.

Waste Containers/storage bins.

The design of an efficient waste collection system requires careful consideration of the type, size and location of containers at the point of waste generation for storage of wastes until they are collected. While single-family households generally use small containers, residential units, commercial units, institutions and industries require large containers. Smaller containers are usually handled manually whereas the larger, heavier ones require mechanical handling. The containers may fall under either of the following two categories:

(i) **Stationary containers:** These are used for contents to be transferred to collection vehicles at the site of storage.

(ii) **Hauled containers:** These are used for contents to be directly transferred to a processing plant, transfer station or disposal site for emptying before being returned to the storage site.

The desirable characteristics of a well-designed container are low cost, size, weight, shape, resistance to corrosion, water tightness, strength and durability. For example, a container for manual handling by one person should not weigh more than 20 kg, otherwise it may lead to occupational health hazards such as muscular strain, etc. Containers that weigh more than 20 kg, when full, require two or more crew members to manually load & unload the wastes, and which result in low collection efficiency. Containers should not have rough or sharp edges, and preferably have a handle and a wheel to facilitate mobility. They should be covered to prevent rainwater from entering (which increases the weight & rate of decomposition of organic materials) into the solid wastes. The container body must be strong enough to resist & discourage stray animals & scavengers from ripping it as well as withstand rough handling by the collection crew and mechanical loading equipment. Containers should be provided with a lifting bar, compatible with the hoisting mechanism of the vehicle. The material used should be light, recyclable, easily moulded and the surface must be smooth & resistant to corrosion. On the one hand, steel and ferrous containers are heavy and subject to corrosion; the rust peels off exposing sharp edges, which could be hazardous to the collection crew. On the other, wooden containers (*e.g.*, bamboo, rattan and wooden baskets) readily absorb & retain moisture and their surfaces are generally rough, irregular & difficult to clean.

Communal containers.

Generally, the containers used for waste storage are communal/public containers which a compactor collection vehicle can lift and empty mechanically. Communal containers may be fixed on the ground (stationary) or movable (hauled). Movable containers are provided with hoists and tails compatible with lifting mechanism of collection vehicles and such containers have capacities of 1-4 m^3. The waste management authority must monitor, maintain and upgrade the communal containers. In residential and commercial areas in India, the communal containers are often made of concrete. In areas with very high waste generation rates, *i.e.*, rates exceeding two truckloads daily, such as wet markets, large commercial centres & large business establishments, roll-on-roll or hoisted communal containers with capacities of 12-20 m^3 and a strong superstructure with wheels are used. Normally, the collection vehicle keeps an empty container as a replacement before it hauls the filled container. When a truck is used as a collection vehicle, the use of communal containers may be appropriate.

It is advisable to place the containers 100-200 m apart for economic reasons. The communal containers are usually staggered such that the effective distance of 100 m is maintained. This means that the farthest distance the householder will have to walk is 50 meters. However, in narrow streets with low traffic, where the house owner can readily cross the street, a longer distance is advisable. If the collection vehicle has to stop frequently, say, at every 50 m or so, fuel consumption increases, and this must be avoided.

Disadvantages of communal container.

The major disadvantage of communal containers is the potential lack of maintenance and upgrading. The residuals & scattered solid wastes emit foul odours, which discourage residents from using the containers properly. In addition, if fixed containers are built below the vehicle level, the collection crew may be held responsible for sweeping & loading the solid wastes into transfer containers before being loaded into the collection vehicle. Sweeping and cleaning the communal containers of residuals obviously impinge on the time of the crew members and take a longer time than if the wastes are placed in smaller containers. As fixed communal containers have higher rates of failure, their use is not advisable.

To overcome the problem of maintaining communal containers, individual residents should maintain their own containers and locate them in designated areas. The communal area must have the facilities of water & drains to facilitate the cleaning of the containers. This has the advantage of reducing the number of collection stops and at the same time maintaining the householder's responsibility for cleaning them. The residents must also be properly educated on the importance of good housekeeping as the containers in the communal area are subject to vandalism.

Waste Collection vehicles.

Almost all waste collections are based on collector and collection crew, which move through the collection service area with a vehicle for collecting the waste material. The collection vehicle selected must be appropriate to the terrain, type & density of waste generation points, the way it travels and type & kind of material. The collection vehicle may be small and simple (*e.g.*, two-wheeled cart pulled by an individual) or large, complex and energy intensive (*e.g.*, rear loading compactor truck). The most commonly used collection vehicle is the dump truck fitted with a hydraulic lifting mechanism. A description of some vehicle types is given below:

(i) **Small-scale collection and muscle-powered vehicles:** These are common vehicles used for waste collection in many countries and are generally used in rural hilly areas. These can be small rickshaws, carts or wagons pulled by people or animals, and are less expensive, easier to build & maintain compared to other vehicles. They are suitable for densely populated areas with narrow lanes & squatter settlements, where there is relatively low volume of waste generated. Some drawbacks of these collection vehicles include limited travel range of the vehicles and weather exposure that affect humans & animals.

(ii) **Non-compactor trucks:** Non-compactor trucks are efficient & cost effective in small cities and in areas where wastes tend to be very dense and have little potential for compaction. When these trucks are used for waste collection, they need a dumping system to easily discharge the waste. It is generally required to cover the trucks in order to prevent residue flying off or rain soaking the wastes. Trucks with capacities of 10-12 m^3 are effective, if the distance between the disposal site and the collection area is less than 15 km. If the distance is longer, a potential transfer station closer than 10 km from the collection area is required. Non-compactor trucks are generally used, when labour cost is high. Controlling & operating cost is a deciding factor, when collection routes are long and relatively sparsely populated.

(iii) **Compactor truck:** Compaction vehicles are more common these days, generally having capacities of 12-15 m^3 due to limitations imposed by narrow roads. Although the capacity of a compaction vehicle, is similar to that of a dump truck, the weight of solid wastes collected per trip is 2 to 2.5 times larger since the wastes are hydraulically compacted. The success of waste management depends on the level of segregation at source. A compactor truck allows waste containers to be emptied into the vehicle from the rear, front or sides and inhibits vectors (of disease) from reaching the waste during collection & transport. It works poorly when waste stream is very dense, wet, collected materials are gritty or abrasive, or when the roads are dusty. The advantages of the compactor collection vehicle include the following:

- Containers are uniform, large, covered and relatively visually inoffensive;
- Waste is set out in containers so that the crew can pick them up quickly;
- Health risk to the collectors and odour on the streets are minimised;
- Waste is relatively inaccessible to the waste pickers.

30. Describe the functions and types of waste transfer station.

Ans. Waste transfer station is a centralised facility, where waste is unloaded from smaller collection vehicles and re-loaded into large vehicles for transport to a disposal or processing site. This transfer of waste is frequently accompanied by removal, separation or handling of waste. In areas, where wastes are not already dense, they may be compacted at a transfer station. The technical limitations of smaller collection vehicles and the low hauling cost of solid waste, using larger vehicles, make a transfer station viable. Also, the use of transfer station proves reasonable, when there is a need for vehicles servicing a collection route to travel shorter distances, unload and return quickly to their primary task of collecting the waste.

Limitations in hauling solid wastes are the main factors to be considered, while evaluating the use of transfer stations. These include the additional capital costs of purchasing trailers, building transfer stations and the extra time, labour & energy required for transferring wastes from collection truck to transfer trailer.

The main problem in the establishment of a transfer station, however, is securing a suitable site. Stored solid wastes and recyclable materials, if not properly handled, will attract flies & other insect vectors. Odours from the transferred solid wastes will also be a nuisance, if not properly controlled. Besides, the traffic and noise due to collection vehicles, collectors, drivers, etc., invite the resentment of the communities living in the vicinity of transfer stations.

Types of waste transfer stations.

Depending on the size, transfer stations can be either of the following two types:

(i) **Small to medium transfer stations:** These are direct-discharge stations that provide no intermediate waste storage area. The capacities are generally small (less than 100 tonnes/day) and medium (100 to 500 tonnes/day). Depending on weather, site aesthetics and environmental concerns, transfer operations of this size may be located either indoor or outdoor. More complex small transfer stations are usually attended during hours of operation and may include some simple waste and materials processing facilities. For example, it includes a recyclable material separation and processing centre. The required overall station capacity (*i.e.*, the number and size of containers) depends on the size & population density of the area served and the frequency of collection.

(ii) **Large transfer stations:** These are designed for heavy commercial use by private and municipal collection vehicles. The typical operational procedure for a larger station is as follows:

- When collection vehicles arrive at the site, they are checked in for billing, weighed and directed to the appropriate dumping area;

- Collection vehicles travel to the dumping area and empty the wastes into a waiting trailer, a pit or a platform;
- After unloading, the collection vehicle leaves the site, and there is no need to weigh the departing vehicle, if its weight (empty) is known;

Transfer vehicles are weighed either during or after loading. If weighed during loading, trailers can be more consistently loaded to just under maximum legal weights and this maximises payloads and minimises weight violations.

Designs for larger transfer operations.

Several different designs for larger transfer operations are common, depending on the transfer distance and vehicle type. Most designs, however, fall into one of the following three categories:

(i) **Direct-discharge non-compaction station:** In these stations, waste is dumped directly from collection vehicle into waiting transfer trailers and is generally designed with two main operating floors. In the transfer operation, wastes are dumped directly from collection vehicles (on the top floor) through a hopper and into open top trailers on the lower floor. The trailers are often positioned on scales so that dumping can be stopped when the maximum payload is reached. A stationary crane with a bucket is used to distribute the waste in the trailer. After loading, a cover or tarpaulin is placed over the trailer top. Because of the use of little hydraulic equipment, a shutdown is unlikely and this station minimises handling of waste.

(ii) **Platform/pit non-compaction station:** In this arrangement, the collection vehicles dump their wastes onto a platform or into a pit using waste handling equipment, where wastes can be temporarily stored, and if desired, picked through for recyclables or unacceptable materials. The waste is then pushed into open-top trailers, usually by front-end loaders. Like direct discharge stations, platform stations have two levels. If a pit is used, however, the station has three levels.A major advantage of these stations is that they provide temporary storage, which allows peak inflow of wastes to be levelled out over a longer period. Construction costs for this type of facility are usually higher because of the increased floor space. This station provides convenient and efficient storage area and due to simplicity of operation and equipment, the potential for station shutdown is less.

(iii) **Compaction station:** In this type of station, the mechanical equipment is used to increase the density of wastes before they are transferred. The most common type of compaction station uses a hydraulically powered compactor to compress wastes. Wastes are fed into the compactor through a chute, either directly from collection trucks or after intermediate use of a pit. The hydraulic ram of the compactor pushes waste into the transfer trailer, which is usually mechanically linked to the compactor. Compaction stations are used when:

- Wastes must be baled for shipment;
- Open-top trailers cannot be used because of size restrictions;
- Site topography or layout does not accommodate a multi-level building.

The main disadvantage of a compaction facility is that the facility's ability to process wastes is directly dependent on the operation of the compactor.

31. What are the objectives of solid waste processing?

Ans. The processing of solid wastes helps in achieving the best possible benefit from every functional element of the solid waste management (SWM) system and, therefore, requires proper selection of techniques and equipment for every element. Accordingly, the wastes that are considered suitable for further use need to be paid special attention in terms of processing, in order that we could derive maximum economical value from them. The objectives of solid waste processing are:

(i) **Improving efficiency of Solid Waste Management (SWM) system:** Various processing techniques are available to improve the efficiency of SWM system. For example, before waste papers are reused, they are usually baled to reduce transporting and storage volume requirements. In some cases, wastes are baled to reduce the haul costs at disposal site, where solid wastes are compacted to use the available land effectively. If solid wastes are to be transported hydraulically and pneumatically, some form of shredding is also required. Shredding is also used to improve the efficiency of the disposal site.

(ii) **Recovering material for reuse:** Usually, materials having a market, when present in wastes in sufficient quantity to justify their separation, are most amenable to recovery and recycling. Materials that can be recovered from solid wastes include paper, cardboard, plastic, glass, ferrous metal, aluminium and other residual metals.

(iii) **Recovering conversion products and energy:** Combustible organic materials can be converted to intermediate products and ultimately to usable energy. This can be done either through incineration, pyrolysis, composting or bio-digestion. Initially, the combustible organic matter is separated from the other solid waste components. Once separated, further processing like shredding and drying is necessary before the waste material can be used for power generation.

32. What are the purpose and equipments used for volume reduction (compaction) of solid waste?

Ans. Volume and size reduction is an important factor in the development & operation of any Solid Waste Management (SWM) system. The main purpose is to reduce the volume (amount) and size of the solid waste, as compared to its original form, and produce waste of uniform size. Volume reduction or compaction refers to densifying wastes in order to reduce their volume. The benefits of waste compaction include:

- Reduction in the quantity of materials to be handled at the disposal site;
- Improved efficiency of collection and disposal of wastes;
- Increased life of landfills;
- Economically viable waste management system.

However, following disadvantages are associated with compaction:

- Poor quality of recyclable materials sorted out of compaction vehicle;
- Difficulty in segregation or sorting (since the various recyclable materials are mixed and compressed in lumps);
- Bio-degradable materials (*e.g.*, left over food, fruits & vegetables) destroy the value of paper & plastic material.

Equipment used for compaction. Based on their mobility, the compaction equipment used in volume reduction are the following:

(i) **Stationary equipment:** This represents the equipment in which wastes are brought to, and loaded into, either manually or mechanically. In fact, the compaction mechanism used to compress waste in a collection vehicle, is a stationary compactor. According to their application, stationary compactors can be described as light duty (*e.g.*, those used for residential areas), commercial or light industrial, heavy industrial and transfer station compactors. Usually, large stationary compactors are necessary, when wastes are to be compressed into:

- Steel containers that can be subsequently moved manually or mechanically;
- Chambers where the compressed blocks are banded or tied by some means before being removed;
- Chambers where they are compressed into a block and then released and hauled away untied;
- Transport vehicles directly.

(ii) **Movable equipment:** This represents the wheeled and tracked equipment used to place and compact solid wastes, as in a sanitary landfill.

According to their compaction pressure, we can divide the compactors used at transfer stations as follows:

(a) **Low-pressure (less than 7 kg/cm^2) compaction:** This includes those used at apartments & commercial establishments, bailing equipment used for waste papers & cardboards and stationary compactors used at transfer stations. In low-pressure compaction, wastes are compacted in large containers. Portable stationary compactors are being used increasingly by a number of industries in conjunction with material recovery options, especially for waste paper and cardboard.

(b) **High-pressure (more than 7 kg/cm^2) compaction:** Compact systems with a capacity up to 350 kg/cm^2 come under this category. In such systems, specialised compaction equipment are used to compress solid wastes into blocks or bales of various sizes. In some cases, pulverised wastes are extruded after compaction in the form of logs. The volume reduction achieved with these high-pressure compaction systems varies with the characteristics of the waste. Typically, the reduction ranges from about 3 to 1 through 8 to 1. When wastes are compressed, their volume is reduced, which is normally expressed in percentage.

33. What are the purpose and equipments used for size reduction of solid waste?

Ans. **Size reduction or shredding:** This is required to convert large sized wastes (as they are collected) into smaller pieces. Size reduction helps in obtaining the final product in a reasonably uniform and considerably reduced size in comparison to the original form. But size reduction does not necessarily imply volume reduction, and this must be accounted into the design & operation of SWM systems as well as in the recovery of materials for reuse and conversion to energy. In the overall process of waste treatment and disposal, size reduction is implemented ahead of:

- Landfilling to provide a more homogeneous product. This may require less cover material and less frequent covering than that without shredding. This can be of economic importance, where cover material is scarce or needs to be brought to the landfill site from some distance.
- Recovering materials from the waste stream for recycling.
- Baling the wastes—a process sometimes used ahead of long distance transport of solid wastes—to achieve a greater density.
- Making the waste a better fuel for incineration waste energy recovery facilities. (The size reduction coupled with screening, results in a more homogeneous mixture of relatively uniform size, moisture content & heating value, and thereby improving the steps of incineration & energy recovery reducing moisture, *i.e.*, drying & dewatering of wastes).

Mode of action & applications of various size reduction equipments is tabulated below.

Size Reduction

Equipment Type	Mode of action	Application
Small grinders	Grinding, mashing	Organic residential solid wastes
Chippers	Cutting, slicing	Paper, cardboard, tree trimmings, yard waste, wood, plastics
Large grinders	Grinding, mashing	Brittle and friable materials, used mostly in industrial operation
Jaw crushers	Crushing, breaking	Large solids
Rasp mills	Shredding, tearing	Moistened solid wastes
Shredders	Shearing, tearing	All types of municipal wastes
Cutters, Clippers	Shearing, tearing	All types of municipal wastes
Hammer mills	Breaking, tearing, cutting, crushing	All types of municipal wastes, most commonly used equipment for reducing size and homogenizing composition of wastes

Hydropulper	Shearing, tearing	Ideally suited for use with pulpable wastes, including paper, wood chips. Used primarily in the paper making industry. Also used to destroy paper records

The most frequently used shredding equipment are the following:

(i) **Hammer mill:** These are used most often in large commercial operations for reducing the size of solid wastes. Hammer mill is an impact device consisting of a number of hammers, fastened flexibly to an inner disk , which rotates at a very high speed.

Solid wastes, as they enter the mill are hit by sufficient force, which crush or tear them with a velocity so that they do not adhere to the hammers. Wastes are further reduced in size by being struck between breaker plates and/or cutting bars fixed around the periphery of the inner chamber. This process of cutting & striking action continues, until the required size of material is achieved and after that it falls out of the bottom of the mill.

(ii) **Hydropulper:** An alternative method of size reduction involves the use of a hydropulper. Solid wastes and recycled water are added to the hydropulper. The high-speed cutting blades, mounted on a rotor in the bottom of the unit, convert pulpable and friable materials into slurry with a solid content varying from 2.5 to 3.5%. Metal, tins, cans and other non-pulpable or non-friable materials are rejected from the side of the hydropulper tank. The rejected material passes down a chute that is connected to a bucket elevator, while the solid slurry passes out through the bottom of the pulper tank and is pumped to the next processing operation.

34. What is the purpose of component separation of solid wastes?

Ans. Component separation is a necessary operation in which the solid waste components are identified and sorted either manually or mechanically to aid further processing. This is required for the:

- Recovery of valuable materials for recycling;
- Preparation of solid wastes by removing certain components prior to incineration, energy recovery, composting and biogas production.

The most effective way of separation is manual sorting in households prior to collection. The municipality generally provides separate, easily identifiable containers into which the householder deposits segregated recyclable materials such as paper, glass, metals, etc. Usually, separate collections are carried out for the recyclable material. At curbside, separate areas are set aside for each of the recyclable materials for householders to deliver material – when there is no municipal collection system. In case the separation is not done prior to collection, it could be sorted out through mechanical techniques such as air separation, magnetic separation, etc., to recover the wastes.

35. Describe some important component separation techniques from solid waste.

Ans. Some of the component separation techniques are described below:

Air separation: This technique is in use in industrial operations for segregating various components from dry mixture of solid waste. Air separation is primarily used to separate lighter materials (usually organic) from heavier (usually inorganic) ones. The lighter material may include plastics, paper & paper products and other organic materials. Generally, there is also a need to separate the light fraction of organic material from the conveying air streams, which is usually done in a cyclone separator. In this technique, the heavy fraction is removed from the air classifier (*i.e.*, equipment used for air separation) to the recycling stage or to land disposal, as appropriate. The light fraction may be used, with or without further size reduction, as fuel for incinerators or as compost material. There are various types of air classifiers commonly used, some of which are listed below:

(i) **Conventional chute type:** This is one of the simplest types of air classifiers. In this type, when the processed solid wastes are dropped into the vertical chute, the lighter material is carried by the airflow to the top while the heavier materials fall to the bottom of the chute. The control of the percentage split between the light & heavy fraction is accomplished by varying the waste loading rate, airflow rate and the cross section of chute. A rotary air lock feed mechanism is required to introduce the shredded wastes into the classifier.

(ii) **Zigzag air classifier:** A zigzag air classifier consists of a continuous vertical column with internal zigzag deflectors through which air is drawn at a high rate. Shredded wastes are introduced at the top of the column at a controlled rate, and air is introduced at the bottom of the column. As the wastes drop into the air stream, the lighter fraction is fluidised and moves upward & out of column, while the heavy fraction falls to the bottom. Best separation can be achieved through proper design of the separation chamber, airflow rate and influent feed rate.

(iii) **Open inlet vibrator type:** In this type of air classifier, the separation is accomplished by a combination of the following actions:

Vibration: This helps to stratify the material fed to the separator into heavy and light components. Due to this agitation, the heavier particles tend to settle at the bottom as the shredded waste is conveyed down the length of the separator.

Inertial force: In this action, the air pulled in through the feed inlet imparts an initial acceleration to the lighter particle, while the wastes travel down the separator as they are being agitated.

Air pressure: This action refers to the injection of fluidising air in two or more high velocity and low mass flow curtains across the bed. A final stripping of light particles is accomplished at the point where the heavy fraction discharges from the elutriators. The resulting separation is less sensitive to particle size than a conventional vertical air classifier, be it of straight or zigzag design.

An advantage of this classifier is that an air lock feed mechanism is not required and wastes are fed by gravity directly into the separator inlet.

Magnetic separation: The most common method of recovering ferrous scrap from shredded solid wastes involves the use of magnetic recovery systems. Ferrous materials are usually recovered either after shredding or before air classification. When wastes are mass fired in incinerators, the magnetic separator is used to remove the ferrous material from the incinerator residue. Magnetic recovery systems have also been used at landfill disposal sites. The specific locations, where ferrous materials are recovered will depend on the objectives to be achieved, such as reduction of wear & tear on processing & separation equipment, degree of product purity achieved and the required recovery efficiency.

Equipment used for magnetic separation: Various types of equipment are in use for the magnetic separation of ferrous materials. The most common types are the following:

(i) **Suspended magnet:** In this type of separator, a permanent magnet is used to attract the ferrous metal from the waste stream. When the attracted metal reaches the area, where there is no magnetism, it falls away freely. This ferrous metal is then collected in a container. This type of separation device is suitable for processing raw refuse, where separators can remove large pieces of ferrous metal easily from the waste stream.

(ii) **Magnetic pulley:** This consists of a drum type device containing permanent magnets or electromagnets over which a conveyor or a similar transfer mechanism carries the waste stream. The conveyor belt conforms to the rounded shape of the magnetic drum and the magnetic force pulls the ferrous material away from the falling stream of solid waste.

Screening: Screening is the most common form of separating solid wastes, depending on their size by the use of one or more screening surfaces. Screening has a number of applications in solid waste resource and energy recovery systems. Screens can be used before or after shredding and after air separation of wastes in various applications dealing with both light & heavy fraction materials. The most commonly used screens are rotary drum screens and various forms of vibrating screens. Rotating wire screens with relatively large openings are used for separation of cardboard & paper products, while vibrating screens & rotating drum screens are typically used for the removal of glass & related materials from the shredded solid wastes.

Besides the mechanical techniques described above for segregating wastes, there are other separation techniques also which is discussed below:

(i) **Hand-sorting or previewing:** Previewing of the waste stream and manual removal of large sized materials is necessary, prior to most types of separation or size reduction techniques. This is done to prevent damage or stoppage of equipment such as shredders or screens, due to items such as rugs, pillows, mattresses, large metallic or plastic objects, wood or other construction materials, paint cans, etc.

(ii) **Inertial separation:** Inertial separation methods rely on ballistic or gravity separation principles to separate shredded solid wastes into light (*i.e.*, organic) & heavy (*i.e.*, inorganic) particles.

(iii) **Flotation:** In the flotation process, glass-rich feedstock, which is produced by screening the heavy fraction of the air-classified wastes after ferrous metal separation, is immersed in water in a tank. Glass chips, rocks, bricks, bones and dense plastic materials that sink to the bottom are removed with belt scrappers for further processing. Light organic and other materials that float are skimmed from the surface. These materials are taken to landfill sites or to incinerators for energy recovery. Chemical adhesives (flocculants) are also used to improve the capture of light organic & fine inorganic materials.

(iv) **Optical sorting:** Optical sorting is used mostly to separate glass from the waste stream, and this can be accomplished by identification of the transparent properties of glass to sort it from opaque materials (*e.g.*, stones, ceramics, bottle caps, corks, etc.) in the waste stream. Optical sorting involves a compressed air blast that removes or separates the glasses - plain or coloured. An optical sorting machinery is, however, complex and expensive.

36. What is the purpose of drying and dewatering of solid waste?

Ans. Drying and dewatering operations for solid wastes are used primarily for incineration systems, with or without energy recovery systems. These are also used for drying of sludges in waste water treatment plants, prior to their incineration or transport to land disposal. The purpose of drying and dewatering operation is to remove moisture from wastes and thereby make it a better fuel. Sometimes, the light fraction is pelletised after drying to make the fuel easier to transport and store, prior to use in an incinerator or energy recovery facility.

37. What are the methods and equipments used for drying and dewatering of solid wastes?

Ans. Drying: The following three methods are used to apply the heat required for drying the wastes:

(i) **Convection drying:** In this method, hot air is in direct contact with the wet solid waste stream.

(ii) **Conduction drying:** In this method, the wet solid waste stream is in contact with a heated surface.

(iii) **Radiation drying:** In this method, heat is transmitted directly to the wet solid waste stream by radiation from the heated body. Of these three methods, convection drying is used most commonly.

A rotary drum dryer is composed of a rotating cylinder, slightly inclined from the horizontal through which the material to be dried and the drying gas are passed simultaneously. The drying of material in a direct rotary dryer occurs in the following stages:

- Heating the wet material and its moisture content to the constant-rate drying temperature.
- Drying the material substantially at this temperature.
- Heating of material to its discharge temperature and evaporation of moisture remaining at the end of the stage.

The retention time in the rotary drum is about 30-45 minutes.

Dewatering. Dewatering is more applicable to the problem of sludge disposal from wastewater treatment of plants, but may also be applicable in some cases to municipal/industrial waste problems. When drying beds, lagoons or spreading on land are not feasible, other mechanical means of dewatering are used. The emphasis in the dewatering operation is often on reducing the liquid volume. Once dewatered, the sludge can be mixed with other solid waste, and the resulting mixture can be:

- Incinerated to reduce volume;
- Used for the production of recoverable by-products;
- Used for production of compost;
- Buried in a landfill.

Centrifugation and filtration are the two common methods for the dewatering of sludge. Sludges with solid content of a few percent can be thickened to about 10-15% in centrifugation and about 20-30% in pressure filtration or vacuum filtration.

38. What are the various technologies involved in solid waste management?

Ans. Solid waste management technologies include, technologies associated with the control of generation, storage, collection, transfer & transportation, processing, marketing, incineration and disposal of solid wastes. All of these processes have to be carried out within existing legal and social guidelines that protect the public health and environment and are aesthetically acceptable. The various techniques employed in solid waste management include:

- Composting
- Sanitary landfilling (Controlled tipping)
- Thermal process (Incineration and pyrolysis)
- Recycling and reuse.

39. Describe in detail various solid waste disposal disposal options and their selection criteria.

Ans. The most common disposal option practised currently in many countries is either uncontrolled dumping or dumping with moderate control. The environmental costs of uncontrolled dumping include breeding of disease causing vectors (*e.g.*, flies, mosquitoes and rodents), pollution, odour and smoke.

Solid waste disposal options:

Some of the options available for waste disposal, are as follows:

(i) **Uncontrolled dumping:** This is the most common method being practised in many parts of the world, including India. In this method, wastes are dumped at a designated site without any environmental control. They remain there for a long period of time, pose health risks and cause environmental degradation. Due to the adverse health & environmental impact associated with it, this non-engineered disposal method is not a viable and safe option.

(ii) **Sanitary landfill:** Sanitary landfill is a fully engineered disposal option in that the selected location or wasteland is carefully engineered in advance before it is pressed into service. Operators of sanitary landfills can minimise the effects of leachate (*i.e.*, polluted water which flows from a landfill) and gas production through proper site selection, preparation and management. This particular option of waste disposal is suitable when the land is available at an affordable price, and adequate workforce & technical resources are available to operate & manage the site.

(iii) **Composting:** This is a biological process of decomposition in which organisms, under controlled conditions of ventilation, temperature & moisture, convert the organic portion of solid waste into humus-like material. If this process is carried out effectively, what we get as the final product is a stable, odour-free soil conditioner. Generally, the option of composting is considered, when a considerable amount of biodegradable waste is available in the waste stream and there is use or market for composts. Composting can be either centralised or small-scale. Centralised composting plants are possible, if adequate skilled workforce and equipments are available. And, small-scale composting practices can be effective at household level, but this needs public awareness.

(iv) **Incineration:** This refers to the controlled burning of wastes, at a high temperature (roughly 1200-1400°C), which sterilises and stabilises the waste in addition to reducing its volume. In the process, most of the combustible materials (*i.e.*, self-sustaining combustible matter, which saves the energy needed to maintain the combustion) such as paper or plastics get converted into carbon dioxide and ash. Incineration may be used as a disposal option, when land filling is not possible and the waste composition is highly combustible. An appropriate technology, infrastructure and skilled workforce are required to operate and maintain the plant.Incineration is generally limited to hospital & other biological wastes.

(v) **Gasification:** This is the partial combustion of carbonaceous material (through combustion) at high temperature (roughly 1000°C) forming a gas, comprising mainly carbon dioxide, carbon monoxide, nitrogen, hydrogen, water vapour and methane, which can be used as fuel.

(vi) **Refuse-derived fuel (RDF):** This is the combustible part of raw waste, separated for burning as fuel. Various physical processes such as screening, size reduction, magnetic separation, etc., are used to separate the combustibles.

(vii) **Pyrolysis:** This is the thermal degradation of carbonaceous material to gaseous, liquid & solid fraction in the absence of oxygen. This occurs at a temperature between 200 and 900°C. The product of pyrolysis is a gas of relatively high calorific value of 20,000 joules per gram with oils, tars & solid burned residue.

Selection criteria of waste disposal options: We can assess the effectiveness of each of the waste disposal options with the help of proper frameworks which represents an aid to decision-making and helps to ensure the key issues are considered. A sub-framework explains how and why the necessary information should be obtained. A framework contains a list of issues and questions pertaining to the technical, institutional, financial, social & environmental features of a waste disposal system to assess the capacity of a disposal option to meet the requirements.

An appraisal of waste disposal option must include the following factors:

(i) **Technical:** This feature, involving efficient and effective operation of the technology being used, evaluates the following components of a SWM system:

- Composition of wastes, *e.g.*, type, characteristics and quantity.
- Existing practices, *e.g.*, collection, transport, and recycling process.
- Siting, *e.g.*, location of disposal site, engineering material, etc.
- Technology, *e.g.*, operation, maintenance, technical support, etc.
- Impact, *e.g.*, anticipated by-product, requirement for their treatment and disposal, etc.

(ii) **Institutional:** This involves the ability and willingness of responsible agencies to operate & manage the system by evaluating the following:

- Structures, roles and responsibilities, *e.g.*, current institutional frameworks.
- Operational capacity, *e.g.*, municipal capacities, local experience and staff training.
- Incentives, *e.g.*, management improvement and waste disposal practices.
- Innovation and partnership.

(iii) **Financial:** This assesses the ability to finance the implementation, operation & maintenance of the system by evaluating the following:

- Financing and cost recovery, *e.g.*, willingness to raise finance for waste management.
- Current revenue and expenditure on waste management.
- Potential need for external finance for capital cost.

(iv) **Social:** This helps in avoiding adverse social impact by evaluating the following:

- Waste picking, which has an impact on livelihood and access to waste pickers.
- Health and income implication.
- Public opinions on the existing and proposed system.

(v) **Environmental:** This means setting up an environment friendly disposal system by evaluating the following:

- Initial environmental risks, *i.e.*, impact of existing and proposed disposal option.
- Long-term environmental risks, *i.e.*, long-term implication (future impacts).

40. Describe briefly the techniques of treatment and disposal of municipal solid waste (MSW).

Ans. Various techniques of MSW treatment & disposal are described below:

- **Composting.** Composting is the controlled biological decomposition of organic matter, such as food and yard wastes, into humus, a soil-like material. Composting is nature's way of recycling organic wastes into new soil used in vegetable and flower gardens, landscaping, and many other applications. Organic matter constitutes 35%-40% of the municipal solid waste generated. It is the natural process of decomposition of organic waste that yields manure or compost, which is very rich in nutrients. Composting is a biological process in which micro-organisms, mainly fungi and bacteria, convert degradable organic waste into humus like substance. This finished product, which looks like soil, is high in carbon & nitrogen and is an excellent medium for growing plants. Vermi-composting has become very popular in the last few years. In this method, worms are added to the compost. These help to break the waste and the added excreta of the worms makes the compost very rich in nutrients.
- **Landfills.** Landfills are generally located in urban areas where a large amount of waste is generated and has to be dumped in a common place. Unlike an open dump, it is a pit that is dug in the ground. At the end of each day, a layer of soil is scattered on top of it and usually an earth-moving equipment is used to compress the garbage, which now forms a cell. The contamination of groundwater and soil through landfills is known as leaching.
- **Sanitary landfills.** An alternative to landfills which will solve the problem of leaching to some extent, is a sanitary landfill which is more hygienic and built in a methodical manner. These are lined with materials that are impermeable such as plastics & clay, and are also built over impermeable soil. The major problem is the development of methane gas, which occurs when little oxygen is present, *i.e.* during anaerobic decomposition. Methane gas produced from sanitary landfills is tapped and sold as fuel.
- **Incineration plants.** To reduce waste volume, a controlled burning process called combustion or incineration is practiced to minimizing volume. Combustors, when properly equipped, can convert water into steam to fuel heating systems or generate electricity. The ash that is buried at the landfills leaches the area and cause severe contamination.

41. What is composting of solid waste?

Ans. Composting is an environment friendly process to convert solid wastes into valuable agricultural inputs. Composts are excellent source of humus and plant nutrients, the application of which improves soil biophysical properties and organic matter status of the soil. Composting is defined as the biological conversion of organic wastes into an amorphous dark brown to black colloidal humus like substance under conditions of optimum temperature, moisture & aeration. Nutrient content of compost depends largely on the nutrient content of the wastes. Composting is a process in which the organic portion of solid waste is allowed to decompose under carefully controlled conditions. It is a biological process of decomposition & transformation of the waste material accomplished by the action of bacteria, fungi, and other microorganisms.

Composting is the aerobic, thermophilic degradation of organic matter present in the refuse by microbes, predominantly by fungi and actinomycetes, which are favoured by semi moist condition that prevail in the process. The control parameters for optimum composting include, temperature (40°C), moisture (40.7%), pH (4.5-9.5), nutrients (C:N ratio 40:1); C:P ratio (100:1), air (0.5-0.8 m^3/d/kg volatile solid) and particle size (6-25 mm).

With proper control of moisture, temperature, and aeration, a composting plant can reduce the volume of raw organic material by as much as 50 per cent. In addition, composting can stabilize the waste and produce an end product that may be recycled for beneficial use. The end product is called compost or humus. It resembles potting soil in texture and earthy odor, and it may be used as a soil conditioner.

A complete municipal solid waste (MSW) composting operation includes sorting & separating, shredding & pulverizing, digestion, product upgrading, and finally marketing. Sorting and separation operations are required to isolate organic, decomposable waste materials from the plastic, glass, metal, and other non biodegradable substances. Solid waste sorting and separation methods are a key part of MSW recycling operations. Shredding and pulverizing serve to reduce the size of the individual pieces of the organic waste, resulting in a relatively uniform mass of material. This facilitates handling, moisture control, and aeration of the decomposing waste. Size reduction also helps optimize bacterial activity and increases the rate of decomposition. After size reduction, the wastes are ready for the actual composting or digestion step. Digestion may take place in open windrow or in an enclosed mechanical facility.

42. What are benefits of Composting of Municipal Solid Waste?

Ans. Composting is a controlled biological process that uses natural aerobic processes to increase the rate of biological decomposition of organic materials. It is carried out by successive microbial populations that brak down organic materials into carbon dioxide, water, minerals, and stabilized organic matter. Carbon dioxide and water are released into the atmosphere, while minerals and organic matter are converted into a potentially reusable soil-like material called compost. The loss of water and carbon dioxide typically reduces the volume of remaining material by 30 to 60%. Compost can be used as a soil amendment in a variety of agricultural, horticultural or landscaping applications.

Benefits of Composting are:

- Increases overall waste diversion from final disposal, especially since as much as 80% of the waste stream in low and middle-income countries is compostable.
- Enhances recycling and incineration operations by removing organic matter from the waste stream.
- Produces a valuable soil amendment-integral to sustainable agriculture.

- Promotes environmentally sound practices, such as the reduction of methane generation at landfills.
- Enhances the effectiveness of fertilizer application.
- Can reduce waste transportation requirements.
- Flexible for implementation at different levels, from household efforts to large-scale centralized facilities.
- Can be started with very little capital and operating costs.
- The climate is optimum for composting.
- Addresses significant health effects resulting from organic waste.
- Provides an excellent opportunity to improve a city's overall waste collection program.
- Accommodates seasonal waste fluctuations, such as leaves and crop residue.
- Can integrate existing informal sectors involved in the collection, separation and recycling of wastes.

43. What is windrow composting?

Ans. A windrow is a long, low pile of the prepared organic waste, usually about 3m wide at the base and about 2 m high. Most windrows are conical in cross section and about 50 m in length. The composting waste is aerated by periodically turning each windrow. Turning frequency varies with moisture content and other factors. When moisture content is maintained at about 50 per cent, windrows are turned two or three times a week and in some cases daily.

Generally, open field windrow composting takes about 5 weeks for digestion or stabilization of the waste material. An additional 3 weeks may sometimes be required to ensure complete stabilization. Temperatures in an aerobic compost windrow may reach 65°C because of the natural metabolic action of thermophilic microbes that thrive at such elevated temperatures. The relatively high temperatures destroy most of the pathogenic or disease-causing organisms that may be present in the waste.

Open-field windrow composting requires relatively large land areas. To reduce land requirements, various types of enclosed mechanical systems can be used in lieu of the open-field method. A variety of mechanical type compost systems are available. Oxygen is supplied to the waste material by forced aeration, stirring, or tumbling. In addition to reducing land requirements, enclosed mechanical compost facilities can reduce the time required for stabilization from about 5 weeks to about 1 week.

The digestion of the waste is carried out naturally in an outside decomposition area in windrows (for five weeks) or in mechanized composting plants (for 4 to 6 days). In natural system, the garbage is mixed with nutrient source (sewage sludge/animal manure) and a filler (wood chips) to provide entry of air. The mixture is turned over twice a week and the process is completed in 4-6 weeks. The darkening of refuse, fall in temperature and a musty odour indicate completion of the process.

Before the stabilized compost or humus can be sold for use as a soil conditioner, it must be processed further to upgrade or improve its quality and appearance. This includes drying, screening, and granulating or pelletizing. Sometimes, the compost is placed in bags, although bulk sale is more efficient and economical. Compost can increase the organic & nutrient content of soil and improve its texture & ability to retain moisture.

44. What is Vermicomposting?

Ans. The role of earthworms in improving the soil fertility is well known. Earthworms feed on any organic wastes, consume three to five times their body weight and after using 5 to 10 per cent of the organic wastes for their growth, excrete the mucous coated undigested matter as worm casts. Worm casts consist of organic matter that has undergone physical & chemical breakdown through the activity of the muscular gizzard, that grinds the material to a particle size of 1-2 micron. The nutrients present in the worm casts are readily soluble in water for the uptake of plants. Vermi castings are rich sources of macro & micronutrients, vitamins, enzymes, antibiotics, growth hormones and immobilized micro flora.

Vermicompost refers to organic manure produced by earthworms. It is a mixture of worm castings, including humus, live earthworms, their cocoons and other micro organisms. Vermi composting is an appropriate method for disposal of non-toxic solid and liquid organic wastes. It helps in cost effective & efficient recycling of animal wastes (Poultry droppings, horse, piggery excreta & cattle dung), agricultural residues and industrial wastes using low energy.

Several types of earthworms are found in our soils. Earthworms can be divided into the following two categories:

- Epigeic—the surface living worms
- Endogeic—the burrowing worms

Epigeic: These worms are found on the surface and are reddish brown in colour. They do not process the soil but are efficient in composting of organic wastes. They enhance the rate of organic manure production through biodegradation or mineralization.

e.g. Lampito mauritii, Octochaetona serrata, Perionyx excavatus.

Endogeic: These species burrow and mix the soil, from different horizons in the profile. They ingest organic and mineral fraction of soil, thus promoting the formation of organo mineral complexes. Organo mineral crumbs are brought from deeper parts of the soil profile to the surface. Different species of earthworms show specificity to soil types, moisture content and temperature.

Method of vermicomposting include:

- **Selection of earthworm:** Earthworm that is native to the local soil may be used.
- **Size of pit:** Any convenient dimension such as 2m × 1m × 1m may be prepared.
- **Preparation of vermin bed:** A layer, 15-20 cm thick of good loamy soil above a thin layer of (5 cms) broken bricks and sand should be made.

- **Inoculation of earthworms:** About one hundred earthworms are introduced as an optimum inoculating density into a compost pit of about 2 m × 1 m × 1 m, provided with vermin bed.
- **Organic layering:** It is done on the vermibed with fresh cattle dung. The compost pit is then layered to about 5 cm with dry leaves or hay or organic wastes. Moisture content of the pit is maintained by the addition of water.
- **Wet organic layering:** It is done after four weeks with moist green organic waste, which can be spread over it to a thickness of 5 cm. This practice can be repeated every 4 days. Mixing of wastes periodically without disturbing the vermin bed ensures proper vermicomposting. Wet layering with organic wastes can be repeated till the compost pit is nearly full.

At maturation (after 120 days), the moisture content is brought down, by stopping the addition of water. This ensures drying of compost and migration of worms in to the vermibed. The mature compost, a fine loose granular mass (about 1500 kg), is removed from the pit, sieved, dried and packed. Matured vermin compost is rich in nutrients and recommended to be used @ 50 t ha^{-1}.

Characteristics of vermicompost

pH -7.00

EC dsm^{-1} -1.20

Organic carbon% -30.50

Macronutrients:

Total nitrogen % -0.66

Total P_2O_5% -1.93

Total K_2O% -0.42

Micronutrients

Fe (ppm) -19.8

Zn (ppm) -0.90

Mn (ppm) -16.50

Cu (ppm) -2.30

45. What are thermal treatment processes for solid waste disposal?

Ans. This refers to processes that involve the use of heat to treat waste. Listed below are descriptions of some commonly utilized thermal treatment processes.

Incineration: Incineration is a process of destruction of waste at high temperature. The combustible wastes are converted through controlled combustion to a residue, which contain no combustible matter. If land suitable for solid waste landfilling operations is not available within economic haul distances, then incineration is necessary. After incineration, the wastes are converted to carbon dioxide, water vapour and ash. This method may be used as a means of recovering energy to be used in heating or the supply of electricity. In addition to supplying energy incineration technologies have the advantage of reducing the volume of the waste, rendering it harmless, reducing transportation costs and reducing the production of the green house gas methane.The solid waste is reduced in volume (80% - 90%) and height (98-99%). Incinerator can accept toxic and industrial wastes of any size in solid or powdery form. The other special wastes include hospital wastes, putrifiable organic solids from slaughter houses.

Pyrolysis and gasification: Pyrolysis is the process of conversion of biomass into solid, liquid and gaseous energy. Pyrolysis results in the chemical breakdown of organic carbon material into three basic components: (1) gas phase containing mainly H_2, CO_2, CO and CH_4 (2) tar or oil phase containing simple organic acids, methanol and acetone and (3) char phase made up of pure carbon and inert material. Pyrolysis does not cause pollution of the atmosphere and large quantities of potentially hazardous plastics could be treated. Pyrolysis and gasification are similar processes as they both decompose organic waste by exposing it to high temperatures and low amounts of oxygen. Gasification uses a low oxygen environment while pyrolysis allows no oxygen. These techniques use heat and an oxygen starved environment to convert biomass into other forms. A mixture of combustible and non-combustible gases as well as pyroligenous liquid is produced by these processes. All of these products have a high heat value and can be utilised. Gasification is advantageous since it allows for the incineration of waste with energy recovery and without the air pollution that is characteristic of other incineration methods.

Open burning: Open burning is the burning of unwanted materials in a manner that causes smoke and other emissions to be released directly into the air without passing through a chimney or stack. This includes the burning of outdoor piles, burning in a burn barrel and the use of incinerators which have no pollution control devices and as such release the gaseous by products directly into the atmosphere. Open burning has been practiced by a number of urban centres because it reduces the volume of refuse received at the dump and therefore extends the life of their dumpsite. Garbage may be burnt because of the ease and convenience of the method or because of the cheapness of the method. In countries where house holders are required to pay for garbage disposal, burning of waste in the backyard allows the householder to avoid paying the costs associated with collecting, hauling and dumping the waste.

Open burning has many negative effects on both human health and the environment. This uncontrolled burning of garbage releases many pollutants into the atmosphere. These include dioxins, particulate matter, polycyclic aromatic compounds, volatile organic compounds, carbon monoxide, hexachlorobenzene and ash. All of these chemicals pose serious risks to human health. The Dioxins have adverse effects on reproduction, development, disrupt the hormonal systems or even cause cancer. The polycyclic aromatic compounds and the hexachlorobenzene are carcinogenic. The particulate matter can be harmful to persons with respiratory problems such as asthma or bronchitis and carbon monoxide can cause neurological symptoms. The harmful effects of open burning are also felt by the environment. This process releases acidic gases such as the halo-hydrides; it also may release the oxides of nitrogen and carbon. Nitrogen oxides contribute to acid rain, ozone depletion, smog and global warming. The particulate matter creates smoke and haze which contribute to air pollution.

46. Describe in detail the features of sanitary landfills.

Ans. Land filling is the most common and economic method of solid waste disposal. The indiscriminate land filling of solid waste in open dumps without adequate control and consideration of sanitation & public health as generally followed in India is undesirable. It results in water pollution, bad odour, fire and breeding of flies & rats.

It should be replaced by sanitary land filling or controlled tipping. The construction of sanitary land filling includes:

- Deposition of solid waste in such a way to have a working force of minimum area.
- Spreading and compaction of waste in thin layers.
- Covering of the waste with a layer of compacted cover soil daily.
- Final cover of the entire construction with compacted earth layer of 1.0 m thick.

The solid wastes in sanitary land fill are degraded by soil microbes. In comparison with other biological treatment systems such as activated sludge and anaerobic digestion, the microbial degradation of solid waste proceeds at a slow rate.

Sanitary Landfills are designed to greatly reduce or eliminate the risks that waste disposal may pose to the public health and environmental quality. They are usually placed in areas where land features act as natural buffers between the landfill and the environment. For example the area may be comprised of clay soil which is fairly impermeable due to its tightly packed particles, or the area may be characterised by a low water table and an absence of surface water bodies thus preventing the threat of water contamination.

Besides the strategic placement of the landfill other protective measures are incorporated into its design. The bottom and sides of landfills are lined with layers of clay or plastic to keep the liquid waste, known as leachate, from escaping into the soil. The leachate is collected and pumped to the surface for treatment. Boreholes or monitoring wells are dug in the vicinity of the landfill to monitor groundwater quality. A landfill is divided into a series of individual cells and only a few cells of the site are filled with trash at any one time. This minimizes exposure to wind and rain. The daily waste is spread and compacted to reduce the volume, a cover is then applied to reduce odours and keep out pests. When the landfill has reached its capacity it is capped with an impermeable seal which is typically composed of clay soil.

Some sanitary landfills are used to recover energy. The natural anaerobic decomposition of the waste in the landfill produces landfill gases which include carbon dioxide, methane and traces of other gases. Methane can be used as an energy source to produce heat or electricity. Thus some landfills are fitted with landfill gas collection (LFG) systems to capitalise on the methane being produced. The process of generating gas is very slow, for the energy recovery system to be successful there needs to be large volumes of wastes.These landfills present the least environmental and health risk , however, the cost of establishing these sanitary landfills are high when compared to the other land disposal methods of solid waste .

A sanitary landfill is essentially an engineered waste disposal option, where the environmental risk is controlled at an appropriate and acceptable level. But, if it is not properly managed, it can cause the following problems:

(i) Noise pollution due to vehicles such as earthmovers, compactors, etc.,

(ii) Scavenger birds, vermins, insects, etc., are attracted to the landfill for breeding and they constitute potential health problems,

(iii) Leachates, if not treated or controlled, may pollute groundwater and surface water and

(iv) Gas released, due to degradation or volatilisation of waste components, causes problems such as odour, flammability and damage to health and the environment.

Uncontrolled disposal is a non-engineered waste disposal method in which wastes are dumped at a designated point without any environmental control, and it (i) causes odour problems due to the putrification of biodegradable wastes, (ii) provides a breeding place for disease vectors such as flies, mosquitoes, etc, and (iii) causes visual pollution, etc.

When properly managed, a landfill is a better and safer option of disposing wastes than uncontrolled dumping. Also, it is adaptable to all kinds of wastes and there is potential for by-product recovery.

Controlled dumps: Controlled dumps are disposal sites which comply with most of the requirements for a sanitary landfill but usually have one deficiency. They may have a planned capacity but no cell planning, there may be partial leachate management, partial or no gas management, regular cover, compaction in some cases, basic record keeping and they are fenced or enclosed. These dumps have a reduced risk of environmental contamination, the initial costs are low and the operational costs are moderate. While there is controlled access and use, they are still accessible by scavengers and so there is some recovery of materials through this practice.

Bioreactor Landfills: Recent technological advances have lead to the introduction of the Bioreactor Landfill which use enhanced microbiological processes to accelerate the decomposition of waste. The main controlling factor is the constant addition of liquid to maintain optimum moisture for microbial digestion. This liquid is usually added by re-circulating the landfill leachate. In cases where leachate in not enough, water or other liquid waste such as sewage sludge can be used. The landfill may use either anaerobic or aerobic microbial digestion or it may be designed to combine the two. These enhanced microbial processes have the advantage of rapidly reducing the volume of the waste creating more space for additional waste, they also maximise the production & capture of methane for energy recovery systems and they reduce the costs associated with leachate management. For Bioreactor landfills to be successful the waste should be comprised predominantly of organic matter and should be produced in large volumes.

Landfill is a complex reactor where physical, chemical and biological processes transform polluting wastes into environmentally acceptable deposits. Due to the complexity of these processes and their potential environmental effects, monitoring is needed to confirm that the landfill works as expected. Knowledge of the chemical composition of leachate & gas is required, as leachates may contain toxic substances and, if not prevented, may contaminate the groundwater. Landfill gases that may be flammable, asphyxiating and noxious, pose a health hazard. A continued groundwater-monitoring programme is essential for confirming the integrity of the liner system.

Main features of a modern landfill is shown below in figure.

47. How can we control landfill gases and leachate?

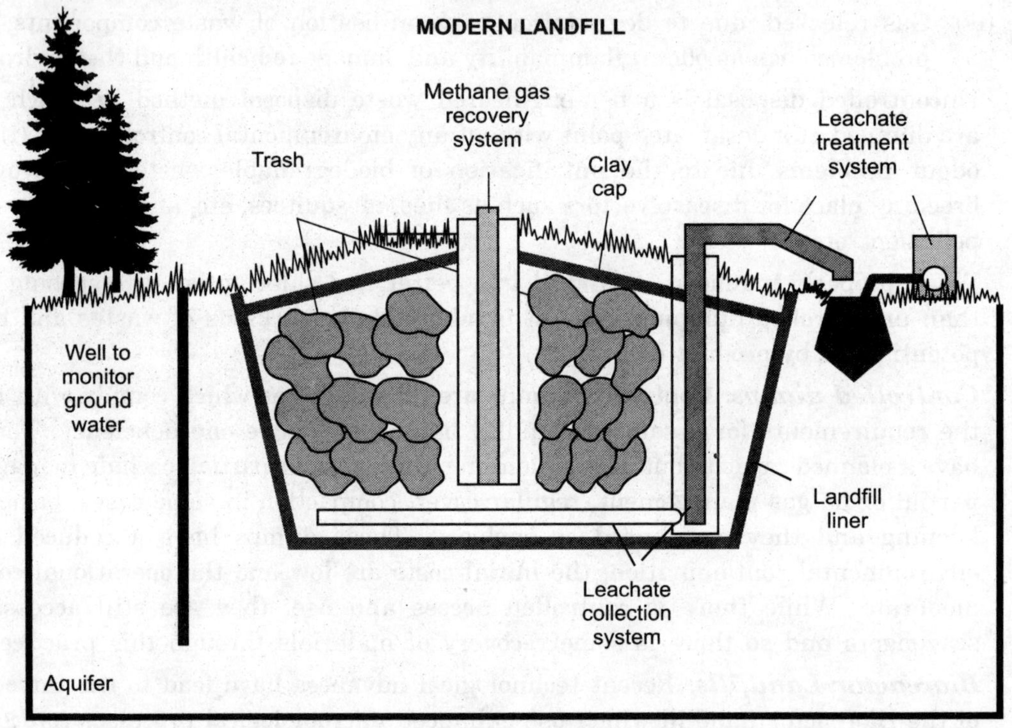

Ans. Landfill gases: Landfill gases include methane, carbon dioxide, oxygen & nitrogen, and these adversely impact on public health & the environment. Methane is flammable in air and can lead to unpredictable & uncontrolled subsidence and production of smoke & toxic fumes. Trace components such as aldehydes, alcohol & esters are toxicants when present in air at concentrations above occupational exposure standards. The landfill gases lead to global warming as these absorb reflected solar radiations.

It is vital that these emissions are controlled, and we can achieve this by controlling:

- Waste inputs (*i.e.*, restrict the amount of organic wastes);
- Processes within the waste (*i.e.*, minimise the moisture content to limit gas production);

- The migration process (*i.e.*, put physical barriers or vents to remove the gas from the site and reduce gas pressure).

Since gas emissions cannot be easily prevented, removal by vents within the waste or stonewalled vents is the preferred option.

Landfill Leachate: The best way to control leachate is through prevention, which can be done with natural liners and synthetic liners. Natural liners, such as compacted clay or shale, bitumen or soil sediments, are less permeable, resistant to chemical attack and have good sorption properties. Synthetic (geo-membranes) liners such as high density or medium density polyethylene, are less permeable, easy to install and relatively strong & have good deformation characteristics.

Natural and synthetic liners can be combined to improve the efficiency of the containment system. The various treatments used to treat leachates are leachate recirculation, biological treatment (*e.g.*, aerated lagoons, activated sludge process, rotating biological contactors, anaerobic treatments that include anaerobic filters, anaerobic lagoons and digesters) and physico-chemical treatment (*e.g.*, flocculation-precipitation process).

48. Describe the factors affecting the production of leachate and landfill gas.

Ans. The factors, which affect the production of leachate and landfill gas, are the following:

Nature of solid waste: The decomposition of waste containing biodegradable matter leads to the production of gas & leachate, and the amount depends on the content of biodegradable material in the waste.

Moisture content: Most micro-organisms require a minimum of approximately 12% (by weight) moisture for growth, and thus the moisture content of landfill waste is an important factor in determining the amount and extent of leachate & gas production.

pH: The methanogenic bacteria within a landfill produce methane gas, which will grow only at low pH range around neutrality.

Particle size and density: The size of waste particle affects the density that can be achieved upon compaction and affects the surface area & hence volume. Both affect moisture absorption and therefore are potential for biological degradation.

Temperature: An increase in temperature tends to increase gas production. The temperature affects the microbial activity to the extent that it is possible to segregate bacteria, according to their optimum temperature operating conditions.

The composition of waste, which varies with region and climate (season), determines the variation in pollution potential. Carbohydrates comprise a large percentage of biodegradable matter within municipal waste, the overall breakdown of which can be represented by the following equation:

$$\underset{\text{(Carbohydrate)}}{C_6H_{12}O_6} \xrightarrow{\text{Bacteria}} CH_4 + CO_2 + \text{Biomass} + \text{Heat}$$

49. Describe the composition & properties, hazards, migration and control of landfill gases.

Ans. Landfill gas contains a high percentage of methane due to the anaerobic decomposition of organic matter, which can be utilised as a source of energy. Composition & properties, hazards, migration and control of landfill gases is described below:

Composition and properties.

The amount & composition of the landfill gas generated for different substrates can be predicted, depending on the general anaerobic decomposition of solid wastes added. Climatic and environmental conditions also influence gas composition. Due to the heterogeneous nature of the landfill, some acid-phase anaerobic decomposition occurs along with the methanogenic decomposition. Since aerobic and acid-phase degradation give rise to carbon dioxide and not methane, there may be a higher carbon dioxide content in the gas generated than what would otherwise be expected. Depending on the moisture distribution, some carbon dioxide goes into solution. This may appear to increase (artificially) the methane content of the gas measured in the landfill. A typical landfill gas contains a number of components such as the following, which tend to occur within a characteristic range:

Methane: This is a colourless, odourless and flammable gas with a density lighter than air, typically making up 50-60% of the landfill gas.

Carbon dioxide: This is a colourless, odourless and non-inflammable gas that is denser than air, typically accounting for 30-40%.

Oxygen: The flammability of methane depends on the percentage of oxygen. It is, therefore, important to control oxygen levels, where gas extraction is undertaken.

Nitrogen: This is inert and will have little effect, except to modify the explosive range of methane.

It is difficult to convert the amount of gas measured to the maximum landfill gas production value because gas is withdrawn from a small part of the landfill only, referred to as zone of influence during measurement. In other words, it is very difficult to determine this zone and relate it to the whole landfill area.

Hazards of landfill gases.

Landfill gas consists of a mixture of flammable, asphyxiating & noxious gases and may be hazardous to health & safety, and hence the need for precautions. Some of the major hazards are listed below:

Explosion and fire hazards: Methane is flammable in air within the range of 5-15% by volume, while hydrogen is flammable within the range of 4.1-7.5% (in the presence of oxygen) and potentially explosive. Fire, occurring within the waste, can be difficult to extinguish and can lead to unpredictable and uncontrolled subsidence as well as production of smoke & toxic fumes.

Trace components: These comprise mostly alkanes & alkenes, and their oxidation products such as aldehydes, alcohols & esters. Many of them are toxicants, when present in air at concentrations above occupational exposure standards.

Global warming: Known also as greenhouse effect, it is the warming of the earth's atmosphere by the accumulation of gases (methane, carbon dioxide and chlorofluorocarbons) that absorbs reflected solar radiation.

Migration of landfill gases.

During landfill development, most of the gas produced is vented to the atmosphere, provided the permeable intermediate cover has been used. While biological and chemical processes affect gas composition through methane oxidation, which converts methane to carbon dioxide, physical factors affect gas migration. The physical factors that affect gas migration include:

Environmental conditions: These affect the rate of degradation and gas pressure build up.

Geophysical conditions: These affect migration pathways. In the presence of fractured geological strata or a mineshaft, the gas may travel large distances, unless restricted by the water table.

Climatic conditions: Falling atmospheric pressure, rainfall and water infiltration rate affect landfill gas migration.

The proportion of void space in the ground, rather than permeability, determines the variability of gas emission. If the escape of landfill gas is controlled and proper extraction system is designed, this gas can be utilised as a source of energy. If landfill gas is not utilised, it should be burnt by means of flaring. However, landfill gas utilisation can save on the use of fossil fuels since its heating value is approximately 6 kWh/m^3 and can be utilised in internal combustion engines for production of electricity and heat. Landfill gas is extracted out of the landfill by means of gas wells, which are normally drilled by auger and are driven into the landfill at a spacing of 40-70 m. In addition, horizontal systems can be installed during operation of the landfill. The gas wells consist mainly of perforated plastic pipes surrounded by coarse gravel and are connected with the gas transportation pipe with flexible tubing. The vacuum necessary for gas extraction and transportation is created by means of a blower. The most important factors influencing planning and construction of landfill gas extraction systems are settling of waste, water tables in landfills and gas quality.

Control of landfill gas emission.

To control gas emission, it is necessary to control the following:

- Waste inputs (*i.e.*, restrict the amount of organic waste).
- Processes within the waste (*i.e.*, minimise moisture content to limit gas production).
- Migration process (*i.e.*, provide physical barriers or vents to remove the gas from the site and reduce gas pressure).
- Since gas migration cannot be easily prevented, removal is often the preferred option. This is done by using vents (extraction wells) within the waste or stone filled vents, which are placed around the periphery of the landfill site. Some of the gas collection systems include impermeable cap, granular material, collection pipes and treatment systems.

50. Describe the composition & properties, migration, control and treatment of leachate produced in landfill.

Ans. Leachate liquid produced in landfill can pollute both groundwater & surface water supplies. The degree of pollution will depend on local geology & hydrogeology, nature of waste and the proximity of susceptible receptors. Once groundwater is contaminated, it is very costly to clean it up. Landfills, therefore, undergo siting, design and construction procedures that control leachate migration.

Composition and properties.

Leachate comprises soluble components of waste and its degradation products enter water, as it percolates through the landfill. The amount of leachate generated depends on:

- Water availability;
- Landfill surface condition;
- Refuse state;
- Condition of surrounding strata.

The major factor, *i.e.,* water availability, is affected by precipitation, surface runoff, waste decomposition and liquid waste disposal.

Common toxic components in leachate are ammonia and heavy metals, which can be hazardous even at low levels, if they accumulate in the food chain. The presence of ammoniacal nitrogen means that leachate often has to be treated off-site before being discharged to a sewer, since there is no natural bio-chemical path for its removal. Leachate composition varies with time and location. Table below shows a typical leachate properties and composition at various stages of waste decomposition:

Properties and Composition of Leachate at Various Stages of Decomposition (mg/L except pH) Components	Fresh wastes	Aged wastes	Wastes with high moisture
pH	6.2	7.5	8.0
COD	23800	1160	1500
BOD	11900	260	500
TOC	8000	465	450
Volatile acid (as C)	5688	5	12
NH3-N	790	370	1000
NO3-N	3	1	1.0
Ortho-P	0.73	1.4	1.0
Cl	1315	2080	1390
Na	9601	300	1900

Mg	252	185	186
K	780	590	570
Ca	1820	250	158
Mn	27	2.1	0.05
Fe	540	23	2.0
Cu	0.12	0.03	-
Zn	21.5	0.4	0.5
Pb	0.40	0.14	-

Leachate migration.

It is difficult to predict the movement of escaped leachate accurately. The main controlling factors are the surrounding geology and hydrogeology. Escape to surface water may be relatively easy to control, but if it escapes to groundwater sources, it can be very difficult both to control and clean up. The degree of ground water contamination is affected by physical, chemical and biological actions. The relative importance of each process may change, however, if the leachate moves from the landfill to the sub-surface region.

Leachate Control.

The best way to control leachate is through prevention, which should be integral to the landfill site design. In most cases, it is necessary to control liquid access, collection and treatment, all of which can be done using the following landfill liners:

Natural liners: These refer to compacted clay or shale, bitumen or soil sealants, etc., and are generally less permeable, resistant to chemical attack & have good sorption properties. They generally do not act as true containment barriers, because sometimes leachate migrates through them.

Synthetic (geo-membrane) liners: These are typically made up of high or medium density polyethylene and are generally less permeable, easy to install,relatively strong & have good deformation characteristics. They sometimes expand or shrink according to temperature and age.

Natural and geo-membrane liners are often combined to enhance the overall efficiency of the leachate containment system. Some of the leachate collection systems include impermeable liner, granular material, collection piping, leachate storage tank; leachate is trucked to a wastewater treatment facility.

Leachate Treatment.

Concentrations of various substances occurring in leachate are too high to be discharged to surface water or into a sewer system. These concentrations, therefore, have to be reduced by removal, treatment or both. The various treatments of leachate include:

Leachate recirculation: It is one of the simplest forms of treatment. Recirculation of leachate reduces the hazardous nature of leachate and helps wet the waste, increasing its potential for biological degradation.

Biological treatment: This removes BOD, ammonia and suspended solids. Leachate from landfilled waste can be readily degraded by biological means, due to high content of volatile fatty acids (VFAs). The common methods are aerated lagoons (*i.e.*, special devices which enhance the aerobic processes of degradation of organic substances over the entire depth of the tank) and activated sludge process, which differs from aerated lagoons in that discharged sludge is recirculated and is often used for BOD and ammonia removal. While under conditions of low COD, rotating biological contactors (*i.e.*, biomass is brought into contact with circular blades fixed to a common axle which is rotated) are very effective in removing ammonia. In an anaerobic treatment system, complex organic molecules are fermented in filter. The common types are anaerobic filters, anaerobic lagoon and digesters.

Physicochemical treatment: After biological degradation, effluents still contain significant concentrations of different substances. Physico chemical treatment processes could be installed to improve the leachate effluent quality. Some of these processes are flocculation-precipitation. (Note that addition of chemicals to the water attracts the metal by floc formation). Separation of the floc from water takes place by sedimentation, adsorption and reverse osmosis.

51. Describe the environmental effects of landfill operations.

Ans. The environmental effects of a landfill operation include wind-blown litter & dust, noise, obnoxious odour, vermin & insects attracted by the waste, surface runoff and inaesthetic conditions. Gas& leachate problems also arise during the operation phase and require significant environmental controls.

The major environmental effects of landfill operations are described below:

(i) Wind-blown litter and dust are continuous problems of the ongoing landfill operation and a nuisance to the neighbourhood. Covering the waste cells with soil and spraying water on dirty roads and waste in dry periods, in combination with fencing and movable screens, may minimise the problem of wind-blown litter and dust. However, the problem will remain at the tipping front of the landfill.

(ii) Movement of waste collection vehicles, emptying of wastes from them, compactors, earthmoving equipment, etc., produce noise. Improving the technical capability of the equipment, surrounding the fill area with soil embankments & plantations, limiting the working hours and appropriately training the workforce will help minimise noise pollution.

(iii) Birds (*e.g.*, scavengers), vermin, insects and animals are attracted to the landfill for feeding and breeding. Since many of these may act as disease vectors, their presence is a potential health problem.

(iv) Surface run-off, which has been in contact with the land filled waste, may be a problem in areas of intense rainfall. If not controlled, heavily polluted run-off may enter directly into creeks and streams. Careful design and maintenance of surface drains and ditches, together with a final soil cover on completed landfill sections, can help eliminate this problem.

(v) An operating landfill, where equipment and waste are exposed, appears inaesthetic. This problem may be reduced by careful design of screening soil embankments, plantings, rapid covering and re-vegetation of filled sections.

(vi) Gas released, as a result of degradation or volatilisation of waste components, causes odour, flammability, health problems and damage of the vegetation (due to oxygen depletion in the root zone). The measures to control this include liners, soil covers, passive venting or active extraction of gas for treatment before discharge into the atmosphere.

(vii) Polluted leachate appears shortly after disposal of the waste. This may cause groundwater pollution and pollution of streams through sub-surface migration. Liners, drainage collection, treatment of leachate, and groundwater & downstream water quality monitoring are necessary to control this problem.

Besides the emissions, incidental events such as flooding, fires, landslides and earthquakes result in severe environmental impacts, and may require preventive measures with respect to landfill site selection, design and operation. In the main, to minimise adverse environmental impacts due to sanitary landfill, proper attention must be paid to the environmental aspects at all stages and phases of landfill management, viz., site selection, design, construction, operation and maintenance.

Regulations for Landfills: Regulations include restrictions on distances from airports, flood plains, and fault areas, as well as limitations on construction in wetlands and others. Prevention of contamination of groundwater and land resources requires synthetic liner and adequate buffer with the restricted activities around the landfill.

52. Describe the criteria for landfill as notified by Ministry of Environment and Forest (MOEF) Government of India.

Ans. For the identification of landfill site the following criteria as suggested by MOEF should be followed:

- The landfill site shall be large enough to last for 20-25 years and preferably within 5 km from present city limits.
- The site shall be at least 500 mt. away from habitation clusters, forest areas, monuments, National Parks, Wetlands and places of important cultural, historical or religious interest.
- No landfill should be constructed within 200 mt of any lake or pond.
- No landfill should be constructed within 100 mt. of a navigable river.
- No landfill should be constructed within 200 mt. of the right of way of any state or national highway.
- A site should be at least 500mt. away from a notified habitated area.
- A buffer zone of 500 mt. around a landfill boundary should be declared as a No development zone after the landfill location is finalized.
- No landfill site should be constructed within critical habitat areas.
- A landfill should not be constructed in areas where water table is less than 2 mt. below ground surface.

- No landfill should be constructed within 500 mt. of any water supply.
- Topographical and geographical features (contour, slope, soil type) of the site should be carefully analyzed in order to prevent soil contamination and disturbance of drainage pattern.
- Transportation and linkages will be clearly defined for waste movement from the city. The influence of increased heavy vehicle traffic due to land filling should be taken care in order to avoid nuisance.

53. Describe in detail the features of Biological waste treatment of solid wastes.

Ans. Features of biological waste treatment methods like composting and anaerobic digestion are described below.

Composting: Composting is the controlled aerobic decomposition of organic matter by the action of micro organisms and small invertebrates. A number of composting techniques being used today include: in vessel composting, windrow composting, vermicomposting and static pile composting. The process is controlled by making the environmental conditions optimum for the waste decomposers to thrive. The rate of compost formation is controlled by the composition and constituents of the materials *i.e.* their Carbon/Nitrogen (C/N) ratio, the temperature, the moisture content and the amount of air.

The C/N ratio is very important for the process to be efficient. The micro organisms require carbon as an energy source and nitrogen for the synthesis of some proteins. If the correct C/N ration is not achieved, then application of the compost with either a high or low C/N ratio can have adverse effects on both the soil and the plants. A high C/N ratio can be corrected by dehydrated mud and a low ratio is corrected by adding cellulose.

Moisture content greatly influences the composting process. The microbes need the moisture to perform their metabolic functions. If the waste becomes too dry the composting is not favoured. If however there is too much moisture then it is possible that it may displace the air in the compost heap depriving the organisms of oxygen and drowning them.

A high temperature is desirable for the elimination of pathogenic organisms. However, if temperatures are too high, above 75°C then the organisms necessary to complete the composting process are destroyed. Optimum temperatures for the process are in the range of 50-60°C.

Aeration is a very important and the quantity of air needs to be properly controlled when composting. If there is insufficient oxygen the aerobes will begin to die and will be replaced by anaerobes. The anaerobes are undesirable since they will slow the process, produce odours and also produce the highly flammable methane gas. Air can be incorporated by churning the compost.

Although compost has been used for a variety of purposes, contaminants in the compost could be detrimental to the environment & public health as they affect the water (*i.e.*, eutrophication and leaching to surface & groundwater), the land (*i.e.*, acidic soil, nitrogen depletion in soil, impacts of acids, organic & metal contamination), the air (*i.e.*, odour) and health (*i.e.*, drinking of contaminated water, toxins in the finished product and pathogens).

Anaerobic Digestion: Anaerobic digestion like composting uses biological processes to decompose organic waste. However, where composting can use a variety of microbes and must have air; anaerobic digestion uses bacteria and an oxygen free environment to decompose the waste. Aerobic respiration, typical of composting, results in the formation of carbon dioxide and water. While the anaerobic respiration results in the formation of carbon dioxide and methane. In addition to generating the humus which is used as a soil enhancer, anaerobic digestion is also used as a method of producing biogas which can be used to generate electricity. Optimal conditions for the process require nutrients such as nitrogen, phosphorous and potassium, it requires that the pH be maintained around 7 and the alkalinity be appropriate to buffer pH changes, temperature should also be controlled.

54. Briefly describe the mechanism of composting.

Ans. Biodegradation is a natural, ongoing biological process that is a common occurrence in both human-made & natural environments. Any organic material that can be biologically decomposed is compostable. Human beings have used this naturally occurring process for centuries to stabilise and recycle agricultural & human wastes. Today, however, composting is a diverse practice that includes a variety of approaches, depending on the type of organic materials being composted & the desired properties of the final product.

To derive the maximum benefit from the natural, slow decomposition process (*e.g.*, grass clippings left in the lawn or food scraps rotting in dustbins, etc.), it is necessary to control the environmental conditions during the composting process.

The overall composting process is as follows:

Organic matter + O_2 + aerobic bacteria $\longrightarrow$ CO_2 + NH_3 + H_2O + other end products + energy

Compost is the end product of the composting process. The by-products of this process are carbon dioxide & water. Compost is peaty humus, dark in colour & has a crumbly texture, an earthy odour, and resembles rich top soil. Composts will not have any resemblance in the physical form to the original waste from which it was derived. High-quality compost is devoid of weed seeds and organisms that may be pathogenic to humans, animals, or plants. Cured compost is also relatively stable and resistant to further decomposition by microorganisms.

The composting process is an environmentally sound and beneficial means of recycling organic materials and not a means of waste disposal. And, it is important to view compostable materials as usable and not as waste requiring disposal.

A complete composting process is shown below in figure.

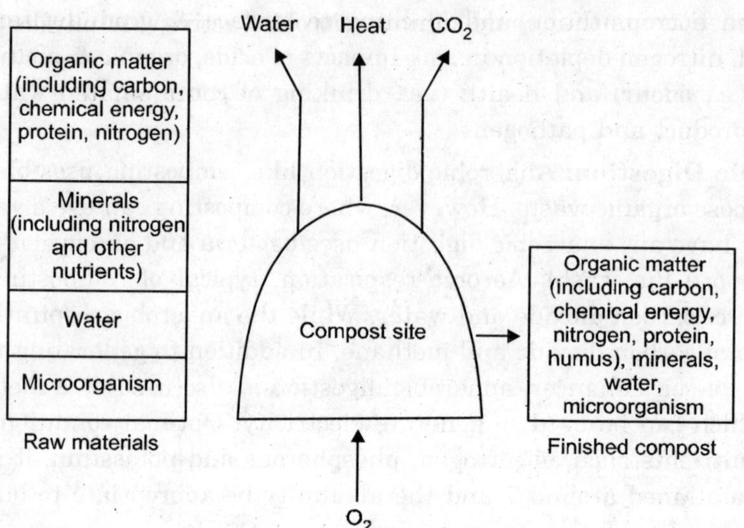

55. Describe the five basic stages involved in composting and three processes of composting.

Ans. There are five basic stages involved in all composting practices, namely, **preparation, digestion, curing, screening & finishing and storage or disposal.** Preparation consists of sorting the recyclables, removal of non-combustibles, shredding, pulping, grinding and the addition of water sludge. There are five techniques of digestion, viz., windrow, aerated, static pile, in-vessel composting & anaerobic processing. These techniques vary in the method of air supply, temperature control, mixing/turning of the material, time required for composting and capital & operating costs. The amount of curing necessary at the initial stabilisation depends on the proposed use of the composted material. If the compost is to be pelletised and/or bagged, it must be completely stable before being finished. The amount of finishing required is also dependent on the final marketing of the compost. Regrinding and rescreening is done, so as to make the compost uniform in size. The efficiency of the composting process, *i.e.*, the success or failure of the operation, depends on the method of disposal. Even where a good compost market exists, provisions must still be made for storage because the use of composting is seasonal.

There are three processes of composting, viz., biological, chemical and physical. In biological processes, microorganisms such as bacteria, fungi and actinomycetes break down the organic matter present in the waste. As microorganisms begin to decompose the organic material, the carbon in it is converted to by-products like carbon dioxide & water and a humic end product called compost. Inoculum is added in case of a lack of microbial organisms. If all conditions are ideal for a given microbial population to perform at its maximum potential, composting will occur rapidly. The chemical environment is largely determined by the composition of material to be composted. Several factors determine the chemical environment for composting: carbon energy source, the correct amount of water, adequate oxygen, appropriate pH and the absence of toxic constituents that could inhibit microbial activity. A physical environment is essential for the composting process to proceed efficiently. This includes factors such as temperature, particle size, mixing and pile size. Smaller particle size is preferred, as it has more surface area per unit weight, and therefore, facilitates more microbial activity, which leads to rapid decomposition. The optimum temperature range is between 32 and 60°C. Temperature above 60°C is not ideal for composting. Mixing is done to distribute moisture & air evenly and promote the breakdown of compost clumps.

56. What is anaerobic composting?

Ans. In the anaerobic composting process, facultative bacteria break down the organic materials in the absence of oxygen and produce methane & carbon dioxide. Single-stage digesters contain the entire process in one airtight container. The feedstock is first shredded, and before being placed in the container, water & possible nutrients are added to the previously shredded material. The single-stage digester may contain agitation equipment, which continuously stirs the liquefied material. As digestion progresses, a mixture of methane and carbon dioxide is produced. These gases are continuously removed from both first and second-stage digesters and are either combusted on site or directed to off site gas consumers. A stabilised residue remains, when the digestion process is completed, which can be removed either by mechanical equipment or pumped out as a liquid. The digested residue may require further curing by windrow or static pile composting.

57. Describe the effects of various factors affecting the biological, processes occurring in composting.

Ans. Several factors contribute to the success of composting including physical, chemical, and biological processes.

Biological processes.

Microorganisms such as bacteria, fungi and actinomycetes as well as larger organisms such as insects & earthworms play an active role in decomposing the organic materials. As microorganisms begin to decompose the organic material, they break down organic matter and produce carbon dioxide, water, heat and humus (the relatively stable organic end product). This humus end product is called compost.

Microorganisms consume some of the carbon to form new microbial cells, as they increase their population. They have, preferences on the type of organic material they consume. When the organic molecules they require are not available, they may become dormant or die. The chain of succession of different types of microbes continues, until there is little decomposable organic material left. At this point, the organic material that is remaining is termed compost. It is largely made up of microbial cells, microbial skeletons and by-products of microbial decomposition, and undecomposed particles of organic & inorganic origin. Decomposition may proceed slowly at first because of smaller microbial populations, but as populations grow in the first few hours or days, they rapidly consume the organic materials present in the feedstock. The number and kind of microorganisms are generally not a limiting environmental factor in composting non-toxic agricultural materials, yard trimmings, or municipal solid wastes, all of which usually contain an adequate diversity of microorganisms.

Under optimal conditions, composting proceeds through the following four phases:

(i) **Mesophilic, or moderate-temperature phase:** Compost bacteria combine carbon with oxygen to produce carbon dioxide and energy. The microorganisms for reproduction & growth use some of the energy and the rest is generated as heat. When a pile of organic refuse begins to undergo the composting process, mesophilic bacteria proliferate, raising the temperature of the composting mass up to 44°C. This is the first stage of the composting process. These mesophilic bacteria can include *E. coli* and other bacteria from the human intestinal tract, but these soon become increasingly inhibited by the temperature, as the thermophilic bacteria take over in the transition range of 44 to 52°C.

(ii) **Thermophilic, or high-temperature phase:** In the second stage of the process, the thermophilic microorganisms are very active and produce heat. This stage can continue up to about 70°C, although such high temperatures are neither common nor desirable in compost. This heating stage takes place rather quickly and may last only a few days, weeks, or months. It tends to remain localised in the upper portion of a compost pile where the fresh material is being added, whereas in batch compost, the entire composting mass may be thermophilic all at once. After the thermophilic heating period, the manure will appear to have been digested, but the coarser organic material will not be digested. This is when the third stage of composting, *i.e.*, the cooling phase, takes place.

(iii) **Cooling phase:** During this phase, the microorganisms that were replaced by the thermophiles migrate back into the compost and digest the more resistant organic materials. Fungi and macroorganisms such as earthworms & sow bugs that break the coarser elements down into humus also move back in.

(iv) **Maturation or curing phase:** The final stage of the composting process is called curing, ageing, or maturing stage, and is a long and important one. A long curing period (*e.g.*, a year after the thermophilic stage) adds a safety net for pathogen destruction. Many pathogens have a limited period of viability in the soil, and the longer they are subjected to the microbiological competition of the compost pile the more likely they will die a swift death. Immature compost can be harmful to plants. Uncured compost can, for example, produce phytotoxins (*i.e.*, substances toxic to plants), robbing the soil of oxygen & nitrogen and contain high levels of organic acids.

Different communities of microorganisms predominate during the various composting phases. Initial decomposition is carried out by mesophilic microorganisms, which rapidly break down the soluble, readily degradable compounds. The heat they produce causes the compost temperature to rise rapidly. As the temperature rises above 40°C, the mesophilic microorganisms become less competitive and are replaced by thermophilic (heat loving) ones. At temperatures of 55°C and above, many microorganisms that are pathogenic to humans or plants are destroyed. Temperatures above 65°C kill many forms of microbes and limit the rate of decomposition. Composters use aeration and mixing to keep the temperature below this point. During the thermophilic phase, high temperatures accelerate the breakdown of proteins, fats, and complex carbohydrates like cellulose & hemicellulose, the major structural molecules in plants. As the supply of these high-energy compounds become exhausted, compost temperature gradually decreases and mesophilic microorganisms once again take over the final phase of curing or maturation of the remaining organic matter.

The composting process, therefore, should cater to the needs of the microorganisms and promote conditions that will lead to rapid stabilisation of the organic materials. While several microorganisms are beneficial to the composting process and may be present in the final product, some microbes are potential pathogens (disease causing) to animals, plants & humans. These pathogenic organisms must be destroyed in the composting process before the compost is distributed in the market place. Most of this destruction takes place by controlling the temperature of composting operations.

58. Describe the factors affecting the chemical processes occurring during composting.

Ans. Factors that determine the chemical environment for composting include the presence of an adequate carbon food/energy source, a balanced amount of nutrients, the correct amount of water, adequate oxygen, appropriate pH and the absence of toxic constituents that could inhibit microbial activity The effects of each of these factors is discussed below:

(i) **Carbon food /energy source:** For their carbon/energy source, microorganisms in the composting process rely on carbon in the organic material, unlike higher plants that rely on carbon dioxide and sunlight. The carbon contained in natural or human-based organic materials may or may not be biodegradable. The relative ease with which a material is biodegraded depends on the genetic makeup of the microorganisms present and the organic molecules that the organism decomposes. Since most municipal & agricultural organics and yard trimmings contain an adequate amount of biodegradable forms of carbon, it is not a limiting factor in the composting process. As more easily degradable forms of carbon are decomposed, a small portion of the carbon is converted into microbial cells, and a significant portion is converted to carbon dioxide and lost to the atmosphere. As the composting process progresses, the loss of carbon results in a decrease in weight & volume of the feedstock. The less easily decomposed forms of carbon will form the matrix for the physical structure of the final product.

(ii) **Nutrients:** Among the plant nutrients (*i.e.*, nitrogen, phosphorus, and potassium), nitrogen is of greatest concern, because it is lacking in some plant materials. The carbon-nitrogen ratio, which is established on the basis of available carbon rather than total carbon, is considered critical in determining the rate of decomposition. Leaves, for example, are a good source for carbon, and fresh grass, manure &

slaughterhouse waste are the sources for nitrogen. To aid the decomposition process, the bulk of the organic matter should be carbon with just enough nitrogen. In general, an initial ratio of 30:1 (Carbon: Nitrogen) is considered ideal. Higher ratios tend to retard the process of decomposition, while ratios below 25:1 may result in odour problems. As the composting process proceeds and carbon is lost to the atmosphere, this ratio decreases.

Finished compost should have ratios of 15 to 20:1. Adding 3- 4 kg of nitrogen material for every 100 kg of carbon should be satisfactory for efficient and rapid composting. To lower the carbon to nitrogen ratios, nitrogen-rich materials such as yard trimmings, animal manures, or bio-solids are added. Adding partially decomposed or composted materials (with a lower carbon: nitrogen ratio) as inoculums may also lower the ratio. As the temperature in the compost pile rises and carbon: nitrogen ratio falls below 25:1, the nitrogen in the fertiliser is lost as gas (ammonia) to the atmosphere. The composting process slows, if there is not enough nitrogen, and too much nitrogen may cause the generation of ammonia gas, which can create unpleasant odours.

(iii) **Moisture:** Water is an essential part of all forms of life, and the microorganisms living in a compost pile are no exception. Since most compostable materials have lower than ideal water content, *i.e.*, 50 to 60% of total weight, the composting process may be slower than desired, if water is not added. However, it should not be high enough to create excessive free flow of water and movement caused by gravity. Excessive moisture and flowing water form leachate, creates potential liquid management problems including water & air pollution (*e.g.*, odour). For example, excess moisture impedes oxygen transfer to the microbial cells, can increase the possibility of developing anaerobic conditions and may lead to rotting & obnoxious odours. Microbial processes contribute moisture to the compost pile during decomposition. Although moisture is added, it is also being lost through evaporation. Since the amount of water evaporated usually exceeds the input of moisture from the decomposition processes, there is generally a net loss of moisture from the compost pile. In such cases, adding moisture may be necessary to keep the composting process performing at its peak.

Controlling the size of piles can minimise evaporation from compost piles, as piles with larger volumes have less evaporating surface/unit volume than smaller piles. The water added must be thoroughly mixed so that the organic fraction in the bulk of the material is uniformly wetted and composted under ideal conditions. Properly wetted compost has the consistency of a wet sponge.

(iv) **Oxygen:** Composting is considered an aerobic process. Decomposition can occur under both aerobic (requiring oxygen) and anaerobic (lacking oxygen) conditions. The compost pile should have enough void space to allow free air movement so that oxygen from the atmosphere can enter the pile and the carbon dioxide and other gases emitted can be exhausted to the atmosphere. To maintain aerobic conditions, in which decomposition occurs at a fast rate, the compost pile is mechanically aerated or turned frequently to expose the microbes to the atmosphere and to create more air spaces by fluffing up the pile. A 10 to 15% oxygen concentration is considered adequate, although a concentration as low as 5% may be sufficient for leaves. While higher concentrations of oxygen will not negatively affect the composting process, circulation of an excessive amount of air can cause problems. For example, excess air removes heat, which cools the pile and also promotes excess evaporation. In other words, excess air slows down the rate of composting. Excess aeration is also an added expense that increases production costs.

(v) **pH:** The pH factor affects the amount of nutrients available for the microorganisms, the solubility of heavy metals and the overall metabolic activity of the microorganisms. A pH between 6 and 8 is optimum, and it can be adjusted upward by the addition of lime, or downward with sulphur, although such additions are normally not necessary. The composting process produces carbon dioxide, which, when combined with water, produces carbonic acid, which could lower the pH of the compost. As the composting process progresses, the final pH varies, depending on the specific type of feedstock used and operating conditions. Wide swings in pH are unusual, since organic materials are naturally well buffered with respect to pH changes. Down swings in pH during composting usually do not occur. The composition of material to be composted largely determines the chemical environment. In addition, several modifications can be made during the composting process to create an ideal chemical environment for the rapid decomposition of organic materials .

59. Describe the factors affecting the physical processes occurring during composting.

Ans. The physical environment in the composting process is affected by factors such as temperature, particle size, mixing and pile size. Each of these is essential for the composting process to proceed in an efficient manner. Their effects are described below:

(i) **Particle size:** As composting progresses, there is a natural process of size reduction and the particle size of the material being composted is critical. Because smaller particles usually have more surface area per unit weight, they facilitate more microbial activity on their surfaces, which leads to rapid decomposition. The optimum particle size has enough surface area for rapid microbial activity and also enough void space to allow air to circulate for microbial respiration. The feedstock composition can be manipulated to create the desired mix of particle size and void space. For instance, through particle size reduction, we can increase the desired combination of void space & surface area for garden trimmings or municipal solid wastes. To improve the aesthetic appeal of finished composts, we can carry out particle size reduction, after the composting process is completed.

(ii) **Temperature:** Composting can occur at a range of temperatures, and the optimum temperature range is between 32 and 60° C. Temperatures above 65° C are not ideal for composting as thermal destruction of cell proteins kill the organisms.

Similarly, temperatures below the minimum required for a group of organisms affect the metabolic activity (*i.e.*, regulatory machinery) of the cells. Temperatures can be lowered, if required, by either increasing the frequency of mechanical agitation or using airflow throttling, temperature feedback control or blowers controlled with timers. Mixing or mechanical aeration also provides air for the microbes.

When compost is at a temperature greater than 55° C for at least three days, pathogen destruction occurs. It is important that all portions of the compost material are exposed to such temperatures to ensure pathogen destruction throughout the compost. At these temperatures, weed seeds are also destroyed. After the complete pathogen destruction, temperatures may be lowered and maintained at slightly lower levels (51 to 55° C). Attaining and maintaining 55° C for three days is not difficult for in-vessel composting systems . However, to achieve pathogen destruction with windrow composting systems , 55° C temperature level must be maintained for a minimum of 15 days, during which time the windrows must be turned at least five times. The longer duration and increased turning are necessary to achieve a uniform pathogen destruction in the entire pile. Care should be taken to avoid contact between materials that have achieved these minimum temperatures and materials that have not.

(iii) **Mixing:** Mixing of feedstock, water & inoculants is important and is done by turning or mixing the piles after composting has begun. Mixing & agitation distribute moisture & air evenly, and promote the breakdown of compost clumps. Excessive agitation of open vessels or piles, however, can cool them and retard microbial activity.

60. Describe briefly various composting technologies.

Ans. Various composting technologies namely windrow composting, aerated static pile composting, in-vessel composting and anaerobic processing - vary in the method of air supply, temperature control, mixing/turning of the material, time required for composting, and capital & operating costs. Besides these general categories of composting technologies, there are also some supporting technologies, which include sorting, screening, and curing.

Four general categories of composting technologies are described below:

Windrow composting.

The windrow system is the least expensive and most common approach. Windrows are defined as regularly turned elongated piles, shaped like a haystack in cross section and up to a hundred meters or more in length. The cross-sectional dimensions vary with feedstock and turning equipment, but most municipal solid waste (MSW) windrows are 1.5 to 3 meters high and 3 to 6 meters wide. Windrows composed of MSW are usually required to be located on an impermeable surface, which greatly improves equipment handling under inclement weather conditions. The optimum size & shape of the windrow depends on particle size, moisture content, pore space and decomposition rate - all of which affect the movement of oxygen towards the centre of the pile.

Process control is normally through pile management, although forced aeration can also be used. Turning the pile re-introduces air into the pile and increases porosity so that efficient passive aeration from atmospheric air continues at all times. The windrow dimensions should allow conservation of the heat generated during the composting process and also allow air to diffuse to the deeper portions of the pile.

Windrows must be placed on a firm surface to turn the piles with ease. They may be turned as frequently as once per week, but more frequent turning may be necessary, if high proportions of bio-solids are present in the feedstock. Turning the piles also moves the materials from the pile surface to the core of the windrow, where they can undergo composting. Machines equipped with augers, paddles or tines are used for turning the piles. Some windrow turners can supplement piles with water, if necessary. When piles are turned, heat is released as steam to the atmosphere. If inner portions of the pile have low levels of oxygen, odours may result when this portion of the pile is exposed to the atmosphere. Piles with initial moisture content within the optimum range have a reduced potential for producing leachate. The addition of moisture from precipitation, however, increases this potential. Any leachate or runoff created must be collected and treated or added to a batch of incoming feedstock to increase its moisture content. To avoid problems with leachate or runoff, piles can be placed under a roof, but doing so adds to the initial costs of the operation.

Aerated static pile composting.

Aerated static pile composting technology requires the composting mixture (*i.e.*, a mixture of pre-processed materials and liquids) to be placed in piles that are mechanically aerated. The piles are placed over a network of pipes connected to a blower , which supplies the air for composting. Air can be supplied under positive or negative pressure. That is to say, the air supply blower either forces air into the pile or draws air out of it. Forcing the air into the pile generates a positive pressure system, while drawing air out of the pile creates a negative pressure. When the composting process is nearly complete, the piles are broken up for the first time since their construction. The compost is then taken through a series of post-processing steps. A timer or a temperature feedback system similar to a home thermostat controls the blowers.

Air circulation in the compost piles provides the needed oxygen for the composting microbes and prevents excessive heat build-up in the pile. Removing excess heat and water vapour cools the pile to maintain optimum temperature for microbial activity. A controlled air supply enables construction of large piles, which decreases the need for land. Odours from the exhaust air could be substantial, but traps or filters can be used to control them. The temperatures in the inner portion of a pile are usually adequate to destroy a significant number of the pathogens and weed seeds present. The surface of piles, however, may not reach the desired temperatures for destruction of pathogens because piles are not turned in the aerated static pile technology. This problem can be overcome by placing a layer of finished compost of 15 to 30 cms thick over the compost pile. The outer layer of finished compost acts as an insulating blanket and helps maintain the desired temperature for destruction of pathogens and weed seeds throughout the entire pile.

Aerated static pile composting systems have been used successfully for MSW, yard trimmings, bio-solids and industrial composting. Aerated static pile composting can also be done under a roof or in the open. Producing compost using this technology usually takes about 6 to 12 weeks. The land requirements for this method are lower than that of windrow composting.

In-vessel composting system.

In-vessel composting systems enclose the feedstock in a chamber or vessel that provides adequate mixing, aeration and moisture. Drums, digester bins and tunnels are some of the common in vessel type systems. In vessel systems vary in their requirements for pre-processing materials. For example, some require minimal pre-processing, while others require extensive MSW pre-processing. These vessels can be single or multi compartment units. In some cases, the vessel rotates, and in others, it is stationary and a mixing/agitating mechanism moves the material around. Most in-vessel systems are continuous-feed systems, although some operate in a batch mode. All in-vessel systems require further composting(curing) after the material has been discharged from the vessel.

A major advantage of in-vessel systems is that all environmental conditions can be carefully controlled to allow rapid composting. The material to be composted is frequently turned & mixed to homogenise the compost and promote rapid oxygen transfer. Retention times range from less than one week to as long as four weeks. These systems, if properly operated, produce minimal odours and little or no leachate. In-vessel systems enable exhaust gases from the vessel to be captured and are subjected to odour control & treatment.

Some of the commonly used in-vessel systems are as follows:

Vertical composting reactor: It is generally over 4 meters high and can be housed in silos or other large structures. Organic material, typically fed into the reactor at the top through a distribution mechanism, moves by gravity to an unloading mechanism at the bottom. Process control is usually by pressure-induced aeration, where the airflow is opposite to the downward materials flow. The height of these reactors makes process control difficult due to the high rates of airflow required per unit of distribution surface area. Neither temperature nor oxygen can be maintained at optimal levels throughout the reactors, leading to zones of non-optimal activity. As with static pile composting, a stable porous structure is important in vertical reactors, which usually lack internal mixing. Tall vertical reactors have been used in the sludge composting industry where uniform feedstock and porous amendments can minimise these difficulties in process control, but are rarely used for heterogeneous materials like MSW.

Horizontal composting reactors: These avoid high temperature, oxygen & moisture gradients of vertical reactors by maintaining a short airflow pathway. They come in a wide range of configurations, including static & agitated, pressure and/or vacuum-induced aeration. Agitated systems generally use the turning process to move the material through the system in a continuous mode, while static systems require a loading & unloading mechanism. Material handling equipment may also shred to a certain degree, exposing new surfaces for decomposition, but excessive shredding may also reduce porosity. Aeration systems are usually set in the floor of the reactor and may use temperature and/or oxygen as control variables. Systems with agitation and bed depths less than two to three meters are effective in dealing with the heterogeneity of MSW.

Rotating drum composting reactors: Rotating drum reactors take the trade-off between reactor cost and compost residence time to an even further extreme than the horizontal or vertical in-vessel systems. These reactors, also known as digesters, retain the material for only a few hours or days. While the tumbling action can help homogenise and shred materials, the short residence time usually means the processing is more physical than biological. While rotating drums can play an important role in MSW composting, they are normally followed by other biological processing, which may include in-vessel, static pile and/or windrow systems.

Anaerobic composting.

In anaerobic processes, facultative bacteria break down the organic materials in the absence of oxygen and produce methane & carbon dioxide. Anaerobic systems, if configured efficiently, will generate sufficient energy in the form of methane to operate the process and have enough surpluses to either market as gas or convert to electricity. Conventional composting systems, on the other hand, need significant electrical or mechanical energy inputs to aerate or turn the piles. Several approaches are available for anaerobic digestion of feedstock.

Single-stage digesters contain the entire process in one airtight container. In this system, the feedstock is first shredded, and before being placed in the container, water and possibly nutrients are added to the previously shredded material. A single-stage digester may contain agitation equipment, which continuously stirs the liquefied material. The amount of water added and presence or absence of agitation equipment depend on the particular process employed.

The two-stage digestion involves circulating a liquid supernatant from a first stage digester, containing the materials, to a second-stage digester. This circulation eliminates the need for agitation equipment and provides the system operator with more opportunity to carefully control the biological process.

As digestion progresses, a mixture of methane and carbon dioxide is produced. These gases are continuously removed from both first & second stage digesters and are either combusted on-site or directed to off-site gas consumers. A portion of the recovered gas may be converted to thermal energy by combustion, which is then used to heat the digester. A stabilised residue remains, when the digestion process is completed. The residue is either removed from the digester with the mechanical equipment or pumped out as a liquid. It is chemically similar to compost, but contains more moisture. Conventional dewatering equipment can reduce the moisture content enough to handle the residue as a solid. The digested residue may require further curing by windrow or static pile composting.

Figure below illustrates an anaerobic digester with an aerobic compost curing.

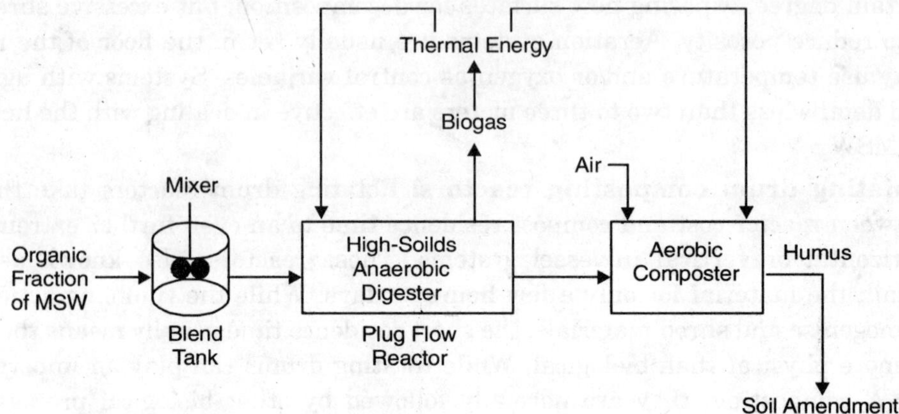

61. Describe the process and features of backyard composting using dry leaves and kitchen & garden waste.

Ans. Backyard composting using dry leaves and kitchen & garden waste can be done with a little time and effort. Any pile of waste organic matter will rot. To produce good compost for one's own garden following steps are to be followed:

- Choose a compost bin which can be of wood, cement, brick or plastic.
- Place the bin on a leveled, well-drained surface as it does not require base. Earthworm and other micro-organisms enter the bin from the base of bin through the soil and act on compost.

Avoid wood bins that may be chemically treated to keep micro-organisms at bay. Carbon nitrogen ratio in the bin should be 25:1. Carbon-rich organic matters are brown colored waste products that include hay, saw dust, old leaves, cardboard, newspaper and straw. Nitrogen-rich organic matters are green colored products that include green grass, manure, coffee, weeds, and vegetable peels. Bottom layer of bin should be around six inches of carbon-rich matter like hay, straw etc. Then top of it should be covered with a three-inch layer of nitrogen-rich organic waste like vegetable scraps, manure etc.

- Water each layer in the bin. Add these layers alternately till it becomes 1 to 1.5 metres high.
- Shred all the waste into smaller particles that you dump in the pile which makes decomposition process faster. A sample pile composition could be four parts of fruit & vegetable scraps, two parts of cow dung, one part of shredded paper, and one part dry leaves.
- Protect the pile from rain. To avoid sogginess of the contents cover the pile and see to it that contents are not too dry either.

- Ensure only biodegradable organic component are added.
- Proper decomposition occurs in presence of proper air and water. Don't saturate the pile with excess water. Turn the contents of the compost bin thoroughly using a shovel. This will aerate its contents, prevent it from stinking and hasten decomposition. It is advisable to mix the compost once in one or two weeks. Under proper temperature and moisture conditions, earthworms and other microbes will do the decomposition.

If these steps are properly followed then compost would be ready in six months.

Spread around two inches of compost on the soil until it mixes well. Though the compost is spread on the top layer of the soil, it releases nutrients to the layers lying underneath.

Compost quality check: Smell sweet like earth, dark in colour and crumbly.

Do not dump diseased or infected plants & vegetables as they may survive even in the bin. Meat, dairy products, bones and fish attract rodents and other undesired creatures to bin. Also, dog, cat or pig feces should not be put in the pile. However, chicken or cow dung is beneficial in a compost bin. Refrain from adding chemically-treated plants from garden.

For monitoring compost: Touch the pile. If it is warm, it means microbes are doing their job. If it is not warmer than temperature outside then feed kitchen waste and manure to the pile. It will increase rate of decomposition. Keep the pile moist and not dry. Air is necessary for organisms working on pile. Insert some tree branches in the pile so that they can be occasionally shaken to allow air circulation. Air and moisture act as pile's lifelines. If pile is still not decomposing, it means too much carbon and too little nitrogen is present in the pile.

The Indian scenario

The first significant development in composting as a systemised process took place in India in 1925, when a process involving the anaerobic degradation of leaves, refuse, animal manure and sewerage were placed in pits. The materials were placed in layers and the pit wall conserved some of the heat of degradation, resulting in high temperature than when composting was carried out in the open. This process (often referred as Indore process) took approximately six months to produce usable compost.

Following this, the Indian Council of Agricultural Research (ICAR) improved the method by laying down alternate layers of waste & sewage and this system (referred to as the Bangalore process) is still being used in India. In India, the high humid degradation that occurs in the land requires a large amount of humus for maintaining soil-fertility, and for that reason, composting is an ideal method for recycling organic wastes.

62. Describe the manual composting methods referred as Bangalore method & Indore methods of composting and compare their features.

Ans. Bangalore Method.

This is an anaerobic composting method conventionally carried out in pits. Formerly the waste was anaerobically stabilised in pits where alternate layers of MSW and night soil were laid. The pit is completely filled and a final soil layer is laid to prevent fly breeding, entry of rain water into the pit and for conservation of the released energy. The material is allowed to decompose for 4 to 6 months after which the stabilised material is taken out and used as compost.

Indore Method.

This method of composting in pits involves filling of alternate layers of similar thickness as in Bangalore method. However, to ensure aerobic condition the material is turned at specific intervals for which a 60 cm strip on the longitudinal side of the pit is kept vacant. For starting the turning operation, the first turn is manually given using long handled rakes 4 to 7 days after filling. The second turn is given after 5 to 10 more days. Further turning is normally not required and the compost is ready in 2 to 4 weeks.

In the urban areas, due to extensive provision of water carriage system of sanitation, night soil is not available. Composting of MSW alone is hence carried out. Aerobic composting of MSW is commonly carried out in windrows.

Comparison of the two Methods.

The Bangalore method requires longer time for stablisation of the material & hence needs larger land space, which is in short supply in urban areas. The gases generated in this anaerobic process also pose smell & odour problems.

The Indore method on the other hand stabilises the material in shorter time & needs lesser land space. As no odourous gases are generated in this process, it is environment friendly & hence commonly preferred. While the organic matter is stabilised during the composting process, the moisture content also changes. The non decomposables are also rejected. Hence the quantity of compost is much lesser than the input & is normally around 50%, and the exact value depends upon the characteristics of the input material.

63. Describe the bio-gasification/bio-methanation process of MSW disposal.

Ans. Biogasification or Biomethanation is the process of conversion of organic matter in the waste (liquid or solid) to BioMethane (sometimes referred to as "Biogas" with high energy density) and manure (bio compost) by microbial action in the absence of air, known as "anaerobic processing or digestion."

Biogas is a mixture of gases composed of methane (CH_4) 40-70 vol.%, carbon dioxide (CO_2) 30-60 vol.%, other gases 1-5 vol.% including, hydrogen (H_2) 0-1 vol.% and hydrogen sulphide (H_2S) 0-3 vol.%. It originates from bacteria in the process of bio-degradation of organic material under anaerobic (without air) conditions. The natural generation of biogas is an important part of the biogeochemical carbon cycle.

Biogasification is particularly suitable for wet substrates, such as sludges or food waste, which present difficulties in composting, as the lack of structural material restricts air circulation. The anaerobic process is used sometimes to digest sewage sludge, and this has been extended to fractions of household solid waste.

In contrast to aerobic processes (*i.e.*, composting), biogasification is mildly exothermic. Thus, the heat needs to be supplied to maintain the process temperature, especially for thermophilic processes. The advantage of high temperature is that the reaction will occur at a faster rate, and so a shorter residence time is required in the reactor vessel.

The conditions for biogasification is anaerobic, for which a totally enclosed process vessel is required. Although this necessitates a higher level of technology than compared to composting, it allows a greater control over the process itself and the emission of noxious odours. Greater process control, especially of temperature, allows a reduction in treatment time, when compared to composting. Since a biogas plant is usually vertical, it also requires less area than a composting plant.

Anaerobic processing of organic material is a two-stage process, where large organic polymers are fermented into short-chain volatile fatty acids. These acids are then converted into methane and carbon dioxide. Both the organic polymers fermentation process and acid conversion occur at the same time, in a single-phase system. And, the separation of the acid-producing (acidogenic) bacteria from the methane producing (methanogenic) bacteria results in a two-phase system.

The main feature of anaerobic treatment is the concurrent waste stabilisation and production of methane gas, which is an energy source. The retention time for solid material in an anaerobic process can range from a few days to several weeks, depending upon the chemical characteristics of solid material and the design of the biogasification system (*e.g.*, single stage, two stage, multi- stage, wet or dry, temperature and pH control).

In the absence of oxygen, anaerobic bacteria decompose organic matter as follows:

Organic matter + anaerobic bacteria $\longrightarrow$ $CH_4 + CO_2 + H_2S + NH_3$ + other end products + energy

Some of the benefits of biogasification of solid wastes are as follows:

- Production of energy (heat, light, electricity);
- Transformation of organic waste into high quality fertiliser;
- Improvement of hygienic conditions through reduction of pathogens, worm eggs and flies;
- Reduction of workload in firewood collection and cooking;
- Environmental advantages through protection of soil, water, air and woody vegetation;
- Micro-economical benefits through energy & fertiliser substitution, additional income generation and increasing yields of animal husbandry & agriculture;
- Macro-economic benefits through decentralised energy generation, import substitution and environmental protection.

Biogas technology can substantially contribute to energy conservation and development, if the economic viability & social acceptance of biogas technology are favourable.

64. Describe various bio-gasification /anaerobic digestion process of organic waste present in MSW.

Ans. According to the solid content of the material digested and the temperature at which the process operates, the various biogasification processes can be classified as under:

Dry anaerobic digestion.

In dry anaerobic digestion, semi-solid wastes are digested to produce biogas in a single stage, either as a batch process or a continuous process. It takes place at a total solid concentration of over 25%, and below this level of solid, the process is described as wet digestion. With regard to temperature, the processes are either described as mesophilic (operating between 30 and 40°C) or thermophilic (operating between 50 and 65°C), and anaerobic microorganisms have optimum growth rates within these temperature ranges.

The dry fermentation process means that only little process water has to be added or heated, which favours thermophilic operation. No mixing equipment is necessary, and crust formation is not possible due to the relatively solid nature of the digester contents. This anaerobic process usually takes between 12 and 18 days, followed by several days in post-digestion for residue stabilisation & maturation.

Wet anaerobic digestion.

This process consists of a single stage in a completely mixed mesophilic digester, operating at a total solid content of around 3-8%. To produce this level of dilution, water has to be added & heated, and then removed after the digestion process. This method is used to digest sewage sludge, and animal & house hold wastes. The single-stage wet process suffers from problems such as the formation of a hard scum layer in the digester and difficulty in keeping the content completely mixed.

The major problem with the single-stage process is that the different reactions in the process cannot be separately optimised. The acidogenic microorganisms grow fast and lower the pH of the reaction mixture, whereas the methanogens, which grow slowly, have a pH optimum around 7.0.

The development of the two-stage digestion process solves this problem as hydrolysis & acidification occur in the first reactor vessel, kept at a pH of around 6.0 and methanogenesis occurs in the second vessel, operated at a pH of 7.5-8.2. The whole process can run with a retention time of 5 to 8 days.

Maturing or refining: The residues of both wet & dry biogasification processes require extensive maturing under aerobic conditions. However, effective aeration can reduce this time considerably.The maturation processes facilitate the release of entrapped methane, elimination of phytotoxins (*i.e.*, substances that are harmful for plant growth, such as volatile organic acids) and reduce the moisture content to an acceptable level. These residues contain a high level of water - even the dry process residue contains around 65% water. Filtering or pressing can reduce excess water, and further drying can be achieved using waste heat from the gas engine, if the biogas is burnt onsite to produce electricity. The digested residue, initially anaerobic, will also contain many volatile organic acids and reduced organic materials. These need to be matured aerobically to oxidise & stabilise the compounds, in the process similar to the maturation of aerobic compost, prior to sale as compost or disposal as residue.

Odour production is measured as the total amount of volatile organics produced per tonne of bio-waste during composting and the final aerobic maturation after anaerobic digestion.

65. Describe the various factors affecting biogasification of solid waste.

Ans. As with composting, a number of factors affect biogasification, which are described below:

Temperature: A temperature range of about 25-40°C (mesophilic) is generally optimal. It can be achieved without additional heating, thus being very economical. In some cases, additional energy input is provided to increase temperature to 50-60°C (thermophilic range) for greater gas production. Often digesters are constructed below ground to conserve heat.

pH and alkalinity: pH close to neutral, *i.e.*, 7, is optimum. At lower pH values (below 5.5), some bacteria carrying out the process are inhibited. Excess loading and presence of toxic materials will lower pH levels to below 6.5 and can cause difficulties. When pH levels are too low, stopping the loading of the digester and/or use of lime is recommended. The presence of alkalinity between 2500 and 5000 mg/L will provide good buffering against excessive pH changes.

Nutrient concentration: An ideal C: N ratio of 25:1 is to be maintained in any digester. It is an important parameter, as anaerobic bacteria need nitrogen compound to grow and multiply. Too much nitrogen, however, can inhibit methanogenic activity. If the C: N ratio is high, then gas production can be enhanced by adding nitrogen, and if the C: N ratio is low, it can be increased by adding carbon, *i.e.*, adding chicken manure, etc., which reduces the possibility of toxicity. Anaerobic digestion not only breaks down plant materials into biogas, but also releases plant nutrients, such as nitrogen (N), potassium (K) & phosphorous (P), and converts them into a form that can be easily absorbed by plants.

Loading: When any digester is designed, the main variable to be defined is the internal volume. The digester volume is related to, feed rate (Q, measured in m^3/day) and hydraulic loading or retention time (R, measured in days). The feed rate (Q) is given by the mass of total solid (m, kg) fed daily, divided by the proportion of total solid (TS) in the mixed slurry. The retention time (R) of any digester is given by the volume of the digester pit (V, m^3), divided by the volume of the daily feed (Q, m^3/day). The loading rate of a digester is defined as the mass of volatile solids added each day per unit volume of digester. The typical values for the loading rate are between 0.2 and 2.0 kg VS/m^3/day.

Effect of toxins: The main cause of biogas plants receiving flak is the presence of toxic substance. Chlorinated hydrocarbons, such as chloroforms and other organic solvents, are particularly toxic to biogas digestion. If the digester has been badly poisoned, it may be difficult to remove the toxins without removing most of the bacteria. In that case, the digester must be emptied, cleaned with water and refilled with fresh slurry.

66. Describe the main Components of biogas plant.

Ans. A typical biogas plant has the following components:

- A digester in which the slurry (*e.g.*, dung mixed with water) is fermented;
- An inlet tank used to mix the feed and let it into the digester;
- A gas holder/dome in which the generated gas is collected;
- An outlet tank to remove the spent slurry;
- Distribution pipeline(s) to carry the gas into the kitchen;
- A manure pit, where the spent slurry is stored.

In India, the objective of setting up bio gas plant has been:

- To provide fuel for cooking purposes and organic manure to rural households through biogas plants;
- To mitigate the drudgery of rural women, reduce pressure on forest and accentuate social benefits;
- To improve sanitation in villages by linking toilets with biogas plants.

67. Describe the various types of biogas plants model used in India.

Ans. There are various biogas plant models approved by National Project on Biogas Development (NPDB) initiated by the ministry of non conventional energy resources for implementation. All these models are based on the basic designs available: floating metal drum type, fixed masonry dome type, and FLEXI, a portable model made of rubberised nylon fabric, which has been approved for promotion in hilly and other terrains.

Some of the NPDB approved models of biogas are described below:

KVIC floating drum: Khadi and Village Industries Commission (KVIC) developed this model in the early 1960s. This model has an underground cylindrical digester with inlet and outlet connections at the bottom on either side of a masonry wall. An inverted metal drum, which serves as the gasholder, rests on a wedge type support on top of the digester and, as the gas begins to accumulate, the drum starts rising in height. The weight of the drum applies pressure on the gas to make it pass through the pipeline to the point of use. As the gas flows out, the drum gradually moves down. Due to this smooth two-way motion, the gas remains at constant pressure, which ensures efficient use of gas. Though KVIC has been a very popular model since the beginning, it has two major drawbacks: the plant cost is very high and the metal gasholder has to be painted regularly for protecting it against corrosion, which means high running cost.

Deenbandhu: Action for Food Production, a voluntary organisation based in New Delhi developed this model in 1984. The cost of the Deenbandhu bio gas plant is nearly 50% less than that of the KVIC plant, which has brought the biogas technology within the reach of even the poorer sections of the population. The cost reduction was achieved by minimising the surface area through joining the segments of two spheres of different diameters at their bases. This structure acts as a digester, and pressure is exerted on the slurry, which is pushed into a displacement chamber. Once the gas is drawn from the outlet, the slurry again enters the digester. The brick masonry dome, which is fixed, requires skilled workmanship and quality material to ensure no leakage.

Pragati: A Pune-based NGO has developed this model, which is a combination of KVIC & Deenbandhu designs. In this model, the lower part of the digester is semi-spherical in shape with a conical bottom. However, instead of a fixed dome, it has a floating drum acting as gas storage chamber. The spread of Pragati model has been confined mainly to the state of Maharashtra.

KVIC plant with ferro-cement digester: The Structural Engineering Research Centre, Ghaziabad, has developed the ferro-cement digester design in order to overcome the problems encountered in the construction of traditional models of biogas plants. In this digester, layers of thin steel wire mesh, distributed throughout, are impregnated with rich mortar. Ferro-cement (*i.e.*, concrete made of welded mesh, sand & cement) as a building material offers several advantages like 10 to 15% reduction in cost over KVIC digesters, usage of locally available material, less labour and little or no maintenance. The only limitation though is ferro-cement is vulnerable to damage due to the impact of pointed loads, which, however, can be easily repaired.

Plant with fiber reinforced plastic (FRP) gas holder: FRP is used in place of metal in the floating drum gasholder. Contact Moulding Process, a technique of moulding without the application of external pressure, is adopted to manufacture the FRP gas holder . It employs one of the less expensive types of moulds, resulting in lower cost of the plant. The major advantage of FRP is its resistance to corrosion, which saves the recurring expenditure on painting the drum.

FLEXI: Developed by Swastik Rubber Products Ltd., Pune, this is a portable model in which the digester is made of rubberised nylon fabric. The model is particularly suitable for hilly areas, where high transportation cost of construction materials, such as cement and bricks substantially increases the cost of installing the regular type of biogas plants.

68. Describe the environmental effects of composting and biogasification.

Ans. The compost produced and slurry from biogas plants is often used as a soil amendment in a variety of applications. Since the product is used for a variety of purposes, contaminants in the compost could be detrimental to the environment. This is particularly true when one considers that the environmental pollutants are easily minimised through simple treatment procedures (*i.e.*, waste segregation, proper turning and sufficient composting time). The composting facilities of solid waste with manure, sewage sludge and residue from processing create some significant environmental effects as described below:

(i) **Water impacts:** Water runoff from garden waste composting facilities could contain large concentration of nutrients (*i.e.*, nitrates & phosphorous), volatile organics and metals that cause algal blooms in the nearby surface water. Retention basins may be used at facilities to limit water runoff. Water impacts are not serious at yard waste composting facilities. Municipal waste composting, sludge composting and co-composting involve a large amount of potential contaminants, and water impact could be greater at these facilities. Leachate from MSW compost facilities can contain high concentration of nutrients, volatile organics and metals. Leachate affects both surface & groundwater.

(ii) **Land impacts:** At garden waste composting facilities, soil may become more acidic, due to the presence of certain leaves and pine needles in the compost pile. Nitrogen depletion may also occur, which can be limited by proper turning. MSW and co-composting facilities carry the potentially harmful impacts of acids, and organic & metal contamination. Again careful pre-processing to divert much of the potentially hazardous materials from the compost facility is an important quality control procedure.

(iii) **Odour pollution:** Odour is one of the most frequent problems at composting facilities. Frequent turning of compost piles has proven to be effective in limiting odour problems. When in-vessel systems are used, odour control devices (*e.g.*, air scrubber, etc.) can minimise the problem.

(iv) **Health impact:** The primary public health concerns associated with composting operation result from:

- Drinking contaminated water;
- Toxins in the finished product (applied on land);
- Pathogens.

Nitrate contamination of drinking water can affect the oxygen-carrying capacity of the blood in infants, *e.g.*, blue baby syndrome (methemoglobinemia) and in elderly, but again under proper composting conditions, this risk can be minimised. Insects and vermin can spread pathogens. Note that because of the high temperature achieved during the normal composting operations, pathogens found in manure, sewage sludge or municipal waste are usually destroyed. There are risks to workers as well (*e.g.*, aggravation of respiratory problem). However, proper training and health monitoring as well as proper apparel and equipment can minimise these risks .

69. What are the benefits of composting?

Ans. Composting is one of the important components of solid waste management (SWM). It is á form of source reduction or waste prevention, as the materials are completely diverted from the disposal facilities and require no management or transportation. Community-yard trimming composting programme, source-separated organic composting and mixed municipal solid waste (MSW) composting constitute the various recycling processes. A major portion of municipal solid wastes in India contain up to 70% by weight of organic materials. In addition, certain industrial by-products - those from food processing, agricultural & paper industries - are mostly composed of organic materials.

Composting, being an organic material, can significantly reduce waste stream volume. Diverting such materials from the waste stream frees up landfill space needed for materials that cannot be composted. Composting owes its current popularity to several factors, including increased landfill tipping fees, shortage of landfill capacity and increasingly restrictive measures imposed by regulatory agencies. In addition, recycling mandates indirectly encourage composting, as they consider it an acceptable strategy for achieving mandatory goals.

Composting may also offer an attractive economic advantage for communities where the costs of using other options are high. However, it is considered a viable option only when the compost can be marketed. In some cases, nevertheless, the benefits of reducing disposal needs through composting may be adequate to justify choosing this option, even if the compost is only used as a landfill cover. Compost, because of its high organic matter content, makes a valuable soil amendment and is used to provide nutrients for plants. When mixed with soil, compost promotes a proper balance between air & water in the resulting mixture, helps reduce soil erosion and serves as a slow release fertiliser.

70. What do you mean by thermal treatment of solid waste?

Ans. Thermal treatment of solid wastes, which is pre-treatment of waste prior to final disposal includes both the burning of mixed MSW (municipal solid waste) in incinerators and the burning of selected parts of the waste stream as fuel for energy recovery. Various incineration technologies such as mass burning system, refuse derived fuel (RDF) system, modular incineration and fluidised bed incineration are in practice. Emission of air pollutants is a major concern of incineration facilities.

71. What is incineration of solid waste?

Ans. Incineration is a chemical reaction in which carbon, hydrogen and other combustible elements in the solid waste mix with oxygen in the combustion zone and generates heat. The air requirements for combustion of solid wastes is approximately 5000 kg of air is required for each tonne of solid wastes burned. Usually, excess air is supplied to the incinerator to ensure complete mixing and combustion and to regulate operating temperature and control emissions. Excess air requirements, however, differ with moisture content of waste, heating values and the type of combustion technology employed. The principal gaseous products of combustion are carbon dioxide, carbon monoxide, water, oxygen and oxides of nitrogen.

Many incinerators are designed to operate in the combustion zone of 900°C-1100°C. This temperature is selected to ensure good combustion, complete elimination of odours and protection of the walls of the incinerator. Incinerator systems are designed to maximise waste burn out & heat output, while minimising emissions by balancing the oxygen (air) and the three "Ts", *i.e.*, time, temperature and turbulence. Complete incineration of solid wastes produces virtually an inert residue, which constitutes about 10% of the initial weight of waste and a larger reduction in volume. The residue is generally landfilled. The incineration facility along with combustion of waste emits air pollutants (*i.e.*, fine particulate and toxic gases), which are an environmental concern, and, therefore, their control is necessary. Other concerns relating to incineration include the disposal of the liquid wastes from floor drainage, quench water, scrubber effluents and the problem of ash disposal in landfills because of heavy metal residues. By optimising the combustion process, we can control the emission of combustible, carbon-containing pollutants . Oxides of nitrogen & sulphur, and other gaseous pollutants are not considered a problem because of their relatively smaller concentration.

72. Describe the main objectives of incineration of solid wastes.

Ans. The purpose of incineration is to combust solid wastes to reduce their volume to about one-tenth, without producing offensive gases and ashes. Key objectives of incineration of solid wastes are described below:

Waste Volume reduction: Depending on its composition, incineration reduces the volume of solid wastes to be disposed of by about 90%. The weight of the solid wastes to be dealt with is reduced by about 70 %. This has both environmental & economic advantages since there is less demand for final disposal to landfill, as well as reduced costs and environmental burdens due to transport, if a distant landfill is used.

Waste Stabilisation: Incinerator output (*i.e.*, ash) is considerably more inert than incinerator input (*i.e.*, solid wastes), mainly due to the oxidation of the organic components of the waste stream. This leads to a reduction of landfill management problems (since the organic fraction is responsible for landfill gas production) and the organic compounds present in landfill leachate.

Recovery of energy from waste: Energy recovered from burning the wastes is used to generate steam for use in on-site electricity generation. Combined heat and power plants increase the efficiency of energy recovery by producing electricity as well as utilising the residual heat. Solid waste incineration can replace the use of fossil fuels for energy generation. As a large part of the energy content of solid wastes comes from renewable resources (*e.g.*, biomass), there should be a lower overall net carbon dioxide production than that from burning fossil fuels, since carbon dioxide is absorbed in the initial growing phase of the biomass.

Sterilisation of waste: This is of primary importance in the incineration of hospital waste. Incineration of solid wastes will also ensure destruction of pathogens prior to final disposal in a landfill.

Waste volume reduction for both environmental & economic reasons and sterilisation of waste is the main objectives of incineration. Due to the growing concern over the production of landfill gas and the organic compounds in leachate from landfill receiving untreated waste, in future there will be more emphasis on using incineration for stabilising wastes for subsequent landfilling. Landfill gas and leachate arise mainly from the organic fraction of solid wastes, which will be effectively converted to gases & mineralised ash by incineration.

73. Describe the main factors to be considered in site selection for waste incineration facility.

Ans. The important factors to be considered for siting the incineration facility are described below:

Effect on residents: Residents will be concerned with the health effects associated with incinerator plant, decreased property value and increased traffic (*e.g.*, due to truck movement).

Environmental impact: Incineration has the potential to create a variety of environmental concerns like air, water & noise pollution and ash disposal.

Development plans: It is important to evaluate future land use plans at the possible site.

Proximity to waste source: Transportation cost is one of the most significant expenditures in waste management system.

Proximity to energy market: The energy products will have to be delivered to buyers. The location of power line must be considered.

Logistic concerns: Area zoning and access route must be considered.

Residual ash disposal: Access to a secure landfill is necessary.

74. Describe various waste incineration technologies in detail.

Ans. The four important waste incineration technologies mass burning system, refuse derived fuel system, modular incineration and fluidised bed incineration. The two most widely used and technically proven incineration technologies are mass-burning incineration and modular incineration. Fluidised-bed incineration has been employed to a lesser extent and Refuse Derived Fuel (RDF) production & incineration has also been used, with limited success. Some facilities are used in conjunction with pyrolysis, gasification and other related processes that convert solid waste to gaseous, liquid, or solid fuel through thermal processing. These incineration technologies are described below:

Mass-burning system.

Mass-burning systems facility consists of a reciprocating grate combustion system and a refractory-lined, water-walled steam generator. Mass-burn systems generally consist of either two or three incineration units ranging in capacity from 50 to 1,000 tonnes per day. That means the facility capacity ranges from about 100-150 to 2,000-3,000 tonnes per day. These facilities can accept refuse that has undergone little preprocessing other than the removal of oversized items. Although this versatility makes mass-burn facilities convenient & flexible, local programmes to separate household hazardous wastes (*e.g.*, cleaners & pesticides) and recover certain materials (*e.g.*, iron scrap) are necessary to help ensure environmentally viable incineration & resource conservation.

To achieve greater combustion & heat recovery efficiency, the larger field-erected incinerators are usually in-line furnaces with a grate system. The steam generator generally consists of refractory-coated water wall systems, *i.e.*, walls comprised of tubes through which water circulates to absorb the heat of combustion.

Mass-burning of waste can also be done by the use of a rotary kiln. Rotary kilns use a turning cylinder, either refractory or water wall design, to tumble the waste through the system. The kiln is inclined, with waste entering at the high elevation end and ash & non-combustibles leaving at the lower end. The waste intake area includes a tipping floor, pit, crane and sometimes conveyors. Trucks enter the tipping floor and tip their wastes either onto the floor itself, or directly into the pit. When wastes are tipped onto the floor, a front-end loader or a bulldozer is used to push them into the pit or onto a conveyor. MSW is continuously fed to a grate system, from a feed chute, which moves the waste through a combustion chamber using a tumbling motion. A travelling or reciprocating grate may follow rotary combustors to further complete combustion.

At least two combustor units are included to provide a level of redundancy and to allow waste processing at a reduced rate during periods of scheduled and unscheduled maintenance. Mass-burn facilities today generate a higher quality of steam (*i.e.*, pressure & temperature), which is then passed through a turbine generator to produce electricity or through an extraction turbine to generate electricity as well as provide process steam for heating or other purposes.

Figure below shows a typical mass-burn facility.

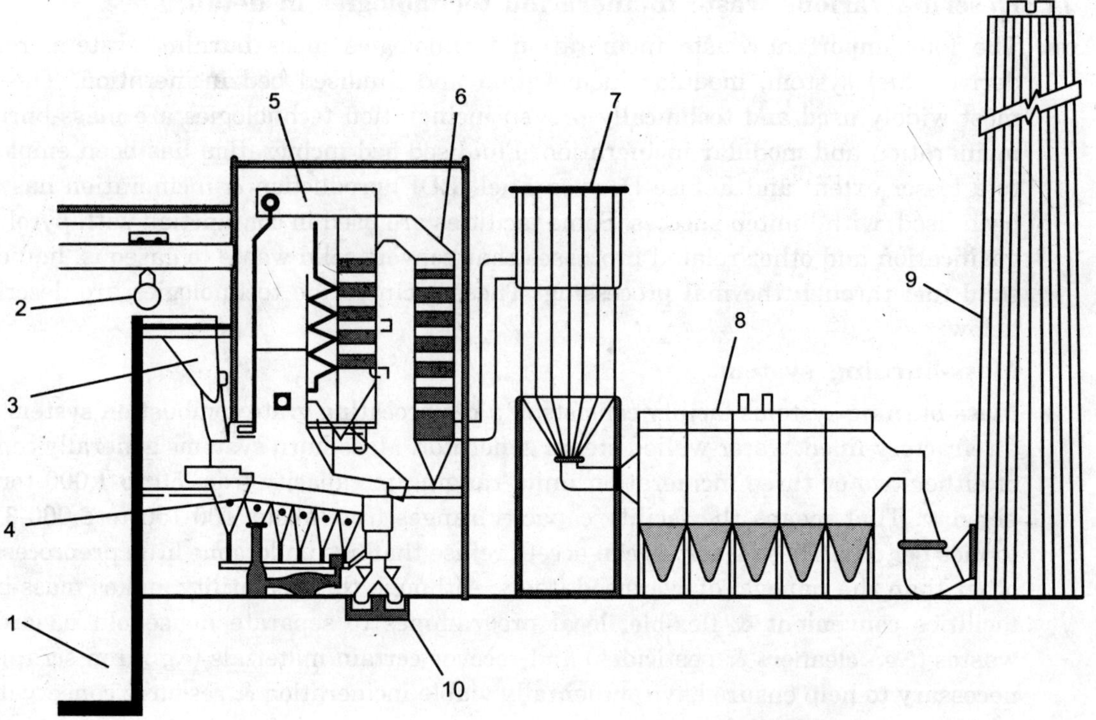

Refuse derived fuel (RDF) system.

Refuse-derived fuel (RDF) refers to solid wastes in any form that is used as fuel. The term RDF, however, is commonly used to refer to solid waste that has been mechanically processed to produce a storable, transportable and more homogeneous fuel for combustion. RDF systems have two basic components: RDF production and RDF incineration.

RDF production facilities make RDF in various forms through material separation, size reduction and pelletising. Although RDF processing has the advantage of removing recyclables and contaminants from the combustion stream, on an average, capital costs per tonne for incineration units that use RDF are higher than for other incineration options. RDF production plants like mass-burn incinerators have an indoor tipping floor. Instead of being pushed onto a pit, the waste in an RDF plant is typically fed onto a conveyor, which is either below grade or hopper fed. In some plants, the loader doing the feeding will separate corrugated and bulky items, like carpets.

Once on the conveyor, the waste travels through a number of processing stages, usually beginning with magnetic separation. The processing steps typically include one or more screening stages, using trammel or vibrating screens, shredding or hammer milling of waste with additional screening steps, pelletising or baling of burnable wastes, and, depending on the local recycling markets and the design of the facility, a manual separation line.

A typical RDF facility scheme is shown below in figure.

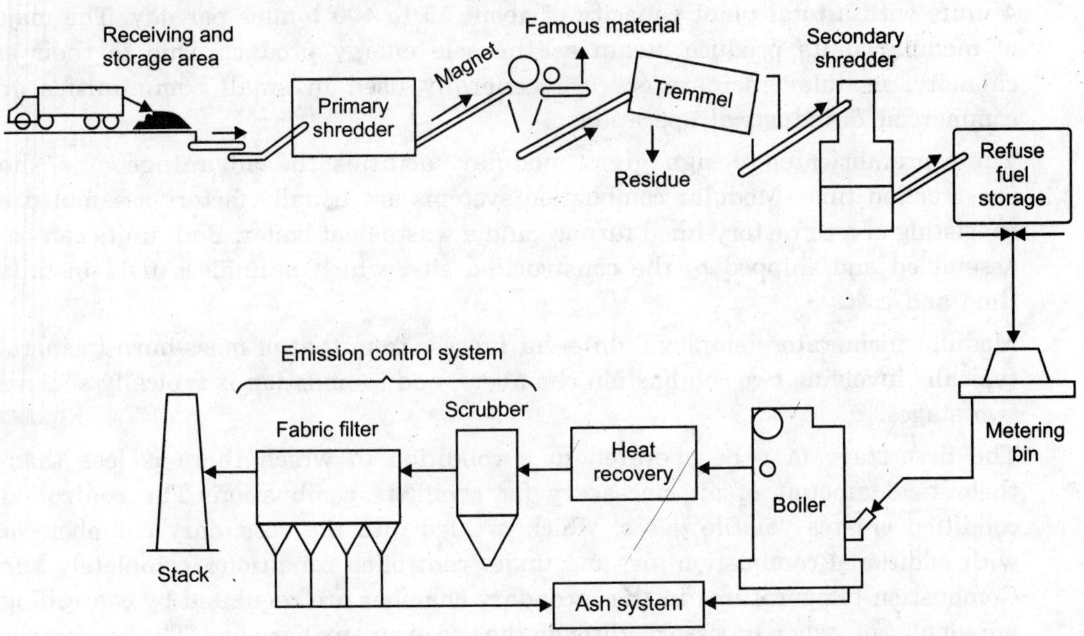

There are two primary types of RDF systems in operation, and these are:

(i) **Shred-and-burn RDF systems:** Shred-and-burn systems are the simplest form of RDF production. The process system typically consists of shredding the MSW to the desired particle size that allows effective feeding to the combustor and magnetic removal of ferrous metal, with the remaining portion delivered to the combustor. There is no attempt to remove other non-combustible materials in the MSW before combustion. This, in essence, is a system with minimal processing and removal of non-combustibles.

(ii) **Simplified process RDF systems:** This is a system that removes a significant portion of the non-combustibles. A simplified process system involves processing the MSW to produce an RDF with a significant portion of the non-combustibles removed before combustion. The MSW process removes more than 85% of the ferrous metals, a significant percentage of the remaining non-combustible (*i.e.*, glass, nonferrous metals, dirt, sand, etc.), and shreds the material to a nominal particle top size of 10 to 15 cm to allow effective firing in the combustion unit .

Depending on the type of combustor to be used, a significant degree of separation can be achieved to produce a high-quality RDF (*i.e.*, low ash), which typically results in the loss of a higher percentage of combustibles when compared to systems that can produce a low-quality fuel (*i.e.*, slightly higher ash content) for firing in a specially designed combustor. These types of systems recover over 95% of the combustibles in the fuel fraction.

Modular incineration.

Modular incinerator units are usually prefabricated units with relatively small capacities between 5 and 120 tonnes of solid waste per day. Typical facilities have between 1 and 4 units with a total plant capacity of about 15 to 400 tonnes per day. The majority of modular units produce steam as the sole energy product. Due to their small capacity, modular incinerators are generally used in small communities or for commercial & industrial operations.

Their prefabricated design gives modular facilities the advantage of a shorter construction time. Modular combustion systems are usually factory-assembled units consisting of a refractory-lined furnace and a waste heat boiler. Both units can be pre-assembled and shipped to the construction site, which minimises field installation time and cost.

Modular incinerators employ a different process from that of mass-burn incinerators, typically involving two combustion chambers, and combustion is typically achieved in two stages.

The first stage may be operated in a condition in which there is less than the theoretical amount of air necessary for complete combustion. The controlled air condition creates volatile gases, which are fed into the secondary chamber, mixed with additional combustion air, and under controlled conditions, completely burned. Combustion temperatures in the secondary chamber are regulated by controlling the air supply, and when necessary, through the use of an auxiliary fuel. The hot combustion gases then pass through a waste heat boiler to produce steam for electricity generation or for heating purposes. The combustion gases and products are processed through air emission control equipment to meet the required emission standards.

In general, modular incineration systems are a suitable alternative and may, for smaller-sized facilities, be more cost-effective than other incinerators. But modular incineration has become less common, partly due to concerns over the consistency and adequacy of air pollution controls.

Fluidised-bed incineration.

Fluidised-bed incineration of MSW is typically medium scale, with processing capacity from 50 to 150 tonnes per day. In this system, a bed of limestone or sand that can withstand high temperatures, fed by an air distribution system, replaces the grate. The heating of the bed and an increase in the air velocities cause the bed to bubble. There are two types of fluidised-bed technologies, viz., bubbling bed and circulating bed. The differences are reflected in the relationship between air flow and bed material, and have implications for the type of wastes that can be burned, as well as the heat transfer to the energy recovery system.

Unlike mass-burn incinerators, fluidised-bed incinerators require fuel preparation. They are generally associated with source separation because glass & metals do not fare well in these systems and also they can successfully burn wastes of widely varying moisture & heat content, so that the inclusion of paper and wood, which are both recyclable & burnable, is not a crucial factor in their operation. Fluidised bed systems are more consistent in their operation than mass burn and can be controlled more effectively to achieve higher energy conversion efficiency, less residual ash & lower air emissions. However, these systems operate efficiently on smaller scales than mass-burn incinerators, which may make them attractive in some situations. For this reason, fluidised-bed technology may be a sound choice for high-recycling cities in developing countries when they first adopt incineration.

Out of most recent Waste to energy technologies adopted in India such as Biomethanation, landfill with gas recovery, gasification/pyrolysis, incineration and composting; incineration is selected as last option.

75. Describe basic types of waste to energy recovery systems following incineration of municipal solid waste (MSW).

Ans. Most of the MSW incineration currently practice energy recovery in the form of steam, which is used either to drive a turbine to generate electricity or directly for heating . In the past, it was common to simply burn MSW in incinerators to reduce its volume & weight, but energy recovery has become more prevalent now.

In waste-to-energy (WTE) plants, heat from the burning waste is absorbed by water in the wall of the furnace chamber, or in separate boilers to produce steam which is used either for heating or to turn turbines to generate electricity. The amount of energy recovered from waste is a function of the amount of waste combusted, energy value of the waste stream and the efficiency of the combustion process.

The three basic types of waste to energy incineration of MSW are described below:

(i) **Generation of electricity:** Electricity is the most common form of energy produced and sold from WTE facilities constructed today. By directing the steam produced from a WTE system through a turbine generator, electricity can be produced and sold. A process flow diagram of an incinerator and electrical generation system is shown below in figure.

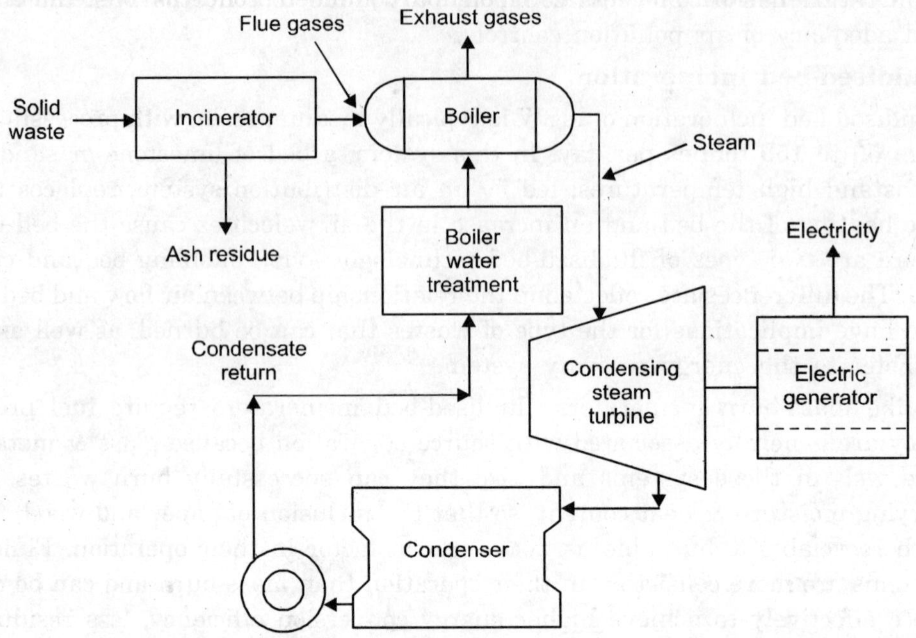

Of the electricity produced in incineration facilities, about one-fifth is used at the facility for general operations, and the remainder can be sold.

(ii) Steam generation: Steam is used widely in a variety of industrial applications. Steam generated in incineration facilities can also be used directly by a customer for manufacturing operations. Steam generated in an incinerator is supplied to a customer through a steam line, and a separate line sometimes returns the condensed steam. It can be used to drive machinery such as compressors, for space heating and generating electricity. Industrial plants, dairies, cheese plants, public utilities, paper mills, tanneries, breweries, public buildings and many other businesses use steam for heating and air conditioning.

When assessing potential markets for steam, it is important to consider a market's proximity to the WTE facility and the quantity of steam produced. Proximity is important because steam cannot usually be economically transported more than 1.5 to 3.0 km. The WTE facility, therefore, should be as close as possible to the potential market. The advantages of transmitting steam over a long distance to an end user must be weighed against energy losses that will occur in transmission. Installation of a pipeline connecting the facility and the customer can also be prohibitively expensive in certain circumstances .The quantity of steam produced from a given amount of waste will decrease, as the steam temperature & pressure increase, but the equipment using the steam will operate more efficiently. To ensure the continuous availability of high quantity & quality steam, supplementary fuels, may occasionally be used, but this will result in an increase in the operating costs.

(iii) **Co-generation:** Co-generation refers to combined production of steam & electricity and can occur in two ways. If the steam conditions (pressure & temperature) required by the customer are less than the incineration plant's design specifications, a turbine-generator is used to produce electricity and thus reduce steam conditions to appropriate levels for the customer. If the steam purchaser cannot accept all the steam produced by the facility, the excess can be converted to electricity. In co-generation, high-pressure steam is used first to generate electricity; the steam leaving the turbine is then used to serve the low pressure steam users for heating purposes.

Co-generation provides greater overall energy efficiency, even though the output of the major energy product - whether electricity or steam - may be less than that generated by producing one type of energy alone.

Co-generation allows flexibility, so that seasonal variations in steam demand can be offset by increases in electricity production, and can provide the project a financial base by selling electricity, should the steam customer become unavailable.

Co-generation System for Producing Electricity and Steam from incineration of MSW is shown below in figure .

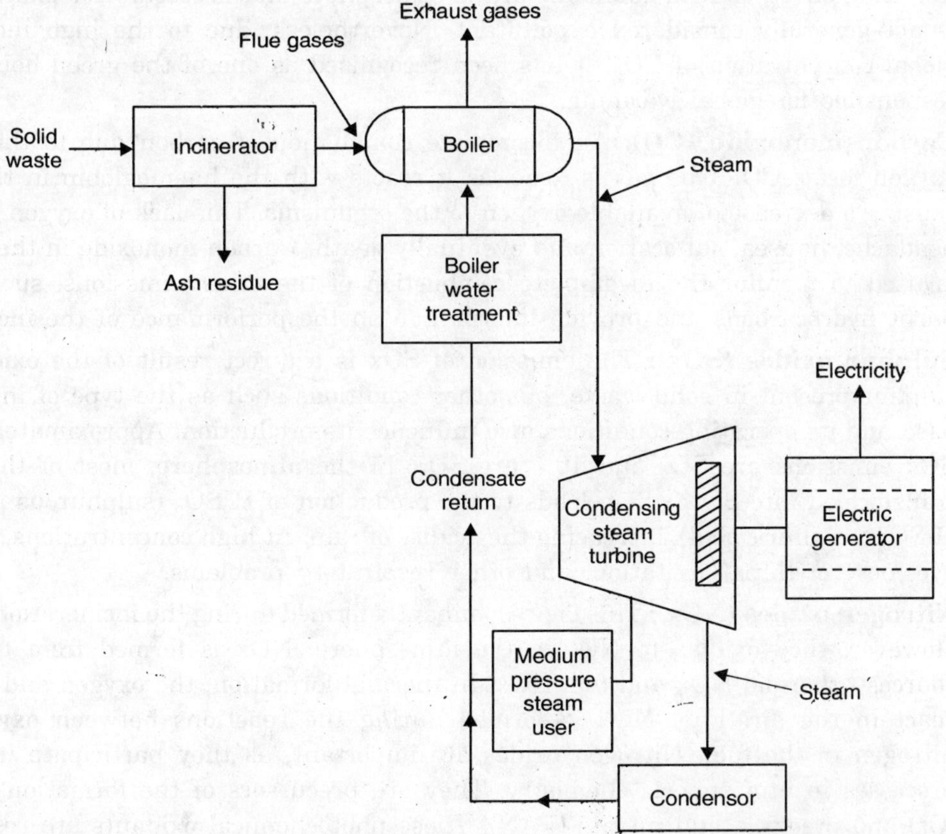

The major risks of incinerators are the potential emission of contaminants into the air through exhaust stack or into the water through ash leachate. Proper planning to minimise these problems are essential for a successful incineration programme.

76. What are the various air pollutants emitted from waste incineration plants?

Ans. The operation of the combustion process plays an important role in the formation of pollutants, which are carbon monoxide, NOx (oxides of nitrogen), hydrocarbons and other volatile organic compounds. It also produces gaseous stream containing dust, acid gases (HCl, SOx, HF), heavy metals and traces of dioxins. The modern incinerators, however, produce less particulate & gaseous pollutants than the older plants. Also, emissions from incinerators are controlled by a combination of measures that use both the pollution prevention approach and various control equipment.

The main pollutants emitted from incineration plants are described below:

Gaseous pollutants.

The various gaseous pollutants formed due to incineration processes are:

Carbon dioxide (CO_2): This is one of the main products of incineration, and the other main product is water. At low concentrations, CO_2 has no short-term toxic or irritating effect, as it is abundant in the atmosphere and necessary for plant life and is not generally considered a pollutant. Nevertheless, due to the high increase in global concentration of CO_2, it has been recognised as one of the green house gases responsible for global warming.

Carbon monoxide (CO): An incomplete combustion of carbon due to the lack of oxygen forms CO. This gas is toxic, as it reacts with the haemoglobin in the blood, causing a decrease of available oxygen to the organisms. This lack of oxygen produces headache, nausea, suffocation and eventually death. Carbon monoxide in the flue gas is used to monitor the incomplete combustion of the other emissions, such as unburnt hydrocarbons and provide information on the performance of the incinerator.

Sulphur oxides (SOx): The emission of SOx is a direct result of the oxidation of sulphur present in solid waste, but other conditions such as the type of incinerator used and its operating conditions also influence its production. Approximately 90% of SOx emissions are SO_2 and 10% are SO_3. In the atmosphere, most of the SO_2 is transformed into SO_3, which leads to the production of H_2SO_3 (sulphurous acid) and H_2SO_4 (sulphuric acid), increasing the acidity of rain. At high concentrations, it causes eye, nose & throat irritation, and other respiratory problems.

Nitrogen oxides (NOx): This is predominantly formed during the incineration process. However, they oxidise to NO_2 in the atmosphere. NOx is formed from two main sources - thermal NOx and fuel NOx. In thermal formation, the oxygen and nitrogen react in the air. Fuel NOx is formed during the reactions between oxygen and nitrogen in the fuel. Nitrogen oxides are important, as they participate in several processes in atmospheric chemistry. They are precursors of the formation of ozone (O_3) and preoxy acetal nitrate (PAN). These photochemical oxidants are responsible for smog formation and cause acid rain.

Particulates: This is formed during the combustion process by several mechanisms. The turbulence in the combustion chambers may carry some ash into the exhaust flow. Other inorganic materials present in the waste volatilise at combustion temperature and later condense downstream to form particles or deposits on ash particles. The main component of fly ash is chemically inert silica; but it may also contain toxic metal and organic substances.

Hydrochloric acid (HCl): Hydrochloric acid results from the high concentration of chlorine containing materials (*e.g.*, some type of plastics like polyvinyl chloride) in solid waste. Chlorine easily dissolves in water to form HCl. Its presence in the gaseous state may increase the acidity of local rain & ground water, which can damage exposed & unprotected metal surfaces, erode buildings and may affect the mobilisation of heavy metals in soil.

Hydrogen fluoride (HF): Hydrogen fluoride is more toxic & corrosive than HCl, although its presence in the emissions from solid waste incinerators occurs in much smaller quantities. It is formed due to the presence of trace amounts of fluorine in the waste.

Heavy metals (Hg, Cd, Pb, Zn, Cu, Ni, Cr): Solid waste contains heavy metals and metallic compounds in the combustible & incombustible fractions. During the incineration process, metals may vaporise directly or form oxides or chlorides at high temperatures in the combustion zone. They condense over other particles and leave the incineration process in the flue gas.

Dioxins and furans: Polychlorinated dibenzo-p-dioxins (PCDD) and polychlorinated dibenzofurans (PCDF) have been detected in the emissions from solid waste incinerators. Dioxins can be formed in all combustion processes, where organic carbon, oxygen and chlorine are present. The concern over dioxins & furans has increased after a number of animal studies have shown that for some species, they are carcinogenic and highly toxic, even at very low levels of exposure.

77. Describe the various pollution control flue gas cleaning equipments used in waste incinerators.

Ans. Gas-cleaning equipments employed to carry out the necessary flue gas cleaning in waste incinerator plants are described below:

Electrostatic precipitators (ESP): These are used for particulate control. ESP use electric forces to move the particle flowing out of the gas stream on to the collector electrodes. The particles get a negative charge, when they pass through an ionised field. The electric field that forces the charged particles to the walls comes from discharged electrodes maintained at high voltage in the centre of the flue gas flow lane.

When particles are collected, they must be carefully removed to avoid their reentry into the gaseous stream. This is achieved by knocking them loose from the plates or by intermittent and continuous washing with water. The removal efficiency is more than 99% with a low-pressure drop. Particle size and other physical characteristics such as gas stream temperature, flue gas volume, moisture content, gas stream composition, particle composition and particle surface characteristics affect the performance of the equipment. ESP's come in one or two stage designs and can have different configurations: plate wire, flat plate and tubular. These configurations can be wet or dry, depending on the method of dust collection.

Fabric/bag filters: In fabric filtration, the gas flows through a number of filter bags placed in parallel, leaving the dust captured by the fabric. Extended operation of fabric filters requires periodic cleaning of the cloth surface. After a new fabric goes through a number of cycles of use and cleaning, it forms a residual cake of dust that becomes the filter medium, which is responsible for highly efficient filtering of small particles that characterises fabric filter. They are widely accepted for controlling particulate matter.

The type of cloth fabric limits the temperature of operation of fabric cloth: cotton is least resistant (800°C) while fabric glass is the most resistant (275°C). This temperature requirement makes the use of a cooling system necessary for the gas, before it enters the filter, but it is also necessary that the temperature of the exhaust gas stream be maintained above the dew point because liquid particles block the pores in the fabric very quickly. The major difference between different configurations of fabric filters is the cleaning method used during operating cycles such as shaker, reverse-air and pulse-jet cleaning.

Scrubbers: Scrubbers are used to control particulate matter and acid gases leaving the incinerator. Particulates and gases are removed from the gas stream mainly by absorption and adsorption. The particles are moved to the vicinity of the water droplets and collide with each other. The particles adhere to the liquid media and precipitate to the bottom of the unit containing the dust particle from the gas phase. In addition to removing entrapped particulate matter, scrubbers can also remove gases by absorption and adsorption. Any other type of particulate control equipment does not possess this capability of scrubber. It can remove particles of size 0.1 to 200 m efficiently. The various types of scrubbers can be dry, semi-dry or wet, depending on the composition of flue gas.

78. Describe the various environmental concerns related to MSW incineration plants.

Ans. Apart from air pollution, there are other environmental concerns related to waste incineration which are described below:

(i) **Water pollution:** Wastewater in an incineration facility can be generated in various forms. These include tipping floor runoff system wash water, ash quench water and water from pollution control systems. For most incineration facilities, wastewater can be recycled in a closed-loop system. In these systems, water from floor drains, ash dewatering, water softener recharge and other process wastewaters are collected and stored in a tank. This water is then reused for ash quenching. Sanitary waste can be directed to municipal sewer systems. In some cases, regulatory authorities may require that the waste stream be pretreated before discharge.

(ii) **Land-retained pollution:** Land-retained pollutants originate as stack or fugitive emissions and are of increasing concern. Bioaccumulation and subsequent ingestion from food is an indirect exposure route resulting from land-retained emissions. To provide better understanding of land-retained pollutants, it may be desirable to establish baseline contaminant levels, before incineration plant construction so that changes in those levels throughout the plant's operating lifetime can be monitored.

(iii) **Residue disposal:** An incineration facility & its emission control system produce a variety of residues such as large quantity of bottom ash, the unburned & not burnable materials discharged from the incinerator at the end of the burning cycle. The process also produces a lighter emission known as fly ash. Fly ash consists of products in particulate form, which are either produced as a result of the chemical decomposition of burnable materials or are unburned (or partially burned) materials drawn upward by thermal air currents in the incinerator and trapped in pollution control equipment. Fly ash normally comprises only a small proportion (ranging from 10 to 20%) of the total volume of residue from an incineration facility.

Constituents in both ash and scrubber product vary, depending on the materials burned. In systems burning a homogeneous fuel such as coal, oil, or tires, the level of pollutants in residues may be relatively constant. Systems burning a more heterogeneous mixture, such as municipal, industrial, or medical waste may experience wide swings in the chemical composition of residues. The major constituents of concern in municipal waste combustion ash are heavy metals, particularly lead, cadmium & mercury. These metals may impact human health and the environment; if improperly handled, stored, transported, disposed of or reused.

(iv) **Noise pollution:** Truck traffic is the greatest source of noise pollution in incineration plant operations. Well-maintained and responsibly operated trucks will help minimise this problem. Local regulations may restrict truck traffic to certain hours of the day and to specified truck corridors. Under these conditions, noise pollution should not be a significant factor. Noise resulting from plant operations and air handling fans associated with the combustion and emission control equipment is also a potential problem. Noise levels are likely to be the highest in front of waste tipping floor doors, ash floor doors and the vicinity of air emission stacks. Walls, fences, trees and landscaped earthen barriers can serve to reduce noise levels.

(v) **Aesthetic impact:** Proper site landscaping and building design can help minimise or prevent negative aesthetic impacts. Such impacts are much less problematic, if the facility is sited in an industrial area and not adjacent to residential or commercial areas. Keeping the process building at negative pressure can prevent undesirable odours from escaping outside of the building. The use of internal air for combustion in the plant processes will destroy most odours.

Some facilities may emit visible steam or vapour plumes. Smoke, resulting from improper conditions in the combustion chamber, can also be problematic. Air emission stacks & cooling towers may also be unappealing anomalies in the skyline of some areas. If external lights on buildings prove objectionable to neighbours, perimeter lights (on stands) directed towards the plant may be preferable.

79. Describe in detail the solid waste management hierarchy.

Ans. Solid waste is the unwanted or useless solid materials generated from combined residential, industrial and commercial activities . It may be categorized according to its origin (domestic, industrial, commercial, construction or institutional wastes); according to its contents (organic material, glass, metal, plastic paper etc); or according to hazard potential (toxic, non-toxic, flammable, radioactive, infectious etc). Management of solid waste reduces or eliminates adverse impacts on the environment & human health and supports economic development and improved quality of life. A number of processes are involved in effectively managing waste for a municipality. These include monitoring, collection, transport, processing, recycling and disposal of wastes.

Reduce, Reuse, Recycle.

Methods of waste reduction, waste reuse and recycling are the preferred options when managing waste. There are many environmental benefits that can be derived from the use of these methods. They reduce or prevent green house gas emissions, reduce the release of pollutants, conserve resources, save energy and reduce the demand for waste treatment technology & landfill space. Therefore that these methods should be adopted and incorporated as part of the waste management plan.

Waste reduction and reuse.

Waste reduction and reuse of products are both methods of waste prevention. They eliminate the production of waste at the source of generation and reduce the demands for large scale treatment and disposal facilities. Methods of waste reduction include manufacturing products with less packaging, encouraging customers to bring their own reusable bags for packaging, encouraging the public to choose reusable products such as cloth napkins and reusable plastic & glass containers, backyard composting and sharing & donating any unwanted items rather than discarding them.All of the methods of waste prevention require public participation. Also the government may need to regulate the types & amount of packaging used by manufacturers and make the reuse of shopping bags mandatory.

Recycling.

Recycling refers to the removal of items from the waste stream to be used as raw materials in the manufacture of new products. Recycling occurs in three phases: first the waste is sorted and recyclables collected, the recyclables are used to create raw materials. These raw materials are then used in the production of new products.

The sorting of recyclables may be done at the source (*i.e.* within household or office) for selective collection by the municipality or to be dropped off by the waste producer at a recycling centres. The pre-sorting at the source requires public participation which may not be forthcoming if there are no benefits to be derived. Also a system of selective collection by the government can be costly. It would require more frequent circulation of trucks within neighbourhood to facilitate the waste collection.

Another option is to mix the recyclables with the general waste stream for collection andthen sorting & recovery of recyclable materials can be performed by the municipality at a suitable site. The sorting by the municipality has the advantage of eliminating the dependence on the public and ensuring that the recycling does occur. Disadvantage however, is that the value of the recyclable materials is reduced since being mixed in and compacted with other garbage can have adverse effects on the quality of the recyclable material.

Waste Collection.

Waste from homes is generally collected by local authorities through regular waste collection, or by special collections for recycling. Within hot climates the waste should be collected at least twice a week to control fly breeding, and the harbouring of other pests in the community. Other factors to consider when deciding on frequency of collection are the odours caused by decomposition and the accumulated quantities.

Waste treatment.

Waste treatment techniques transform the waste into a form that is more manageable, reduce the volume or reduce the toxicity of the waste thus making the waste easier to dispose of. Treatment methods are selected based on the composition, quantity, and form of the waste material. Some waste treatment methods being used today include subjecting the waste to extremely high temperatures, dumping on land or land filling and use of biological processes to treat the waste. It should be noted that treatment and disposal options are chosen as a last resort to the previously mentioned management strategies of reducing, reusing and recycling of waste.

Solid waste management hierarchy is shown below in figure.

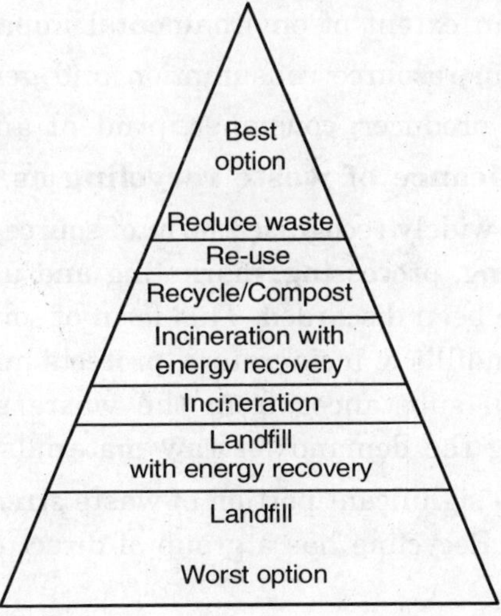

80. What is the purpose and advantages of prevention of waste generation by source reduction.

Ans. Source reduction can serve several purposes, including the following:

(i) **Product reuse:** Using reusable products, instead of their disposal equivalents, reduce the amount of materials that are to be managed as wastes. An example of product reuse is the reusable shopping bag.

(ii) **Material volume reduction:** Reducing the volume of material used changes the amount of waste entering the waste stream. This helps in controlling the waste generated and its disposal. For example, buying in bulk or using large food containers reduces the amount of packaging waste generated.

(iii) **Toxicity reduction:** Source reduction reduces the amount of toxic constituents in products entering the waste stream and reduces the adverse environmental impacts of recycling or other waste management activities. For example, substitution of lead and cadmium in inks (solvent-based to water-based) and paints is a source reduction activity.

(iv) **Increased product lifetime:** Source reduction facilitates the use of products with longer lifetime over short-lived alternatives that are designed to be discarded at the end of their useful lives. It encourages a product design that allows for repair and continued use rather than disposal. Manufacturing long-life tyres is a good example of increasing product lifetime.

(v) **Decreased consumption:** This refers to the reduced consumption of materials that are not reusable (*e.g.*, using a reusable shopping bag instead of picking up plastic bags from the store). Consumer education about the materials that are difficult to dispose of or are harmful to the environment is essential. Buying practices can thus be altered (*e.g.*, buying in bulk) to reflect environmental consciousness.

Main advantages of source reduction are:

- Reduction in extent of environmental impacts.
- Reduction in resource consumption and generation of pollution.
- It includes producer, consumer, prudent and efficient activities.

81. Describe the significance of waste recycling as a form of source reduction.

Ans. Recycling is the most widely recognised form of source reduction involving the process of separating, collecting, processing, marketing and ultimately using a material that would have otherwise been discarded. This form of source reduction, like other forms, lessens reliance on landfills & incinerators, protects human health & the environment by removing harmful substances from the waste stream and conserves natural resources by reducing the demand for raw materials.

Recycling can divert a significant portion of waste stream from disposal in landfill and combustion facilities. Recycling has a group of direct & indirect significance which is described below:

(i) **Economic significance:** Economic assessment of waste recycling is a difficult task as many of the beneficial environmental & social impacts of recycling are long-term & are intangible, and, therefore, are difficult to quantify. Some of the short and long term economic benefits are:

- **Cost reduction:** Resource recovery through recycling of solid waste could be of interest to waste management authorities as a means of reducing the waste disposal cost. Any saving in waste management cost could be a significant incentive to the authorities to increase the coverage of service areas and improve the service level. They can save cost from fuel for transportation, operation & maintenance, and generate revenue by sale of recyclables, etc.
- **Employment:** Recycling of waste is a labour intensive activity, and its potential to ease the unemployment problem is high. Enhanced recycling activities, for example, can create an additional job market for skilled & unskilled workforce, and they can adapt to any of the occupations such as a labourer in recycling business or industry or a dealership.
- **Energy saving:** Use of recyclables in some industrial processes is known to consume less energy than the use of any other raw material. The reduction in energy consumption in one industry could mean its availability for some other industry in need.
- **Reduced health care costs:** Improved health and sanitary conditions in urban areas resulting from indirect benefits of waste recycling can reduce the investment in public health programme.
- **Saving costs for other public utilities:** Enhanced solid waste recycling practices can reduce the frequency of sewer clogging, blocking of natural watercourses and pollution of water bodies. This will benefit the concerned public utilities through reduced cost in cleaning sewers & improved public safety due to blocked sewers and narrowing of natural watercourses.

(ii) **Environmental and health significance:** The volume of waste is increasing rapidly because of population growth and economic development. The composition of waste is also changing, leading to waste production with more recyclables. At the same time, polluted waste fractions are increasing because of increasing complex processes being used in industries, and these contribute to environmental degradation. This notwithstanding, recycling helps, among others, in the following ways, to facilitate effective waste management:

- **Improved environment:** The environmental pollution may be due to inadequate SWM as well as due to its effect on other urban infrastructure. Recycling reduces the volume of waste that has to be finally dumped, and thereby causing reduction in pollution at the waste disposal sites. When there is reduction in volume of waste because of its increased reuse, different types of pollution (*e.g.*, water, air & land) will get abated.

- **Natural resource conservation:** Industries with natural products as their raw material for production are depleting natural resources. Use of more and more recyclable solid wastes in industrial production will relieve the tremendous pressure on these precious resources. For example, recycling of waste paper means a lower demand for wood, which means less cutting of trees and an enhanced possibility for sustainable use of the forest. Using recyclable items in the production process would reduce the demand for energy as well.

(iii) **Social significance:** People engaged in waste collection activities are normally of low social and economic standing. Different groups of people engaged in waste recycling have a hierarchical social and economic status, in which, processors are at the top of the hierarchy followed by waste dealers & wholesalers, waste buyers and waste collectors in that very order, while scavengers are at the bottom. Although there is this social and economic hierarchy within the waste recycling business, the overall social esteem of waste recycling operators is low.

A formal recycling arrangement will help promote the social esteem of waste workers and facilitate their upward social mobility due to increased earning. In addition, the improved recycling activity will increase the economic value of the waste and will reduce waste scavenging activity providing opportunity for scavengers to switch to a more socially acceptable occupation. In short, institutionalised recycling programmes will help remove the stigma associated with waste scavenging and transform it to an economic enterprise.

82. Describe various elements of a waste recycling programme.

Ans. Recycling includes a mix of strategies, ranging from single material drop off centres to large scale, centralised processing facilities. Elements of a recycling programme include source separation, buy back. Curbside (kerbside) collection, storage & collection of recyclables, collection vehicle & processing equipment, material resource facilities and full stream processing which are described below:

Source separation.

Source separation refers to the segregation of the recyclable & reusable materials at the point of generation. This requires that several designated materials be separated into their own specific containers, while other programmes use only two containers—one for the storage of mixed recyclables and the other for regular wastes.

Drop-off/buy-back.

A drop-off programme requires residents to separate the recyclable materials and bring them to a specified drop-off or collection centre. However, we must take into account local conditions when designing a collection programme. For a community that does not provide a curbside pickup, for example, educating and encouraging citizens to deliver materials to a drop-off site may be all that is needed. A recycling centre can be established at the same location where residents deliver waste. Mobile recycling drop-off trailers can also be used. Drop-off recycling, however, is less convenient than curbside pickup.

Buy-back refers to a drop-off programme that provides monetary incentives to participate. In this type of programme, the residents are paid back for their recyclable material directly or indirectly through the reduction in collection & disposal fees. Establishing a buy-back centre (*i.e.*, a place where recyclables are purchased) may help induce citizens to recycle. Some buy back centres purchase some materials depending on current market conditions.Mobile buy-back operations can serve some areas, purchasing recyclables from small communities or from neighbourhoods of large metropolitan areas on a regular schedule.

Curbside programme.

In a curbside system, source separated recyclables are collected separately from regular refuse from the curbside, alley, or commercial facility. Curbside programmes vary greatly from community to community. Some programmes require residents to separate different materials that are stored in their own containers and collected separately. Other programmes use only one container to store recyclables or two containers, one for paper and the other for heavy recyclables (*e.g.*, glass aluminium, etc.).

Storage & collection of recyclables.

Collection of source-separated materials is a necessary component of recycling programme. Establishing a collection system for source-separated materials will require more careful planning than regular trash collection. Some principles of sound recyclables storage and collection programme include:

- **Resident convenience:** The easier it is for residents to separate materials, the higher the participation and recovery rates will be.
- **Collection crew convenience:** The system should be convenient for collection crews. For example, loading and sorting activities should be as simple as possible.
- **Cost effectiveness:** Equipment and procedures must be designed to maximise collection crew and vehicle productivity.
- **Integrity of materials:** The storage and collection system should keep recyclables in the best shape possible. It should be properly handled, dry and contaminant free.

How residents store recyclables in a household and curb has a direct impact on the success of a recycling programme. The storage container should provide a handy way to store materials until collected, and it must be easy for the collector to distinguish recyclables from garbage.

Collection vehicles for recycling.

Collection vehicles that are designed specifically for collecting recyclables have several storage bins,which can be easily loaded and often equipped with automatic container-tipping devices. A dedicated, closed-body collection vehicle for recycling with sufficient capacity offers advantages such as easy loading and unloading, flexible compartments and protection from weather. Of course, this warrants a substantial initial investment.

Processing equipments for recycling.

Recycling involves a number of processing techniques and these processes require different equipments. Some of the special equipments used in recycling are:

- **Balers:** Balers can be used to densify many types of materials including paper, cardboard, plastics and cans. Balers can improve space utilisation and reduce material transportation costs.
- **Can densifiers:** Can crushers are used to densify aluminium and steel cans prior to transport.
- **Glass crushers:** These are used to process glass fraction separated by colour and break it into small pieces.This crushed material is called cullet,and can be reprocessed into new glass products.
- **Magnetic separators:** These are used to remove ferrous material from a mixture of materials.
- **Wood grinders:** These are chippers and are used to shred large pieces of wood into chips that can be used as mulch or as fuel.
- **Scales:** These are used to measure the quantity of materials recovered or sold.

Material recovery facilities (MRF).

MRF is a centralised facility that receives, separates, processes and markets recyclable material. It can be operated with both drop off and curbside programmes. The primary advantage of MRF is that it allows materials directly from the municipalities and processes them uniformly. It is generally designed to handle all type of recyclables. Implementation of MRF in a municipality depends upon a number of factors as given below:

- **Market demand:** When additional processing is required, MRF is more useful as buyers may have certain material specifications.
- **Separate collection:** In systems that require residents to separate their recyclables, intermediate separation and processing is required.
- **Number of different recyclables:** In general, a MRF will be more beneficial when a large number of different recyclables are collected.
- **Quantities of materials:** Because MRF involves substantial capital and operating costs (*e.g.*, buildings, equipment & labour), it is expected to handle a significant amount of materials to justify its operation.

Full stream processing.

This is a high technology separation technique, which processes all components of municipal waste. The materials recovered by this process tend to be of lower quality than those recovered or source separated in MRF because the former is a mix of various types of wastes. To achieve a better quality, the materials obtained through the full stream processing must be cleaned, which is a costly process.

However, this technique remains attractive because it does not require source separation, and it is used in the following applications:

(i) **Refuse derived fuel (RDF) preparation:** In this application, it is used to extract the combustible portion of municipal waste.

(ii) **Municipal waste composting:** In this application, it is used to concentrate the compostable portion of municipal solid waste.This is sometimes performed as part of RDF preparation.

(iii) **Material recovery:** In this application, it is used to recover& resell certain materials, and thereby making material recovery a recycling technology as well.

In full stream processing, depending on the facility design, the materials are separated either mechanically or by hand, and size & weight are the main characteristics used to separate the materials. For example:

When the material is dumped, oversized materials such as furniture, etc., are removed; rotating screens are used to separate materials of different sizes (small and large); ferrous material is extracted using a magnet system; air classifier is used to separate the lighter material; light materials including plastic and paper are further processed into RDF; heavy fraction is mechanically or manually sorted to recover saleable materials such as cardboard, etc.

83. Describe the Salient Features of Municipal Solid Waste (MSW) Rules, 2000.

Ans. Main features of Indian MSW rules, 2000 are given below:

- **Responsibility of the Urban Local Body**
  - ❑ The Rule designates the Urban Local Bodies as sole responsible to manage solid waste in their area and dictates that "within the territorial area of the municipality, be responsible for the implementation of the provisions of these rules, and for any infrastructure development for collection, storage, segregation, transportation, processing and disposal of municipal solid wastes"
  - ❑ Prohibits waste to be exposed to open atmosphere;
  - ❑ Prohibits waste disposal by burning (garbage, dry leaves) in open;
- **Collection of MSW**
  - ❑ Mandates collection of waste from slums and open squatter areas, hotels/restaurants/ office complexes and commercial areas;
  - ❑ Avoid Manual handling of waste, and ensure that the waste is collected and removed from the municipal area daily;
  - ❑ Vehicles used for transportation of wastes to be covered;
  - ❑ Biodegradable waste and non bio-degradable waste must be collected in separate bins from source. Waste bins for biodegradable waste shall be painted 'Green', those for storage of recyclable wastes shall be painted 'White' and those for storage of other wastes shall be painted 'Black':
  - ❑ Construction/demolition wastes/debris to be separately collected and disposed off following proper norms;
  - ❑ Stray animals are to be kept out from the waste storage facilities
- **Processing of MSW**
  - ❑ Recover recyclables from the waste mass before treating for biodegradable portion of the waste;

- Treatment of organic waste through biodegradation such as vermi composting, mechanical composting by windrow method or any other suitable methods such as anaerobic digestion etc as approved by Central Pollution Control Board (CPCB) may be adopted;
- In case the municipal body is engaged in any other treatment technology, such as incineration, energy recovery from waste etc. it must be duly approved by CPCB;
- Chlorinated plastics should not to be incinerated.

• **Disposal of MSW**

- Municipal body to develop scientifically designed landfill as disposal facility for residues out of waste processing facilities, as well as pre-processing rejects or unprocessed mixed waste (applicable if the waste is not fit for any treatment) in a scientifically designed sanitary landfill for a long term of 20-25 years.
- Site suitability criteria to be ensured for selection of landfill sites.
- Land filling of mixed waste must be avoided, unless the waste is found unsuitable for waste processing. Under unavoidable circumstances or till installation of alternate facilities, land-filling shall be done following proper norms.

• **Monitoring of Pollution**

- Municipality to take adequate pollution prevention steps for all its waste management and handling units
- Measures to reduce air pollution in case the unit has a waste to energy units.
- Environment Monitoring (ground & surface water, air quality) for waste handling site.

• **Awareness Programs**

- The municipality to be engaged in encouraging citizens, by organizing awareness programs for segregation of waste at source and promote recycling or reuse of segregated materials through community participation program involving representatives of local resident welfare associations, community based organizations and non governmental organizations .

84. What is the role of Municipal Body Towards bio-medical waste management?

Ans. Hospital waste/Bio-medical waste is generated during the diagnosis, treatment, or immunization of human beings or animals or in research activities in these fields or in the production or testing of biological waste. Hospital/Bio-medical waste must be managed through "Bio-Medical Waste (Management and Handling) Rules, 1998 .

The biomedical waste management rule directs biomedical waste incineration ash to be disposed into municipal landfills. Also, the municipal body must be a member of the 'Advisory Committee' in the state to advice on steady implementation of biomedical waste management and handling in their areas.

85. What is the role of Municipal Body towards e-waste management?

Ans. E-waste or electronic waste means waste from electrical and electronic equipment, whole or in part or rejects from their manufacturing and repair process, which are intended to be discarded. The E-waste (Management and Handling) Rules 2011 has been been published by the Ministry of Environment and Forest.

86. Discuss the problems related to plastic waste management.

Ans. Problems related to plastic waste management are listed below:

- The plastic content of the municipal waste is picked up by rag pickers for recycling either at primary collection centers or at dumpsites.Since the rag-picking sector is not formalized, not all the recyclables, particularly plastic bags, get picked up and are found littered everywhere.
- Littering is a very common phenomenon in India. One of the offshoots of littering is the choking of drains, streams, etc.
- Plastic films, bags are not permeable, and so they tend to hold other type of wastes thus blocking the way. This gives rise to flooding of the streets in the urban low lying areas with wastewater emanating foul smell and causing breakthrough of serious health hazards.
- Recently, cow deaths have been reported due to the consumption of scattered plastic bags along with the organic matter.
- Plastics are recycled mostly in factories, which do not have adequate technologies to process them in a safe manner. This exposes the workers to toxic fumes and unhygienic conditions.
- Dioxin, a highly carcinogenic and toxic by-product of the manufacturing process of plastics, is one of the chemicals believed to be passed on through breast milk of the mother to the nursing infant. Burning of plastics, especially PVC releases this dioxin and also furan into the atmosphere.
- Since toxic dyes and chemicals are used as additives during the recycling, the workers engaged in the recycling of plastic are constantly exposed to various toxic compounds.
- Polybag recycling is carried out in shanties, this problem is compounded due to poor ventilation, as workers find themselves inhaling contaminated air . Indian collection sector employ children below the age of 15 to collect them because of the low wages to be paid to the child and the ease of availability of child labour.
- Backyard smelters and plastic recycling units dot India's suburban/urban sites, taking lead battery scrap and plastic waste imported from developed countries . The dangerous toxins emitting from the smelters affects human, animal and plant life.
- The current situation is that the plastic recycling in the country is creating more problems and with the influx of plastic waste import it is getting aggravated. If imported, India should also import the technology along with the waste.
- Although plastics contribute only about 7% by weight to MSW, they may contribute 15% or more to the total heat content of MSW. Hydrogen chloride gas is emitted during combustion of polyvinyl chloride (or other chlorinated polymers), and may result in corrosion of municipal waste combustor internal surfaces.

87. Describe the environmental issues related to disposal of plastic waste.

Ans. Plastic products have become an integral part in our daily life as a basic need. Its production crosses the 150 million tonnes per year globally. In India approximately 15 Million tonnes plastic products are consumed every year. Its broad range of application is in packaging films, wrapping materials, shopping and garbage bags, fluid containers, clothing, toys, household & industrial products, and building materials. Plastics never degrades and remains on landscape for several years. The recycled plastics are more harmful to the environment than the virgin products due to mixing of colour, additives, stabilizers, flame retardants etc.

The recycling of a virgin plastic material can be done 2-3 time only, because, after every recycling, the strength of plastic material is reduced due to thermal degradation.

Environmental issues on disposal of Plastic Waste:

Indiscriminate littering of unskilled recycling/reprocessing and non-biodegradability of plastic waste raises the following environmental issues:

- During polymerization process fugitive emissions are released.
- During product manufacturing various types of gases are released.
- Indiscriminate dumping of plastic waste on land makes the land infertile due to its barrier properties.
- Burning of plastics generates toxic emissions such as Carbon Monoxide, Chlorine, Hydrochloric Acid, Dioxin, Furans, Amines, Nitrides, Styrene, Benzene, 1, 3- butadiene, CCl_4, and Acetaldehyde.
- Lead and Cadmium pigments, commonly used in LDPE, HDPE and PP as additives are toxic and are known to leach out.
- Non-recyclable plastic wastes like multilayer, metalised pouches and other thermoset plastic poses disposal problems.
- Sub-standard plastic carry bags, packaging films (<40?) etc. pose problem in collection and recycling.
- Littered plastics give unaesthetic look in the city, choke the drain and may cause flood during monsoon.
- Garbage mixed with plastics interferes in waste processing facilities and also cause problems in landfill operations.
- Recycling industries operating in non-conforming areas are posing threat to environment to unsound recycling practices.

Disposal of plastic waste is a sericus concern in India and such no technology has been validated, however, several experiments have been conducted on reuse of plastic waste in road construction, co-processing of plastic waste in cement kilns. Currently, World wide accepted technology used for the plastic disposal is incineration, however, due to poor maintenance of incinerators, it releases several harmful gases including dioxins & furans in case of chlorinated and brominated plastic waste therefore, raising several environmental issues. In India, for safer disposal of plastic waste, various technologies have been experimented such as Utilization of plastic waste in road construction, Co-processing of Plastic waste in Cement Kilns.

88. What are activities involved in solid waste management ?

Ans. Activities involved are:

- Waste generation,
- Onsite handling ,storage and processing
- Collection
- Transfer and transport
- Processing and recovery & disposal

89. What is meant by commercial/industrial waste collection services?

Ans. The use of large movable & stationary containers and also large stationary compactors are done in this method. Compactors are used to compress the material directly into the large containers or in the form of bales which are then placed in the large containers.

90. What is hauled container waste collection system?

Ans. Waste collection system in which containers used for storage of waste are hauled to the processing, transfer, emptied and returned to either their original location or some other location are defined as hauled container system.

91. What is stationary container waste collection system?

Ans. The collection system in which the containers are used for storage of waste remains at the point of waste generation except when moved for collection are defined as stationary container system.

92. Mention the advantages of composting.

Ans. The entire process involving both the separation and bacterial conversion of the organic solid waste is called composting. Its advantages include:

- Compost contains nitrogen essential for plant growth.
- Used for agricultural field.
- Used for recycling.
- Increasing water retention.
- Increases ion exchange capacity of soil.

93. Describe briefly the sources, effects and management of solid waste.

Ans. Higher standards of living of ever increasing population have resulted in an increase in the quantity & variety of solid waste generated. Management of solid waste is very important in order to minimize the adverse effects of solid wastes. Sold waste can be classified as municipal, industrial, agriculture, medical & mining waste and sewage sludge.

Sources of Urban and Industrial Wastes.

Urban waste consists of medical waste from hospitals; municipal solid wastes from homes, offices, markets, small cottage units, and horticulture waste from parks, gardens, orchards etc.

- Waste from homes contains a variety of discarded materials like polyethylene bags, empty metal & aluminum cans, scrap metals, glass bottles, waste paper, diapers, cloth/rags, food waste etc.
- Waste from shops mainly consists of waste paper, packaging material, cans, bottles, polyethylene bags, peanut shells, eggshells, tea leaves etc.
- Biomedical waste includes anatomical wastes, pathological wastes, infectious wastes etc.
- Construction/demolition waste includes debris and rubbles, wood, concrete etc.
- Horticulture waste and waste from slaughter houses include vegetable parts, residues and remains of slaughtered animals, respectively.

The urban solid waste materials that can be degraded by micro-organisms are called biodegradable wastes. Examples of this type of waste are vegetable wastes, stale food, tea leaves, egg shells, peanut shells, dry leaves etc. Wastes that cannot be degraded by micro-organisms are called non-biodegradable wastes eg, polyethylene bags, scrap metal, glass bottles etc.

- **Industrial wastes:** Industrial wastes consists of a large number of materials including factory rubbish, packaging material, organic wastes, acids, alkalis and metals etc. During some industrial processing large quantities of hazardous and toxic materials are produced. The main sources of industrial wastes are chemical industries, metal and mineral processing industries. Radioactive wastes are generated by nuclear power plants. Thermal power plants produce fly ash in large quantities. Solid wastes from other types of industries include scrap metal, rubber, plastic, paper, glass, wood, oils, paints, asphalt, tars, dyes, scrap leather, ceramics. Abrasives slag, heavy metals, asbestos, batteries.

Effects of Solid Wastes.

Municipal solid wastes heap up on the roads due to improper disposal system. People clean their own houses and dump in their immediate surroundings which affects the community including themselves. This type of dumping allows biodegradable materials to decompose under uncontrolled and unhygienic conditions. This produces foul smell and breeds various types of insects & infectious organisms besides spoiling the aesthetics of the site.

Industrial solid wastes are sources of toxic metals and hazardous wastes, which may spread on land and can cause changes in physico chemical and biological characteristics thereby affecting productivity of soils. Toxic substances may leach or percolate to contaminate the ground water.

In refuse mixing the hazardous wastes are mixed with garbage and other combustible wastes. This makes segregation and disposal more difficult & risky. Various types of wastes like cans, pesticides, cleaning solvents, batteries, radioactive materials, and plastics are mixed up with paper, scraps and other non-toxic materials which could be recycled.

Management of Solid Waste:

For waste management we stress on 'three R's'—Reduce, reuse and recycle before destruction and safe storage of wastes.

(i) **Reduction in use of raw materials:** Reduction in the use of raw materials will correspondingly decrease the production of waste. Reduced demand for any metallic product will decrease the mining of their metal and cause less production of waste.

(ii) **Reuse of waste materials:** The refillable containers which are discarded after use can be reused. Villagers make casseroles and silos from waste paper and other waste materials. Making rubber rings from the discarded cycle tubes which are used by the newspaper vendors, instead of rubber bands, reduces the waste generation during manufacturing of rubber bands. Because of financial constraints poor people reuse their materials to the maximum.

(iii) **Recycling of materials:** Recycling is the reprocessing of discarded materials into new useful products.

- Formation of some old type products *e.g.* old aluminum cans and glass bottles are melted and into recast new cans and bottles .
- Formation of new products: Preparation of cellulose insulation from paper, preparation of fuel pellets from kitchen waste, Preparation of automobiles and construction material from steel cans.

The process of reducing, reusing & recycling saves money, energy, raw materials, land space and also reduces pollution. Recycling of paper will reduce cutting of trees for making fresh paper. Reuse of metals will reduce mining & melting of ores for recovery of metals from ores & prevent pollution.

For discarding wastes the following methods can be adopted:

(i) **Sanitary landfill:** In a sanitary landfill, garbage is spread out in thin layers, compacted and covered with clay or plastic foam. In the modern landfills the bottom is covered with an impermeable liner, usually several layers of clay, thick plastic and sand. The liner protects the ground water from being contaminated due to percolation of leachate. Leachate from bottom is pumped and sent for treatment. When land is full it is covered with clay, sand, gravel and top soil to prevent seepage of water. Several well are drilled near the landfill site to monitor if any leakage is contaminating groundwater.

(ii) **Composting:** Due to shortage of space for landfill in bigger cities, the biodegradable yard waste is allowed to degrade or decompose in an oxygen rich medium. A good quality nutrient rich and environmental friendly manure called compost is formed which improves the soil conditions and fertility.

(iii) **Incineration:** Incinerators are burning plants capable of burning a large amount of solid waste materials at high temperature. The initial cost is very high. During incineration high levels of toxic dioxins, furans, lead and cadmium may be emitted with the fly ash of incinerator. Dioxin level may reach many times more than in the ambient environment. waste landfill plant is an engineered facility used for disposing of solid wastes on land or within the earth's mantle without creating nuisance or hazard to public health or safety, such as breeding of rodents & insects and contamination of groundwater.

94. Describe Six Functional Elements of Municipal Solid Waste Management.

Ans. The activities associated with the management of municipal solid wastes from the point of generation to final disposal is grouped into the six functional elements as described below:

(a) **Waste generation:** Waste generation encompasses activities in which materials are identified as no longer being of value (in their present form) and are either thrown away or gathered together for disposal. Waste generation is, at present, an activity that is not very controllable. In the future, more control is likely to be exercised over generation of wastes. Reduction of waste at source, although not controlled by solid waste managers, is now included in system evaluations as a method of limiting the quantity of waste generated.

(b) **Waste handling and sorting, storage, and processing at the source:** Waste handling and sorting involves the activities associated with management of wastes until they are placed in storage containers for collection. Handling also encompasses the movement of loaded containers to the point of collection. Sorting of waste components is an important step in the handling and storage of solid waste at the source. For example, the best place to separate waste materials for reuse and recycling is at the source of generation. Households are becoming more aware of the importance of separating newspaper & cardboard, bottles/glass, kitchen wastes and ferrous & non-ferrous materials.On site storage is of primary importance because of public health concerns and aesthetic consideration. Unsightly makeshift containers and even open ground storage, both of which are undesirable, are seen at many residential and commercial sites. The cost of providing storage for solid wastes at the source is normally borne by the household in the case of individuals, or by the management of commercial and industrial properties. Processing at the source involves activities such as backyard waste composting.

(c) **Waste collection:** Funcional element of waste collection includes not only the gathering of solid wastes and recyclable materials, but also the transport of these materials, after collection, to the location where the collection vehicle is emptied. This location may be a material processing facility, a transfer station, or a landfill disposal site.

(d) **Waste Sorting, processing and transformation:** The recovery of sorted materials, processing of solid waste and transformation of solid waste that occurs primarily in locations away from the source of waste generation are encompassed by this functional element. Sorting of mixed wastes usually occurs at a materials recovery facility, transfer stations, combustion facilities, and disposal sites. Sorting includes the separation of bulky items, separation of waste components by size using screens, manual separation of waste components, and separation of ferrous & non-ferrous metals. Waste processing is undertaken to recover conversion products and energy. The organic fraction of Municipal Solid Waste (MSW) can be transformed by a variety of biological & thermal processes. The most commonly used biological transformation process is aerobic composting. The most commonly used thermal transformation process is incineration. Waste transformation is undertaken to reduce the volume, weight, size or toxicity of waste without resource recovery. Transformation may be done by a variety of mechanical (eg shredding), thermal (*e.g.* incineration without energy recovery) or chemical (*e.g.* encapsulation) techniques.

(d) **Waste transfer and transport:** It involves two steps: (i) the transfer of wastes from the smaller collection vehicle to the larger transport equipment and (ii) the subsequent transport of the wastes, usually over long distances, to a processing or disposal site. The transfer usually takes place at a transfer station.

(e) **Waste disposal:** The disposal of wastes by landfilling or uncontrolled dumping is the ultimate fate of all solid wastes, whether they are residential wastes collected & transported directly to a landfill site, residual materials from Materials Recovery Facilities residue from the combustion of solid waste, rejects of composting, or other substances from various solid waste processing facilities. A municipal solid waste landfill plant is an engineered facility used for disposing of solid wastes on land or within the earth's mantle without creating nuisance or hazard to public health or safety, such as breeding of rodents and insects and contamination of groundwater.

95. Describe the hierarchy of solid waste management options.

Ans. Current thinking on the best methods to deal with waste is centred on a broadly accepted 'hierarchy of waste management' (arrangement in order of rank) which gives a priority listing of the waste management options available. The hierarchy usually adopted is (a) waste minimisation/reduction at source, (b) recycling, (c) waste processing (with recovery of resources *i.e.* materials (products) and energy), (d) waste transformation (without recovery of resources) and (e) disposal on land (landfilling). The highest rank of the ISWM hierarchy is waste minimisation or reduction at source, which involves reducing the amount (and/or toxicity) of the wastes produced. Reduction at source is first in the hierarchy because it is the most effective way to reduce the quantity of waste, the cost associated with its handling, and its environmental impacts.

The second highest rank in the hierarchy is recycling, which involves (a) the separation and sorting of waste materials; (b) the preparation of these materials for reuse or reprocessing; and (c) the reuse and reprocessing of these materials. Recycling is an important factor which helps to reduce the demand on resources and the amount of waste requiring disposal by landfilling.

The third rank in the ISWM hierarchy is waste processing which involves alteration of wastes to recover conversion products (*e.g.*, compost) and energy. The processing of waste materials usually results in the reduced use of landfill capacity.

Transformation of waste, without recovery of products or energy, may have to be undertaken to reduce waste volume (*e.g.* shredding and baling) or to reduce toxicity. This is usually ranked fourth in the ISWM hierarchy.

Ultimately, something must be done with (a) the solid wastes that cannot be recycled and are of no further use; (b) the residual matter remaining after solid wastes have been pre-sorted at a materials recovery facility; and (c) the residual matter remaining after the recovery of conversion products or energy.

Landfilling is the fifth rank of the ISWM hierarchy and involves the controlled disposal of wastes on or in the earth's mantle. It is by far the most common method of ultimate disposal for waste residuals. Landfilling is the lowest rank in the ISWM hierarchy because it represents the least desirable means of dealing with wastes.

96. Describe various methods of Waste minimization.

Ans. Waste minimisation or reduction at source is the most desirable activity, since the community does not incur expenditure for waste handling, recycling & disposal of waste that is never created and delivered to the waste management system. To reduce the amount of waste generated at the source, the methods are:

- The adoption of industry standards for product manufacturing and packaging that use less material,
- The passing of laws that minimise the use of virgin materials in consumer products, and
- The levying of cess/fees for waste management services that penalise generators in case of increase in waste quantities.

Modifications in product packaging standards can result in reduction of waste packaging material or use of recyclable materials. Minimisation of use of virgin raw materials by the manufacturing industry promotes substitution by recycled materials. Sorting at source, recycling at source and processing at source (*e.g.* yard composting) help in waste minimisation. One waste management strategy used in some communities in developed countries is to charge a variable rate per can (or ton) of waste, which gives generators a financial incentive to reduce the amount of waste set out for collection. Issues related to the use of variable rates include the ability to generate the revenues required to pay the costs of facilities, the administration of a complex monitoring & reporting network for service, and the extent to which wastes are being put in another place by the generator and not reduced at source .

97. What is the Relationship between Climate Change and Solid Waste?

Ans. Even before a material or product becomes solid waste, it goes through a long cycle that involves removing and processing raw materials, manufacturing the product, transporting the materials and products to markets, and using energy to operate the product. Each of these activities has the potential to generate greenhouse gas emissions through one ormore of the following means:

- **Energy consumption.** Extracting and processing raw materials, manufacturing products, and transporting materials and products to markets all generate greenhouse gas emissions by consuming energy from fossil fuels.
- **Methane emissions.** When organic waste decomposes in landfills, it generates methane, a greenhouse gas.
- **Carbon storage.** Trees absorb carbon dioxide, a greenhouse gas, from the air and store it in wood through carbon sequestration. Waste prevention and recycling of wood and paper products allow more trees to remain standing in the forest, where they can continue to remove carbon dioxide from the air, which helps minimize climate change impacts.

Different wastes and waste management activities have varying impacts on energy consumption, methane emissions, and carbon storage. For example, recycling reduces greenhouse gas emissions by preventing methane emissions from landfills or open dumps and by preventing the consumption of energy for extracting and processing raw materials. Communities looking for ways to help prevent climate change can start by implementing an integrated solid waste management program.

Carbon dioxide is released to the atmosphere when solid waste, fossil fuels (oil, natural gas, and coal), and wood and wood products are burned. Methane is emitted during the production and transport of coal, natural gas, and oil; the decomposition of organic wastes in municipal solid waste landfills; and by livestock. Nitrous oxide is emitted during agricultural and industrial activities, as well as during the combustion of solid waste and fossil fuels. Each greenhouse gas differs in its ability to trap heat in the atmosphere. Methane traps over 21 times more heat than carbon dioxide, and nitrous oxide absorbs 310 times more than carbon dioxide. The higher the heat trapping potential of the green house gas, the greater the impact on climate change. Efforts to decrease emissions of these gases help reduce climate change impacts.

98. What can you do on personal level to reduce solid waste?

Ans. Following actions can help reduce solid waste:

- Carry your own cloth or jute bag when you go shopping.
- Say no to all plastic bags as far as possible.
- Reduce the use of paper bags also.
- Reuse the soft drinks poly bottles for storing water.
- Segregate the waste in the house - keep two garbage bins and see to it that the biodegradable & the non biodegradable waste is put into separate bins and dispose off separately.
- Dig a compost pit in your garden and put all the bio degradable into it.

- See to it that all garbage is thrown into the municipal bin as the collection is generally done from there.
- When you go out do not throw paper and other wrappings or even left over food here & there, make sure that it is put in the correct place that is into a dustbin.
- Not to throw the waste/litter on the streets, drains, open spaces, water bodies etc.
- Storage of organic/bio-degradable and recyclable waste separately at source.
- Community storage/collection of waste in flats, multi-storied buildings, societies, commercial complexes, etc.
- Managing excreta of pet dogs and cats appropriately.
- Waste processing/disposal at a community level.
- Pay adequately for the services provided.
- Public education to be organized.

99. Describe the role of rag pickers in solid waste management and occupational hazards associated with it.

Ans. Rag pickers are the people who are actually going through the garbage bins, dumping sites to pick out the 'rags'. These rag pickers: women, children, and men from the lowest rung in the society, are a common sight in most cities and towns around the country. Rag picking is considered the most menial of all activities and it is people who have no other alternative that are generally driven to it. Rag pickers contribute a great deal towards waste management as they scavenge the recyclable matter thereby saving the municipality of the cost & time of collecting & transporting this to the dumps.

They are one of the focal points for the recycling of waste. They are the persons who, in spite of all the dangers that they face, goes on relentlessly picking through the garbage bin, looking for waste that could be useful to them. They sell all the material they picked to the whole sellers and retailers who in turn sell it to the industry that uses this waste matter as raw material. The main items of collection are plastics, paper, bottles, and cans.

While picking through waste, the rag pickers puts themself at a great risk and is always prone to disease as the waste that they handle can be infectious. We can indirectly help the rag pickers by carefully segregating the waste that is generated at our homes, thereby facilitating their search for materials that are useful to them. They will not have to scavenge in the bins/yards for long hours.

Occupational hazards associated with waste handling Infections:

- Skin & blood infections resulting from direct contact with waste, and from infected wounds.
- Eye and respiratory infections resulting from exposure to infected dust.
- Different diseases that results from the bites of animals feeding on the waste.
- Intestinal infections that are transmitted by flies feeding on the waste.

100. Describe the actions to be taken for waste management at source.

Ans. Waste Management at source is given below in table.

Source of waste generation	**Action to be taken**
Household	• Not to throw any solid waste in the neighbourhood, on the streets, open spaces, and vacant lands, into the drains or water bodies. • Keep food waste/biodegradable waste in a non corrosive container with a cover (lid). • Keep dry, recyclable waste in a bin or bag or a sack. • Keep domestic hazardous waste if and when generated separately for disposal at specially notified locations.
Multi-storeyed buildings, commercial complexes, private societies	• Provide separate community bin or bins large enough to hold food/biodegradable waste and recyclable waste generated in the building or society. • Direct the members of the association to deposit their waste in community bin.
Slums	• Use community bins provided by local body for deposition of food and biodegradable waste.
Shops,offices, institutions, etc	• If situated in a commercial complex, deposit the waste in bins provided by the association.
Hotels & restaurants	• The container used should be strong, not more than 100 litre in size, should have a handle on the top or handles on the sides and a rim at the bottom for easy handling.
Vegetable & Fruit Markets	• Provide large containers, which match with transportation system of the local body. • Shop keepers not to dispose of the waste in front of their shops or open spaces. Deposit the waste as and when generated into the large container placed in the market.
Meat & fish markets	• Not to throw any waste in front of their shops or open spaces around. Keep non-corrosive container/containers not exceeding 100-litre capacity with lid handle and the rim at the bottom and deposit the waste in the said containers as and when generated. • Transfer the contents of this container into a large container provided by the association.

Street food vendors	• Not to throw any waste on the street, pavement or open spaces. Keep bin or bag for the storage of waste that generates during street vending activity. • Preferably have arrangements to affix the bin or bag with the hand-cart used for vending.
Marriage halls, community halls, kalyana mandapas	• Not to throw any solid waste in their neighbourhood, on the streets, open spaces, and vacant lands, into the drains or water bodies. • Provide a large container with lid which may match with the transportation system of the local body and deposit all the waste generated in the premises in such containers.
Hospitals, Nursing homes, etc.	• Not to throw any solid waste in their neighbourhood, on the streets,open spaces, and vacant lands, into the drains or water bodies. • Not to dispose off the biomedical waste in the municipal dust bins or other waste collection or storage site meant for municipal solid waste. • Store the waste as per the directions contained in the government of India, Ministry of Environment Biomedical Waste (Management & Handling) Rules, 1998.
Construction/ demolition waste	• Not to deposit construction waste or debris on the streets, footpaths, pavements, open spaces, water bodies etc. • Store the waste within the premises or with permission of the authorities just outside the premises without obstructing the traffic preferably in a container if available through the local body or private contractors.
Garden waste	• Compost the waste within the garden, if possible Trim the garden waste once in a week on the days notified by the local body. • Store the waste into large bags or bins for handing over to the municipal authorities appointed for the purpose on the day of collection notified.

101. List out the Application of some important industrial solid wastes.

Ans. Industrial solid wastes applications are tabulated below.

S.No.	Solid waste	Areas of application
1	Fly ash	• Cement • Raw material in Ordinary Portland Cement (OPC) manufacture • Manufacture of oil well cement • Making sintered fly ash light-weight aggregates • Cement / silicate bonded fly ash/clay binding bricks and insulating bricks • Cellular concrete bricks and blocks, lime and cement fly ash concrete • Precast fly ash concrete building units • Structural fill for roads, construction on sites, land reclamation, etc. • As filler in mines, in bituminous concrete • As plasticiser • As water reducer in concrete and sulphate resisting concrete
2	Blast Furnace Slags	• Manufacture of slag cement, super sulphated cement, metallurgical cement • Non-portland cement • Making expansive cement, oil well, coloured cement and high early-strength cement • In refractory and in ceramic as sital • As a structural fill (air-cooled slag) • As aggregate in concrete
3	Ferro-alloy & other metallurgical slags	• As structural fill • In making pozzolona metallurgical cement
4	By product gypsum	• In making of gypsum plaster, plaster boards and slotted tiles • As set controller in the manufacture of portland cement • In the manufacture of expensive or non-shrinking cement, super sulphated and anhydrite cement • As mineraliser • Simultaneous manufacture of cement and sulphuric acid

5	Lime sludge (phosphochalk paper and sugar sludges)	• As a sweetener for lime in cement manufacture • Manufacture of lime pozzolana bricks/binders • For recycling in parent industry • Manufacture of building lime • Manufacture of masonry cement
6	Chromium sludge	• As a raw material component in cement manufacture • Manufacture of coloured cement as a chromium-bearing material
7	Red mud	• As a corrective material • As a binder • Making construction blocks • As a cellular concrete additive • Coloured composition for concrete • Making heavy clay products and red mud bricks • In the formation of aggregate • In making floor and all tiles • Red mud polymer door
8	Pulp and paper	• Lignin

102. Describe various acts, rules and notifications for Solid Waste Management in India.

Ans. Laws concerning solid waste are passed to improve the solid waste management and to regulate the disposal activity, which causes problems in public health, the environment and economics. Many laws apply to the control of solid waste management problems which are given below:

Acts, Rules and Notification regarding Solid Waste Management in India

- Constitution of India, 1950
- Code of Criminal Procedure, 1973
- Water (Prevention and Control of Pollution) Act, 1974
- The Air (Prevention and Control of Pollution) Act, 1981
- Environment Protection Act, 1986
- Hazardous waste (Management & Handling) Rules, 1989
- Coastal Regulation Zone Notification, 1991
- Bio-medical wastes (Management & Handling) Rules, 1998.
- Recycled plastics (Manufacture and Usage) Rules, 1999
- Municipal Waste (Management and Handling) Rules 2000

The right to live in a clean and healthy environment is not only a fundamental right guaranteed under Article 21 of our Constitution but also a right recognized and enforced by the courts of law under different laws, like Law of Torts, Indian Penal Code, 1860 Civil Procedure Code, 1908 and Criminal Procedure Code, 1973. **The Constitution of India, 1950 the earliest legislation and which is the supreme law of the land has imposed a fundamental duty on every citizen of India under Article 51-A(g) to protect and improve the environment.**

At the national policy level, the ministry of environment and forests has legislated the Municipal Waste Management and Handling Rules 2000 in exercise of the power conferred under sections 3, 6 and 25 of the Environment Protection Act, 1986. These rules shall apply to every municipal authority responsible for collection, segregation, storage, transportation, processing and disposal of municipal solid wastes.

Composting of wastes is a legal requirement provided under the Municipal Solid Waste Management (MSW) Rules 2000 for all municipal bodies in the country. The MSW Rules 2000 requires that "biodegradable wastes shall be processed by composting, vermi-composting, anaerobic digestion or any other appropriate biological processing for the stabilization of wastes".

Every municipal authority shall, within the territorial area of the municipality, be responsible for the implementation of the provisions of these rules, and for any infrastructure development for collection, storage, segregation, transportation, processing and disposal of municipal solid wastes.

The Central Government, to perform its functions effectively as contemplated under sections 6, 8, and 25 of the Environment Protection Act, 1986, and has made various Rules, Notifications and Orders including the Bio-medical wastes (Management & Handling) Rules, 1998.

Recycled plastics (Manufacture and Usage) Rules, 1999.

- Prohibit the usage of carry bags or containers made of recycled plastics for storing, carrying, dispensing or packaging of foodstuffs.
- Prescribe that the minimum thickness of carry bags made of recycled plastics shall not be less than 20 microns.
- Directs the manufacturers of carry bags that the carry bags and containers shall be in natural shape or white in colour.
- Stipulate that recycling of plastics shall be undertaken strictly in accordance with the standards prescribed by the Bureau of Indian Standards. The manufacturers of recycled plastics carry bags shall mark their products as "recycled".

This notification also provides that the Plastics Industries Association through member units shall undertake self-regulatory measures. The State Pollution Control Board exercise powers to implement and control the above rules.

Preliminary surveys on municipalities' preparedness in implementing the MSW Rules 2000 show that the majority of the cities have embarked on city-wide implementation of door-to-door collection of waste, source segregation, composting of organics, recycling and creating engineered and safe landfill sites for residual waste disposal.

Segregation of municipal solid waste.

In order to encourage the citizens, municipal authority shall organize awareness programmes for segregation of wastes and shall promote recycling or reuse of segregated materials. The municipal authority shall undertake phased programme to ensure community participation in waste segregation. For this purpose, the municipal authorities shall arrange regular meetings at quarterly intervals with representatives of local resident welfare associations and non-governmental organizations.

Storage of municipal solid wastes.

Municipal authorities shall establish and maintain storage facilities in such a manner, as they do not create unhygienic and unsanitary conditions around it. Following criteria shall be taken into account while establishing and maintaining storage facilities, namely:

- Storage facilities shall be created and established by taking into account quantities of waste generation in a given area and the population densities. A storage facility shall be so placed that it is accessible to users.
- Storage facilities to be set up by municipal authorities or any other agency shall be so designed that wastes stored are not exposed to open atmosphere and shall be aesthetically acceptable and user-friendly.
- Storage facilities or 'bins' shall have 'easy to operate' design for handling, transfer and transportation of waste. Bins for storage of bio-degradable wastes shall be painted green, those for storage of recyclable wastes shall be painted white and those for storage of other wastes shall be painted black.

Manual handling of waste shall be prohibited. If unavoidable due to constraints, manual handling shall be carried out under proper precaution with due care for safety of workers.

Processing of municipal solid wastes.

Municipal authorities shall adopt suitable technology or combination of such technologies to make use of wastes so as to minimize burden on landfill. Following criteria shall be adopted, namely

- The biodegradable wastes shall be processed by composting, vermicomposting, anaerobic digestion or any other appropriate biological processing for stabilization of wastes.
- Mixed waste containing recoverable resources shall follow the route of recycling. Incineration with or without energy recovery can also be used for processing wastes in specific cases. Municipal authority or the operator of a facility wishing to use other state-of-the-art technologies shall approach the Central Pollution Control Board to get the standards laid down before applying for grant of authorization.

Disposal of municipal solid wastes.

Landfilling shall be restricted to non-biodegradable, inert waste and other waste that are not suitable either for recycling or for biological processing. Landfilling shall also be carried out for residues of waste processing facilities as well as pre-processing rejects from waste processing facilities. Landfilling of mixed waste shall be avoided unless the same is found unsuitable for waste processing. Under unavoidable circumstances or till installation of alternate facilities, landfilling shall be done following proper norms.

Managing Non-biodegradable solid waste.

Non-biodegradable solid waste (NBDSW) or refuse is a carpet word. It eovers a variety of materials ranging from asbestos to Zinc batteries. Polythene and its related compounds are the most commonly found solid waste materials in urban environs. Many non-biodegradable solid waste materials are known to cause considerable environmental hazards when released into land, water and atmosphere.

Coastal environment and solid waste management.

Solid waste related problems prevail more in megalopolis and the dangers reach great heights in coastal cities. Solid wastes of domestic and industrial units are considered major pollutants of coastal regions of ndia. Nearly 44000 m^3 of domestic sewage and 440 m^3 of industrial waste are discharged every year into the seas of India.

103. Describe the Salient Features of the Indian Plastic Waste Management (PWM) Rules, 2011.

Ans. Important features of PWM rules, 2011 are given below:

(i) The plastic carry bags shall be used for the purpose of carrying or dispensing commodities but don't include these bags which are integral part of packaged products. The thickness of bag shall not be <40μ;

(ii) Carry bags can also be made from compostable plastics conforming IS/ISO:17088:2008;

(iii) Prescribed Authority for registration, manufacture & recycling shall be State Pollution Control Board (SPCB) or Pollution Control Committee (PCC). And for enforcement of Rules relating to use, collection, segregation, transportation & disposal of plastic waste, shall be concerned Municipal Authority;

(iv) Multilayered pouches or sachets used for packaging of gutkha etc. shall not use plastic material in any form;

(v) Every carry bags made from plastic shall bear a label or mark "recycled" as per IS:14534:1998. Each carry bag made from "Compostable Material" shall bear a label "Compostable" & shall conform to IS/ISO:17088:2008;

(vi) No carry bag shall be made available free of cost by retailers to consumers. The concerned Municipal Authority may be notification determine the minimum price for carry bags in order to encourage re-use so as to minimize plastic waste generation;

(vii) Each State Government shall for constitute a State Level Advisory (SLA) Body to monitor implementation of Rules. This body shall meet once in a year and may invite experts, if it considers necessary.

(viii) The Plastic Waste Management (PWM) shall be as under;

(a) Recycling, recovery or disposal of plastic waste shall be carried out as per the rules, regulations and standards stipulated by the central government from time to time;

(b) Recycling of plastics shall be carried out in accordance with the Indian Standard IS 14534:1998 titled as Guidelines for Recycling of Plastics, as amended from time to time;

(c) The Municipal Authority shall be responsible for setting up, operationalisation and coordination of the waste management system and for performing the associated functions, namely:- (i) to ensure safe collection, storage, segregation, transportation, processing and disposal of plastic waste; (ii) to ensure that no damage is caused to the environment during this process; (iii) to ensure setting up of collection centres for plastic waste involving manufacturers; (iv) to ensure its channelisation to recyclers; (v) to create awareness among all stakeholders about their responsibilities; (vi) to engage agencies or groups working in waste management including waste pickers, and (vii) to ensure that open burning of plastic waste is not permitted;

(d) For setting up plastic waste collection centres, the Municipal Authority may ask the manufacturers, either collectively or individually in line with the principle of Extended Producer's Responsibility (EPR) to provide the required finance to establish such collection centre;

(e) Recyclers shall ensure that recycling facilities are in accordance with the Indian Standard: IS 14534:194 titled as Guidelines for Recycling of Plastics and in compliance with the rules under the Environment (Protection) Ad, 1986, as amended from time to time;

(f) The concerned Municipal Authority shall ensure that the residues generated from recycling processes are disposed of in compliance with Schedule II (Management of Municipal Solid Wastes) and Schedule III (Specifications for Landfill Sites) of the Municipal Solid Wastes (Management and Handling) Rules, 2000 made under the Environment (Protection) Act, 1986, as amended from time to time;

(g) The Municipal Authority shall incorporate the said rules in the Municipal Bye-laws of all the Urban Local Bodies;

(h) The Municipal Authority shall encourage the use of plastic waste by adopting suitable technology such as in Road Construction, Co-incineration etc. The Municipal Authority or the operator intending to use such technology shall ensure the compliance with the prescribed standards including pollution norms prescribed by the Competent Authority in this regard.

(ix) Each SPCB or PCC shall prepare and submit Annual Report to CPCB by 30th day of September each year. The Central Pollution Control Board (CPCB) shall consolidate the report on use of plastic carry bags, sachets/pouches etc. and management of plastic waste. The consolidated report alongwith recommendations on implementation of the Plastic Waste (Management & Handling) (Amendment) Rules, 2011 will be submitted to MoEF by 30th Day of December.

104. What are various hazardous wastes we generate?

Ans. Hazardous wastes are those wastes that are highly toxic to humans, animals, & plants; are corrosive, highly inflammable, or explosive; and reactive when exposed to certain things *e.g.* gases. Industrial & hospital waste is considered hazardous as they may contain toxic substances. Certain types of household waste are also hazardous. India generates around 10 million tonnes of hazardous wastes every year.

Hazardous wastes refer to wastes that may cause adverse health effects on the ecosystem and human beings. These wastes pose risks to human health or living organisms, due to the fact that they: are non-degradable or persistent in nature; can be biologically magnified; are highly toxic and even lethal at very low concentrations. The criteria used to determine the nature of hazard include toxicity, phytotoxicity, genetic activity and bio-concentration. The threat to public health & the environment of a given hazardous waste is dependent on the quantity & characteristics of the waste involved.

Household wastes that can be categorized as hazardous waste include old batteries, shoe polish, paint tins, old medicines, and medicine bottles.

In the industrial sector, the major generators of hazardous waste are the metal, chemical, paper, pesticide, dye, refining, and rubber goods industries. Direct exposure to chemicals in hazardous waste such as mercury and cyanide can be fatal.

Hospital waste is generated during the diagnosis, treatment, or immunization of human beings or animals or in research activities in these fields or in the production or testing of biologicals. It may include wastes like sharps, soiled waste, disposables, anatomical waste, cultures, discarded medicines, chemical wastes, etc. These are in the form of disposable syringes, swabs, bandages, body fluids, human excreta, etc. This waste is highly infectious and can be a serious threat to human health if not managed in a scientific and discriminate manner. It has been roughly estimated that of the 4 kg of waste generated in a hospital at least 1 kg would be infected.

Hospital waste contaminated by chemicals used in hospitals is considered hazardous. These chemicals include formaldehyde & phenols, which are used as disinfectants, and mercury, which is used in thermometers or equipment that measure blood pressure. Most hospitals in India do not have proper disposal facilities for these hazardous wastes.

105. What are four characteristics of hazardous wastes?

Ans. Four characteristics of hazardous wastes are ignitability, corrosivity, reactivity and toxicity which are described below:

(i) **Ignitability:** A waste is an ignitable hazardous waste, if it has a flash point of $< 600°C$; readily catches fire & burns so vigorously as to create a hazard; or is an ignitable compressed gas or an oxidiser. A simple method of determining the flash point of a waste is to review the material safety data sheet, which can be obtained from the manufacturer or distributor of the material. Naphtha, lacquer thinner, epoxy resins, adhesives and oil based paints are all examples of ignitable hazardous wastes.

(ii) **Corrosivity:** A liquid waste which has a pH of less than or equal to 2 or greater than or equal to 12.5 is considered to be a corrosive hazardous waste. Sodium hydroxide, a caustic solution with a high pH, is often used by many industries to clean or degrease metal parts. Hydrochloric acid, a solution with a low pH, is used by many industries to clean metal parts prior to painting. When these caustic or acid solutions are disposed of, the waste is a corrosive hazardous waste.

(iii) **Reactivity:** A material is considered a reactive hazardous waste, if it is unstable, reacts violently with water, generates toxic gases when exposed to water or corrosive materials, or if it is capable of detonation or explosion when exposed to heat or a flame. Examples of reactive wastes are waste gunpowder, sodium metal or wastes containing cyanides or sulphides.

(iv) **Toxicity:** To determine if a waste is a toxic hazardous waste, a sample of the material must be subjected to a test conducted in a certified laboratory.The toxic characteristic identifies wastes that are likely to leach dangerous concentrations of toxic chemicals into ground water.

106. In the regulatory definition of solid waste, which criteria a material must fall in to be classified as Hazardous Waste?

Ans. Hazardous wastes refer to wastes that may cause adverse health effects on the ecosystem, human being or living organisms, due to the fact that they:

- are non-degradable or persistent in nature;
- can be biologically magnified;
- are highly toxic and even lethal at very low concentrations.

The above list relates only to the intrinsic hazard of the waste, under uncontrolled release, to the environment, regardless of quantity or pathways to humans, plants and animals. These Wastes are secondary materials, which are generally classified into six categories as inherently waste: like materials, spent materials, sludges, by-products, commercial chemical products and scrap metals. Solid wastes form a subset of all secondary materials and hazardous wastes form a subset of solid waste. However, certain secondary materials are not regulated as wastes, as they are recycled and reused.

A material to be classified as a hazardous waste, must also meet the criteria specified in the regulatory definition of solid waste. By using either or both of the following criteria, we can identify as to whether or not a waste is hazardous:

(i) The list provided by government agencies declaring that substance as hazardous.

(ii) Characteristics such as ignitibility, corrosivity, reactivity and toxicity of the substance.

These two criteria are explained below:

Listed hazardous wastes (priority chemicals)

A specific list showing certain materials as hazardous wastes minimises the need to test wastes as well as simplifies waste determination. In other words, any waste that fits the definition of a listed waste is considered a hazardous waste. Four separate lists cover wastes from generic industrial processes, specific industrial sectors, unused pure chemical products & formulations that are either acutely toxic or toxic, and all hazardous waste regulations apply to these lists of wastes.These wastes, classified in the F, K, P, and U industrial waste codes, respectively are described below:

F-list: The F-list contains hazardous wastes from non-specific sources, that is, various industrial processes that may have generated the waste. The list consists of solvents commonly used in degreasing, metal treatment baths & sludges, wastewaters from metal plating operations and dioxin containing chemicals or their precursors. Examples of solvents that are F-listed hazardous wastes, include benzene, carbon tetrachloride, cresylic acid, methyl ethyl ketone (MEK), methylene chloride, 1, 1, 1, trichloroethane, toluene, and trichloroethylene. Solvent mixtures or blends, which contain greater than 10% of one or more of the solvents listed above are also considered F-listed wastes.

K-list: The K-list contains hazardous wastes generated by specific industrial processes. Examples of industries, which generate K-listed wastes include wood preservation, pigment production, chemical production, petroleum refining, iron & steel production, explosive manufacturing and pesticide production.

P and U lists: The P and U lists contain discarded commercial chemical products, off specification chemicals, container residues and residues from the spillage of materials. These two lists include commercial pure grades of the chemical, any technical grades of the chemical that are produced or marketed, and all formulations in which the chemical is the sole active ingredient. An example of a P or U listed hazardous waste is a pesticide, which is not used during its shelf-life and requires to be disposed in bulk. The primary distinction between the two lists is the quantity at which the chemical is regulated. The P-list consists of acutely toxic wastes that are regulated when the quantity generated per month, or accumulated at any time, exceeds one kilogram , while U-listed hazardous wastes are regulated when the quantity generated per month exceeds 25 kilograms. Examples of businesses that typically generate P or U listed wastes include pesticide applicators, laboratories and chemical formulators.

Characteristics of hazardous wastes.

The regulations define characteristic hazardous wastes as wastes that exhibit measurable properties posing sufficient threats to warrant regulation. For a waste to be deemed a characteristic hazardous waste, it must cause, or significantly contribute to, an increased mortality or an increase in serious irreversible or incapacitating reversible illness, or pose a substantial hazard or threat of a hazard to human health or the environment, when it is improperly treated, stored, transported, disposed of, or otherwise mismanaged. In other words, if the wastes generated at a facility are not listed in the F, K, P, or U lists, the final step to determine whether a waste is hazardous is to evaluate it against the four hazardous characteristics *i.e.*, ignitability, corrosivity, reactivity and toxicity.

107. Describe the classification of various hazardous wastes?

Ans. There are many compounds, products & product combinations that fit within the definition of hazardous waste. These groups of hazardous waste are classified into the following five general categories:

(i) **Radioactive substance:** Substances that emit ionising radiation are radioactive. Such substances are hazardous because prolonged exposure to radiation often results in damage to living organisms. Radioactive substances are of special concern because they persist for a long period. The period in which radiation occurs is commonly measured and expressed as half-life, *i.e.*, the time required for the radioactivity of a given amount of the substance to decay to half its initial value. For example, uranium compounds have half-lives that range from 72 years for U232 to 23,420,000 years for U236. The management of radioactive wastes is controlled by regulatory agencies. Disposal sites that are used for the long-term storage of radioactive wastes are not used for the disposal of any other solid waste.

(ii) **Chemicals:** Most hazardous chemical wastes can be classified into four groups: synthetic organics, inorganic metals, salts, acids & bases, and flammables & explosives. Some of the chemicals are hazardous because they are highly toxic to most life forms.When such hazardous compounds are present in a waste stream at levels equal to, or greater than, their threshold levels, the entire waste stream is identified as hazardous.

(iii) **Biomedical wastes:** The principal sources of hazardous biological wastes are hospitals and biological research facilities. The ability to infect other living organisms and the ability to produce toxins are the most significant characteristics of hazardous biological wastes. This group mainly includes malignant tissues discarded during surgical procedures and contaminated materials, such as hypodermic needles, bandages & outdated drugs. This waste can also be generated as a by-product of industrial biological conversion processes.

(iv) **Flammable wastes:** Most flammable wastes are also identified as hazardous chemical wastes.This dual grouping is necessary because of the high potential hazard in storing, collecting and disposing of flammable wastes. These wastes may be liquid, gaseous or solid, but most often they are liquids. Typical examples include organic solvents, oils, plasticisers and organic sludges.

(v) **Explosives:** Explosive hazardous wastes are mainly ordnance (artillery) materials, *i.e.*, the wastes resulting from ordnance manufacturing and some industrial gases.Similar to flammables, these wastes also have a high potential for hazard in storage, collection & disposal, and hence, they should be considered separately in addition to being listed as hazardous chemicals. These wastes may exist in solid, liquid or gaseous form.

(vi) **Household hazardous wastes:** Household wastes such as cleaning chemicals, batteries, nail polish etc in MSW constitute hazardous waste. Especially batteries contain mercury which are alkaline which is dangerous enough to kill people.

Generic household hazardous material include non chlorinated organic, chlorinated organic, pesticides, latex paint, oil based paints, waste oil, automobile battery and household battery.

108. What are the community sources of Generation of various categories of hazardous wastes?

Ans. Hazardous wastes are generated in limited amounts in a community and very little information is available on the quantities of hazardous waste generated within a community and in various industries. Hazardous waste generation outside the industry is irregular and very less in amount.

Table below gives a list of hazardous waste generation sources:

Waste category	Sources
Radioactive substances	Biomedical research facilities, colleges and university laboratories, offices, hospitals, nuclear power plants, etc.
Toxic chemicals	Agricultural chemical companies, battery shops, car washes, chemical shops, college and university laboratories, construction companies, electric utilities, hospitals and clinics, industrial cooling towers, newspaper and photographic solutions, nuclear power plants, pest control agencies, photographic processing facilities, plating shops, service stations, etc.
Biological wastes	Biomedical research facilities, drug companies, hospitals, medical clinics, etc.
Flammable wastes	Dry cleaners, petroleum reclamation plants, petroleum refining and processing facilities, service stations, tanker truck cleaning stations, etc.
Explosives	Construction companies, dry cleaners, ammunition production facilities, etc.

In addition to the sources listed, the spillage of containerised hazardous waste is also considered an important source. The quantities of hazardous wastes that are involved in spillage are usually not known. The effects of spillage are visible to the community. Because the occurrence of spillage cannot be predicted, the potential threat to human health and environment is greater than that from routinely generated hazardous wastes.

109. Describe the methods of Storage and collection of Hazardous wastes.

Ans. When large quantities of hazardous wastes are generated, special facilities are used that have sufficient capacity to hold wastes accumulated over a period of several days. When only a small amount is generated, the waste can be containerised, and limited quantity may be stored. Containers and facilities used in hazardous waste storage and handling are selected on the basis of waste characteristics. For example, corrosive acids or caustic solutions are stored in fibreglass or glass-lined containers to prevent deterioration of metals in the container. Care is required to avoid storing incompatible wastes in the same container or locations.

The waste generator, or a specialised hauler, generally collects the hazardous waste for delivery to a treatment or disposal site. The loading of collection vehicles is completed in either of the following ways:

(i) Wastes stored in large-capacity tanks are either drained or pumped into collection vehicles;

(ii) Wastes stored in sealed drums or sealed containers are loaded by hand or by mechanical equipment onto flatbed trucks.

The stored containers are transported unopened to the treatment and disposal facility. To avoid accidents and loss of life, two collectors should be assigned when hazardous wastes are to be collected.

The equipment used for collection vary with the waste characteristics, and the typical collection equipment are listed in Table below:

Waste Category	Waste Collection equipment and accessories
Radioactive substances	Various types of trucks and railroad equipment depending on characteristics of wastes; special marking to show safety hazard; heavy loading equipment to handle concrete-encased lead containers.
Toxic chemicals	Flatbed trucks for wastes stored in drums; tractor-trailer tank truck combination for large volumes of wastes; railroad tank cars; special interior linings such as glass, fibreglass or rubber.
Biological wastes	Standard packers' collection truck with some special precautions to prevent contact between wastes and the collector; flatbed trucks for wastes stored in drums.
Flammable wastes	Same as those for toxic chemicals, with special colourings and safety warning printed on vehicles.
Explosives	Same as those for toxic chemicals with some restriction on transport routes, especially through residential areas.

For short-haul distances, drum storage and collection with a flatbed truck is often used. As hauling distances increase, the larger tank trucks, trailers and railroad tank cars are used.

110. Describe the transfer and transport methods for hazardous wastes.

Ans. The economic benefits derived by transferring smaller vehicle loads to larger vehicles, for non-hazardous solid wastes are equally applicable to hazardous wastes. However, the facilities of a hazardous waste transfer station are quite different from non hazardous solid waste transfer station. Typically, hazardous wastes are not compacted (*i.e.*, mechanical volume reduction) or delivered by numerous community residents. Instead, liquid hazardous wastes are generally pumped from collection vehicles and sludge or solids are reloaded without removal from the collection containers for transport to processing and disposal facilities.

It is unusual to find a hazardous waste transfer facility, where wastes are simply transferred to larger transport vehicles. Some processing and storage facilities are often part of the material handling sequence at a transfer station. For example, neutralisation of corrosive wastes might result in the use of a lower-cost holding tank on transport vehicles. As in the case of storage , care is required to avoid the danger of mixing incompatible wastes.

111. What is the purpose of processing of hazardous wastes?

Ans. Processing of hazardous waste is done for purposes of recovering useful materials and preparing the wastes for disposal. Processing can be accomplished on-site or off-site. The variables affecting the selection of processing site include the characteristics of wastes, the quantity of wastes, the technical, economical & environmental aspects of available on-site treatment processes and the availability of the nearest off-site treatment facility (*e.g.*, haul distance, fees, and exclusions). The treatment of hazardous waste can be accomplished by physical, chemical, thermal or biological means.

Table below gives the various individual treatment processes in each category:

Operation/Proesses	Functions performed[3]	Types of wastes*	Forms of wastes[4]
Physical Treatment			
Aeration	Se	1, 2, 3, 4	L
Ammonia stripping	VR, Se	1, 2, 3, 4	L
Carbon sorption	VR, Se	1, 2, 3, 5	L, G
Centrifugation	VR, Se	1, 2, 3, 4, 5	L
Dialysis	VR, Se	1, 2, 3, 4	L
Distillation	VR, Se	1, 2, 3, 4, 5	L
Electro dialysis	VR, Se	1, 2, 3, 4, 6	L
Encapsulation	St	1, 2,3, 4, 6	L, S
Evaporation	Vr, Se	1, 2, 5	L
Filtration	Vr, Se	1, 2, 3, 4, 5	L, G
Flocculation/Settling	VR, Se	1, 2, 3, 4, 5	L
Flotation	Se	1, 2, 3, 4	L
Reverse osmosis	VR, Se	1, 2, 4, 6	L
Sedimentation	VR, Se	1, 2, 3, 4, 5	L
Thickening	Se	1, 2, 3, 4	L
Vapour scrubbing	VR, Se	1, 2, 3, 4	L
Chemical Treatment			
Calcination	VR	1, 2, 5	L
Ion exchange	VR, Se, De	1, 2, 3, 4, 5	L

Neutralisation	De	1, 2, 3, 4	L
Oxidation	De	1, 2, 3, 4	L
Precipitation	VR, Se	1, 2, 3, 4, 5	L
Reduction	De	1, 2	L
Solvent extraction	Se	1, 2, 3, 4, 5	L
Sorption	De	1, 2, 3, 4	L
Thermal treatment			
Incineration	VR, De	3, 5, 6, 7, 8	S, L, G
Pyrolysis	VR, De	3, 4, 6	S, L, G
Biological treatment			
Activated sludges	De	3	L
Aerated lagoons	De	3	L
Anaerobic digestion	De	3	L
Anaerobic filters	De	3	L
Trickling filters	De	3	L
Waste stabilisation pond	De	3	L

$ Functions: VR= volume reduction; Se = separation; De = detoxification; St = storage; * Waste types: 1 = inorganic chemical without heavy metals; 2 = inorganic chemical with heavy metal; 3 = organic chemical without heavy metal; 4 = organic chemical with heavy metal; 5 = radiological; 6 = biological; 7 = flammable and 8 = explosive; # Waste forms: S = solid; L = liquid and G = gas

In practice, the physical, chemical and thermal treatment operations are the most commonly used. (Biological treatment processes are used less often because of their sensitivity.) Depending on the type of wastes being treated, one or more of these methods may be used.

112. Describe various Disposal methods for hazardous wastes.

Ans. Regardless of their form (*i.e.*, solid, liquid, or gas), most hazardous waste is disposed off either near the surface or by deep burial. Table below shows the various hazardous waste disposal methods:

Operation/Proesses	Functions performed[3]	Types of wastes*	Forms of wastes[4]
Deep well injection	Di	1, 2, 3, 4, 5, 6, 7	L
Detonation	Di	6, 8	S, L, G
Engineered storage	St	1, 2, 3, 4, 5, 6, 7, 8	S, L, G
Land burial	Di	1, 2, 3, 4, 5, 6, 7, 8	S, L
Ocean dumping	Di	1, 2, 3, 4, 7, 8	S, L, G

$ Functions: Di= disposal; St = storage; * Waste types: 1= inorganic chemical without heavy metals; 2 = inorganic chemical with heavy metal; 3 = organic chemical without heavy metal; 4 = organic chemical with heavy metal; 5 = radiological; 6 = biological; 7 = flammable and 8 = explosive.

Waste form: S = solid; L = liquid and G = gas

Although, controlled landfill methods have been proved adequate for disposing of municipal solid waste and limited amounts of hazardous waste, they are not suitable enough for the disposal of a large quantity of hazardous waste, due to the following reasons:

- Possible percolation of toxic liquid waste to the ground water;
- Dissolution of solids followed by leaching and percolation to the ground water;
- Dissolution of solid hazardous wastes by acid leachate from solid waste, followed by leaching and percolation to the ground water;
- Potential for undesirable reactions in the landfill that may lead to the development of explosive or toxic gases;
- Volatilisation of hazardous waste leading to the release of toxic or explosive vapours to the atmosphere;
- Corrosion of containers with hazardous wastes.

Care is therefore required both in the selection of a hazardous waste disposal site and its design. In general, disposal sites for hazardous wastes should be separate from those for municipal solid wastes. As hazardous wastes can exist in the form of liquids, sludges, solids and dusts, a correct approach for co-disposal for each of the hazardous wastes should be determined. To avoid the co-disposal of incompatible wastes, separate storage areas within the total landfill site should be designated for various classes of compatible wastes.

Liquid wastes are usually stored in a tank near the site and can be introduced into the landfill by means of trenches or lagoons, injection or irrigation. Sludges are also placed in trenches. During disposal of lightweight wastes, the disposal area must be kept wet to prevent dust emissions.

Hazardous solid waste characterised by a high degree of impermeability as such must not be disposed of over large areas. When containerised wastes are to be disposed of, precautions must be taken to avoid the rupturing of containers during the unloading operation and the placement of incompatible waste in the same location. To avoid rupturing, the containers are unloaded and placed in position individually. The covering of the containers with earth should be monitored and controlled carefully to ensure that a soil layer exists between each container and the equipment placing the soil does not crush or deform the container.

While designing a landfill site for hazardous waste, provision should be made to prevent any leachate escaping from landfill site. This requires a clay liner, and in some cases, both clay and impermeable membrane liners are used. A layer of limestone is placed at the bottom of the landfill to neutralise the pH of leachate. A final soil cover of 25 cm or more should be placed over the liner. The completed site should be monitored continuously, both visually and with sample wells.

113. Describe the various physical and chemical treatment methods of hazardous wastes?

Ans. Physical and chemical treatments are an essential part of most hazardous waste treatment operations,and the treatments include the following:

(i) **Filtration and separation:** Filtration is a method for separating solid particles from a liquid using a porous medium. The driving force in filtration is a pressure gradient, caused by gravity, centrifugal force, vacuum, or pressure greater than atmospheric pressure. The application of filtration for treatment of hazardous waste fall into the following categories:

Clarification, in which suspended solid particles less than 100 ppm (parts per million) concentration are removed from an aqueous stream. This is usually accomplished by depth filtration and cross-flow filtration and the primary aim is to produce a clear aqueous effluent, which can either be discharged directly, or further processed. The suspended solids are concentrated in a reject stream.

Dewatering of slurries of typically 1% to 30% solids by weight. Here, the aim is to concentrate the solids into a phase or solid form for disposal or further treatment. This is usually accomplished by cake filtration. The filtration treatment, can be used for neutralisation of strong acid with lime or limestone, or precipitation of dissolved heavy metals as carbonates or sulphides followed by settling and thickening of the resulting precipitated solids as slurry. The slurry can be dewatered by cake filtration and the effluent from the settling step can be filtered by depth filtration prior to discharge.

(ii) **Chemical precipitation:** This is a process by which the soluble substance is converted to an insoluble form either by a chemical reaction or by change in the composition of the solvent to diminish the solubility of the substance in it. Settling and/or filtration can then remove the precipitated solids. In the treatment of hazardous waste, the process has a wide applicability in the removal of toxic metal from aqueous wastes by converting them to an insoluble form. This includes wastes containing arsenic, barium, cadmium, chromium, copper, lead, mercury, nickel, selenium, silver, thallium and zinc. The sources of wastes containing metals are metal plating & polishing, inorganic pigment, mining and the electronic industries. Hazardous wastes containing metals are also generated from cleanup of uncontrolled hazardous waste sites, *e.g.*, leachate or contaminated ground water.

(iii) **Chemical oxidation and reduction (redox):** In these reactions, the oxidation state of one reactant is raised, while that of the other reactant is lowered. When electrons are removed from an ion, atom, or molecule, the substance is oxidised and when electrons are added to a substance, it is reduced.Such reactions are used in treatment of metal bearing wastes, sulphides, cyanides and chromium and in the treatment of many organic wastes such as phenols, pesticides and sulphur containing compounds. Since these treatment processes involve chemical reactions, both reactants are generally in solution. However, in some cases, a solution reacts with a slightly soluble solid or gas.

There are many chemicals, which are oxidising agents; but relatively few of them are used for waste treatment. Some of the commonly used oxidising agents are sodium hypochlorite, hydrogen peroxide, calcium hypochlorite, potassium permanganate and ozone. Reducing agents are used to treat wastes containing hexavalent chromium, mercury, organo metallic compounds and chelated metals. Some of the compounds used as reducing agents are sulphur dioxide, sodium borohydride, etc. In general, chemical treatment costs are highly influenced by the chemical cost. This oxidation and reduction treatment tends to be more suitable for low concentration (*i.e.*, less than 1%) in wastes.

(iv) **Solidification and stabilization (S/S):** In hazardous waste management, solidification and stabilisation is a term normally used to designate a technology employing activities to reduce the mobility of pollutants, thereby making the waste acceptable under land disposal requirements. Solidification and stabilisation are designed to improve waste handling and physical characteristics, decrease surface area across which pollutants can transfer or leach, limit the solubility or detoxify the hazardous constituent. To understand this technology, it is important to understand the following terms:

Solidification: This refers to a process in which materials are added to the waste to produce a solid. It may or may not involve a chemical bonding between the toxic contaminant and the additive.

Stabilisation: This refers to a process by which a waste is converted to a more chemically stable form. Subsuming solidification, stabilisation represents the use of a chemical reaction to transform the toxic component to a new, non-toxic compound or substance.

Chemical fixation: This implies the transformation of toxic contaminants to a new non-toxic compound.

Encapsulation: This is a process involving the complete coating or enclosure of a toxic particle or waste agglomerate with a new substance (*e.g.*, S/S additive or binder). The encapsulation of the individual particles is known as micro-encapsulation, while that of an agglomeration of waste particles or micro-encapsulated materials is known as macro-encapsulation.

In S/S method, some wastes can be mixed with filling and binding agents to obtain a dischargeable product. This simple treatment can only be used for waste with chemical properties suitable for landfilling. With regard to wastes with physical properties, it changes only the physical properties, but is unsuitable for landfilling. The most important application of this technology, is the solidification of metal containing waste. S/S technology could potentially be an important alternative technology with a major use being to treat wastes in order to make them acceptable for land disposal. Lower permeability, lower contaminant leaching rate and such similar characteristics may make hazardous wastes acceptable for land disposal after stabilisation.

(v) **Evaporation:** Evaporation is defined as the conversion of a liquid from a solution or slurry into vapour. All evaporation systems vaporise the volatile solvent. Evaporation is used in the treatment of hazardous waste and the process equipment is quite flexible and can handle waste in various forms - aqueous, slurries, sludges and tars. Evaporation is commonly used as a pre-treatment method to decrease quantities of material for final treatment. It is also used in cases where no other treatment method is found to be practical, such as in the concentration of trinitrotoluene (TNT) for subsequent incineration.

(vi) **Ozonation:** Ozone is one of the strongest oxidising agents known. It can be substituted for conventional oxidants such as chlorine, hydrogen peroxide and potassium permanganate. Ozone and UV radiations have been used to detoxify industrial organic wastes, containing aromatic & aliphatic polychlorinated compounds, ketones and alcohols.

114. Describe various thermal treatment methods of hazardous wastes.

Ans. The two main thermal treatments used for hazardous wastes are:

(i) **Incineration:** Incineration can be regarded as either a pre-treatment of hazardous waste, prior to final disposal or as a means of valorising waste by recovering energy. It includes both the burning of mixed solid waste or burning of selected parts of the waste stream as a fuel. The concept of treating hazardous waste is similar to that of municipal solid waste.

(ii) **Pyrolysis:** This is defined as the chemical decomposition or change brought about by heating in the absence of oxygen. This is a thermal process for transformation of solid & liquid carbonaceous materials into gaseous components and the solid residue containing fixed carbon & ash.

The application of pyrolysis to hazardous waste treatment leads to a two-step process for disposal. In the first step, wastes are heated separating the volatile contents (*e.g.*, combustible gases, water vapour, etc.) from non-volatile char and ash. In the second step volatile components are burned under proper conditions to assure incineration of all hazardous components.

Pyrolysis is applicable to hazardous waste treatment, as it provides a precise control of the combustion process. The first step of pyrolysis treatment is endothermic and generally done at 425 to 760°C. The heating chamber is called the pyrolyser. Hazardous organic compounds can be volatilised at this low temperature, leaving a clean residue. In the second step, the volatiles are burned in a fume incinerator to achieve destruction efficiency of more than 99%. The pyrolysis process can be applied to solids, sludges and liquid wastes.

Wastes with the following characteristics are especially amenable to pyrolysis:

- Sludge material that is either too viscous, too abrasive or varies too much in consistency to be atomised in an incinerator.
- Wastes such as plastic, which undergo partial or complete phase changes during thermal processing.
- High-residue materials such as high ash liquid and sludges, with light, easily entrained solids that will generally require substantial stack gas clean up.

- Materials containing salts & metals, which melt & volatilise at normal incineration temperatures. Materials like sodium chloride, zinc and lead, when incinerated may cause refractory spalling and fouling of the heat exchanger surface.

115. Describe the biological treatment methods for hazardous waste?

Ans. On the basis of the fact that hazardous materials are toxic to living beings, it is not uncommon assume that biological treatment is not possible for hazardous wastes.

Some of the techniques used for biological treatment of hazardous waste are:

(i) **Land treatment:** This is a waste treatment and disposal process, where a waste is mixed with or incorporated into the surface soil and is degraded, transformed or immobilised through proper management. The other terminologies used commonly include land cultivation, land farming, land application and sludge spreading. Compared to other land disposal options (*e.g.*, landfill and surface impoundments), land treatment has lower long term monitoring, maintenance & potential clean up liabilities and because of this, it has received considerable attention as an ultimate disposal method. It is a dynamic, management intensive process involving waste, site, soil, climate and biological activity as a system to degrade and immobilise waste constituents.

In land treatment, the organic fraction must be biodegradable at reasonable rates to minimise environmental problems associated with migration of hazardous waste constituents.

The various factors involved in the operation of the system are as follows:

Waste characteristics: Biodegradable wastes are suitable for land treatment. Radioactive wastes, highly volatile, reactive, flammable liquids & inorganic wastes such as heavy metals, acids & bases, cyanides and ammonia are not considered for land treatment. Land treatability of organic compound often follows a predictable pattern for similar type of compounds. Chemical structure, molecular weight, water solubility and vapour pressure are few of the characteristics that determine the ease of biodegradation.

Soil characteristics: The rate of biodegradation and leaching of waste applied, the availability of nutrients & toxicants to microorganisms and the fate of hazardous waste constituents are determined largely by application rate as well as the soil's chemical & physical characteristics or reaction. Principal soil characteristics affecting land treatment processes are pH, salinity, aeration, moisture holding capacity, soil temperature, etc. Some of the characteristics can be improved through soil amendments (*e.g.*, nutrients, lime, etc.), tillage or through adjustments of loading rate, frequency, etc., at the time of waste application.

Microorganisms: Soil normally contains a large number of diverse microorganisms, consisting of several groups that are predominantly aerobic in well drained soil. The types and population of microorganisms present in the waste amended soil depend on the soil moisture content, available oxygen, nutrient composition and other characteristics. The key groups of the microorganisms present in the surface soil are bacteria, actinomycetes, fungi, algae and protozoa. In addition to these groups, other micro and macro fauna, such as nematodes and insects are often present.

Waste degradation: Conditions favourable for plant growth are also favourable for the activity of soil microorganisms. The factors affecting waste degradation that (may be adjusted in the design and operation of a land treatment facility) are soil pH (near 7), soil moisture content (usually between 30 to 90%), soil temperature (activity decreases below 10°C) and nutrients.

(ii) **Enzymatic systems:** Enzymes are complex proteins proteins, composed of amino acids, are linked together via peptide bonds. Enzymes capable of transforming hazardous waste chemicals to non-toxic products can be harvested from microorganisms grown in mass culture. Such crude enzyme extracts derived from microorganisms convert pesticides into less toxic and persistent products. The reaction of detoxifying enzymes are not limited to intracellular conditions but have been demonstrated through the use of immobilised enzyme extracts on several liquid waste streams. The factors of moisture, temperature, aeration, soil structure, organic matter content, seasonal variation and the availability of soil nutrients influence the presence and abundance of enzymes.

(iii) **Composting:** The principles involved in composting organic hazardous wastes are the same as those in the composting of all organic materials , though with moderate modifications. The mi~~robiology of hazardous wastes differs from that of composting in the use of inoculums. The reaction is that certain types of hazardous waste molecules can be degraded by only one or a very few microbial species, which may not be widely distributed or abundant in nature. The factors important in composting of hazardous wastes are those that govern biological reactions. The principal physical parameters are the shape & dimensions of the particles of the material to be composted and the environmental factors of interest in an operation are temperature, pH, available oxygen, moisture, and nutrient availability.

The compost technology can be divided into two broad classes - windrow (open pile) & in vessel (enclosed), and the former may be further subdivided into turned & forced aeration (static pile). Composting, by no means, is a panacea for the hazardous waste problem. When considering the future of hazardous waste composting needs, attention must be paid to the advantages and disadvantages inherent in composting as compared to those inherent in physical, chemical & thermal method of waste treatment.

(iv) **Aerobic and anaerobic treatment:** Hazardous materials are present in low to high concentration in wastewaters, leachate and soil. These wastes are characterised by high organic content (*e.g.*, up to 40,000 mg/L total organic carbon), low & high pH (2 to 12), elevated salt levels (sometimes, over 5%), and presence of heavy metals & hazardous organics. Hazardous wastes can be treated using either aerobic or anaerobic treatment methods.

In aerobic treatment, under proper conditions, microorganisms grow. They need a carbon and energy source, which many hazardous wastes satisfy, nutrients such as nitrogen, phosphorus & trace metals and a source of oxygen. Some organisms can use oxidised inorganic compounds (*e.g.* nitrate) as a substitute for oxygen. Care is to be taken such that all the required nutrients and substances are supplied in sufficient quantities. Temperature and pH must be controlled as needed and the substances that are toxic to the organisms (*e.g.*, heavy metals) must be removed.

Anaerobic treatment is a sequential biologically destructive process in which hydrocarbons are converted, in the absence of free oxygen, from complex to simpler molecules, and ultimately to carbon dioxide & methane. The process is mediated through enzyme catalysis and depends on maintaining a balance of population within a specific set of environmental conditions. Hazardous waste streams often consist of hydrocarbons leading to higher concentrations of chemical oxygen demand (COD). Depending upon the nature of waste, the organic constituents may be derived from a single process stream or from a mixture of streams.

The treatability of the waste depends upon the susceptibility of the hydrocarbon content to anaerobic biological degradation, and on the ability of the organisms to resist detrimental effect of biologically recalcitrant and toxic organic & inorganic chemicals. The metabolic interactions among the various groups of organisms are essential for the successful and complete mineralisation of the organic molecules. Various parameters such as the influent quality, the biological activity of the reactor and the quality of the reactor environment are monitored to maintain efficient operating conditions within the reactor.

116. Describe various methods and advantages of pollution prevention & waste minimization.

Ans. Pollution prevention is the use of materials, processes, or practices that reduce or eliminate the generation of pollutants or wastes at the source. It includes practices that reduce the use of hazardous & non-hazardous materials, energy, water or other resources as well as those that protect natural resources through conservation or more efficient use. Pollution prevention is the maximum feasible reduction of all wastes generated at production sites. It involves the judicious use of resources through source reduction, energy efficiency, reuse of input materials and reduced water consumption.

Waste minimisation means the reduction of hazardous waste that is generated prior to treatment, storage and disposal. It is defined as any source reduction or recycling activity that results in the reduction of the total volume of hazardous waste, or toxicity of hazardous waste, or both. Practices in waste minimisation include recycling, source separation, product substitution, manufacturing process changes and the use of less toxic raw materials.

Pollution prevention and waste minimisation makes us environmentally responsible. While pollution prevention reduces waste at its source, waste minimisation, including recycling & other methods, reduces the amount of waste.

The factors that can contribute to pollution prevention and waste minimization include the following:

(i) **Management support & employee participation:** Management commitment through policy, communications & resources for waste minimisation and pollution prevention is essential to earn the dedication of all employees. A formal policy statement must be drafted and adopted. for this purpose to reflect commitment and attitude towards protecting the environment, minimising or eliminating waste and reusing or recycling materials by the laboratories, departments and industries.

(ii) **Training:** Employees must be provided with formal and on the job training to increase awareness of operating practices that reduce both solid and hazardous waste generation. The training programme should include the industries' compliance requirements, occupational health & safety requirements, waste minimisation and pollution prevention.

(iii) **Waste audits:** Waste audits will help industries to identify areas of potential waste reduction. The audit programme includes the identification of hazardous wastes and their sources, prioritisation of various waste reduction actions to be undertaken, evaluation of some technically, economically & ecologically feasible approaches to waste minimisation & pollution prevention, development of an economic comparison of waste minimisation & pollution prevention options and evaluation of their results.

(iv) **Good operating practices:** These practices involve the procedural or organisational aspects of industry, changes in operating practices, in order to reduce the amount of waste generated. These practices may include, material handling improvements, scheduling improvements, spill & leak prevention, preventive maintenance, corrective maintenance, material/waste tracking or inventory control & waste stream segregation, according to the toxicity, type of contaminant & their physical state.

(v) **Material substitution:** The purpose is to find substitute materials, which are less hazardous than those currently utilised and which result in the generation of waste in smaller quantities and/or of less toxicity.

(vi) **Technological modification:** These practices are oriented towards process and equipment modifications to reduce waste generation and can range from changes that can be implemented in a matter of days at low cost to the replacement of process equipment involving large capital expenditures.

(vii) **Recycling of materials:** These options are characterised as reclaimation , use/ reuse and resource recovery techniques. Which involve the return of a waste material either to the originating process or to another process as a substitute for an input material.

(viii) **Surplus chemical waste exchange options:** Inter- and intra-department chemical exchange is to be implemented and encouraged by employers/employees. Material exchanges not only reduce wastes but also save money.

In addition, by auditing each department or section, a knowledge base of chemical purchase and usage can be developed, allowing each department to develop and implement controls on the purchase of chemicals, institute intra departmental chemical sharing/swapping programmes and eliminate excessive purchase & usage.

Facility operations should be examined to determine whether changes in practices and procedures will result in the generation of non-hazardous or less hazardous waste, or waste reduced in toxicity or volume. The specifics in this context include the substitution of non-toxic materials for toxic ones, distillation or evaporation of water-based chemical end-products, reclamation & reuse of common solvents, use of non-chromate cleaners as a standard part of doing business to generate non-hazardous end products. By implementing and adhering to the guidelines for handling and storing wastes at the point of generation, the costs associated with hazardous waste disposal will also be minimised .

117. Describe the provisions and status of hazardous wastes management in india.

Ans. In the USA, about 70% of the hazardous waste generated are produced from chemical and petrochemical industries. As industrialisation proceeds, the management of hazardous wastes is increasingly becoming a serious problem in India as well. The Indian chemical industry, which accounts for about 13% of the total industrial production and about 10% of the GNP, employs about 6% of the nation's industrial workforce and is one of the major generators of toxic & hazardous wastes. There are about 15000 industrial units located in 400 districts, out of which 12,000 units have been granted authorization for multiple disposal practices including incineration, storage, land disposal and other disposal options. However, Small and Medium sized Enterprises (SMEs) are the major sources of hazardous wastes. And, the States of Andhra Pradesh, Assam, Gujarat, Karnataka, Kerala, Madhya Pradesh, Maharashtra, Orissa, Rajasthan and Tamil Nadu generate the majority of all hazardous wastes.

India is the first country that has made provisions for the protection and improvement of environment in its Constitution.One of the Fundamental Duties of every citizen of India is to protect & improve the natural environment including forests, lakes, rivers & wild life and to have compassion for living creatures.

India has enacted the following laws, regulations and standards governing the country's environmental protection:

(i) The Water (Prevention and Control of Pollution) Act, 1974 as amended in 1988.
(ii) Water (Prevention and Control of Pollution) Rules, 1975.
(iii) The Water (Prevention and Control of Pollution) Cess Act, 1977, amended in 1991.
(iv) The Water (Prevention and Control of Pollution) Cess Rules, 1978.
(v) The Air (Prevention and Control of Pollution) Act, 1984, amended in 1987.
(vi) The Air (Prevention and Control of Pollution) Rules 1982 and 1983.
(vii) The Environment (Protection) Act, 1986.

(viii) Hazardous Waste (Management and Handling) Rules, 1989 as amended in 2000.

(ix) Management, Storage and Import of Hazardous Chemical Rules, 1989.

(x) Manufacture, Use, Import, Export and Storage of Hazardous Microorganisms, Genetically Engineered Microorganisms or Cells Rules, 1989.

(xi) The Public Liability Insurance Act, 1991.

(xii) The Public Liability Insurance Rules, 1991.

(xiii) The Biomedical Wastes (Management and Handling) Rules, 1995.

(xiv) Municipal Wastes (Management and Handling) Draft Rules, 1999.

(xv) Hazardous Waste (Management and Handling) Amendment Rules 2000.

(xvi) E-waste Management and Handling Rules, 2008

Because of these amendments, the legal management of hazardous substances in India will now apply to 50 industrial processes.

The penal provisions for non-compliance under Hazardous Waste (Management and Handling) Amended Rules 2000 and Environment (Protection) Act, 1986 are:

The State Pollution Control Board may cancel an authorisation issued under these rules or suspend it for such period as it thinks fit, if, in its opinion, the authorised person has failed to comply with any of the conditions of the authorisation or with any provisions of the Act of these rules, after giving the authorised person an opportunity to show cause and after recording reasons therefore.

The occupier, transporter and operator of a facility shall be liable for damages caused to the environment resulting due to improper disposal of hazardous waste listed in Schedule 1, 2 and 3 of The Hazardous Waste (Management and Handling) Amendment Rules, 2000. The occupier and operator of a facility shall also be liable to reinstate or restore damaged or destroyed elements of the environment. The occupier and operator of a facility shall be liable to pay a fine as levied by the SPCB with the approval of the Central Pollution Control Board (CPCB) for any violation of the provisions under these rules. An appeal shall lie against any order of grantor refusal of an authorisation by the Member Secretary, SPCB, etc., to the Secretary, Department of Environment of the State.

Besides the aforementioned provisions for non-compliance(s), the Penalty Provisions, delineated under Sections 15 (1, 2) and 16 of the Environmental (Protection) Act, 1986 are also applicable.

Furthermore, the Union Ministry of Environment and Forests, through the Gazette Notification of March 24, 1992, introduced Public Liability Insurance Act Policy, which is specially designed to protect any person, firm, association, or company who owns or has control over handling any hazardous substance at the time of accident. These include 179 hazardous substances along with three categories of inflammable substances. The term handling means manufacturing, processing, treatment, packaging, storing, transportation by vehicle, use, collection, destruction, conversion, offering for sale, transfer or any other similar form of dealing with hazardous substances.

Hazardous Waste (Management, Handling and Transboundary Movement) Rules 2008

Changes to the Hazardous waste Rules Existing Regulation.

The Ministry had notified the Hazardous Wastes (Management and Handling) Rules, 1989 as amended in 2000 and 2003 for regulating management and handling of hazardous waste. Based on the experience gained in the implementation of these Rules, the Hazardous Waste (Management, Handling and Transboundary Movement) Rules, 2008 have been notified repealing the earlier Rules with a view to ensuring effective implementation. The Ministry has also provided financial assistance for strengthening the State Pollution Control Boards (SPCBs) for facilitating implementation of the Rules. Financial assistance has also been provided for setting up Common Treatment, Storage and Disposal Facilities for hazardous waste management. In addition, the Ministry and the Central Pollution Control Board (CPCB) from time to time sponsor training programmes for creation of awareness about the provisions laid down in the Rules. The CPCB has also published guidelines on various aspects of the hazardous waste management for ensuring compliance of the Rules.

In new rules, categories of wastes banned for export and import had also been defined, fulfilling the Basel Convention, ratified by India in 1992. The basic objectives of the Basel Convention are for the control and reduction of transboundary movements of hazardous and other wastes subject to the Convention, prevention & minimization of their generation, environmentally sound management of such wastes and for active promotion of the transfer & use of cleaner technologies.

Current Indian Scenario.

The hazardous waste generated in the country per annum currently is around 8 million tonnes out of which 70% is being generated by five states, namely Gujarat, Maharashtra, Tamil Nadu, Karnataka and Andhra Pradesh. Only three States have developed common TSDF (Treatment, Storage, Disposal Facility), which are essential component of proper hazardous waste management activity for ultimate disposal of the hazardous wastes in an environmentally sound manner. These 10 facilities are currently operational only in Gujarat, Andhra Pradesh and Maharashtra.

Though the Hazardous Wastes (Management & Handling) Rules were notified in 1989, the implementation on the ground has left a lot to be desired. Lack of proper infrastructure and strict enforcement mechanism has led to hazardous waste still remaining a grave problem. New emerging wastes and loopholes in the current legislation have also contributed to this. There are still problems of hazardous waste not being managed in sound environmental conditions, improper dumping and lack of proper treatment & disposal facilities.

However, the new draft claims to address sustainable development and also enable the recovery and/or reuse of useful materials from hazardous materials generated from a process, thereby, reducing the hazardous wastes destined for final disposal and to ensure the environmentally sound management of all hazardous materials.

118. Describe the ways and means of properly managing hazardous wastes.

Ans. Management of hazardous waste follows the functional elements of solid waste, viz., generation, storage & collection, transfer & transport, processing and disposal. Special facilities are used that have sufficient capacity to hold wastes accumulated over a period of several days. Small amounts are containerised, and limited quantities may be stored for periods covering months or years. The waste generator or a specialised hauler normally does the collection of hazardous wastes for delivery to a treatment or disposal facility. All storage containers remain unopened till they reach the treatment and disposal facility. Processing of waste can be done to recover useful materials and to prepare the wastes for disposal. Processing can be accomplished either on-site or off-site. Regardless of their forms, most hazardous wastes are disposed of either near the surface or by deep burial. When landfills are used for such wastes, precautions must be taken to avoid the rupturing of containers during the unloading operation and the placement of incompatible wastes in the same location. Also provisions should be made to prevent any leachate from escaping from landfills, which can be done both visually and by monitoring wells.

119. Describe the advantages of waste minimisation and pollution prevention.

Ans. Waste minimisation means reduction, to the extent feasible, of hazardous waste that is generated prior to treatment storage and disposal. The advantages include reduction of the total volume and toxicity of hazardous waste or reduction in both. By using materials carefully so as to reduce the generation of waste, pollution is reduced, resources are conserved and costs of waste disposal are minimised. Pollution prevention is the use of materials, processes or practices that reduce or eliminate the creation of pollutants or wastes at the source. The advantages include reduction of the use of hazardous and non-hazardous materials, energy, water or other resources as well as those that protect natural resources through conservation or that is more efficient.

120. Describe the three stage hierarchy of options for handling and management of hazardous waste.

Ans. A three stage hierarchy of options for handling and managing hazardous wastes are as follows:

- The top tier includes in plant options such as process manipulation, recycle and reuse options that reduce the production of hazardous waste in the first place. It also contains most desirable options.
- Middle stage highlights processes that convert hazardous waste to less hazardous or non hazardous substances that include:
  - (a) Incineration
  - (b) Land treatment
  - (c) Ocean and atmospheric assimilation
  - (d) Chemical, physical and biological treatments
  - (e) Thermal treatments

- Last stage which is the least desirable tier is perpetual storage- cheapest alternative. Few process include landfill, underground injection, arid region unsaturated zone, surface impoundments, salt formations and waste piles.

121. What is the need and benefits of Integrated Solid Waste Management (ISWM)?

Ans. Integrated solid waste management refers to the strategic approach to sustainable management of solid wastes covering all sources and all aspects, covering generation, segregation, transfer, sorting, treatment, recovery and disposal in an integrated manner, with an emphasis on maximizing resource use efficiency.

Need for ISWM:

- Cities are facing an increasing growth in population, and shares in GDP growth, resulting in - among other things - increasingquantities of waste being generated.
- Due to changing lifestyles and consumption patterns, the quantity of waste generated has increased with quality and composition of waste becoming more varied and changing.
- Industrialization and economic growth has produced more amounts of waste, including hazardous and toxic wastes.
- There is a growing realization of the negative impacts that wastes have had on the local environment (air, water, land, human health etc.)
- Complexity, costs and coordination of waste management has necessitated multi-stakeholder involvement in every stage of the waste stream. This calls for an integrated approach to waste management.
- Local Governments are now looking at waste as a business opportunity, (a) to extract valuable resources contained within it that can still be used and (b) to safely process and dispose wastes with a minimum impact on the environment.

Benefits of ISWM:

- Cleaner and safe neighborhoods
- Higher resource use efficiency
- Resource augmentation
- Savings in waste management costs due to reduced levels of final waste for disposal
- Better business opportunities and economic growth
- Local ownership & responsibilities/participation.

122. What are the elements of Integrated Solid Waste Management (ISWM)?

Ans. Integrated Solid Waste Management takes an overall approach to creating sustainable systems that are economically affordable, socially acceptable and environmentally effective. An integrated solid waste management system involves the use of a range of different solid waste treatment methods, and key to the functioning of such a system is the collection and sorting of the waste. It is important to note that no one single treatment method can manage all the waste materials in an environmentally effective way. Thus all of the available treatment & disposal options must be evaluated equally and the best combination of the available options suited to particular community chosen. Effective management schemes therefore need to operate in ways which best meet current social, economic, and environmental conditions of the municipality. Elements of ISWM is shown below in the figure.

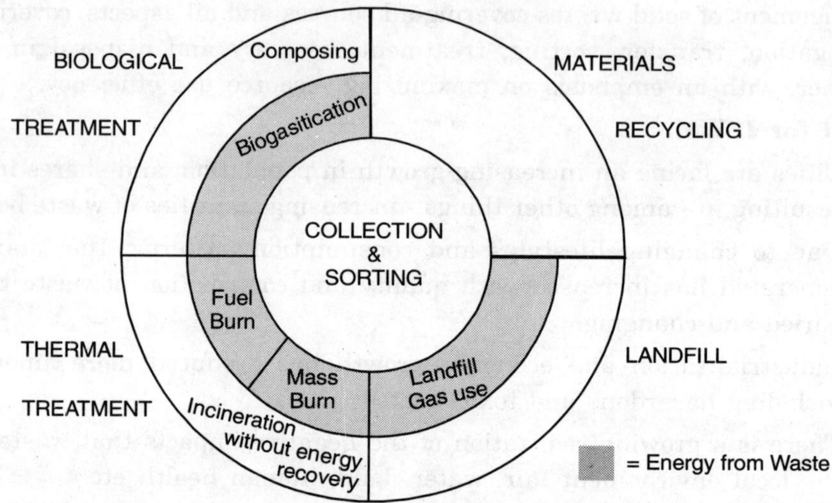

SOURCES AND TYPES OF MUNICIPAL SOLID WASTES

1. Write short notes on solid waste.

Ans. Solid waste refers to non-soluble material such as agricultural refuse, industrial waste, mining residues, demolition waste, municipal garbage or even sewage sludge. Most of these kinds of wastes cannot be recycled or rehabilitated for further use.

2. What are the sources of solid waste?

Ans. (i) Residential, Commercial, Institutional

(ii) Industrial

(iii) Agricultural

(iv) Hazardous waste

3. What is solid waste management?

Ans. Solid waste management is the entire process involved in the recycling process. Solid waste management starts with the trucks picking up recyclables, delivering them to the recycling.

4. What is municipal solid waste?

Ans. Municipal solid waste is the solid waste, or garbage, collected from the residents of a city. It is composed of mostly paper, plastic, food scraps and other household wastes.

5. What are the types of solid wastes?

Ans. Solid waste can be classified into different types depending on their source:

(i) Household waste is generally classified as municipal waste

(ii) Industrial waste as hazardous waste

(iii) Biomedical waste or hospital waste as infectious waste

6. Define toxic waste.

Ans. Old medicines, paints, chemicals, bulbs, spray cans, fertilizer and pesticide containers, batteries, shoe polish.

7. Differentiate between (a) Hazardous and (b) Non-hazardous solid wastes.

Ans. (a) Substance that is ignitable, corrosive, reactive, infectious or explosive

(b) Easily decomposable/ biodegradable solid waste

8. Define Legislation.

Ans. Legislation is the process or act of making law or a set of laws by the legislation body or governing body in a country.

9. What are the impacts of solid waste on health?

Ans. The group at risk from the unscientific disposal of solid waste includes – the population in areas where there is no proper waste disposal method, especially the pre-school children, waste workers, and workers in facilities producing toxic and infectious material. Other high-risk group includes population living close to a waste dump and those, whose water supply has become contaminated either due to waste dumping or leakage from landfill sites. Uncollected solid waste also increases risk of injury, and infection.

10. What is meant by domestic wastes?

Ans. Domestic wastes mean any solid waste derived from households including single and multiple residences, hotels and motels, bunkhouses, ranger stations, crew quarters, campgrounds, picnic grounds and day use recreation areas.

11. What is meant by farming wastes?

Ans. Farming wastes means the wastes from the customary and generally accepted activities, practices, and procedures that farmers adopt, use or engage in during the production and preparation for market of poultry, livestock and associated farm products and in the production and harvesting of agricultural crops which include agronomic, horticultural & silvicultural crops and wastes resulting from aquaculture activities. However, the term does not include special wastes such as waste oils or other lubricants, unused fertilizers or pesticide containers or residues.

12. What is meant by industrial wastes?

Ans. An industrial waste means solid waste produced in or generated by industrial or manufacturing processes. The term does not include commercial, domestic, mining or hazardous waste regulated under subtitle C or RCRA or oil and gas waste.

13. What is meant by institutional wastes?

Ans. Institutional wastes mean all the solid waste which are not special wastes, emanating from institutions such as but not limited to hospitals, health care facilities, nursing homes, laboratories, orphanages, correctional institutions, schools and universities.

14. What is meant by medical wastes?

Ans. A medical waste means the solid wastes generated by hospitalized patients who are isolated to protect others from communicable diseases.

ON-SITE STORAGE & PROCESSING OF SOLID WASTE

1. What is meant by "Construction/demolition wastes"?

Ans. "Construction/demolition wastes" means wastes, other than special wastes, resulting from construction, remodeling, repair and demolition of structures and from road building. Such wastes include but are not limited to bricks, concrete and other masonry materials, soil, rock an lumber, road spoils, rebar, paving material.

2. What is meant by "Convenience center"?

Ans. "Convenience center" means any area which is staffed and fenced that has waste receptacles on site that are open to the public, when an attendant is present, to receive domestic waste, municipal solid waste and recyclable materials.

3. What is meant by "Curing area"?

Ans. "Curinv area" means an area where organic material that has undergone the rapid initial stage of composting is further stabilized into a humus-like material.

4. What is onsite handling?

Ans. Onsite handling refers to the activities associated with the handling of solid wastes until they are placed in the containers used for the storage before collection.

5. What are the types of equipments used for the onsite handling of solid waste?

Ans.
- House hold compactors
- Gravity chutes
- Service Elevators
- Collection carts
- Pneumatic conveyors
- Container trains

COLLECTION AND TRANSFER OF SOLID WASTE

1. What are the methods for transfer of solids?

Ans. Motor vehicles, railroads and ocean-going vessels are the principle means used to transport solid wastes.

2. Explain about waste transfer stations.

Ans. Waste transfer stations are facilities where municipal solid waste is unloaded from collection vehicles and briefly held while it is reloaded onto larger long-distance transport vehicles for shipment to landfills or other treatment or disposal facilities.

3. What are the types of trucks used for collection of solid wastes?

Ans. (i) Residential waste collection trucks:

(a) Automated

(b) Semi-automated

(c) Rear loading

(ii) Commercial refuse collection trucks:

(a) Front loading

(b) Roll off compactor

(c) Roll of style doors

(d) Semi-automated

(e) Automated

4. What are transfer stations?

Ans. Waste transfer stations are facilities where municipal solid waste is unloaded from collection vehicles and briefly held while it is reloaded onto larger long-distance transport vehicles for shipment to landfills or other treatment or disposal facilities.

5. How to select transfer station locations?

Ans. Identifying a suitable site for a waste transfer station can be a challenging process. Site suitability depends on numerous technical, environmental, economic, social and political criteria.

6. What are the transfer station operations?

Ans. This section describes transfer station operations issues and suggests operational practices intended to minimize the facilities impact on its host community. Issues covered include:

(a) Operations and maintenance plans

(b) Facility operating hours

(c) Interacting with public

(d) Waste screening

(e) Emergency situations

(f) Record keeping

7. What are the steps involved in collection of solid waste?

Ans.
- Types of collection services
- Types of collection systems
- Analysis of collection systems
- General methodology involved in setting up collection routes.

8. What is meant by Compactor?

Ans. Compactors are the types that can be used compress material directly in to large containers or to form bales are then placed in large containers.

9. What are the types of collection systems?

Ans.
- Hauled container systems
- Stationary container systems.

10. What are the types of hauled container system?

Ans.
- Tilt frame container
- Trash trailer

11. Define at site time

Ans. The time spent at the disposal site, including the time spent in waiting to unload as well as the time spent unloading.

12. What is meant by off-route?

Ans. It includes (1) time spent checking in and out in the morning and at the end of the day. (2) Time lost due to unavoidable congestion. (3) Time spent on equipment repairs and maintenance.

OFF-SITE PROCESSING OF SOLID WASTE

1. What are the principles of municipal solid waste management?

Ans. Municipal Solid Waste Management involves the application of principle of integrated Solid Waste Management (ISWM) to municipal waste. ISWM is the application of suitable techniques, technologies and management programs covering all types of solid wastes from all sources to achieve the twin objectives of (a) waste reduction and (b) effective management of waste still produced after waste reduction.

2. Give the processing techniques of Municipal Solid Wastes.

Ans. The commonly practiced technologies for SWM can be grouped under three major categories, *i.e.*, bio-processing, thermal processing and sanitary landfill. The bio-processing method includes aerobic and anaerocic composting. Thermal methods are incineration and pyrolysis. Sanitary Landfill is generally used to dispose off the final rejects coming out of the biological and thermal waste processing units.

3. Define "Incinerator".

Ans. "Incinerator" means an enclosed device using controlled flame combustion, the primary purpose of which is to thermally break down solid waste. Examples of incinerators are rotary kiln, fluidized bed, and liquid injection incinerators.

4. Define "Solid waste processing".

Ans. "Solid waste processing" means any process that modifies the characteristics or properties of solid waste, including, but not limited to, treatment, incineration, composting, separation, grinding, shredding, and volume reduction; provided, that it does not include the grinding or shredding of landscaping or land clearing wastes or unpaineted, unstained, and untreated wood into mulch or other useful products.

5. Define "Source reduction".

Ans. "Source reduction" means any action or activity that reduces or eliminates the generation of waste.

6. Define "Energy recovering facility".

Ans. "Energy recovery facility" means a facility for the recovery of energy or energy producing materials from the controlled proecessing of solid waste and the production of energy from said solid waste and other materials, including coal, for a heating & cooling system and/or for the production of electricity & process steam.

7. Define Electrostatic Precipitators.

Ans. It is a system to reduce air pollution during incineration. Sanitary landfillng, refuse is carried and dumped into low lying area under an engineered operation.

8. Define Vermiculture.

Ans. Organic Solid wastes are converted into natural manure with help of earthwarm.

9. What is Indore process?

Ans. Indore method uses manual turning of piled up mass for its decomposition under aerobic conditions.

10. What is Aerobic Composting?

Ans. Organic materials are subjected to aerobic micro bacterial decomposition. Aerobic means presence of oxygen.

DISPOSAL OF SOLID WASTE

1. Define Landfill?

Ans. Landfill means a facility, other than a land application unit, where solid wastes are disposed off by burial in excavated pits or trenches or by placement on land and covering with soil or other approved material.

2. Explain Leachate?

Ans. Leachate means a liquid that has passed through or emerged from solid waste and contains soluble, suspended, or miscible materials removed from such wastes.

3. Explain apparent "Sanitary landfill"?

Ans. "Sanitary landfill" means a method of disposing of solid waste into or on land without creating nuisances or hazards to public health or to the environment by utilizing the principles of engineering to confine the solid waste to the smallest practical area, to reduce it to the smallest practical volume, and to cover it with a layer(s) of an approved material.

4. Define 'Sludge'.

Ans. 'Sludge' means any solid, semi-solid or liquid waste generated from a municipal, commercial, industrial wastewater treatment plant, water supply treatment plant, or air pollution control facility, exclusive of the treateed effluent from a wastewater treatment plant.

5. What is meant by Solid Waste Landfill?

Ans. "Solid Waste Landfill (SWLF) Unit" means a discrete area of land or an excavation that receives waste and that is not a land application unit, surface impoundment, injection well, or waste pile.

6. What is meant by Pyrolysis?

Ans. Pyrolysis is a thermochemical decomposition of organic material at elevated temperatures in the absence of oxygen (or any halogen). It involves the simultaneous change of chemical composition and physical phase, and is irreversible. The word is coined from the Greek-derived elements pyro "fire" and lysis "separating".

7. What is meant by "Fill area"?

Ans. "Fill Area" means the area containing waste placed for final disposal not including earthern beams or other facility appurtenances.

8. What are the factors to be considered for effective site selection for disposal of Solid waste?

Ans.
- Available land area.
- Impact of processing and resource recovery
- Haul distance
- Soil conditions
- Topography
- Climate
- Surface and sub-surface water conditions
- Geological and local environmental conditions.

9. Mention the types of land filling method.

Ans.
1. Area
2. Trench
3. Depression

10. What are the gases found in Landfills?

Ans. Ammonia, Carbon dioxide, Carbon monoxide, Hydrogen, Hydrogen sulfide, Methane, Nitrogen and Oxygen.

11. Mention the methods to control seepage.

Ans.
1. The use of impermeable cover materials.
2. The interception of high groundwater before it reaches the fill.
3. Equalization of the water levels within and outside the landfill.
4. The use of an impervious layer of clay material or other materials.

12. What are the equipments used for Sanitary landfills?

Ans. Crawler and rubber-tired tractors, scrapers, compactors, draglines, and motor graders.

SOURCES AND TYPES OF MUNICIPAL SOLID WASTES

1. Classify the types of solid wastes

Ans. (a) Source-based classification

(i) **Residential:** This refers to wastes from dwellings, apartments, etc., and consists of leftover food, vegetable peels, plastic, clothes, ashes, etc.

(ii) **Commercial:** This refers to wastes consisting of leftover food, glasses, metals, ashes, etc., generated from stores, restaurants, markets, hotels, motels, auto-repair shops, medical facilities, etc.

(iii) **Institutional:** This mainly consists of paper, plastic, glasses, etc., generated from educational, administrative and public buildings such as schools, colleges, offices, prisons, etc.

(iv) **Municipal:** This includes dust, leafy matter, building debris, treatment plant residual sludge, etc., generated from various municipal activities like construction and demolition, street cleaning, landscaping, etc.

(v) **Industrial:** This mainly consists of process wastes, ashes, demolition and construction wastes, hazardous wastes, etc., due to industrial activities.

(vi) **Agricultural:** This mainly consists of spoiled food grains and vegetables, agricultural remains, litter, etc., generated from fields, orchards, vineyards, farms, etc.

(vii) **Open areas**: this includes wastes from areas such as Streets, alleys, parks, vacant lots, playgrounds, beaches, highways, recreational areas, etc.

(b) Type-based classification

(i) **Garbage:** This refers to animal and vegetable wastes resulting from the handling, sale, storage, preparation, cooking and serving of food. Garbage comprising these wastes contains putrescible (rotting) organic matter, which produces an obnoxious odour and attracts rats and other vermin. It, therefore, requires special attention in storage, handling and disposal.

(ii) **Ashes and residues:** These are substances remaining from the burning of wood, coal, charcoal, coke and other combustible materials for cooking and heating in houses, institutions and small industrial establishments. When produced in large quantities, as in power-generation plants and factories, these are classified as industrial wastes. Ashes consist of fine powdery residue, cinders and clinker often mixed with small pieces of metal and glass.

(iii) **Combustible and non-combustible wastes:** These consist of wastes generated from households, institutions, commercial activities, etc., excluding food wastes and other highly putrescible material. Typically, while *combustible material* consists of paper, cardboard, textile, rubber, garden trimmings, etc., *non-combustible material* consists of such items as glass, crockery, tin and aluminium cans, ferrous and non-ferrous material and dirt.

(iv) **Bulky wastes:** These include large household appliances such as refrigerators, washing machines, furniture, crates, vehicle parts, tyres, wood, trees and branches. Since these household wastes cannot be accommodated in normal storage containers, they require a special collection mechanism.

(v) **Street wastes:** These refer to wastes that are collected from streets, walkways, alleys, parks and vacant plots, and include paper, cardboard, plastics, dirt, leaves and other vegetable matter. Littering in public places is indeed a widespread and acute problem in many countries including India, and a solid waste management system must address this menace appropriately.

(vi) **Biodegradable and non-biodegradable wastes:** *Biodegradable wastes* mainly refer to substances consisting of organic matter such as leftover food, vegetable and fruit peels, paper, textile, wood, etc., generated from various household and industrial activities. Because of the action of micro-organisms, these wastes are degraded from complex to simpler compounds. *Non-biodegradable wastes* consist of inorganic and recyclable materials such as plastic, glass, cans, metals, etc.

2. Explain about the solid waste management (SWM) system.

Ans. A SWM system refers to a combination of various functional elements associated with the management of solid wastes. The system, when put in place, facilitates the collection and disposal of solid wastes in the community at minimal costs, while preserving public health and ensuring little or minimal adverse impact on the environment. The functional elements that constitute the system are:

(i) **Waste generation:** Wastes are generated at the start of any process, and thereafter, at every stage as raw materials are converted into goods for consumption. The source of waste generation, determines quantity, composition and waste characteristics.

(ii) **Waste storage:** Storage is a key functional element because collection of wastes never takes place at the source or at the time of their generation. The heterogeneous wastes generated in residential areas must be removed within 8 days due to shortage of storage space and presence of biodegradable material. Onsite storage is of primary importance due to aesthetic consideration, public health and economics involved. Some of the options for storage are plastic containers, conventional dustbins (of households), used oil drums, large storage bins (for institutions and commercial areas or servicing depots), etc. Obviously, these vary greatly in size, form and material.

(iii) **Waste collection:** This includes gathering of wastes and hauling them to the location, where the collection vehicle is emptied, which may be a transfer station (*i.e.*, intermediate station where wastes from smaller vehicles are transferred to larger ones and also segregated), a processing plant or a disposal site. Collection depends on the number of containers, frequency of collection, types of collection services and routes. Typically, collection is provided under various management arrangements, ranging from municipal services to franchised services, and under various forms of contracts.

(iv) **Waste Transfer and transport:** This functional element involves the transfer of wastes from smaller collection vehicles, where necessary to overcome the problem of narrow access lanes, to larger ones at transfer stations. The subsequent transport of the wastes, usually over long distances, to disposal sites.

The factors that contribute to the designing of a transfer station include the type of transfer operation, capacity, equipment, accessories and environmental requirements.

(v) **Waste Processing:** Processing is required to alter the physical and chemical characteristics of wastes for energy and resource recovery and recycling. The important processing techniques include compaction, thermal volume reduction, manual separation of waste components, incineration and composting. We will discuss the various functions involved in waste processing in detail in Unit 5.

(vi) **Waste Recovery and recycling:** This includes various techniques, equipment and facilities used to improve both the efficiency of disposal system and recovery of usable material and energy. Recovery involves the separation of valuable resources from wastes, delivered at transfer stations or processing plants. It also involves themixed solid size reduction and density separation by air classifier, magnetic device for iron and screens for glass. The selection of any recovery process is a function of economics, *i.e.*, costs of separation versus the recovered-material products.

(vii) **Waste disposal:** Disposal is the ultimate fate of all solid wastes, be they residential wastes, semi-solid wastes from municipal and industrial treatment plants, incinerator residues, composts or other substances that have no further use to the society. Thus, land use planning becomes a primary determinant in the selection, design and operation of landfill operations. A modern sanitary landfill is a method of disposing solid waste without creating a nuisance and hazard to public health. Generally, engineering principles are followed to confine the wastes to the smallest possible area, reduce them to the lowest particle volume by compaction at the site and cover them after each day's operation to reduce exposure to vermin. One of the most important functional elements of SWM, therefore, relates to the final use of the reclaimed land.

3. Write the factors which affects the Solid waste management system.

Ans. Many factors influence the decision-making process in the implementation of a SWM system. Some of the factors that need to be considered in developing a SWM system are listed below:

(i) **Quantities and characteristics of wastes:** The quantities of wastes generated generally depend on the income level of a family, as higher income category tends to generate larger quantity of wastes, compared to low-income category. The quantity ranges from about 0.25 to about 2.3 kg per person per day, indicating a strong correlation between waste production and per capita income. One of the which ranges from 150 kg/m^3 measures of waste composition (and characteristics) is density, to 600 kg/m^3. Proportion of paper and packaging materials in the waste largely account for the differences. When this proportion is high, the density is low and vice versa. The wastes of high density reflect a relatively high proportion and of organic matter moisture and lower levels of recycling.

(ii) **Climate and seasonal variations:** There are regions in extreme north (>70 N Latitude) and south (> 60S Latitude), where temperatures are very low for much of the year. In cold climates, drifting snow and frozen ground interfere with landfill operations, and therefore, trenches must be dug in summer and cover material stockpiled for winter use. Tropical climates, on the other hand, are subject to sharp seasonal variations from wet to dry season, which cause significant changes in the moisture content of solid waste, varying from less than 50% in dry season to greater than 65% in wet months. Collection and disposal of wastes in the wet months are often problematic.

High temperatures and humidity cause solid wastes to decompose far more rapidly than they do in colder climates. The frequency of waste collection in high temperature and humid climates should, therefore, be climate, there is no significant higher than that in cold climates. In sub-tropical or desert variation in moisture content of wastes (due to low rainfall) and low production of leachate from sanitary landfill. High winds and windblown sand and dust, however, cause special problems at landfill sites. While temperature inversions can cause airborne pollutants to be trapped near ground level, landfill sites can affect groundwater by altering the thermal properties of the soil.

(iii) **Physical characteristics of an urban area:** In urban areas (*i.e.*, towns and cities), where the layout of streets and houses is such that access by vehicles is possible and door-to-door collection of solid wastes is the accepted norm either by large compaction vehicle. The pictureis, however, quite different in the inner and older vehicle or smaller city areas where narrow lanes make service by vehicles difficult and often impossible. Added to this is the problem of urban sprawl in the outskirts (of the cities) where population is growing at an alarming rate. Access ways are narrow, unpaved and tortuous, and therefore, not accessible to oollection vehicles. Problems of solid waste storage and collection are most acute in such areas.

(iv) **Financial and foreign exchange constraints:** Solid waste management accounts for sizeable proportions of the budgets of municipal corporations. This is allocated for capital resources, which go towards the purchase of equipments, vehicles, and fuel and labour costs. Typically, 10% to 40% of the revenues of municipalities are allocated to solid waste management. In regions where wage rates are low, the aim is to optimise vehicle productivity. The unfavourable financial situation of some countries hinders purchase of equipment and vehicles, and this situation is further worsened by the acute shortage of foreign exchange. This means that the balance between the degree of mechanisation and the size of the labour force becomes a critical issue in arriving at the most cost-effective solution.

(v) **Cultural constraints:** In some regions, long-standing traditions preclude the intrusion of waste collection on the precincts of households, and therefore, influence the collection system. In others, where the tradition of caste persists, recruits to the labour force for street cleaning and handling of waste must be drawn from certain sections of the population, while others will not consent to placing storage bins in their immediate vicinity. Social norms of a community more often than not over-ride what many may consider rational solutions. Waste management should, therefore, be sensitive to such local patterns of living and consider these factors in planning, design and operation.

(vi) **Management and technical resources:** Solid waste management, to be successful, requires a wide spectrum of workforce in keeping with the demands of the system. The best system for a region is one which makes full use of indigenous crafts and professional skills and/or ensures that training programmes are in place to provide a self-sustaining supply of trained workforce.

4. Write the effects of solid waste disposal to human health and environment.

Ans. **(a) Health impacts:** The volume of waste is increasing rapidly as a result of increasing population and improving economic conditions in various localities. This increased volume of wastes is posing serious problems due to insufficient workforce and other constraints in disposing of it properly. What are the consequences of improper management and handling of wastes? Consider the following:

(i) **Disease vectors and pathways:** Wastes dumped indiscriminately provide the food and environment for thriving populations of vermin, which are the agents of various diseases. The pathways of pathogen transmission from wastes to humans are mostly indirect through insects – flies, mosquitoes and roaches and animals – rodents and pigs. Diseases become a public health problem when they are present in the human and animal population of surrounding communities, or if a carrier transmits the etiological agent from host to receptor.

(ii) **Flies:** Most common in this category is the housefly, which transmits typhoid, salmonellosis, gastro-enteritis and dysentery. Flies have a flight range of about 10 km, and therefore, they are able to spread their influence over a relatively wide area. The four stages in their life-cycle are egg, larva, pupa and adult. Eggs are deposited in the warm, moist environment of decomposing food wastes. When they hatch, the larvae feed on the organic material, until certain maturity is reached, at which time they migrate from the waste to the soil of other dry loose material before being transformed into pupae. The pupae are inactive until the adult-fly emerges. The migration of larvae within 4 to 10 days provides the clue to an effective control measure, necessitating the removal of waste before migration of larvae.

Consequently, in warm weather, municipal was te should be collected twice weekly for effective control. In addition, the quality of household and commercial storage containers is very significant. The guiding principle here is to restrict access to flies. Clearly, the use of suitable storage containers and general cleanliness at their location, as well as frequent collection of wastes, greatly reduces the population of flies. Control is also necessary at transfer stations, composting facilities and disposal sites to prevent them from becoming breeding grounds for flies. Covering solid wastes with a layer of earth at landfill sites at the end of every day arrests the problem of fly breeding at the final stage.

(iii) **Mosquitoes:** They transmit diseases such as malaria, filaria and dengue fever. Since they breed in stagnant water, control measures should centre on the elimination of breeding places such as tins, cans, tyres, etc. Proper sanitary practices and general cleanliness in the community help eliminate the mosquito problems caused by the mismanagement of solid waste.

(iv) **Roaches:** These cause infection by physical contact and can transmit typhoid, cholera and amoebiasis. The problems of roaches are associated with the poor storage of solid waste.

(v) **Rodents:** Rodents (rats) proliferate in uncontrolled deposits of solid wastes, which provide a source of food as well as shelter. They are responsible for the spread of diseases such as plague, murine typhus, leptospirosis, histoplasmosis, rat bite fever, salmonellosis, trichinosis, etc. The fleas, which rats carry, also cause many diseases. This problem is associated not only with open dumping but also poor sanitation.

(vi) **Occupational hazards:** Workers handling wastes are at risk of accidents related to the nature of material and lack of safety precautions. The sharp edges of glass and metal and poorly constructed storage containers may inflict injuries to workers.

(vii) **Animals:** Apart from rodents, some animals (*e.g.*, dogs, cats, pigs, etc.) also act as carriers of disease. For example, pigs are involved in the spread of diseases like trichinosis, cysticerosis and toxoplasmosis, which are transmitted through infected pork, eaten either in raw state or improperly cooked. Solid wastes, when fed to pigs, should be properly treated (cooked at 100 °C for at least 50 minutes with suitable equipment).

(b) Environmental impacts:

Atmospheric Pollution: When refuse is burnt in an open area, a dense smoke often covers the site and neighboring land. Old-fashioned incinerators without air pollution control equipment are little better than open burning. Apart from particulate matter that constitutes smoke, the gaseous discharges from the incomplete combustion may include SO_2, NOx and various gases. If PVC is a constituent of the refuse, the gases may include hydrogen chloride. In addition to pest nuisance and health hazards, the solid wastes also cause air pollution. Burning of solid wastes in open dumps or use of improperly designed incinerators produce excessive pollution. Studies revealed that emission from the uncontrolled burning leads to the production of particulate matter, sulfur oxides, nitrogen oxides, carbon monoxides, lead and mercury. Discharge of arsenic and dibenzofurans are called as cadmium are to be controlled. dioxins and furans. These are of more Polychlorinated concern about their toxicity as carcinogens and mutagens.

Visual Pollution: The aesthetic feeling is offended by the unsightfullness of piles of wastes on the roadsides. Thissituation animals, especially in the was being made worst by the presence of scavenging third world countries. The scavenging animals search their food in the waste and spread it around places. Similarly the rag pickers in India also create such unhygienic scene while collecting recyclables. This creates an ugly situation and under such conditions apart form cleaning the waste, there is a need to educate the public about environmental health. Undesirable noise and traffic sound is also produced while operating the landfills and incinerators. This is due to the movement of vehicles and large machines.

Tourism/Ethics/Recreation: Uncontrolled refuse and sanitary tips in full public view are eye corers. If tourism is important in such cases esthetic nuisance may reduce the number of visitors with the resultant economic loss. There can be depreciation of the value of property nearer to a garbage area or incinerator spillage from vehicle. In addition to this, bad smell, increase of flies, rats, windblown dust, paper and plastics all of which are harmful to the locality. On the other hand, refuse can be used in a well-planned controlled way to improve low lying and derelict or arid lands and property values may then increase in the vicinity.

Water Pollution: When the rain run-off joins the surface water sources there is an inevitably pollution due to suspended solid particles. Organic matters exert high oxygen demand and pathogen load can create a health risk to downstream users. Unless the water table is not high or underlying rock is not fissured, the ground water will be hardly affected. Dumps should not be close to shallow wells. A distance of 12 kms is suggested. On the other hand avoidance of ground water pollution is of paramount importance in the dumping of refuse.

In addition to occupational health, injury issues and environmental health also need to be mentioned in the context of waste management. Contaminated leachate and surface run-off from land disposal facilities affects ground and surface water quality. Volatile organic compounds and dioxins in air-emissions are attributed to increasing cancer incidence and psychological stress for those living near incinerators or land disposal facilities. Drain clogging due to uncollected wastes leading to stagnant waters and subsequent mosquito vector breeding are a few of the environmental health issues, which affect the waste workers as well as the public. The pneumonic plague that broke out in November 1994 in India (Surat, Gujarat) is a typical example of solid waste mismanagement.

5. **Write about the characteristics of solid wastes.**

Ans. 1. PHYSICAL CHARACTERISTICS

Density: It is expressed as mass per unit volume (kg/m^3). This parameter is required for designing a solid waste management program. A reduction in volume by 75% is achieved through normal compaction equipment, so that an initial density of 100kg/m^3 may readily be increased to 400 kg/m^3. Significant changes in the density occur as waste moves from sources to disposal site, as a result of scavenging, handling, wetting, and drying by the weather and vibration during transport. Density is critical in the design of sanitary landfill as well as for storage, collection and transport of wastes. Efficient operation of landfill requires compaction of wastes to optimum density.

Moisture Content: Values greater than 40% are also not common. Moisture increases the weight of the solid wastes and therefore the cost of collection and transport increases. Consequently, waste should be insulated from rain or other extraneous water source. Moisture content is critical determinant in the economic feasibility of waste treatment by incineration. During incineration energy must be supplied for evaporation of water and raising the temperature of vapor.

CHEMICAL CHARACTERISTICS

Information of chemical characteristics is important in evaluating alternative processing and recovery options. Typically, waste is considered as combination of combustible and noncombustible components. If solid waste is to be used as a fuel or for any other use we should know its chemical components.

Lipids: These are included in the class of fats, oils and grease. The principal sources of lipids in the garbage are cooking oil and fats. Lipids have high heating values about 38,000 kJ/kg (kilojoules/kilograms), which makes the waste with high lipid content suitable for energy recovery. Since lipids become liquids at temperature slightly above ambient they add to the liquid content during waste decomposition. They are biodegradable, but they have low solubility in water and hence the rate of biodegradation is slow.

Carbohydrates: These are primarily originated from the food sources rich in starch and celluloses. These readily biodegrade into carbon dioxide, water and methane. Decomposition of carbohydrates attracts the flies and rats and hence should not be left exposed for long duration.

Proteins: These are the compounds containing carbon, hydrogen, nitrogen and oxygen and organic acid with amino groups. They are primarily found in food and garden wastes, but their partial decomposition result in the production of amines, which impart unpleasant odors.

Natural Fibers: These are the natural products contain cellulose and lignins that are relatively resistant to biodegradation. These are found in paper products, food and yard wastes. Paper is almost 100% cellulose, cotton over 95% and wood products over 40-50%. These are highly combustible products most suitable for incineration. The calorific value of oven dried paper products are in the range 12000-18000 kJ/kg.

Synthetic Organic Materials: In the recent years plastics have become a significant components of solid waste, accounting for 1-10%. They are highly resistant to the biodegradation; hence their presence in the waste is objectionable. Currently much attention is given to reduce this component at disposal sites. Plastics have a high heating value, about 32000 kJ/kg, which makes them very suitable for incineration. However, among the plastics Polyvinyl chloride (PVC) when burnt produces dioxin and acid gas. The trace gases produced during the burning of plastic are proved to be carcinogenic.

ON-SITE STORAGE & PROCESSING OF SOLID WASTE

1. Explain about the hauled and stationary containers.

Ans. The design of an efficient waste collection system requires careful consideration of the type, size and location of containers at the point of generation for storage of wastes until they are collected. While single-family households generally use small containers, residential units, commercial units, institutions and industries require large containers. Smaller containers are usually handled manually whereas the larger, heavier ones require mechanical handling. The containers may fall under either of the following two categories:

(i) **Stationary containers:** These are used for contents to be transferred to collection vehicles at the site of storage.

(ii) **Hauled containers:** These are used for contents to be directly transferred to a processing plant, transfer station or disposal site for emptying before being returned to the storage site.

The desirable characteristics of a well-designed container are low cost, size, weight, shape, resistance to corrosion, water tightness, strength and durability. For example, a container for manual handling by one person should not weigh more than 20 kg, lest it may lead to occupational health hazards such as muscular strain, etc. Containers that weigh more than 20 kg, when full, require two or more crew members to manually load and unload the wastes, and which result in low collection efficiency.

Containers should not have rough or sharp edges, and preferably have a handle and a wheel to facilitate mobility. They should be covered to prevent rainwater from entering (which increases the weight and rate of decomposition of organic materials) into the solid wastes. The container body must be strong enough to resist and discourage stray animals and scavengers from ripping it as well as withstand rough handling by the collection crew and mechanical loading equipment.

Containers should be provided with a lifting bar, compatible with the hoisting mechanism of the vehicle. The material used should be light, recyclable, easily moulded and the surface must be smooth and resistant to corrosion. On the one hand, steel and ferrous containers are heavy and subject to corrosion; the rust peels off exposing sharp edges, which could be hazardous to the collection crew. On the other, wooden containers (*e.g.*, bamboo, rattan and wooden baskets) readily absorb and retain moisture and their surfaces are generally rough, irregular and difficult to clean.

2. Write the benefits of the waste processing technique.

Ans. The processing of wastes helps in achieving the best possible benefit from every functional element of the solid waste management (SWM) system and, therefore, requires proper selection of techniques and equipment for every element. Accordingly, the wastes that are considered suitable for further use need to be paid special attention in terms of processing, in order that we could derive maximum economical value from them.

(i) **Improving efficiency of SWM system:** Various processing techniques are available to improve the efficiency of SWM system. For example, before waste papers are reused, they are usually baled to reduce transporting and storage volume requirements. In some cases, wastes are baled to reduce the haul costs at disposal site, where solid wastes are compacted to use the available land effectively. If solid wastes are to be transported hydraulically and pneumatically, some form of shredding is also required. Shredding is also used to improve the efficiency of the disposal site.

(ii) **Recovering material for reuse:** Usually, materials having a market, when present in wastes in sufficient quantity to justify their separation, are most amenable to recovery and recycling. Materials that can be recovered from solid wastes include paper, cardboard, plastic, glass, ferrous metal, aluminium and other residual metals.

(iii) **Recovering conversion products and energy:** Combustible organic materials can be converted to intermediate products and ultimately to usable energy. This can be done either through incineration, pyrolysis, composting or bio-digestion. Initially, the combustible organic matter is separated from the other solid waste components. Once separated, further processing like shredding and drying is necessary before the waste material can be used for power generation.

3. Explain about the critical waste evaluation options in India.

Ans. The problem of municipal solid waste management has acquired alarming dimensions in India especially over the last decade, before which waste management was hardly considered an issue of concern as the waste could be easily disposed of in an environmentally safe manner.

The physical and chemical characteristics of Indian city refuse, nonetheless, show that about 80% of it is compostable and ideal for *biogas* generation due to adequate nutrients (NPK), moisture content of 50-55% and a carbon-to-nitrogen ratio of 25-40:1. Therefore, the development of appropriate technologies for utilisation of wastes is essential to minimise adverse health and environmental consequences.

Against this backdrop, let us discuss below the quantum of wastes generated in India, their composition, disposal methods, recycling aspects, and health and environment impacts:

(i) **Waste quantum:** The per capita waste generation rate is about 500 g/day. This along with increased population has contributed to higher total waste generation quantum.

(ii) **Waste composition:** Studies reveal that the percentage of the organic matter has remained almost static at 41% in the past 3 decades, but the recyclables have increased from 9.56% to 17.18%. Garbage in Indian cities is estimated to contain about 45-75% biodegradable waste (as against 25% of US city-garbage) with 50-55%

moisture; 35-45% being fruits, vegetable and food biomass; and 8-15% non organic materials like plastic, metal, glass, stones, etc. Refuse from Indian cities also contains high organic and low combustible matter, if the studies carried out in six cities are of any indication. Presenting the findings of these studies, Table 1.6 below shows that the highest organic content is found in Bangalore waste (75%) and the lowest in Kolkata (46%).

(iii) **Waste disposal methods:** Waste disposal is the final stage of the waste management cycle. About 90% of the municipal waste collected by the civic authorities in India is dumped in low-lying areas outside the city/town limits, which have no provision of *leachate collection* and treatment, and landfill gas collection and use.

(iv) **Recycling:** This involves collection of recyclables from various sources, which ultimately reach recycling units. It is estimated that about 40-80% of plastic waste gets recycled in India, as compared to 10-15% in the developed nations of the world. However, due to lack of suitable government policies, incentives, subsidies, regulations, standards, etc., related to recycling, this industry is still far behind its western counterparts in terms of technology and quality of manufactured goods. Nevertheless, recycling in India is a highly organised and profit-making venture, though informal in nature.

(v) **Health impacts:** Due to the absence of standards and norms for handling municipal wastes, municipal workers suffer occupational health hazards of waste handling. At the dumpsites in the city of Mumbai, for example, 95 workers were examined and it was found that about 80% of them had eye problems, 73% respiratory ailments, 51% gastrointestinal ailments and 27% skin lesions. Also, municipal workers and rag pickers who operate informally for long hours rummaging through waste also suffer from similar occupational health diseases ranging from respiratory illnesses (from ingesting particulates and bio-aerosols), infections (direct contact with contaminated material), puncture wounds (leading to tetanus, hepatitis and HIV infection) to headaches and nausea, etc. Studies among the 180 rag pickers at open dumps of Kolkata city reveal that average quarterly incidence of diarrhoea was 85%, fever 72% and cough and cold 63%.

(vi) **Environmental impacts:** In addition to occupational health, injury issues and environmental health also need to be mentioned in the context of waste management. Contaminated leachate and surface run-off from land disposal facilities affects ground and surface water quality. Volatile organic compounds and dioxins in air-emissions are attributed to increasing cancer incidence and psychological stress for those living near incinerators or land disposal facilities. Drain clogging due to uncollected wastes leading to stagnant waters and subsequent mosquito vector breeding are a few of the environmental health issues, which affect the waste workers as well as the public. The pneumonic plague that broke out in November 1994 in India (Surat, Gujarat) is a typical example of solid waste mismanagement.

4. Explain about the collection vehicle storage method

Ans. Collection vehicles: Almost all collections are based on collector and collection crew, which move through the collection service area with a vehicle for collecting the waste material. The collection vehicle selected must be appropriate to the terrain, type and density of waste generation points, the way it travels and type and kind of material. It also depends upon strength, stature and capability of the crew that will work with it. The collection vehicle may be small and simple (*e.g.*, two-wheeled cart pulled by an individual) or large, complex and energy intensive (*e.g.*, rear loading compactor truck). The most commonly used collection vehicle is the dump truck fitted with a hydraulic lifting mechanism. A description of some vehicle types follows:

(i) **Small-scale collectionand muscle-powered vehicles:** These are common vehicles used for waste collection in many countries and are generally used in rural hilly areas. As Figure illustrates, these can be small rickshaws, carts or wagons pulled by people or animals, and are less expensive, easier to build and maintain compared to other vehicles.

Small-scale Collection Vehicles: An Illustration

They are suitable for densely populated areas with narrow lanes, and squatter settlements, where there is relatively low volume of waste generated. Some drawbacks of these collection vehicles include limited travel range of the vehicles and weather exposure that affect humans and animals.

(ii) **Non-compactor trucks:** Non-compactor trucks are efficient and cost effective in small cities and in areas where wastes tend to be very dense and have little potential for compaction.

Figure illustrates a non-compactor truck.

When these trucks are used for waste collection, they need a dumping system to easily discharge the waste. It is generally required to cover the trucks in order to prevent residue flying off or rain soaking the wastes. Trucks with capacities of 10–12 m^3 are effective, if the distance between the disposal site and the collection area is less than 15 km. If the distance is longer, a potential transfer station closer than 10 km from the collection area is required. Non-compactor trucks are generally used, when labour cost is high. Controlling and operating cost is a deciding factor, when collection routes are long and relatively sparsely populated.

(iii) **Compactor truck:** Compaction vehicles are more common these days, generally having capacities of 12–15 m^3 due to limitations imposed by narrow roads. Although the capacity of a compaction vehicle, illustrated in Figure, is similar to that of a dump truck, the weight of solid wastes collected per trip is 2 to 2.5 times larger since the wastes are hydraulically compacted.

Non-compactor Trucks

Compactor Truck

The success of waste management depends on the level of segregation at source. One of the examples for best collection method is illustrated in the figure below.

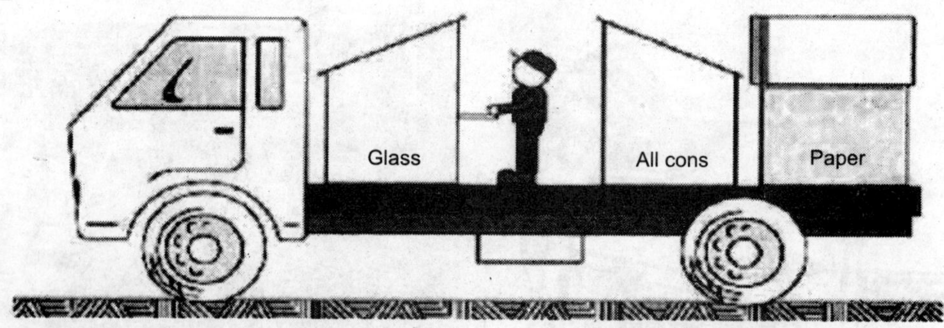

A compactor truck allows waste containers to be emptied into the vehicle from the rear, front or sides and inhibits vectors (of disease) from reaching the waste during collection and transport. It works poorly when waste stream is very dense, wet, collected materials are gritty or abrasive, or when the roads are dusty.

5. Write about the factors affects the waste collection.

Ans. (i) Finalising and implementing the system management plan: For proper implementation of collection and transfer system, it is necessary to have clear organisational structures and management plans. The organizational structure should be simple, with a minimum of administrative and management layers between collection crews and top management. All workers in the department should clearly understand the department's mission and their roles. Through training, incentives and reinforcement by management, workers should be encouraged to be customer-oriented and team contributors. Feedback mechanisms must be introduced to help the crew review their performance and help managers monitoring the performance of crews, equipment, etc. It is also important to periodically review the management plans and structures, as implementation of collection services continues.

(ii) Purchasing and managing equipment: For purchasing equipment, most municipalities issue bid specifications. Detailed specifications include exact requirements for equipment sizes and capacities, power ratings, etc. Performance specifications often request that equipment be equivalent to certain available models and meet standards for capacity, speed, etc. Municipalities may either perform equipment maintenance themselves, contract with a local garage, or in some cases, contract with the vehicle vendor at the time of purchase. As part of the preventive maintenance programme, the collection crew should check the vehicle chassis, tyres and body daily and report any problems to maintenance managers.

(iii) Hiring and training personnel: As in all organisations, good personnel management is essential to an efficient, high-quality waste collection system. Authorities responsible for SWM should, therefore, strive to hire and keep well-qualified personnel. The recruitment programme should assess applicants' abilities to perform the types of physical labour required for the collection, equipment and methods used. To retain employees, management should provide a safe working environment that emphasises career advancement, participatory problem solving and worker incentives. Worker incentives should be developed to recognise and reward outstanding performance by employees. Ways to accomplish motivation include merit-based compensation, awards programme and a work structure. Feedback on employee performance should be regular and frequent.

Safety is especially important because waste collection employees encounter many hazards during each workday. As a result of poor safety records, insurance costs for many collection services are high. To minimise injuries, haulers should have an ongoing safety programme. This programme should outline safety procedures and ensure that all personnel are properly trained on safety issues. Haulers should develop an employee-training programme that helps employees improve and broaden the range of their job-related skills. Education should address such subjects as driving skills, first aid, safe lifting methods, identification of household hazardous wastes, avoidance of substance abuse and stress management.

(iv) Providing public information: Maintaining good communication with the public is important to a well-run collection system. Residents can greatly influence the performance of the collection system by co-operating in separation requirements, and by keeping undesirable materials from entering the collected waste stream.

Commonly used methods of communicating information include brochures, articles in community newsletters, newspaper articles, announcements, and advertisements on radio and television, information attachments to utility bills (either printed or given separately) and school handouts. Communication materials should be used to help residents understand the community waste management challenges and the progress in meeting them. Residents should also be kept informed about issues such as the availability and costs of landfill capacity so that they develop an understanding of the issues and a desire to help meet their waste management needs.

(v) **Monitoring system cost and performance:** Collection and transfer facilities should develop and maintain an effective system for cost and performance reporting. Each collection crew should complete a daily report containing the following information. Collected data should be used to forecast workloads, truck costs, identify changes in the generation of wastes and recyclables, trace the origin of problematic waste materials and evaluate crew performance. Just as the goals of a collection programme set its overall directions, a monitoring system provides the short-term feedback necessary to identify the corrections needed to achieve those goals.

COLLECTION AND TRANSFER OF SOLID WASTE

1. Write the types of waste collection equipments.

Ans. Collection vehicles: Almost all collections are based on collector and collection crew, which move through the collection service area with a vehicle for collecting the waste material. The collection vehicle selected must be appropriate to the terrain, type and density of waste generation points, the way it travels and type and kind of material. It also depends upon strength, stature and capability of the crew that will work with it. The collection vehicle may be small and simple (*e.g.*, two-wheeled cart pulled by an individual) or large, complex and energy intensive (*e.g.*, rear loading compactor truck). The most commonly used collection vehicle is the dump truck fitted with a hydraulic lifting mechanism. A description of some vehicle types follows:

(i) **Small-scale collection and muscle-powered vehicles:** These are common vehicles used for waste collection in many countries and are generally used in rural hilly areas. These can be small rickshaws, carts or wagons pulled by people or animals, and are less expensive, easier to build and maintain compared to other vehicles. They are suitable for densely populated areas with narrow lanes, and squatter settlements, where there is relatively low volume of waste generated. Some drawbacks of these collection vehicles include limited travel range of the vehicles and weather exposure that affect humans and animals.

(ii) **Non-compactor trucks:** Non-compactor trucks are efficient and cost effective in small cities and in areas where wastes tend to be very dense and have little potential for compaction. When these trucks are used for waste collection, they need a dumping system to easily discharge the waste. It is generally required to cover the trucks in order to prevent residue flying off or rain soaking the was tes. Trucks with capacities of 10–12 m^3 are effective, if the distance between the disposal site and the collection area is less than 15 km. If the distance is longer, a potential transfer station closer than 10 km from the collection area is required. Non-compactor trucks are generally used, when labour cost is high.

(iii) Compactor truck: Compaction vehicles are more common these days, generally having capacities of 12–15 m^3 due to limitations imposed by narrow roads. Althoughthe capacity of a compaction vehicle, illustrated in Figure, is similar to that of a dump truck, the weight of solid wastes collected per trip is 2 to 2.5 times larger since the wastes are hydraulically compacted. The success of waste management depends on the level of segregation at source.

2. Briefly discuss about waste collection vehicle routing.

Ans. Collection vehicle routing: Efficient routing and re-routing of solid waste collection vehicles can help decrease costs by reducing the labour expended for collection. Routing procedures usually consist of the following two separate components:

(i) Macro-routing: Macro-routing, also referred to as route-balancing, consists of dividing the total collection area into routes, sized in such a way as to represent a day's collection for each crew. The size of each route depends on the amount of waste collected per stop, distance between stops, loading time and traffic conditions. Barriers, such as railroad embankments, rivers and roads with heavy competing traffic, can be used to divide route territories. As much as possible, the size and shape of route areas should be balanced within the limits imposed by such barriers.

(ii) Micro-routing: Using the results of the macro-routing analysis, micro-routing can define the specific path that each crew and collection vehicle will take each collection day. Results of micro-routing analyses can then be used to readjust macro-routing decisions. Micro-routing analyses should also include input and review from experienced collection drivers.

Districting is the other method for collection route design. For larger areas it is not possible for one institution to handle it then the best way is to subdivide the area and MSW collection districting plan can be made. This routing will be successful only when road network integrity is good and the regional proximity has been generated.

The heuristic (*i.e.*, trial and error) route development process is a relatively simple manual approach that applies specific routing patterns to block configurations. The map should show collection, service garage locations, disposal or transfer sites, one-way streets, natural barriers and areas of heavy traffic flow.

Services on dead-end streets can be considered as services on the street segment that they intersect, since they can only be collected by passing down that street segment. To keep right turns at a minimum, (in countries where driving is left-oriented) collection from the dead-end streets is done when they are to the left of the truck. They must be collected by walking down, reversing the vehicle or taking a U-turn.

3. Explain in detail about transfer station.

Ans. Transfer station is a centralised facility, where waste is unloaded from smaller collection vehicles and re-loaded into large vehicles for transport to a disposal or processing site. This transfer of waste is frequently accompanied by removal, separation or handling of waste. In areas, where wastes are not already dense, they may be compacted at a transfer station. The technical limitations of smaller collection vehicles and the low hauling cost of solid waste, using larger vehicles, make a transfer station viable. Also, the use of transfer station proves reasonable, when there is a need for vehicles servicing a collection route to travel shorter distances, unload and return quickly to their primary task of collecting the waste. Limitations in hauling solid wastes are the main factors to be considered, while evaluating the use of transfer stations. These include the additional capital costs of purchasing trailers, building transfer stations and the extra time, labour and energy required for transferring wastes from collection truck to transfer trailer.

The main problem in the establishment of a transfer station, however, is securing a suitable site. Stored solid wastes and recyclable materials, if not properly handled, will attract flies and other insect vectors. Odours from the transferred solid wastes will also be a nuisance, if not properly controlled. In addition, the traffic and noise due to small and large collection vehicles, collectors, drivers, etc., invite the resentment of the communities living in the vicinity of transfer stations.

Depending on the size, transfer stations can be either of the following two types:

(i) **Small to medium transfer stations:** These are direct-discharge stations that provide no intermediate waste storage area. The capacities are generally small (less than 100 tonnes/day) and medium (100 to 500 tonnes/day). Depending on weather, site aesthetics and environmental concerns, transfer operations of this size may be located either indoor or outdoor. More complex small transfer stations are usually attended during hours of operation and may include some simple waste and materials processing facilities. For example, it includes a recyclable material separation and processing centre. The required overall station capacity (*i.e.*, the number and size of containers) depends on the size and population density of the area served and the frequency of collection.

(ii) **Large transfer stations:** These are designed for heavy commercial use by private and municipal collection vehicles. The typical operational procedure for a larger station is as follows: Several different designs for larger transfer operations are common, depending on the transfer distance and vehicle type. Most designs, however, fall into one of the following three categories:

(a) **Direct-discharge non-compaction station:** In these stations, waste is dumped directly from collection vehicle into waiting transfer trailers and is generally designed with two main operating floors. In the transfer operation, wastes are dumped directly from collection vehicles (on the top floor) through a hopper and into open top trailers on the lower floor. The trailers are often positioned on scales so that dumping can be stopped when the maximum payload is reached. A stationary crane with a bucket is often used to distribute the waste in the trailer. After loading, a cover or tarpaulin is placed over the trailer top. However, some provision for waste storage during peak time or system interruptions should be developed. Because of the use of little hydraulic equipment, a shutdown is unlikely and this station minimises handling of waste.

(b) **Platform/pit non-compaction station:** In this arrangement, the collection vehicles dump their wastes onto a platform or into a pit using waste handling equipment, where wastes can be temporarily stored, and if desired, picked through for recyclables or unacceptable materials. The Like direct discharge stations, platform stations have two levels. If a pit is used, however, the station has three levels. A major advantage of these stations is that they provide temporary storage, which allows peak inflow of wastes to be levelled out over a longer period. Construction costs for this type of facility are usually higher because of the increased floor space. This station provides convenient and efficient storage area and due to simplicity of operation and equipment, the potential for station shutdown is less.

(c) **Compaction station**: In this type of station, the mechanical equipment is used to increase the density of wastes before they are transferred. The most common type of compaction station uses a hydraulically powered compactor to compress wastes. Wastes are fed into the compactor through a chute, either directly from collection trucks or after intermediate use of a pit.

4. Explain about capacity and viability of transfer station.

Ans. Capacity: A transfer station should have enough capacity to manage and handle the wastes at the facility throughout its operating life. While selecting the design capacity of a transfer station, we must, therefore, consider trade-offs between the capital costs associated with the station and equipment and the operational costs. Designers should also plan adequate space for waste storage and, if necessary, waste processing. Transfer stations are usually designed to have 1.5–2 days of storage capacity. The collection vehicle unloading area is usually the waste storage area and sometimes a waste sorting area. When planning the unloading area, designers should allow adequate space for vehicle and equipment manoeuvring. To minimise the space required, the facility should be designed such that the collection vehicle backs into the unloading position. Adequate space should also be available for offices, employee facilities, and other facility-related activities. Factors that should be considered in determining the appropriate capacity of a transfer facility include.

Viability: Transfer stations offer benefits such as lower collection costs (because crews waste less time travelling to the site), reduced fuel and maintenance costs for collection vehicles, increased flexibility in selection of disposal facilities, opportunity to recover recyclables or compostables at the transfer site and the opportunity to shred or scoop wastes prior to disposal. These benefits must be weighed against the costs to develop and operate the facility.

The classical approach to arrive at the economic viability of operating a transfer station, is to add the unit cost of the transfer station to the cost of hauling using large vehicles, and to compare this cost with the cost of hauling directly to the disposal site using the smaller vehicles that service the collection area. The cost of hauling using small vehicles is the sum of the depreciation cost of the vehicle, driver's salary, salary of the collection crew (if they are on standby waiting for the vehicle to return to the collection area) and fuel cost. The transfer station cost is the sum of the transfer station's depreciation cost and the operating and maintenance costs divided by the capacity of the station. The cost of using the large vehicle is the sum of the vehicle depreciation, fuel cost and driver's salary.

The cost-effectiveness of a transfer station depends on the distance of disposal site from the generation area, and a distance of 10–15 km is usually the minimum cost-effective distance. The distance between the disposal site and collection area is one of the principal variables in deciding whether to use a transfer station or haul the solid wastes directly from the collection area to the disposal site.

5. Discuss about implementation of collection and transfer system.

Ans. (i) Finalising and implementing the system management plan: For proper implementation of collection and transfer system, it is necessary to have clear organisational structures and management plans. The organisational structure should be simple, with a minimum of administrative and management layers between collection crews and top management. All workers in the department should clearly understand the department's mission and their roles. Through training, incentives and reinforcement by management, workers should be encouraged to be customer-oriented and team contributors. Feedback mechanisms must be introduced to help the crew review their performance and help managers monitoring the performance of crews, equipment, etc. It is also important to periodically review the management plans and structures, as implementation of collection services continues.

(ii) Purchasing and managing equipment: For purchasing equipment, most municipalities issue bid specifications. Detailed specifications include exact requirements for equipment sizes and capacities, power ratings, etc. Performance specifications often request that equipment be equivalent to certain available models and meet standards for capacity, speed, etc. Municipalities may either perform equipment maintenance themselves, contract with a local garage, or in some cases, contract with the vehicle vendor at the time of purchase. As part of the preventive maintenance programme, the collection crew should check the vehicle chassis, tyres and body daily and report any problems to maintenance managers. In addition, each vehicle should have an individual maintenance record.

(iii) Hiring and training personnel: As in all organisations, good personnel management is essential to an efficient, high-quality waste collection system. Authorities responsible for SWM should, therefore, strive to hire and keep well-qualified personnel. The recruitment programme should assess applicants' abilities to perform the types of physical labour required for the collection, equipment and methods used. To retain employees, management should provide a safe working environment that emphasises career advancement, participatory problem solving and worker incentives. Worker incentives should be developed to recognise and reward outstanding performance by employees. Ways to accomplish motivation include merit-based compensation, awards programme and a work structure. Feedback on employee performance should be regular and frequent.

Safety is especially important because waste collection employees encounter many hazards during each workday. As a result of poor safety records, insurance costs for many collection services are high. To minimise injuries, haulers should have an ongoing safety programme. This programme should outline safety procedures and ensure that all personnel are properly trained on safety issues. Haulers should develop an employee-training programme that helps employees improve and broaden the range of their job-related skills. Education should address such subjects as driving skills, first aid, safe lifting methods, identification of household hazardous wastes, avoidance of substance abuse and stress management.

(iv) Providing public information: Maintaining good communication with the public is important to a well-run collection system. Residents can greatly influence the performance of the collection system by co-operating in separation requirements, and by keeping undesirable materials from entering the collected waste stream. Commonly used methods of communicating information include brochures, articles in community newsletters, newspaper articles, announcements, and advertisements on radio and television, information attachments to utility bills (either printed or given separately) and school handouts. Communication materials should be used to help residents understand the community waste management challenges and the progress in meeting them. Residents should also be kept informed about issues such as the availability and costs of landfill capacity so that they develop an understanding of the issues and a desire to help meet their waste management needs.

(v) Monitoring system cost and performance: Collection and transfer facilities should develop and maintain an effective system for cost and performance reporting. Collected data should be used to forecast workloads, truck costs, identify changes in the generation of wastes and recyclables, trace the origin of problematic waste materials and evaluate crew performance. Just as the goals of a collection programme set its overall directions, a monitoring system provides the short-term feedback necessary to identify the corrections needed to achieve those goals.

OFF-SITE PROCESSING OF SOLID WASTE

1. Write about the purposes of source reduction

Ans. (i) **Product reuse:** Using reusable products, instead of their disposal equivalents, reduce the amount of materials that are to be managed as wastes. An example of product reuse is the reusable shopping bag.

(ii) **Material volume reduction:** Reducing the volume of material used changes the amount of waste entering the waste stream. This helps in controlling the waste generated and its disposal. For example, buying in bulk or using large food containers reduces the amount of packaging waste generated.

(iii) **Toxicity reduction:** Source reduction reduces the amount of toxic constituents in products entering the waste stream and reduces the adverse environmental impacts of recycling or other waste management activities. For example, substitution of lead and cadmium in inks (solvent-based to water-based) and paints is a source reduction activity.

(iv) **Increased product lifetime:** Source reduction facilitates the use of products with longer lifetime over short-lived alternatives that are designed to be discarded at the end of their useful lives. Put differently, it encourages a product design that allows for repairand continued use rather than disposal. Manufacturing long-life tyres is a good example of increasing product lifetime.

(v) **Decreased consumption:** This refers to the reduced consumption of materials that are not reusable (*e.g.*, using a reusable shopping bag instead of picking up plastic bags from the store). Consumer education about the materials that are difficult to dispose of or are harmful to the environment is essential. Buying practices can thus be altered (*e.g.*, buying in bulk) to reflect environmental consciousness.

2. Discuss in detail about full stream processing technique

Ans. This is a high technology separation technique, which processes all components of municipal waste. The materials recovered by this process tend to be of lower quality than those recovered or source separated in MRF because the former is a mix of various types of wastes. To achieve a better quality, the materials obtained through the full stream processing must be cleaned, which is a costly process. However, this technique remains attractive because it does not require source separation, and it is used in the following applications:

(i) **Refuse derived fuel (RDF) preparation:** In this application, it is used to extract the combustible portion of municipal waste.

(ii) **Municipal waste composting:** In this application, it is used to concentrate the compostable portion of municipal solid waste. Note that this is sometimes performed as part of RDF preparation.

(iii) **Material recovery:** In this application, it is used to recover and resell certain materials, and thereby making material recovery a recycling technology as well.

In full stream processing, depending on the facility design, the materials are separated either mechanically or by hand, and size and weight are the main characteristics used to separate the materials.

3. Explain in detail about the recovery of wastes.

Ans. Recycling is perhaps the most widely recognised form of source reduction involving the process of separating, collecting, processing, marketing and ultimately using a material that would have otherwise been discarded. Recycling is fundamental parts of the waste management plan. Although it alone one of the cannot solve a community's municipal SWM problem, it can divert a significant portion of waste stream from disposal in landfill and combustion facilities.

(i) **Economic significance:** Economic assessment of waste recycling is a difficult task as many of the beneficial environmental and social impacts of recycling are long-term and are intangible, and, therefore, are difficult to quantify.

Some of the short- and long-term economic benefits are:

Cost reduction: Resource recovery through recycling of solid waste could be of interest to waste management authorities as a means of reducing the waste disposal cost. Any saving in waste management cost could be a significant incentive to the authorities to increase the coverage of service areas and improve the service level. They can save cost from fuel for transportation, operation and maintenance, and generate revenue by sale of recyclables, etc.

Employment: Recycling of waste is a labour intensive activity, and its potential to ease the unemployment problem is high. Enhanced recycling activities, for example, can create an additional job market for skilled and unskilled workforce, and they can adapt to any of the occupations such as a labourer in recycling business or industry or a dealership.

Energy saving: Use of recyclables in some industrial processes is known to consume less energy than the use of any other raw material. The reduction in energy consumption in one industry could mean its availability for some other industry in need.

Reduced health care costs: Improved health and sanitary conditions in urban areas resulting from indirect benefits of waste recycling can reduce the investment in public health programme.

Saving costs for other public utilities: Enhanced solid waste recycling practices can reduce the frequency of sewer clogging, blocking of natural watercourses and pollution of water bodies. This will benefit the concerned public utilities through reduced cost in cleaning sewers and improved public safety due to blocked sewers and narrowing of natural watercourses.

(ii) **Environmental and health significance:** The volume of waste is increasing rapidly because of population growth and economic development. The composition of waste is also changing, leading to waste production with more recyclables. At the same time, polluted waste fractions are increasing because of increasing complex processes being used in industries, and these contribute increasingly to environmental degradation. This notwithstanding, recycling helps, among others, in the following ways, to facilitate effective waste management.

Improved environment: The environmental pollution may be due to inadequate SWM as well as due to its effect on other urban infrastructure. Recycling reduces the volume of waste that has to be finally dumped, and thereby causing reduction in pollution at the waste disposal sites. When there is reduction in volume of waste because of its increased reuse, different types of pollution (*e.g.*, water, air and land) will get abated.

Natural resource conservation: Industries with natural products as their raw material for production are depleting natural resources. Use of more and more recyclable solid wastes in industrial production will relieve the tremendous pressure on these precious resources. For example, recycling of waste paper means a lower demand for wood, which means less cutting of trees and an enhanced possibility for sustainable use of the forest. Using recyclable items in the production process would reduce the demand for energy as well.

(iii) **Social significance:** People engaged in waste collection activities are normally of low social and economic standing. This is especially true with scavengers, which is evident from persisting poor quality of their living and working conditions. Different groups of people engaged in waste recycling have a hierarchical social and economic status, in which, processors are at the top of the hierarchy followed by waste dealers and wholesalers, waste buyers and waste collectors in that very order, while scavengers are at the bottom. Although there is this social and economic hierarchy within the waste recycling business, the overall social esteem of waste recycling operators is low.

A formal recycling arrangement will help promote the social esteem of waste workers and facilitate their upward social mobility due to increased earning. In addition, the improved recycling activity will increase the economic value of the waste and will reduce waste scavenging activity providing opportunity for scavengers to switch to a more socially acceptable occupation. In short, institutionalised recycling programmes will help remove the stigma associated with waste scavenging and transform it to an economic enterprise.

4. Discuss about recycling program.

Ans. Numerous recycling options are available, and recycling programme development requires strategic planning. Planning for recycling involves understanding markets, assessing local expertise, setting goals and fostering public participation. An efficient recycling programme requires a systematic approach to all programme components, which are interrelated, and therefore, decisions about one must be made taking into consideration other components. As a successful recycling requires public participation, programmes must be designed keeping in view public convenience and support.

(i) **Build local expertise:** Small projects help build local expertise in recycling and minimise the problems associated with poor planning. With small- scale projects, it is easy to compare and evaluate the programmes and techniques that are considered most successful within the community. When the time comes to develop a large-scale programme, there will be practical experience and an established decision-making framework, which will enhance the programme's success.

(ii) **Understand and develop a recycling market:** While planning for a recycling programme, it is important to find an outlet for the recyclable material. Market analysis is both a planning and ongoing activity, as even the most successful recycling programme can be severely affected by market fluctuations. Recycling programmes must, therefore, be designed with the flexibility to handle fluctuating markets and uncertain outlets for material.

(iii) **Foster public education and involvement:** Public participation is one of the most important factors deciding a programme's success. The public has a right and a responsibility to understand the full costs and liabilities of managing the waste they produce. A well-planned public education and involvement programme will foster public interest in recycling.

(iv) **Assess local waste stream:** Planning any recycling programme requires the knowledge of the local waste stream. Choosing the right material to recycle and designing the logistics of the programme are the important parts of the planning process.

(v) **Augment existing programme:** Recycling should augment the success that has been attained by other groups operating recycling programmes. This is very important for planning and success. Other programmes may be run by local volunteer organisations to raise funds or as a community service.

(vi) **Set goals and objectives:** Part of the planning process involves setting goals and objectives. The preliminary assessment of waste stream helps in deciding long-term goals for a community. Planning objectives may include determining the type of waste stream component that should be programmed, investigating the feasibility of the curbside (kerbside) programme, public outreach avenues, etc.

(vii) **Coordinate the programme:** Recycling programme is considered a public service. Therefore, local governments are required to ensure that all services are provided properly. Like any other public service, recycling programmes should be consistent, predictable, equitable and efficient.

(viii) **Evaluate the programme:** New programmes and technologies are evolving continuously, which make the planning for recycling an ongoing process. This requires experiment and evaluation. Even the best recycling programmes experiment with new techniques to improve on their current efforts. If recycling programmes are properly planned and implemented, they would then add to the overall municipal waste management activity.

5. Discuss in detail about Processing equipment for recycling

Ans. **Balers:** Balers can be used to densify many types of materials including paper, cardboard, plastics and cans. transportation costs. Balers can improve space utilisation and reduce material.

Can densifiers: Can crushers are used to densify aluminium and steel cans prior to transport.

Glass crushers: These are used to process glass fraction separated by colour and break it into small pieces. This crushed material is then called cullet, and can be reprocessed into new glass products.

Magnetic separators: These are used to remove ferrous material from a mixture of materials.

Wood grinders: These are chippers and are used to shred large pieces of wood into chips that can be used as mulch or as fuel.

Scales: These are used to measure the quantity of materials recovered or sold.

6. Explain about Material recovery facilities (MRF).

Ans. MRF (pronounced 'murf') is a centralised facility that receives, separates, processes and markets recyclable material. It can be operated with both drop off and curbside programmes. The primary advantage of MRF is that it allows materials directly from the municipalities and processes them uniformly. It is generally designed to handle all type of recyclables. Implementation of MRF in a municipality depends upon a number of factors as follows:

Market demand: When additional processing is required, MRF is more useful as buyers may have certain material specifications.

Separate collection: In systems that require residents to separate their recyclables, intermediate separation and processing is required.

Number of different recyclables: In general, a MRF will be more beneficial when a large number of different recyclables are collected.

Quantities of materials: Because MRF involves substantial capital and operating costs (*e.g.*, buildings, equipment and labour), it is expected to handle a significant amount of materials to justify its operation.

DISPOSAL OF SOLID WASTE

1. Explain about solid waste Disposal methods.

Ans. (i) **Uncontrolled dumping or non-engineered disposal:** As mentioned, this is the most common method being practised in many parts of the world, and India is no exception. In this method, wastes are dumped at a designated site without any environmental control. They tend to remain there for a long period of time, pose health risks and cause environmental degradation. Due to the adverse health and environmental impact associated with it, the non-engineered disposal is not considered a viable and safe option.

(ii) **Sanitary landfill:** Unlike the non-engineered disposal, sanitary landfill is a fully engineered disposal option in that the selected location or wasteland is carefully engineered in advance before it is pressed into service. Operators of sanitary landfills can minimise the effects of leachate (*i.e.*, polluted water which flows from a landfill) and gas production through proper site selection, preparation and management. This particular option of waste disposal is suitable when the land is available at an affordable price, and adequate workforce and technical resources are available to operate and manage the site.

(iii) **Composting:** This is a biological process of decomposition in which organisms, under controlled conditions of ventilation, temperature and moisture, convert the organic portion of solid waste into humus-like material. If this process is carried out effectively, what we get as the final product is a stable, odour-free soil conditioner. Generally, the option of composting is considered, when a considerable amount of biodegradable waste is available in the waste stream and there is use or market for composts. Composting can be either centralised or small-scale. Centralised composting plants are possible, if adequate skilled workforce and equipments are available. And, small-scale composting practices can be effective at household level, but this needs public awareness.

(iv) **Incineration:** This refers to the controlled burning of wastes, at a high temperature (roughly 1200–1500°C), which sterilises and stabilises the waste in addition to reducing its volume. In the process, most of the combustible materials (*i.e.*, self-sustaining combustible matter, which saves the energy needed to maintain the combustion) such as paper or plastics get converted into carbon dioxide and ash. Incineration may be used as a disposal option, when land filling is not possible and the waste composition is highly combustible. An appropriate technology, infrastructure and skilled workforce are required to operate and maintain the plant.

(v) **Gasification:** This is the partial combustion of carbonaceous material (through combustion) at high temperature (roughly 1000°C) forming a gas, comprising mainly carbon dioxide, carbon monoxide, nitrogen, hydrogen, water vapour and methane, which can be used as fuel.

(vi) **Refuse-derived fuel (RDF):** This is the combustible part of raw waste, separated for burning as fuel. Various physical processes such as screening, size reduction, magnetic separation, etc., are used to separate the combustibles.

(vii) **Pyrolysis:** This is the thermal degradation of carbonaceous material to gaseous, liquid and solid fraction in the absence of oxygen. This occurs at a temperature between 200 and 900°C.

2. Discuss about sanitary landfill.

Ans. The term landfill generally refers to an engineered deposit of wastes either in pits/ trenches or on the surface. And, a sanitary landfill is essentially a landfill, where proper mechanisms are available to control the environmental risks associated with the disposal of wastes and to make available the land, subsequent to disposal, for other purposes. However, you must note that a landfill need not necessarily be an engineered site, when the waste is largely inert at final disposal, as in rural areas, where wastes contain a large proportion of soil and dirt. This practice is generally designated as non-engineered disposal method. When compared to uncontrolled dumping, engineered landfills are more likely to have pre-planned installations, environmental monitoring, and organised and trained workforce. Sanitary landfill implementation, therefore, requires careful site selection, preparation and management.

Principle: The purpose of landfilling is to bury or alter the chemical composition of the wastes so that they do not pose any threat to the environment or public health. Landfills are not homogeneous and are usually made up of cells in which a discrete volume of waste is kept isolated from adjacent waste cells by a suitable barrier. The barriers between cells generally consist of a layer of natural soil (*i.e.*, clay), which restricts downward or lateral escape of the waste constituents or leachate.

Landfilling relies on containment rather than treatment (for control) of wastes. An environmentally sound sanitary landfill comprises appropriate liners for protection of the groundwater (from contaminated leachate), run-off controls, leachate collection and treatment, monitoring wells and appropriate final cover design.

3. Explain about Landfill gas and leachate.

Ans. Leachate and landfill gas comprise the major hazards associated with a landfill. While leachate may contaminate the surrounding land and water, landfill gas can be toxic and lead to global warming and explosion leading to human catastrophe. (Note that global warming, also known as greenhouse effect, refers to the warming of the earth's atmosphere by the accumulation of gases (*e.g.*, methane, carbon dioxide and chlorofluorocarbons) that absorbs reflected solar radiation.) The factors, which affect the production of leachate and landfill gas, are the following:

Nature of waste: The deposition of waste containing biodegradable matter invariably leads to the production of gas and leachate, and the amount depends on the content of biodegradable material in the waste.

Moisture content: Most micro-organisms require a minimum of approximately 12% (by weight) moisture for growth, and thus the moisture content of landfill waste is an important factor in determining the amount and extent of leachate and gas production.

pH: The methanogenic bacteria within a landfill produce methane gas, which will grow only at low pH range around neutrality.

Particle size and density: The size of waste particle affects the density that can be achieved upon compaction and affects the surface area and hence volume. Both affect moisture absorption and therefore are potential for biological degradation.

Temperature: An increase in temperature tends to increase gas production. The temperature affects the microbial activity to the extent that it is possible to segregate bacteria, according to their optimum temperature operating conditions.

4. Discuss about landfill gas emission.

Ans. Landfill gas contains a high percentage of methane due to the anaerobic decomposition of organic matter, which can be utilised as a source of energy.

(i) Composition and properties: We can predict the amount and composition of the gas generated for different substrates, depending on the general anaerobic decomposition of wastes added. Climatic and environmental conditions also influence gas composition. Due to the heterogeneous nature of the landfill, some acid phase anaerobic decomposition occurs along with the methanogenic decomposition. Since aerobic and acid-phase degradation give rise to carbon dioxide and not methane, there may be a higher carbon dioxide content in the gas generated than what would otherwise be expected. Furthermore, depending on the moisture distribution, some carbon dioxide goes into solution. This may appear to increase (artificially) the methane content of the gas measured in the landfill. A typical landfill gas contains a number of components such as the following, which tend to occur within a characteristic range:

Methane: This is a colourless, odourless and flammable gas with a density lighter than air, typically making up 50–60% of the landfill gas.

Carbon dioxide: This is a colourless, odourless and non-inflammable gas that is denser than air, typically accounting for 30–40%.

Oxygen: The flammability of methane depends on the percentage of oxygen. It is, therefore, important to control oxygen levels, where gas abstraction is undertaken.

Nitrogen: This is essentially inert and will have little effect, except to modify the explosive range of methane.

It is difficult to convert the amount of gas measured to the maximum landfill gas production value because gas is withdrawn from a small part of the landfill only, referred to as *zone of influence* during measurement. In other words, it is very difficult to determine this zone and relate it to the whole landfill area.

(ii) Hazards: Landfill gas consists of a mixture of flammable, asphyxiating and noxious gases and may be hazardous to health and safety, and hence the need for precautions.

Some of the major hazards are listed below:

Explosion and fire: Methane is flammable in air within the range of 5–15% by volume, while hydrogen is flammable within the range of 4.1–7.5% (in the presence of oxygen) and potentially explosive. Fire, occurring within the waste, can be difficult to extinguish and can lead to unpredictable and uncontrolled subsidence as well as production of smoke and toxic fumes.

Trace components: These comprise mostly alkanes and alkenes, and their oxidation products such as aldehydes, alcohols and esters. Many of them are recognised as toxicants, when in air at concentrations above occupational exposure standards.

Global warming: Known also as greenhouse effect, it is the warming of the earth's atmosphere by the accumulation of gases (methane, carbon dioxide and chlorofluorocarbons) that absorbs reflected solar radiation.

Migration: During landfill development, most of the gas produced is vented to the atmosphere, provided the permeable intermediate cover has been used. While biological and chemical processes affect gas composition through methane oxidation, which converts methane to carbon dioxide, physical factors affect gas migration. The physical factors that affect gas migration include:

Environmental conditions: These affect the rate of degradation and gas pressure build up.

Geophysical conditions: These affect migration pathways. In the presence of fractured geological strata or a mineshaft, the gas may travel large distances, unless restricted by the water table.

Climatic conditions: Falling atmospheric pressure, rainfall and water infiltration rate affect landfill gas migration.

The proportion of void space in the ground, rather than permeability, determines the variability of gas emission. If the escape of landfill gas is controlled and proper extraction system is designed, this gas can be utilised as a source of energy. If landfill gas is not utilised, it should be burnt by means of flaring. However, landfill gas utilisation can save on the use of fossil fuels since its heating value is approximately 6 kWh/m^3 and can be utilised in internal combustion engines for production of electricity and heat.

It is important that landfill gas is extracted during the operation phase. It is extracted out of the landfill by means of gas wells, which are normally drilled by auger and are driven into the landfill at a spacing of 40–70 m. In addition, horizontal systems can be installed during operation of the landfill. The gas wells consist mainly of perforated plastic pipes surrounded by coarse gravel and are connected with the gas transportation pipe with flexible tubing. The vacuum necessary for gas extraction and transportation is created by means of a blower. The most important factors influencing planning and construction of landfill gas extraction systems are settling of waste, water tables in landfills and gas quality.

5. Discuss about environmental effects of landfilling.

Ans. The environmental effects of a landfill include wind-blown litter and dust, noise, obnoxious odour, vermin and insects attracted by the waste, surface runoff and in aesthetic conditions. Gas and leachate problems also arise during the operation phase and require significant environmental controls. In what follows, we will describe some of the major environmental effects below:

(i) Wind-blown litter and dust are continuous problems of the ongoing landfill operation and a nuisance to the neighbourhood. Covering the waste cells with soil and spraying water on dirt roads and waste in dry periods, in combination with fencing and movable screens, may minimise the problem of wind-blown litter and dust. However, note that the problem will remain at the tipping front of the landfill.

(ii) Movement of waste collection vehicles, emptying of wastes from them, compactors, earthmoving equipment, etc produce noise. Improving the technical capability of the equipment, surrounding the fill area with soil embankments and plantations, limiting the working hours and appropriately training the workforce will help minimise noise pollution.

(iii) Birds (*e.g.*, scavengers), vermin, insects and animals are attracted to the landfill for feeding and breeding. Since many of these may act as disease vectors, their presence is a potential health problem.

(iv) Surface run-off, which has been in contact with the land filled waste, may be a problem in areas of intense rainfall. If not controlled, heavily polluted run-off may enter directly into creeks and streams. Careful design and maintenance of surface drains and ditches, together with a final soil cover on completed landfill sections, can help eliminate this problem.

(v) An operating landfill, where equipment and waste are exposed, appears in aesthetic. This problem may be reduced by careful design of screening soil embankments, plantings, rapid covering and re-vegetation of filled sections.

(vi) Gas released, as a result of degradation or volatilisation of waste components, causes odour, flammability, health problems and damage of the vegetation (due to oxygen depletion in the root zone). The measures to control this include liners, soil covers, passive venting or active extraction of gas for treatment before discharge into the atmosphere.

(vii) Polluted leachate appears shortly after disposal of the waste. This may cause groundwater pollution and pollution of streams through sub-surface migration. Liners, drainage collection, treatment of leachate, and groundwater and downstream water quality monitoring are necessary to control this problem.

CHAPTER

10

APPENDIX B: MULTIPLE CHOICE Q & A ON SOLID & HAZARDOUS WASTE MANAGEMENT

1. Which of the following solid waste disposal methods is ecologically most acceptable?

   (a) Pyrolysis (b) Incineration

   (c) Composting (d) Sanitary landfill.

2. Match the features of various solid waste disposal methods.

   Solid waste disposal methods

   A. Incineration B. Sanitary landfill

   C. Composting D. Salvage by sorting

   Features

   I. Requires presorting, grinding and turning.

   II. Limited to special wastes and selected materials.

   III. High operational maintenance cost

   IV. Tractor

   V. Rat and fly breeding

Codes:	A	B	C	D
(a)	II	V	IV	III
(b)	I	IV	II	III
(c)	III	IV	I	II
(d)	III	V	IV	II

3. Organisms that mineralise organic matter in an ecosystem are called decomposers. Aerobic method of composting is called .... method.

   (a) Nagpur (b) Indore

   (c) Delhi (d) Bangalore

ANSWER

1. (c) 2. (c) 3. (b)

4. The term 'refuse' generally does not include:
   (a) Excreta
   (b) Putrescible (decomposable) solid waste
   (c) Ashes
   (d) Non-putrescible solid waste.
5. For rural areas, most suitable solid waste disposal method is
   (a) Land filling (b) Composting
   (c) Pyrolysis (d) Incineration
6. On mass basis, the largest fraction of the municipal solid waste (MSW) from a typical Indian city is made up of the .... substances.
   (a) Salvagable (b) Composting
   (c) Combustible (d) Toxic & hazardous
7. The most popular method of solid disposal in India is:
   (a) Pyrolysis (b) Incineration
   (c) Landfill (d) Fluidisod bed combustion.
8. Biomedical waste (comprising of both solid & liquid wastes) generated in Indian hospitals is about 1.45 kg/day/patient. Which of the following methods is generally not adopted for safe disposal of biomedical wastes?
   (a) Incineration. (b) Landfilling.
   (c) Hydroclaying. (d) Shredding after disinfection.
9. Pick out the wrong statement.
   Autoclaving of biomedical wastes is:
   (a) Followed by its shredding off and suitable disposal.
   (b) A high heat thermal process.
   (c) Meant for disposal of solid wastes only.
   (d) A low heat thermal process.
10. The aerobic & anaerobic methods or mechanical composting of refuse; disposal as practiced in India, are called .... respectively.
    (a) Indore method and Bangalore method
    (b) Bangalore method and Indore method
    (c) Mangalore method and Nagpur method
    (d) Indore method and Mangalore method
11. The method of' refuse disposal burial in trenches is called:
    (a) Composting (b) Incineration
    (c) Pulverisation (d) Pyrolysis

ANSWER

4. (a) 5. (b) 6. (b) 7. (c) 8. (b) 9. (b) 10. (a) 11. (a)

12. Sanitary landfills may cause troubles during peak monsoons. Leachate is colored liquid that comes out of:

(a) Septic tanks. (b) Compost plants.
(c) Sanitary landfills. (d) Aerated lagoons.

13. Pick out the wrong statement.

(a) Incineration can be adopted for disposal of both solid & liquid biomedical wastes.
(b) Liquid biomedical wastes can be disposed off by disinfection and discharge into sewers.
(c) According to biomedical waste management & handling rules various biomedical waste types are segregated by collecting the wastes into yellow, red & black colored containers.
(d) Biomedical waste (management and handling rules) were enacted in India under Environment Protection Act, 1986 in the year 1986.

14. .... is not having a permanent site for disposal of high level radioactive wastes generated in nuclear power plants .

(a) India (b) Russia
(c) U.S.A (d) Canada.

15. Spent fuels generated in nuclear power plants contain plutonium - 239 (a long life hazardous radioactive substance), which has a very long half life period of the order of ...... years.

(a) 1000 (b) 5000
(c) 10000 (d) 24000

16. The furnace of a municipal incinerator consists of a grate system and combustion chambers. Because of the high temperature and high moisture content of the exhaust stream, ... have not been used to control emission from municipal incinerators.

(a) Baghouses (b) Electrostatic precipitators
(c) Cyclones (d) Wet scrubbers

17. What rubbish material do we throwaway the most?

(a) Plastic (b) Aluminium
(c) Paper (d) Glass

18. Used oil should be disposed of by:

(a) Collecting it in a sealed container and taking it to an oil changing business.
(b) Keeping it in the garage for 10 years before throwing it away in the trash.
(c) Watering it down and spreading it as a fertilizer.
(d) Dumping it on your driveway.

ANSWER

12. (c) 13. (d) 14. (a) 15. (d) 16. (a) 17. (c) 18. (a)

19. How long does it take styrofoam to break down in a landfill?
(a) 10 years (b) 50 years
(c) 100 years (d) 500 years
20. What is the environmentally friendly way to dispose off used tyres?
(a) Recycle them to a playground matting .
(b) Dump them in a ditch along the roadway.
(c) Collect them and put them in a big pile.
(d) Send them to a landfill.
21. Mercury is a hazardous chemical. Which item does not contain mercury?
(a) Clinical thermometers (b) Fluorescent light bulbs
(c) Computer discs (d) Blinking light in sneakers
22. Which of the following items are recyclable?
(a) Plastic milk jugs (b) Cereal boxes
(c) Aluminium soda cans (d) all 'a', 'b' and 'c'
23. Most of the domestic trash thrown away each day ends up getting:
(a) Recycled (b) Burned
(c) Eaten by cattle (d) Landfilled
24. Which of the following is non-biodegradable?
(a) Tea leaves (b) Wool
(c) Animal bones (d) Nylon
25. The most serious environmental effects posed by hazardous waste is:
(a) Increased use of land for landfills (b) Contamination of ground water
(c) Destruction of habitat (d) Air pollution.
26. Vermicomposting of solid waste is done by:
(a) Bacteria (b) Fungus
(c) Animals (d) Worms
27. Which of the following in non-biodegrable?
(a) Fruit (b) Vegetables
(c) Earthworm (d) Aluminium foil
28. If waste materials contaminate the source of drinking water, which of the following disease will spread?
(a) Typhoid (b) Scurvy
(c) Anemia (d) Malaria

ANSWER

19. (d) 20. (a) 21. (c) 22. (d) 23. (b) 24. (d) 25. (b) 26. (d)
27. (d) 28. (b)

29. Which of the following solid waste materials can not be decomposed by bacteria to form compost?
    (a) Dead plants (b) Plastic bags
    (c) Kitchen wastes (d) Bodies of insects living in the soil.
30. Fly ash emitted from chimney of thermal power plant can be used:
    (a) In land as fertiliser (b) For disinfection of water
    c) For brick manufacturing (d) All 'a', 'b', &'c'
31. Pick out the wrong statement about solid waste management.
    (a) Sanitary landfill method of solid waste disposal is suitable for garbage disposal.
    (b) Nuissiance from rodent and fly is controlled in the disposal of solid waste by sanitary landfill method.
    (c) Disposal of solid waste by composting is efficient with temperature & pH control.
    (d) The effective measure of solid waste disposal employs the principle of "4 R's" which includes reduction, recycling, reuse and recovery.
32. Windrow is a method of solid waste disposal by:
    (a) Sanitary landfill (b) Composting
    (c) Incineration (d) None of these
33. Most suitable method of solid waste disposal in rural area is:
    (a) Composting (b) Land filling
    (c) Incineration (d) Pyrolysis
34. The end product formed after separation and anaerobic bacterial digestion of organic municipal solid wastes is called:
    (a) Leachate (b) Humus
    (c) Sewage (d) Refuse
35. Which of the following materials is used as landfill sealant for the control of gas and leachate movement?
    (a) Flyash (b) Sand
    (c) Bentonite (d) Lime
36. The daily cover of municipal solid waste landfills consists of:
    (a) Bentonite (b) Compacted soil
    (c) Lime (d) Sand
37. Which of the following solid waste disposal methods conserves energy most efficiently?
    (a) Fludised bed combustion (b) Incineration with heat recovery
    (c) Pyrolysis (d) Composting.

ANSWER

29. (b) 30. (c) 31. (a) 32. (b) 33. (a) 34. (b) 35. (c) 36. (b)
37. (b)

38. In which of the following methods of solid wastes disposal, methane recovery is a positive trend?
    (a) Open dumping (b) Sanitary landfilling
    (c) Ocean dumping (d) Incineration
39. Most of the municipal solid waste (MSW) generated is:
    (a) Burned (b) Recycled
    (c) Placed in landfills (d) Recovered & reused.
40. .... waste does not come under the category of hazardous waste.
    (a) Reactive (b) Non-toxic
    (c) Inflammable (d) Corrosive
41. Which sequence of responses towards solid waste leads to the least amount of energy used?
    (a) Reduce, recycle reuse (b) Reduce, reuse, recycle
    (c) Recycle, reduce, reuse (d) Reuse, recycle, reduce.
42. Which of the following are biodegradable waste products?
    (a) Rubber, plastic, manure (b) Metal, glass, plastic
    (c) Vegetable peels, garden refuse, paper (d) Glass, wood cuttings, batteries
43. Non-biodegradable means a substance that:
    (a) cannot decompose naturally (b) is thrown away as kitchen refuse
    (c) costs too much to recycle (d) will not dissolve in water
44. The total weight of solid waste generated in a town is 72,850 lbs/week, whose population is 3500 persons. The unit generation rate of solid waste (kg/capita/day) is:
    (a) 1.0 (b) 1.5
    (c) 1.3 (d) 2.0
45. The major gases produced from sanitary landfill are due to:
    (a) Anaerobic decomposition of biodegradable organic matter.
    (b) Aerobic decomposition of biodegradable organic matter.
    (c) Anaerobic decomposition of non-biodegradable organic matter.
    (d) Aerobic decomposition of non-biodegradable organic matter.
46. The minimum area of land desirable for sanitary landfill that is sufficient to operate for at least:
    (a) One year (b) Six months
    (c) None of these (d) five years

ANSWER

38. (b) 39. (c) 40. (b) 41. (b) 42. (c) 43. (a) 44. (c) 45. (a)
46. (a)

47. In general, the organic waste material decomposes rapidly (3 to 5 years) is:

(a) Food waste (b) News paper

(c) Leaves (d) All of these.

48. Sainitary landfilling is an operation in which waste to be disposed off is compacted and covered with a layer of soil at the end of .... day's operation.

(a) two (b) one

(c) three (d) none of these.

49. Improvements to landfill design include:

(a) Large size

(b) Reducing the amount of yard clippings allowed

(c) Leachate collection systems

(d) All of the above

50. In Japan and Switzerland the most common waste disposal methods are:

(a) Landfills and incinration (b) Landfills and recycling

(c) Recycling and incineration (d) None of the above

51. Incinerator ash usually contains which of the following chemicals?

(a) Heavy metals (b) Organic compounds

(c) VOC's (d) All of the above

52. The cheapest method of municipal solid waste disposal in the current time is:

(a) Incineration (b) Land disposal

(c) Recycling (d) None of the above

53. Composting uses ____________ processes to transform organic material into compost.

(a) Industrial (b) Chemical

(c) Natural (d) None of these

54. Banning the sale of one-time-use beverage containers would:

(a) Reduce litter (b) Save energy

(c) Save money (d) All of the above

55. One technological problem with plastic recycling is that:

(a) People do not like to recycle

(b) Different types of plastics cannot be recycled together

(c) The technology to recycle plastics does not exist

(d) All of the above

56. The United States produces one-half of the world's e-waste and recycles .... of it.

(a) none (b) all

(c) one-half (d) 10-15%

ANSWER

47. (d) 48. (b) 49. (c) 50. (c) 51. (a) 52. (b) 53. (c) 54. (d)
55. (d) 56. (d)

57. Which of the following is *not* a type of e-waste?
 (a) Discarded TV sets
 (b) Discarded computer printer paper
 (c) Discarded cell pones
 (d) Discarded computer monitors
58. Waste that includes paper, food waste, cans, bottles, yard, glass, wood, and similar items is called:
 (a) Industrial solid waste
 (b) Hazardous waste
 (c) Municipal solid waste
 (d) Toxic solid waste
59. Hazardous waste includes radioactive waste, which will have to be stored safely for as long .... years.
 (a) 15,00
 (b) 50,000
 (c) 100,000
 (d) 240,000
60. How much of the waste we mix, crush, and bury could actually be recycled?
 (a) 30%
 (b) 50%
 (c) 60%
 (d) 75%
61. With 5% of the world's population, the United States produces about .... of the world's solid waste.
 (a) one-tenth
 (b) one-fifth
 (c) one-forth
 (d) one-third
62. For each one kg. of electronics in a computer, how much solid & liquid wastes are created?
 (a) 9 tons
 (b) 2 tons
 (c) 1 tons
 (d) 0.5 ton
63. Garbage produced directly by households and business account for .... % of the solid waste produced in the United States.
 (a) 2
 (b) 5
 (c) 10
 (d) 15
64. Each discarded computer contains approximately 2 kg of which metal?
 (a) Cadmium
 (b) Lead
 (c) Mercury
 (d) Arsenic
65. The primary emphasis in the US EPA's pollution prevention hierarchy is to:
 (a) Recycle wastes
 (b) Treat wastes to reduce their hazard
 (c) Reduce the amount of pollution generated at the source
 (d) Sell pollution emission permits to other companies

ANSWER

57. (b) 58. (c) 59. (d) 60. (d) 61. (d) 62. (a) 63. (a) 64. (b) 65. (c)

66. What is the most desirable method of dealing with municipal solid waste?
    (a) Landfilling (b) Incineration
    (c) Energy recovery (d) Recycling
67. The US EPA defines hazardous waste by:
    (a) Toxicity and reactivity (b) Corrosivity
    (c) Ignitability (d) All of the above
68. Which of the following statement does *not* describe a problem associated with modern landfills?
    (a) Chemicals leaking out of the waste stored there may pollute wells or groundwater supplies.
    (b) Materials buried in landfills decompose in three years.
    (c) Explosive gases can be produced by landfills and may build up in the basements of nearby buildings.
    (d) All of the above
69. What is the most helpful thing that a consumer can do to make sure that more materials are recycled?
    (a) Encourage friends and neighbors to recycle their newspaper.
    (b) Carefully wash and sort all materials put out for recycling.
    (c) Write letters to legislators asking that recycling be made mandatory.
    (d) Make an effort to buy products made from recycled materials
70. Which of the following produces the maximum solid waste?
    (a) Manufacturing (b) Plastic packaging
    (c) Agriculture (d) Nuclear power plants
71. Which items make up the largest percentage of waste produced by households and business?
    (a) Aluminum cans
    (b) Plastic bottles and packaging
    (c) Paper products
    (d) Yard waste, such as grass clippings and tree limbs
72. What percentage of the energy needed to make aluminum cans from ore is needed to make recycled aluminum cans from used aluminum cans?
    (a) 95% (b) 5%
    (c) 60% (d) None of the above

ANSWER

66. (d) 67. (d) 68. (b) 69. (d) 70. (a) 71. (c) 72. (c)

73. Which of following correctly describes the disposal of waste by composting?
    (a) Composting is a good way for individuals to reduce the amount of garbage they send to landfills, but large scale composting is impractical.
    (b) Composting could reduce the amount of waste that restaurants, food processing plants, and animal feedlots send to landfills.
    (c) Compost made from glass & plastics can be recycled and used as building materials.
    (d) yard wastes, such as grass clippings, are not suitable for composting because they contain low level of nutrients.
74. Which of the following correctly describes biodegradable plastics?
    (a) Some plastics are designed to deteriorate when exposed to sunlight.
    (b) Plastic that contains sugars can be broken down by soil bacteria.
    (c) Degradable plastics usually break down into smaller pieces of plastic.
    (d) All of the above
75. Which of the following is *not* considered hazardous waste?
    (a) Dead batteries such as those used in flashlights and radios
    (b) Rotting meat and other food waste
    (c) Metals such as lead and mercury
    (d) Both (a) and (c)
76. Some hazardous waste is disposed of by deep-well injection. This procedure:
    (a) Pollutes the wells and water supplies of nearby residents.
    (b) Stores wastes in layers of dry rock below the water table.
    (c) Violates state law.
    (d) All of the above
77. The methane found in landfills is a gas that:
    (a) is produced when wastes react with oxygen.
    (b) must be pumped to the surface in leachate pipes.
    (c) is a major contaminant of groundwater supplies.
    (d) may be captured and used to produce energy.
78. Which of the following is a true statement about recycling?
    (a) It takes more energy to make steel from scrap than from newly mined ore.
    (b) Cities have never had trouble finding buyers for their recycled materials.
    (c) After they are collected, recyclable materials are cleaned and processed.
    (d) All of the above
79. The process of composting:
    (a) uses synthetic materials.
    (b) has little potential to conserve landfill space.
    (c) is always carried out in city run facilities .
    (d) could effectively handle a variety of wastes.

ANSWER

73. (b) 74. (d) 75. (b) 76. (b) 77. (d) 78. (c) 79. (d)

80. The main problem with so called biodegradable plastic is that:
   (a) Only its organic portion actually decomposes.
   (b) Animals often choke on the plastic litter that forms.
   (c) It releases toxic compounds as it breaks apart.
   (d) It includes a chemical made by a rare bacterium.

81. Which of the following is *not* a method of reducing hazardous waste?
   (a) Allowing fungi to break down petroleum sludge.
   (b) Burning toxic substance in specially designed incinerators.
   (c) Using nontoxic beads instead of solvents to clean metal parts.
   (d) All of the above.

82. A common characteristic of all hazardous waste land disposal facilities is that they:
   (a) are long-term storage sites. (b) make use of deep well injection.
   (c) pose no threat to the environment. (d) are not regulated by state laws.

83. From 1970 to the present, the percentage of waste that is recycled has increased from 5 to ....%.
   (a) 30 (b) 15
   (c) 50 (d) 70

84. An example of source reduction is:
   (a) Composting. (b) Recycling.
   (c) Using canvas shopping bags. (d) All of the above

85. Making products from recycled materials:
   (a) is limited to metals.
   (b) Saves energy and other resources during the manufacturing
   (c) uses much energy that is not economically workable.
   (d) None of the above

86. An example of something that is biodegradable is:
   (a) a leaf in a compost pile.
   (b) a plastic milk jug in a landfill.
   (c) a polystyrene burger container in a trash can.
   (d) All of the above

87. Which of the following is *not* a requirement for a landfill built today?
   (a) It must be lined with clay and plastic.
   (b) It must be at a specified distance from a city or other populated area.
   (c) It must have system for collecting and treating leachate.
   (d) Vent pipes must be installed for removing methane.

ANSWER

80. (a) 81. (a) 82. (a) 83. (a) 84. (c) 85. (b) 86. (a) 87. (b)

88. Which of the following are problems associated with landfills?
(a) Source reduction and composting
(b) Leachate and methane production
(c) Surface impoundment and leachate
(d) All of the above

89. A material is biodegrable if, it
(a) is made of synthetic material.
(b) is made from petroleum or natural gas.
(c) can be broken down by biological processes.
(d) can be disposed off in a landfill.

90. Materials that are formed naturally are:
(a) Bio-degradable
(b) Non-biodegradable
(c) Non-compostable
(d) Non-combustible

91. An advantage of a solid waste................. is that it reduces the amount of trash destined for landfills.
(a) Sanitary land filing
(b) Incinerator
(c) Composting
(d) Bio-treatment

92. More than half of the solid produced in the United States comes from:
(a) Municipality
(b) Construction
(c) Slaughterhouse
(d) Manufacturing sector

93. The total amount of solid waste generated in the United States in the last 40 years has:
(a) Doubled
(b) Trebled
(c) Quadrupled
(d) Halved

94. Problems associated with .... waste include leachate, methane gas, and inadequate space.
(a) Composting
(b) Landfills
(c) Incineration
(d) Pyrolysis

95. Disposing of hazardous wastes by pumping them into the ground below groundwater level is called:
(a) Burial
(b) Encapsulation
(c) Deep well injection
(d) Composting

96. You can reduce buying power to reduce solid waste by using:
(a) Disposable
(b Recycling
(c) Rechargeable
(d) Solar

97. The steps involved in the recycling of metarials are .... cleaning, and crushing.
(a) Storing
(b) Transferring
(c) Sorting
(d) Disposing

ANSWER

88. (b) 89. (c) 90. (a) 91. (b) 92. (d) 93. (a) 94. (b) 95. (c)
96. (c) 97. (c)

98. An advantage of .... plastic is that its production uses 20 to 50 percent less fossil fuel than does the production of regular plastic.
    (a) green (b) recycled
    (c) biodegradable (d) non-biodegradable
99. Waste containing toxic, corrosive, or flammable materials are considered:
    (a) Radioactive (b) Non-biodegradable
    (c) Bio-degradable (d) Hazardous
100. Polyester is a/an................ material ; and therefore non-biodegradable, material commonly used for clothing.
    (a) natural (b) synthetic
    (c) radioactive (d) non-hazardous
101. A modern landfill has a plastic liner to prevent .... from seeping into the soil and contaminating the groundwater.
    (a) methane gas (b) moisture
    (c) leachate (d) carbon dioxide gas
102. Some landfills generate electricity by burning the .... that is produced by decomposing garbage.
    (a) carbon monoxide (b) acetylene
    (c) sulfur dioxide (d) methane
103. Manufacturers could reduce waste and conserve resources by making products that are more:
    (a) environment friendly (b) non-biodegradable
    (c) durable (d) flexible
104. Reducing solid waste by using less material is called........................ reduction.
    (a) source (b) environment friendly
    (c) straight (d) indirect
105. More companies will use recycled products, if consumers buy recycled products and create an increased .... for such products.
    (a) awareness (b) acceptability
    (c) demand (d) none of these
106. Creating steel from scrap instead of from ore uses about.................. percent less energy.
    (a) 20 (b) 45
    (c) 70 (d) 90

ANSWER

98. (a) 99. (d) 100. (b) 101. (c) 102. (d) 103. (c) 104. (a) 105. (c)
106. (c)

107. Composting provides .... to the soil while keeping organic wastes out of landfills.
   (a) nutrients (b) neutralization
   (c) moisture (d) pest resistance
108. Decomposing yard waste and fruit & vegetable trimmings can be broken down by bacteria to form ...., which reduces the need for fertilizers.
   (a) insecticides (b) leachate
   (c) methane (d) compost
109. Biodegradable plastics never completely:
   (a) Burn (b) Melt
   (c) Decompose (d) Recycled
110. The goal of waste management is:
   (a) Acquiring a labor capable of disposing of garbage.
   (b) Disposing of waste safely & effectively and reducing the amount of waste generated.
   (c) Developing management training for supervisor of disposal companies.
   (d) Developing technology for more efficient incineration.
111. Incineration of waste can be a problem because:
   (a) It takes large areas for storage of waste.
   (b) Most countries have made the practice illegal.
   (c) Hazardous chemicals can be released in the smoke that is generated.
   (d) Leaching to the groundwater table can occur.
112. The best solution to the solid waste problem is:
   (a) Incineration (b) Recycling
   (c) Sources reduction (d) Landfills
113. Which of the following represents the largest waste disposal practice in the United states?
   (a) Landfills (b) Incineration
   (c) Composting (d) Recycling
114. If the recycling loop is to work and become economically sustainable, then:
   (a) The number of recycled products must increase.
   (b) Consumers and businesses must purchase the products made from recycled materials.
   (c) Programs must require recycling in all cities.
   (d) Genetically modified bacteria must be found to consume toxic components.

ANSWER

107. (a) 108. (b) 109. (c) 110. (b) 111. (c) 112. (c) 113. (a) 114. (b)

115. An abandoned waste site that poses a direct threat to health and the environment and is designated to have U.S. government funds applied to its cleanup is a:

(a) Hazardous waste site (b) Superfund site
(c) Landfill leachate producing site (d) Surface impoundment site

116. Consumers can decrease waste generation by:

(a) Purchasing good with the Energy Star label
(b) Choosing to buy locally made goods
(c) Choosing to purchase only imported goods
(d) Choosing minimally packaged goods

117. Which of the following statement about the "pay-as-you-throw" approach to garbage collection is NOT correct?

(a) It will not likely be used due to lack of public support.
(b) It reduces the waste stream.
(c) "Pay-as-you-throw" encourages consumers to reduce the volume of goods purchased.
(d) It uses a financial incentive for influencing consumer behavior.

118. The conversion of organic waste to mulch or humus usable for enriching soil by encouraging natural biological processes of decomposition in a controlled manner, is called:

(a) Combustion (b) Composition
(c) Compromising (d) Composting

119. Which of the following conditions results from the operation and subsequent use of landfills?

(a) Decommissioned landfills cannot be used as locations for schools, industries, parks, and golf courses for 300 years after the closing of the landfills.
(b) Modern sanitary landfills are regulated and lined with a porous materials.
(c) Hydrogen gas is generated by the organic decomposition and can be sold as a by-product.
(d) Leachate from old landfills can contaminate groundwater.

120. Which of the following is an example of a product found in a "throwaways society"?

(a) Reusable cloth diapers (b) Fine silverware
(c) Paper napkin (d) Reusable razor blade

121. What is an important factor that determines whether the average citizen of a developed country will produce more or less trash?

(a) The cost of disposing of trash
(b) How close the country is to the equator
(c) How many people live in the country
(d) The age structure of the country

ANSWER

115. (b) 116. (d) 117. (a) 118. (d) 119. (d) 120. (c) 121. (a)

122. How can "final cover" on landfills reduce decomposition of the trush?
   (a) The cap keeps the landfills moist on the inside, preventing docompositon.
   (b) The cap prevents hawks and blue jays from decomposing the trash.
   (c) The cap causes paper to bond to plastic in the landfill.
   (d) The cap keeps the landfill dry, which decreases the ability of bacteria to decompose trash.

123. Why do industries tend to produce so much waste even though it is not the most efficient way to do business?
   (a) It is more profitable to be efficient with waste.
   (b) In most cases, there is no financial incentive for becoming efficient.
   (c) Industry ecologists do not recommend streamlining industrial waste.
   (d) Most of industry is run by disorganized people.

124. "E-waste" is a growing concern, because:
   (a) Only 60% of waste is recycled.
   (b) Electronic devices die easily so few of the devices thrown out could be re-used.
   (c) There is no financial incentive to recycle E-waste.
   (d) E-Waste contains toxic heavy metals and flame retardants.

125. Our obsession with having only the most current electronic devices and throwing away outdated version despite the fact that they work is an example of:
   (a) Reduce, reuse, recycle (b) Sound science
   (c) Living sustainably (d) Our throwaway society.

126. An advantage of recycling aluminum rather than disposing of it in landfills is that aluminum can be:
   (a) Produced from recycled metal using much less energy than is required for its production from aluminum ore.
   (b) Produced from one that is chemically reactive and dangerous to transport, store & process.
   (c) Produced from ore that is scarce and found primarily in remote, inhospitable region at high latitudes.
   (d) Absorbed by plants and then biomagnified in both terrestrial & aquatic food chains.

127. Critics of incineration of municipal solid waste suggest that it may not be best solution for the future, for which of the following reasons?
   (a) Incineration produces ash that increases landfill volume.
   (b) Incineration generates methane.
   (c) Incineration involves advanced technology.
   (d) Incineration contributes to air pollution.

ANSWER

122. (d) 123. (b) 124. (d) 125. (d) 126. (a) 127. (d)

128. Integrated waste management employs all of the following, EXCEPT
   (a) Using refillable soft-drink bottle.
   (b) Using disposable diapers instead of cloth diapers.
   (c) Using reusable canvas bags instead of plastic or paper bags.
   (d) Using tires for the construction of artificial reefs.
129. Which method reduces the volume of waste but could release toxic emissions into the atmosphere?
   (a) Sanitary landfill (b) Incineration
   (c) Discharge to sewers, streams, and rivers (d) Chemical treatment
130. A flammable gas produced by landfills is:
   (a) Carbon dioxide (b) Carbon monoxide
   (c) Methane (d) Radon
131. All of the following are considered toxic metal pollutants, EXCEPT
   (a) Cadmium (b) Potassium
   (c) Lead (d) Mercury
132. Of the following, which is the most serious immediate problem associated with sanitary landfills?
   (a) Generation of CO_2 gas
   (b) Leachate contamination of groundwater
   (c) Release of disease organisms
   (d) Incomplete degradation of wastes
133. Which of the following correctly orders the methods of solid-waste management in term of energy required?

	Least Energy → Most Energy		
(a)	Reuse	Recycle	Reduce
(b)	Recycle	Reuse	Reduce
(c)	Recycle	Reduce	Reuse
(d)	Reduce	Reuse	Recycle

134. Nuclear wastes comprises paper, rags, tools, clothing, filters etc which contain small amounts of mostly short-lived radioactivity, is called .... waste.
   (a) Medium level (b) Low level
   (c) High Level (d) Transuranic
135. Nuclear waste which requires 100% shielding during disposal is .... waste.
   (a) Medium level (b) Low level
   (c) High Level (d) Transuranic
136. The waste which contain elements having an atomic number greater than Uranium is:
   (a) Medium level waste (b) Low level waste
   (c) High Level waste (d) Transuranic wastes

ANSWER

128. (b) 129. (b) 130. (c) 131. (b) 132. (b) 133. (d) 134. (b) 135. (c)
136. (d)

137. Radioactive pollution that is spread through the earth's atmosphere is called:
    (a) Transuranic (b) Radioactive fallout
    (c) Radionulides (d) Low level waste
138. The disaster at the Chernobyl Nuclear fallout contaminated approximately .... Square miles of farmland and villages in Ukrain, Soviet Union.
    (a) 200 (b) 400
    (c) 800 (d) 1,000
139. The part of human body which is first affected by nuclear radiation is:
    (a) Lungs (b) Brain
    (c) Bone marrow (d) Liver.
140. Vitrification is disposing nuclear waste by:
    (a) Burying below ground. (b) Solidifying in the form of glass
    (c) Ice sheet disposal (d) Deep geological disposal
141. Converting part of the hazardous nuclear waste into a more stable material that decays quickly is called:
    (a) Transmutation (b) Vitrification
    (c) Ice sheet Disposal (d) Deep geological disposal
142. International Agreement is necessary for:
    (a) Ice sheet disposal (b) Deep geological disposal
    (c) Buying below ground (d) space disposal
143. Richness of nutrients in industrial waste water leads to:
    (a) Eutrophic condition (b) Oligotrophic
    (c) Mesotrophic (d) None of the above
144. The main problem associated with managing Indian solid waste is:
    (a) Segregation (b) High moisture content
    (c) Season variation (d) All the above
145. Sludge is treated prior to ultimate disposal for:
    (a) Stabilization of organics (b) Volume reduction
    (c) Pathogen reduction (d) All the above
146. Integrated waste management is:
    (a) Co-composting (b) Composting
    (c) Vermicomposting (d) All the above

ANSWER

137. (b) 138. (d) 139. (c) 140. (b) 141. (a) 142. (d) 143. (a) 144. (d)
145. (d) 146. (a)

147. Incineration of municipal solid waste may not be the best solution for which of the following reasons?

(a) Incineration produces ash that increases landfill volume.

(b) Incineration generates methane.

(c) Incineration involves advanced technology.

(d) No-till agriculture

148. Which material accounts for the greatest percentage of the weight of municipal solid waste?

(a) Plastic **(b) Paper**

(c) Yard waste **(d) Food waste**

149. Which of the following is not a method of sources reduction of solid waste?

(a) Composting **(b) Incineration**

(c) Recycling **(d) Making packages that weigh less**

150. Which of the following may be not true about incineration of solid wastes?

(a) There is a drastic reduction in the volume & weight of the waste.

(b) The incineration of solid wastes should be the last option for its disposal.

(c) The incinerators can be built to generate electricity.

(d) The incinerators ash may contain heavy metals and other toxic substances.

151. Modern municipal solid waste landfills contain:

(a) Impermeable barriers and monitoring wells.

(b) Leachate treatment facilities

(c) Methane retrieval systems

(d) All a, b & c

152. Pick out the wrong statement:

(a) Essentially five techniques-incineration, landfills, source reduction, composting and recycling are used to dispose off solid waste.

(b) Per capita production of municipal solid waste in India is equal to about 10 kg per day.

(c) As compared to 1960, net solid waste generation has increased even with recycling programme in place.

(d) A European concept that uses solid waste to generate electricity is called mass burn.

153. The largest single component of municipal solid waste in the United States is:

(a) Yard waste **(b) Plastics**

(c) Food waste **(d) Paper and paper products**

154. You manage the local landfill and wish for materials to degrade faster. What should you mix in with the waste?

(a) Carbon dioxide **(b) More waste**

(c) Methane **(d) Water**

ANSWER

147. (d) 148. (b) 149. (b) 150. (b) 151. (d) 152. (b) 153. (d) 154. (d)

155. It has been discovered that a local landfill is contaminating the groundwater. What is the most likely reason that this occurred?
   (a) There is a problem with the liner.
   (b) There is a problem with the fill dirt.
   (c) There is a problem with the compactor.
   (d) There is a problem with the waste being added.

156. Which of the following is true?
   (a) It is usually cheaper to dispose of waste at a waste-to-energy facility.
   (b) Waste-to-energy facilities combust all of the materials they receive.
   (c) Waste-to-energy facilities eliminate the need for landfills.
   (d) One of the benefits of a waste-to-energy facility is that waste is considerably reduced in weight and volume.

157. Your city recycles 10 tons of newspaper per week. How many trees does this save?
   (a) about 80 (b) about 170
   (c) about 360 (d) about 640

158. You recycle an aluminum soda can, and it is made into another soda can. What kind of recycling is this?
   (a) primary recycling (b) quaternary recycling
   (c) tertiary recycling (d) secondary recycling

159. You recycle your tires, and they are made into material for a high school track. What kind of recycling is this?
   (a) primary recycling (b) quaternary recycling
   (c) tertiary recycling (d) secondary recycling

160. Eight tons of steel are recycled. About how many tons of coal does this save?
   (a) 1 (b) 4 (c) 8 (d) 16

161. If trends since 1960 continue,what will happen in regard to municipal solid waste?
   (a) The total amount of municipal solid waste recycled will stay the same, but the percentage recycled will increase.
   (b) The total amount of municipal solid waste recycled and the percentage recycled will both decrease.
   (c) The total amount of municipal solid waste recycled and the percentage recycled will both increase.
   (d) The total amount of municipal solid waste recycled will increase, but the percentage recycled will stay the same.

162. Assuming that people are generating the same amount of trash, if a pay-as-you-throw system is working, what should happen to recycling rates?
   (a) Recycling rates should stay the same. (b) Recycling rates should increase.
   (c) Recycling rates should decrease. (d) There should be no recycling at all.

ANSWER

155. (a) 156. (d) 157. (b) 158. (a) 159. (d) 160. (c) 161. (c) 162. (b)

163. At the grocery store, you want to make choices that are best for the environment. When asked, "Paper or plastic?" what should you do?
   (a) Neither. You should bring your own bag to use.
   (b) It doesn't matter. Both bags use resources and are equally harmful to the environment.
   (c) Plastic
   (d) Paper
164. You live near an incineration facility. Which pollutants are likely in the air near your home?
   (a) Endrin and toxaphene (b) Heptachlor and dioxins
   (c) Chlordane and furans (d) Dioxins and furans
165. In deep-well injection, how far down is hazardous waste stored?
   (a) It is stored below the drinking-water source.
   (b) It is stored above the drinking-water source.
   (c) It is stored at the same level as the drinking-water source.
   (d) The storage depth varies based on location.
166. Waste oil easily catches on fire. Therefore, the EPA classifies it as a hazardous material based on its:
   (a) Corrosivity (b) Ignitability
   (c) Toxicity (d) Reactivity
167. Lithium-sulfur batteries are unstable under normal conditions. Therefore, the EPA classifies them as a hazardous material based on their:
   (a) Corrosivity (b) Toxicity
   (c) Ignitability (d) Reactivity
168. Battery acid can cause metal containers to break down. Therefore, the EPA classifies it as a hazardous material based on its:
   (a) Corrosivity (b) Toxicity
   (c) Reactivity (d) Ignitability
169. Bleach is harmful if swallowed. Therefore, the EPA classifies it as a hazardous material based on its:
   (a) Toxicity (b) Corrosivity
   (c) Ignitability (d) Reactivity
170. Which of the following is the most common way of disposing of municipal solid waste?
   (a) Recycling (b) Transporting to other country
   (c) Placing in Landfill (d) Burning

ANSWER

163. (a) 164. (d) 165. (a) 166. (b) 167. (d) 168. (a) 169. (a) 170. (c)

CHAPTER

11

Glossary of Terms Related to Solid & Hazardous Waste Mangement

A

Aerobic composting—A method of com-posting organic wastes using bacteria that need oxygen. This requires that the waste be exposed to air, either via turning or by forcing air through pipes that pass through the material.

Aerobic Treatment—Process by which microbes decompose complex organic compounds in the presence of oxygen and use the liberated energy for reproduction and growth. (Such processes include extended aeration, trickling filtration, and rotating biological contactors.)

Agricultural Waste—Poultry and livestock manure, and residual materials in liquid or solid form generated from the production and marketing of poultry, livestock or fur-bearing animals; also includes grain, vegetable, and fruit harvest residue.

Aerated static pile—Forced aeration method of composting in which a free-standing composting pile is aerated by a blower moving air through perforated pipes located beneath the pile.

Airborne Particulates—Total suspended particulate matter found in the atmosphere as solid particles or liquid droplets. Chemical composition of particulates varies widely, depending on location and time of year. Sources of airborne particulates include: dust, emissions from industrial processes, combustion products from the burning of wood and coal, combustion products associated with motor vehicle or non-road engine exhausts, and reactions to gases in the atmosphere.

Anaerobic—A life or process that occurs in, or is not destroyed by, the absence of oxygen.

Anaerobic Decomposition—Reduction of the net energy level and change in chemical composition of organic matter caused by microorganisms in an oxygen-free environment.

Anaerobic digestion—A method of composting that does not require oxygen. This composting method produces methane. Also known as anaerobic composting.

Ash—The noncombustible solid by-products of incineration or other burning process.

Autoclaving—Sterilization via a pressurized, high-temperature steam process.

B

Bacteria—(Singular: bacterium) Microscopic living organisms that can aid in pollution control by metabolizing organic matter in sewage, oil spills or other pollutants. However, bacteria in soil, water or air can also cause human, animal and plant health problems.

Baghouse—A combustion plant emission control device that consists of an array of fabric filters through which flue gases pass in an incinerator flue. Particles are trapped and thus prevented from passing into the atmosphere.

Bale—A densified and bound cube of recycled materials, such as waste paper, scrap metal, or rags.

Basel Convention—An international agreement on the control of transboundary movements of hazardous wastes and their disposal, drawn up in March 1989 in Basel, Switzerland, with over 100 countries as signatories.

Battery—Device that converts chemical energy into electrical energy, consisting of a group of electric cells that are connected to act as a source of direct current. The term is also now commonly used for a single cell, such as the alkaline dry cell used in flashlights and portable tape players, but strictly speaking batteries are made up of connected cells encased in a container and fitted with terminals to provide a source of direct electric current at a given voltage. A cell consists of two dissimilar substances, a positive electrode and a negative electrode, that conduct electricity, and a third substance, an electrolyte, that acts chemically on the electrodes. The two electrodes are connected by an external circuit (*e.g.*, a piece of copper wire); the electrolyte functions as an ionic conductor for the transfer of the electrons between the electrodes.

Batteries also can be generally divided into two main types—rechargeable and nonrechargeable, or disposable. Disposable batteries, also called primary cells, can be used until the chemical changes that induce the electrical current supply are complete, at which point the battery is discarded. Disposable batteries are most commonly used in smaller, portable devices that are only used intermittently or at a large distance from an alternative power source or have a low current drain. Rechargeable batteries, also called secondary cells, can be reused after being drained. This is done by applying an external electrical current, which causes the chemical changes that occur in use to be reversed. The external devices that supply the appropriate current are called chargers or rechargers .

Biodegradable—Capable of decomposing under natural conditions.

Biodegradable Plastic—A degradable plastic in which the degradation results from the action of naturally occurring microorganisms such as bacteria, fungi, and algae.

Biodegradable material—Any organic material that can be broken down by microorganisms into simpler, more stable com-pounds. Most organic wastes (*e.g.*, food, paper) are biodegradable.

Biological Treatment—A treatment technology that uses bacteria to consume organic waste.

Bottom ash—Relatively coarse, noncombustible, generally toxic residue of incin-eration that accumulates on the grate of a furnace.

Bulking agent—An ingredient in a mixture of composting raw materials included to improve the structure and porosity of the mix. Bulking agents are usually rigid and dry and often have large particles (for example, straw.

Bulky waste—Large wastes such as appliances, furniture, and trees and branches, that cannot be handled by normal MSW processing methods.

Buy-Back Center—Facility where individuals or groups bring recyclables in return for payment.

C

Cap—A layer of clay, or other impermeable material installed over the top of a closed landfill to prevent entry of rainwater and minimize leachate.

Carbon Footprint—A measure of the impact our activities have on the environment, and in particular climate change. It relates to the amount of greenhouse gases produced in our day-to-day lives through burning fossil fuels for electricity, heating and transportation etc. The carbon footprint is a measurement of all greenhouse gases we individually produce and has units of tons (or kg) of carbon dioxide equivalent.

Cell—The basic unit by which a landfill is developed. It is the general area where incoming waste is tipped, spread, compacted, and covered.

Chemocar—A special vehicle for the collection of toxic and hazardous wastes from residences, shops, and institutions.

Cleaner production—Processes designed to reduce the wastes generated by production.

Co-disposal—The disposal of different types of waste in one area of a landfill or dump. For instance, sewage sludges may be disposed of with regular solid wastes.

Collection—The process of picking up wastes from residences, businesses, or a collection point, loading them into a vehicle, and transporting them to a processing, transfer, or disposal site.

Collector—Public or private hauler that collects nonhazardous waste and recyclable materials from residential, commercial, institutional and industrial sources.

Combustibles—Burnable materials in the waste stream, including paper, plastics, wood, and food and garden wastes.

Commercial Wastes—All solid wastes emanating from business establishments such as stores, markets, office buildings, restaurants, shopping centers, and theaters.

Commingled—Mixed recyclables that are collected together after having been separated from mixed MSW.

Commingled recyclables—Mixed recyclables that are collected together .

Communal collection—A system of collection in which individuals bring their waste directly to a central point, from which it is collected.

Compaction—Reduction of the bulk of solid waste by rolling and tamping.

Compactor vehicle—A collection vehicle using high-power mechanical or hydraulic equipment to reduce the volume of solid waste.

Composite liner—A liner system for a land-fill consisting of an engineered soil layer and a synthetic sheet of material.

Compost—A humus or soil-like material created from aerobic, microbial decomposition of organic materials such as food scraps, yard trimmings, and manure.

Compostable—Capable of undergoing biological decomposition in a compost site as part of an available program, such that the material is not visually distinguishable and breaks down into carbon dioxide, water, inorganic compounds, and biomass, at a rate consistent with known compostable materials.

Compostable Plastic—A plastic that undergoes degradation by biological processes during composting to yield CO_2, water, inorganic compounds, and biomass at a rate consistent with other known compostable materials and leave no visible, distinguishable or toxic residue.

Composting—A process of accelerated biological decomposition of organic material under controlled conditions.

Composting Facility—1. An offsite facility where the organic component of municipal solid waste is decomposed under controlled conditions; 2. an aerobic process in which organic materials are ground or shredded and then decomposed to humus in windrow piles or in mechanical digesters, drums, or similar enclosures.

Controlled dump—A planned landfill that incorporates to some extent some of the features of a sanitary landfill: siting with respect to hydrogeological suitability, grading, compaction in some cases, leachate control, partial gas management, regular (not usually daily) cover, access control, basic record-keeping, and controlled waste picking.

Construction and Demolition Waste—Waste building materials and packaging resulting from construction, remodeling, repair and demolition operations on houses, commercial buildings and other structures, excluding asbestos, clean fill, as defined in regulations adopted under section 22a-209, or solid waste containing greater than de minimis quantities, as determined by the Commissioner of Environmental Protection, of (A) radioactive material regulated pursuant to section 22a-148, (B) hazardous waste as defined in section 22a-115, and (C) liquid and semi liquid materials, including, but not limited to, adhesives, paints, coatings, sealants, preservatives, strippers, cleaning agents, oils and tars.

Construction and Demolition Waste Processing Facility—A volume reduction plant, the operations of which involve solely the reduction in volume of construction and demolition waste generated elsewhere.

Contaminant—Any physical, chemical, biological, or radiological substance or matter that has an adverse effect on air, water, or soil.

Contamination—Introduction into water, air, and soil of microorganisms, chemicals, toxic substances, wastes, or wastewater in a concentration that makes the medium unfit for its next intended use. Also applies to surfaces of objects, buildings, and various household and agricultural use products.

Contract Collection—Collection by a private collector under a formal agreement with a municipal authority in which the rights and duties of the respective parties are set forth.

Corrugated cardboard—Cardboard with corrugations (can be glued to flat cardboard on one or both sides).

Cost/Benefit Analysis—A quantitative evaluation of the costs which would have incurred by implementing an environmental regulation versus the overall benefits to society of the proposed action.

Cover Material—Soil used to cover compacted solid waste in a sanitary landfill.

Cradle-to-Grave or Manifest System—A procedure in which hazardous materials are identified and followed as they are produced, treated, transported, and disposed of by a series of permanent, linkable, descriptive documents (*e.g.* manifests). Commonly referred to as the cradle-to-grave system.

Cullet—Broken or waste glass suitable for remelting.

Curbside collection—Collection of compostables, recyclables, or trash at the edge of a sidewalk in front of a residence or shop.

Curing—Allowing partially composted materials to sit in a pile for a specified period of time as part of the maturing process in composting.

D

Decomposition—The breakdown of matter by bacteria and fungi, changing the chemical makeup and physical appearance of materials.

Decontamination—Removal of harmful substances such as noxious chemicals, harmful bacteria or other organisms, or radioactive material from exposed individuals, rooms and furnishings in buildings, or the exterior environment.

Degradable Plastic—A plastic designed to undergo a significant change in its chemical structure under specific environmental conditions, resulting in a loss of some properties that may be measured by standard test methods appropriate to the plastic and the application in a period of time that determines its classification.

Demand-side Waste Management—Prices whereby consumers use purchasing decisions to communicate to product manufacturers that they prefer environmentally sound products packaged with the least amount of waste, made from recycled or recyclable materials, and containing no hazardous substances.

Digestion—The biochemical decomposition of organic matter, resulting in partial gasification, liquefaction, and mineralization of pollutants.

Disposables—Consumer products, other items, and packaging used once or a few times and discarded.

Disposal—Final placement or destruction of toxic, radioactive, or other wastes; surplus or banned pesticides or other chemicals; polluted soils; and drums containing hazardous materials from removal actions or accidental releases. Disposal may be accomplished through use of approved secure landfills, surface impoundments, land farming, deep-well injection, ocean dumping, or incineration.

Diversion rate—The proportion of waste material diverted for recycling, composting, or reuse and away from landfilling or incineration.

Dual Stream—Collection system where recyclables are funneled into two streams–usually one is paper/fiber and the other is containers.

Durable Goods—Sturdy items, like furniture or appliances, that can be used for many years. When people repair these products instead of buying new ones, they save money and reduce waste.

Dump—A site used to dispose of solid waste without environmental controls.

E

End User—Consumer of products for the purpose of recycling. Excludes products for re-use or combustion for energy recovery.

Energy Recovery—Obtaining energy from waste through a variety of processes (*e.g.* combustion).

Environmental Impact Assessment (EIA)—An evaluation designed to identify and predict the impact of an action or a project on the environment and human health and well-being. Can include risk assessment as a component, along with economic and land use assessment.

Environmental Risk Assessment—An evaluation of the interactions of agents, humans, and ecological resources. Comprised of human health risk assessment and ecological risk assessment, typically evaluating the probabilities and magnitudes of harm that could come from environmental contaminants.

Extended Producer Responsibility—Environmental protection strategy to reach an environmental objective of a decreased total environmental impact from a product, by making the manufacturer of the product responsible for the entire life-cycle of the product and especially for the take-back, recycling and final disposal of the product.

F

Ferrous Metals—Magnetic metals derived from iron or steel; products made from ferrous metals include appliances, furniture, containers, and packaging like steel drums and barrels. Recycled products include processing tin/steel cans, strapping, and metals from appliances into new products.

Fill—Man-made deposits of natural soils or rock products and waste materials.

Flaring—The burning of methane emitted from collection pipes at a landfill.

Fluidized bed incinerator—A type of incinerator in which the stoker grate is replaced by a bed of limestone or sand that can withstand high temperatures. The heating of the bed and the high air velocities used cause the bed to bubble, which gives rise to the term fluidized.

Fly Ash—Non-combustible residual particles expelled by flue gas. (EPA Glossary)

Food Processing Waste—Food residues produced during agricultural and industrial operations.

Food Waste—Uneaten food and food preparation wastes from residences and commercial establishments such as grocery stores, restaurants, and produce stands, institutional cafeterias and kitchens, and industrial sources like employee lunchrooms.

Fungus (Fungi)—Molds, mildews, yeasts, mushrooms, and puffballs, a group of organisms lacking in chlorophyll (*i.e.* are not photosynthetic) and which are usually non-mobile, filamentous, and multi-cellular. Some grow in soil, others attach themselves to decaying trees and other plants whence they obtain nutrients. Some are pathogens, others stabilize sewage and digest composted waste.

G

Garbage—Animal and vegetable waste resulting from the handling, storage, sale, preparation, cooking, and serving of foods.

Glass Containers—For recycling purposes, containers like bottles and jars for drinks, food, cosmetics and other products. When being recycled, container glass is generally separated into color categories for conversion into new containers, construction materials or fiberglass insulation.

Grasscycling—Source reduction activities in which grass clippings are left on the lawn after mowing.

Green Remediation—The practice of considering all environmental effects of remedy implementation and incorporating options to maximize the net environmental benefit of cleanup actions.

Ground Water—The supply of fresh water found beneath the Earth's surface, usually in aquifers, which supply wells and springs. Because ground water is a major source of drinking water, there is growing concern over contamination from leaching agricultural or industrial pollutants or leaking underground storage tanks.

H

Hazardous waste—Waste that is reactive, toxic, corrosive, or otherwise dangerous to living things and/or the environment. Many industrial by-products are hazardous.

Hazardous Waste Minimization—Reducing the amount of toxicity or waste produced by a facility via source reduction or environmentally sound recycling.

Hauler—Garbage collection company that offers complete refuse removal service; many will also collect recyclables.

Heavy metals—Metals of high atomic weight and density, such as mercury, lead, and cadmium, that are toxic to living organisms.

High Density Polyethylene (HDPE)—A type of plastic used to make milk jugs and other rigid plastic bottles. A material used to make plastic bottles and other products that produces toxic fumes when burned.

Household Collection—Individualized set out of recyclables where each household or unit sets out its own container of recyclables for collection from a designated location or aggregated centralized collection where residents in a multi-family complex all place their recyclables in central storage containers serving the whole complex.

Household Hazardous Waste (HHW)—Hazardous products used and disposed of by residential as opposed to industrial consumers. Includes paints, stains, varnishes, solvents, pesticides, and other materials or products containing volatile chemicals that can catch fire, react or explode, or that are corrosive or toxic.

Household Waste (Domestic Waste)—Solid waste, composed of garbage and rubbish, which normally originates in a private home or apartment house. Domestic waste may contain a significant amount of toxic or hazardous waste.

Humus—The end product of composting, also called compost.

I

Incineration—The process of burning solid waste under controlled conditions to reduce its weight and volume, and often to produce energy.

Incinerator—A furnace for burning waste under controlled conditions.

Industrial Process Waste—Residues produced during manufacturing operations.

Industrial Source Reduction—Practices that reduce the amount of any hazardous substance, pollutant, or contaminant entering any waste stream or otherwise released into the environment. Also reduces the threat to public health and the environment associated with such releases. Term includes equipment or technology modifications, substitution of raw materials, and improvements in housekeeping, maintenance, training or inventory control.

Industrial Waste—Unwanted materials from an industrial operation; may be liquid, sludge, solid, or hazardous waste.

Institutional Waste—Waste generated at institutions such as schools, libraries, hospitals, prisons, etc.

Integrated solid waste management—Coordinated use of a set of waste management methods, each of which can play a role in an overall MSWM plan.

Intermediate Processing Center —A facility which can recycle an item or items and market or deliver for reuse the resulting material product or products. Such facilities may be owned by the public or private entities or combinations thereof and may offer service on a state, regional, municipal or submunicipal level.

Intermediate Processing Facility—A facility where glass, metals, paper products, batteries, household hazardous waste, fertilizers and other items are removed from the waste stream for recycling or reuse.

In vessel composting—Composting in an enclosed vessel or drum with a controlled internal environment, mechanical mixing, and aeration.

Itinerant waste buyer—A person who moves around the streets buying (or bartering for) reusable and recyclable materials.

L

Landfill gases—Gases arising from the decomposition of organic wastes; principally methane, carbon dioxide, and hydrogen sulfide. Such gases may cause explosions at landfills.

Landfilling—The final disposal of solid waste by placing it in a controlled fashion in a place intended to be permanent. The Source Book uses this term for both controlled dumps and sanitary landflls.

Landfills—1. Sanitary landfills are disposal sites for non-hazardous solid wastes spread in layers, compacted to the smallest practical volume, and covered by material applied at the end of each operating day. 2. Secure chemical landfills are disposal sites for hazardous waste, selected and designed to minimize the chance of release of hazardous substances into the environment.

Land Clearing/Clean Wood Processing Facility—A volume reduction plant, the operations of which involve solely the reduction in volume of land clearing debris or clean wood generated elsewhere.

Land Clearing Debris—Trees, stumps, branches, or other wood generated from clearing land for commercial or residential development, road construction, routine landscaping, agricultural land clearing, storms, or natural disasters.

Leachate—Liquid (which may be partly produced by deromposition of organic matter) that has seeped through a landfill or a compost pile and has accumulated bacteria and other possibly harmful dissolved or suspended materials. If uncontrolled, leachate can contaminate both groundwater and surface water.

Leachate Collection System—A system that gathers leachate and pumps it to the surface for treatment

Leachate pond—A pond or tank constructed at a landfill to receive the leachate from the area. Usually the pond is designed to provide some treatment of the leachate, by allowing settlement of solids or by aeration to promote biological processes.

Leaching—The process by which soluble constituents are dissolved and filtered through the soil by a percolating fluid. Also see Leachate.

Life Cycle of a Product—All stages of a product's development, from extraction of fuel for power to production, marketing, use, and disposal.

Lift—The completed layer of compacted waste in a cell at a landfill.

Liner—A protective layer, made of soil and/or synthetic materials, installed along the bottom and sides of a landfill to prevent or reduce the flow of leachate into the environment.

Litter—1. The highly visible portion of solid waste carelessly discarded outside the regular garbage and trash collection and disposal system. 2. leaves and twigs fallen from forest trees.

M

Manual landfill—A landfill in which most operations are carried out without the use of mechanized equipment.

Manual Separation—Hand sorting of recyclable or compostable materials in waste.

Market waste—Primarily organic waste, such as leaves, skins, and unsold food, discarded at or near food markets.

Mass-burn incinerator—A type of incinerator in which solid waste is burned without prior sorting or processing.

Materials recovery—Obtaining materials that can be reused or recycled.

Materials recovery facility (MRF)—A facility for separating commingled recyclables by manual or mechanical means. Some MRFs are designed to separate recyclables from mixed MSW. MRFs then bale and market the recovered materials.

Methane—An odorless, colorless, flammable, explosive gas, CH,, produced by anaerobically decomposing MSW at landfills.

Microbial Growth—The amplification or multiplication of microorganisms such as bacteria, algae, diatoms, plankton, and fungi.

Mixed Glass—Recovered container glass not sorted into categories (*e.g.* color, grade).

Mixed Metals—Recovered metals not sorted into categories such as aluminum, tin, or steel cans or ferrous or non-ferrous metals.

Mixed Municipal Solid Waste—Municipal solid waste that consists of mixtures of solid wastes which have not been separated at the source of generation or processed into discrete, homogeneous waste streams such as glass, paper, plastic, aluminum or tire waste streams.

Mixed Municipal Solid Waste Composting Facility—A volume reduction plant where mixed municipal solid waste is processed using composting technology.

Mixed Paper—Recovered paper not sorted into categories such as old magazines, old newspapers, old corrugated boxes, etc.

Mixed Plastic—Recovered plastic unsorted by category.

Mixed waste—Unsorted materials that have been discarded into the waste stream.

Modular incinerator—A relatively small type of prefabricated solid waste combustion unit.

Monocell—A variation of the cell construction method whereby only a single type of solid waste is disposed of in any individual cell.

Monofill—A landfill intended for one type of waste only.

Mulch—A protective cover of organic material placed over soil to preserve soil moisture, prevent erosion, or promote the growth of plants.

Municipal Collection—Solid waste collection from all residents thereof by a municipal authority.

Municipality—Any town, city or borough within the state.

Municipal solid waste—All solid waste generated in an area except industrial and agricultural wastes. Sometimes includes construction and demolition debris and other special wastes that may enter the municipal waste stream. Generally excludes hazardous wastes except to the extent that they enter the municipal waste stream. Sometimes defined to mean all solid wastes that a city authority accepts responsibility for managing in some way.

Municipal solid waste management—Planning and implementation of systems to handle MSW.

N

Newspaper—Used or discarded newsprint which has a minimum contamination by food or other material.

NGO—Nongovernmental organization. May be used to refer to a range of organizations from small community groups, through national organizations, to international ones. Frequently these are not-for-profit organizations.

Night soil—Human excreta.

NIMBY—"Not In My Back Yard." An expression of resident opposition to the siting of a solid waste facility based on the particular location proposed.

Nitrate—A compound containing nitrogen that can exist in the atmosphere or as a dissolved gas in water and which can have harmful effects on humans and animals. Nitrates in water can cause severe illness in infants and domestic animals. A plant nutrient and inorganic fertilizer, nitrate is found in septic systems, animal feed lots, agricultural fertilizers, manure, industrial waste waters, sanitary landfills, and garbage dumps.

Nitrogenous Wastes—Animal or vegetable residues that contain significant amounts of nitrogen.

Non-Ferrous Metals—Nonmagnetic metals such as aluminum, lead, and copper. Products made all or in part from such metals include containers, packaging, appliances, furniture, electronic equipment and aluminum foil.

Non-Point Sources—Diffuse pollution sources (*i.e.* without a single point of origin or not introduced into a receiving stream from a specific outlet). The pollutants are generally carried off the land by storm water. Common non-point sources are agriculture, forestry, urban, mining, construction, dams, channels, land disposal, saltwater intrusion, and city streets.

O

Office paper—Used or discarded high grade white paper and manilla paper, including paper utilized for file folders, tab cards, writing, typing, printing, computer printing, and photocopying, which is suitable for recycling and which has a minimum of contamination .

Open Burning—Uncontrolled fires in an open dump.

Open dump—An unplanned "landfill" that incorporates few if any of the characteristics of a controlled landfill. There is typically no leachate control, no access control, no cover, no management, and many waste pickers.

Organic waste—Technically, waste containing carbon, including paper, plastics, wood, food wastes, and yard wastes. In practice in MSWM, the term is often used in a more restricted sense to mean material that is more directly derived from plant or animal sources, and which can generally be decomposed by microorganisms.

Organism—Any form of animal or plant life.

Ort—A small scrap or leaving of food after a meal is completed. Often used in the plural.

Other Ferrous Metals—Recyclable metals from strapping, furniture, and metal found in tires and consumer electronics but does not include metals found in construction materials or cars, locomotives, and ships.

Other Glass—Recyclable glass from furniture, appliances, and consumer electronics. Does not include glass from transportation products (cars trucks or shipping containers) and construction or demolition debris.

Other Nonferrous Metals—Recyclable nonferrous metals such as lead, copper, and zinc from appliances, consumer electronics, and non-packaging aluminum products. Does not include nonferrous metals from industrial applications and construction and demolition debris.

Other Paper—For Recyclable paper from books, third-class mail, commercial printing, paper towels, plates and cups; and other non-packaging paper such as posters, photographic papers, cards and games, milk cartons, folding boxes, bags, wrapping paper, and paperboard. Does not include wrapping paper or shipping cartons.

Other Plastics—Recyclable plastic from appliances, eating utensils, plates, containers, toys, and various kinds of equipment. Does not include heavy-duty plastics such as yielding materials.

Other Solid Waste—Recyclable nonhazardous solid wastes, other than municipal solid waste.

Other Wood—Recyclable wood from furniture, consumer electronics cabinets, and other nonpackaging wood products. Does not include lumber and tree stumps recovered from construction and demolition activities, and industrial process waste such as shavings and sawdust.

P

Packer truck, compacter truck—A refuse or recycling collection vehicle that compacts the materials. This is the most common type of refuse collection vehicle.

Paper—In the recycling business, refers to products and materials, including newspapers, magazines, office papers, corrugated containers, bags and some paperboard packaging that can be recycled into new paper products.

Paper Processor/Plastics Processor—Intermediate facility where recovered paper or plastic products and materials are sorted, decontaminated, and prepared for final recycling.

Passively Aerated Windrow System (PAWS)—A composting method in which windrows are constructed over a series of perforated plastic pipes, which serve as air ducts for passive aeration. Windrows are not turned.

Pathogen—An organism capable of causing disease.

Point Source—A stationary location or fixed facility from which pollutants are discharged; any single identifiable source of pollution; *e.g.* a pipe, ditch, ship, ore pit, factory smokestack.

Pollution—Generally, the presence of a substance in the environment that because of its chemical composition or quantity prevents the functioning of natural processes and produces undesirable environmental and health effects. Under the Clean Water Act, for example, the term has been defined as the man-made or man-induced alteration of the physical, biological, chemical, and radiological integrity of water and other media.

Pollution Prevention—Identification of areas, processes, and activities which create excessive waste products or pollutants in order to reduce or prevent them through, alteration, or eliminating a process.

Polyethylene Terephthalate (PET)—A type of plastic used to make soft drink bottles and other kinds of food containers. PET is also used to make fabric.

Polylactic acid or **Polylactide** (**PLA**)—Polylactic acid or Polylactide (PLA) is a biodegradable, thermoplastic, aliphatic polyester derived from renewable resources. Corn starch (in the U.S.) or sugarcanes are the common feedstock. Bacterial fermentation is used to produce lactic acid, which is oligomerized and then catalytically dimerized to make the monomer for ring-opening polymerization. It can be easily produced in a high molecular weight form through ring-opening polymerization using most commonly a stannous octoate catalyst, but for laboratory demonstrations tin(II) chloride is often employed.

Polyvinyl Chloride (PVC)—A tough, environmentally indestructible plastic that releases hydrochloric acid when burned.

Post Consumer—A term used to describe material that is being reused/recycled after it has been in the consumer's hands (*e.g.*, a newspaper going back to the paper mill to be recycled into new recycled content paper products). Material or product used by the consumer for its original purpose and then discarded.

Post consumer materials—Materials that a consumer has finished using, which the consumer may sell, give away, or discard as wastes.

Post-Consumer Recycling—Use of materials generated from residential and consumer waste for new or similar purposes; *e.g.* converting wastepaper from offices into corrugated boxes or newsprint.

Pre-Consumer—A term used to describe material that is being reused/recycled before it ever goes to market (*e.g.* paper scraps off of a paper mill floor going back into the next batch of paper). Waste material generated during the manufacturing process.

Pre-Consumer Materials/Waste—Materials generated in manufacturing and converting processes such as manufacturing scrap and trimmings and cuttings. Includes print overruns, over issue publications, and obsolete inventories.

Pressed Wood Products—Materials used in building and furniture construction that are made from wood veneers, particles, or fibers bonded together with an adhesive under heat and pressure.

Primary material—A commercial material produced from virgin materials used for manufacturing basic products. Examples include wood pulp, iron ore, and silica sand.

Processing—Preparing MSW materials for subsequent use or management, using processes such as baling, magnetic separation, crushing, and shredding. The term is also sometimes used to mean separation of recyclables from mixed MSW.

Processed Construction and Demolition Wood—The wood portion of construction and demolition waste which has been sorted to remove plastics, plaster, gypsum wallboard, asbestos, asphalt shingles, regulated wood fuel and wood which contains creosote or to which pesticides have been applied or which contains substances defined as hazardous waste .

Producer responsibility—A system in which a producer of products or services takes responsibility for the waste that results from the products or services marketed, by reducing materials used in production, making repairable or recyclable goods, and/or reducing packaging.

Putrefaction—Biological decomposition of organic matter; associated with anaerobic conditions.

Pyrolysis—Chemical decomposition of a substance by heat in the absence of oxygen, resulting in various hydrocarbon gases and carbon-like residue.

R

Reclamation—Restoration of materials found in the waste stream to a beneficial use which may be for purposes other than the original use.

Recovery Rate—Percentage of usable recycled materials that have been removed from the total amount of municipal solid waste generated in a specific area or by a specific business.

Recyclables—Items that can be reprocessed into feedstock for new products. Common examples are paper, glass, aluminum, corrugated cardboard, and plastic containers.

Recycle—Minimizing waste generation by recovering and reprocessing usable products that might otherwise become waste (*.i.e.* recycling of aluminum cans, paper, and bottles, etc.).

Recycled content—Products are made from materials that would otherwise have been discarded. That means these products are made totally or partially from material contained in the products you recycle, like aluminum soda cans or newspaper. Recycled-content products also can be items that are rebuilt or re-manufactured from used products such as toner cartridges or computers.

Recycled Wood—Any wood or wood fuel which is derived from such products or processes as pallets, skids, spools, packaging materials, bulky wood waste or scraps from newly built wood products, provided such wood is not treated wood.

Recycling—The process of transforming materials into raw materials for manufacturing new products, which may or may not be similar to the original product.

Recycling Facility/Recycling Center—Land and appurtenances thereon and structures where recycling is conducted, including but not limited to, an intermediate processing center.

Refuse-derived fuel (RDF)—Fuel produced from MSW that has undergone processing. Processing can include separation of recyclables and noncombustible materials, shredding, size reduction, and pelletizing.

Regulated Wood Fuel—Processed wood from construction and demolition activities which has been sorted to remove plastics, plaster, gypsum wallboard, asbestos, asphalt shingles and wood which contains creosote or to which pesticides have been applied or which contains substances defined as hazardous.

Render, Rendering—To reduce, convert, or melt down (fat) by heating. To try out or extract (oil, lard, tallow, etc.) from fatty animal substances; as, to render tallow. Finished product often used in animal feed, cosmetics and soaps.

Residential Waste—Waste generated in single and multi-family homes, including newspapers, clothing, disposable tableware, food packaging, cans, bottles, food scraps, and yard trimmings other than those that are diverted to backyard composting.

Residual—Amount of a pollutant remaining in the environment after a natural or technological process has taken place; *e.g.*, the sludge remaining after initial wastewater treatment, or particulates remaining in air after it passes through a scrubbing or other process.

Residue—Bottom ash, air pollution control residue, and other residues from the combustion process at resources recovery facilities, wood-burning facilities, municipal solid waste incinerators, and biomedical waste incinerators.

Resource recovery—The extraction and utilization of materials and energy from wastes.

Resources Recovery Facility—A facility utilizing processes to reclaim energy from municipal solid waste.

Reuse—The use of a product more than once in its original form, for the same or a new purpose.

Rubbish—Solid waste, excluding food waste and ashes, from homes, institutions, and workplaces.

Run-Off—That part of precipitation, snow melt, or irrigation water that runs off the land into streams or other surface-water. It can carry pollutants from the air and land into receiving waters.

S

Salvage—The utilization of waste materials.

Sanitary landfill—An engineered method of disposing of solid waste on land, in a manner that meets most of the standard specifications, including sound siting, extensive site preparation, proper leachate and gas management and monitoring, compaction, daily and final cover, complete access control, and record-keeping.

Scrap—Materials discarded from manufacturing operations that may be suitable for reprocessing.

Scrap Metal Processor—Intermediate operating facility where recovered metal is sorted, cleaned of contaminants, and prepared for recycling.

Scrubber—Emission control device in an incinerator, used primarily to control acid gases, but also to remove some heavy metals.

Secondary Materials—Materials that have been manufactured and used at least once and are to be used again.

Secure landfill—A disposal facility designed to permanently isolate wastes from the environment. This entails burial of the wastes in a landfill that includes clay and/or synthetic liners, leachate collection, gas collection (in cases where gas is generated), and an impermeable cover.

Septage—Sludge removed from a septic tank (a chamber that holds human excreta).

Set out container—A box or bucket used for residential waste that is placed outside for collection.

Sewage—the waste matter that passes through sewers.

Sewage sludge—A semi-liquid residue that settles to the bottom of canals and pipes carrying sewage or industrial wastewaters, or in the bottom of tanks used in treating wastewaters.

Sharps—Hypodermic needles, syringes (with or without the attached needle), Pasteur pipettes, scalpel blades, blood vials, needles with attached tubing, and culture dishes used in animal or human patient care or treatment, or in medical, research or industrial laboratories. Also included are other types of broken or unbroken glassware that were in contact with infectious agents, such as used slides and cover slips, and unused hypodermic and suture needles, syringes, and scalpel blades.

Single Stream Collection—Collection system where recyclables are fully commingled, mixing fiber (papers) and containers (glass bottles, metal cans and plastic containers).

Site remediation—Treatment of a contaminated site by removing contaminated solids or liquids or treating them on-site.

Sludge Processing Facility—A volume reduction plant, the operations of which involve solely the reduction in volume of water treatment, sewage treatment or industrial sludge generated elsewhere.

SMART (Save Money And Reduce Trash)—Another name for Pay-As-You-Throw—Systems under which residents pay for municipal waste management and disposal services by weight or volume collected, not a fixed fee.

Solid Waste—Unwanted or discarded solid, liquid, semisolid or contained gaseous material, including, but not limited to, demolition debris, material burned or otherwise processed at a resources recovery facility or incinerator, material processed at a recycling facility and sludges or other residue from a water pollution abatement facility, water supply treatment plant or air pollution control facility.

Solid Waste Facility—means any solid waste disposal area, volume reduction plant, transfer station, wood-burning facility or biomedical waste treatment facility.

Solid Waste Disposal Area—Any location, including a landfill or other land disposal site, used for the disposal of more than ten cubic yards of solid waste. For purposes of this subdivision, "disposal" means the placement of material at a location with the intent to leave it at such location indefinitely, or to fail to remove material from a location within forty-five days, but does not mean the placement of material required to be recycled in a location on the premises of a recycling facility, provided such facility is in compliance with all requirements of state or federal law.

Source reduction—The design, manufacture, acquisition, and reuse of materials so as to minimize the quantity and/or toxicity of waste produced.

Source Separated Organic Material Composting Facility—Land, including structures and appurtenances thereon, where the composting of organic material that has been separated at the point or source of generation from non-organic material, takes place. Organic materials means substances composed primarily of carbon and nitrogen, including but not limited to food scraps, food processing residue, soiled or unrecyclable paper and yard trimmings.

Source separation—Setting aside of compostable and recyclable materials from the waste stream before they are collected with other MSW, to facilitate reuse, recycling, and composting.

Special wastes—Wastes that are ideally considered to be outside of the MSW stream, but which sometimes enter it and must often be dealt with by municipal authorities. These include household hazardous waste, medical waste, construction and demolition debris, war and earthquake debris, tires, oils, wet batteries, sewage sludge, human excreta, slaughterhouse waste, and industrial waste.

Subsidy—Direct or indirect payment from government to businesses, citizens, or institutions to encourage a desired activity.

Sustainability—meeting the needs of the present without compromising the ability of future generations to meet their own needs.

T

Tipping fee—A fee for unloading or dumping waste at a landfill, transfer station, incinerator, or recycling facility.

Tipping floor—Unloading area for vehicles that are delivering MSW to a transfer station or incinerator.

Toxic Substance—A chemical or mixture that may present an unreasonable risk of injury to health or the environment.

Toxic Waste—A waste that can produce injury if inhaled, swallowed, or absorbed through the skin.

Transfer point—A designated point, often at the edge of a neighborhood, where sma collection vehicles transfer waste to larger vehicles for transport to disposal sites.

Transfer station—A major facility at which MSW from collection vehicles is consolidated into loads that are transported by larger trucks or other means to more distant final disposal facilities, typically landfills

Trash—Material considered worthless or offensive that is thrown away. Generally defined as dry waste material, but in common usage it is a synonym for garbage, rubbish, or refuse.

Treated Wood—Wood which contains an adhesive, paint, stain, fire retardant, pesticide or preservative.

U

Used Oil—Spent motor oil from passenger cars and trucks collected at specified locations for recycling (not included in the category of municipal solid waste.

V

Vectors—Organisms that carry disease causing pathogens. At landfills rodents, flies, and birds are the main vectors that spread pathogens beyond the landfill site.

Vermicomposting—The process by which worms convert organic waste into worm castings—the dark, fertile, granular excrement of a worm. Castings are rich in plant nutrients.

Virgin materials—Any basic material for industrial processes that has not previously been used, for example, wood-pulp trees, iron ore, crude oil, bauxite.

Volume Reduction—Processing waste materials to decrease the amount of space they occupy, usually by compacting, shredding, incineration, or composting.

Volume Reduction Plant—Any location or structure, whether located on land or water, where more than two thousand pounds per hour of solid waste generated elsewhere may be reduced in volume, including but not limited to, resources recovery facilities and other incinerators, recycling facilities, pulverizers, compactors, shredders, balers and composting facilities.

W

Waste—1. Unwanted materials left over from a manufacturing process. 2. Refuse from places of human or animal habitation.

Waste Characterization—Identification of chemical and microbiological constituents of a waste material.

Waste collector—A person employed by a local authority or a private firm to collect waste from residences, businesses, and community bins.

Waste dealer—A middleman who buys recyclable materials from waste generators and itinerant buyers and sells them, after sorting and some processing, to wholesale brokers or recycling industries.

Waste Exchange—Arrangement in which companies exchange their wastes for the benefit of both parties.

Waste Feed—The continuous or intermittent flow of wastes into an incinerator.

Waste Generation—The weight or volume of materials and products that enter the waste stream before recycling, composting, landfilling, or combustion takes place. Also can represent the amount of waste generated by a given source or category of sources.

Waste management hierarchy—A ranking of waste management operations according to their environmental or energy benefits. The purpose of the waste management hierarchy is to make waste management practices as environmentally sound as possible.

Waste Management Project—Any solid waste disposal and resources recovery area, plant, works, system, facility or component of a facility, equipment, machinery or other element of a facility which the authority is authorized to plan, design, finance, construct, manage, operate or maintain under the provisions of this chapter, including real estate and improvements thereto and the extension or provision of utilities and other appurtenant facilities deemed necessary by the authority for the operation of a project or portion of a project, including all property rights, easements and interests required.

Waste Minimization—Measures or techniques that reduce the amount of wastes generated during industrial production processes; term is also applied to recycling and other efforts to reduce the amount of waste going into the waste stream.

Waste picker—A person who picks out recyclables from mixed waste wherever it may be temporarily accessible or disposed off .

Waste reduction—All means of reducing the amount of waste that is produced initially and that must be collected by solid waste authorities. This ranges from legislation and product design to local programs designed to keep recyclables and compostables out of the final waste stream.

Waste Stream—The total flow of solid waste from homes, businesses, institutions, and manufacturing plants that is recycled, burned, or disposed of in landfills, or segments thereof such as the "residential waste stream" or the "recyclable waste stream."

Waste Reduction—Reducing the amount of materials entering the waste stream from a specific source by redesigning products or patterns of production or consumption (*e.g.*, using returnable beverage containers). Synonymous with Source Reduction.

Waste-to-energy (WTE) plant—A facility that uses solid waste materials (processed or raw) to produce energy. WTE plants include incinerators that produce steam for district heating or industrial use, or that generate electricity; they also include facilities that convert landfill gas to electricity.

Windrow—An elongated pile of aerobically composting materials that are turned periodically to expose the materials to oxygen and to control the temperature to promote biodegradation.

Wood Packaging—Wood products such as pallets, crates, and barrels.

Working face—The length and width of the row in which waste is being deposited at a landfill. Also known as the tipping face.

Worm castings—The material produced from the digestive tracts of worms as they live in earth or compost piles. The castings are rich in nitrates, potassium, phosphorous, calcium, and magnesium.

Y

Yard Trimmings—Leaves, grass clippings, weeds, branches up to one (1") inch in diameter and prunings from yards or gardens.

Yard waste—Leaves, grass clippings, prunings, and other natural organic matter discarded from yards and gardens.

Z

Zero Waste—Zero Waste is a goal that is both pragmatic and visionary, to guide people to emulate sustainable natural cycles, where all discarded materials are resources for others to use. Zero Waste means designing and managing products and processes to reduce the volume and toxicity of waste and materials, conserve and recover all resources, and not burn or bury them. Implementing Zero Waste will eliminate all discharges to land, water or air that may be a threat to planetary, human, animal or plant health.

Reference/Bibliography/ Further Reading

1. Bhide, A. D. and Sundaresan, B. B., 1983. Solid Waste Management in Developing Countries. New Delhi, India: Indian National Scientific Documentation Center.
2. Central Pollution Control Board (CPCB), 1998. Collection, Transportation and Disposal of Municipal Solid Wastes in Delhi (India)—A Case Study, Central Pollution Control Board, Delhi.
3. Fritz, Jack. 1990. *Comparatives Issues in Solid Waste Management in India and China*. Paper presented at the "International Workshop on Waste Management and Resource Recovery", October 27 - November 4, Kathmandu.
4. Gupta, S., Mohan, K., Prasad, R., Gupta, S., Kansal, A., 1998. Solid waste management in India: Options and opportunities, Resources, conservation and recycling 24, Issue 2, 137-154.
5. Hester, R. E and Harrison, R. M., 2002. *Environmental and Health Impact of Solid Waste Management Activities*, Royal Society of Chemistry, U. K.
6. IPE, 2004. Study of Management of Solid Waste in Indian Cities. Twelfth Finance Commission, Government of India.http://www.infrastructureindia.com/monitoreval_cs2.htm.
7. Marandi, B. L., 1998. *Hazardous Waste Management*. Central Pollution Control Board (CPCB). http://www.cpcb.nic.in/news.htm as on 21st May 2005
8. National Solid waste Association of India, 2003. Urban Municipal Solid Waste Management. Special Bulletin of the National Solid Waste Association of India (inaugural issue), Mumbai.
9. Srinivas, S. V., 2003. Energy from Municipal and Industrial Wastes. Department of Chemical engineering, Indian Institute of Madras, Chennai.
10. Tchnobanoglous, G., Kreith, F., 2002. *Handbook of Solid Waste Management*, 2nd edition, McGraw-Hill Handbooks.

11. Tchobanaglous, G., Theisen, H., and Eliassen, R., 1997. Solid wastes: Engineering principles and management issues. McGrawHill publications, NewYork, USA.
12. The Expert Committee, 2000. *Manual on Municipal Solid Waste Management*, The Ministry of Urban Development, The Government of India, Volume 1 and 2.
13. Vehlow, J., 1996. Municipal Solid Waste Management in Germany. Waste management 16, Issue 5, 367-374
14. Chandrappa, R., Das, D.B. & Springer Link 2012, Solid waste management, Springer, Berlin; New York.
15. Davis, M.L., and Cornell, D.A., 1991. Introduction to Environmental Engineering, 2nd edn., McGraw-Hill, New York.
16. Hung, Y., Shammas, N.K. & Wang, L.K. 2014, Handbook of environment and waste management, World Scientific, New Jersey.
17. LaGrega, et al., 2001. Hazardous Waste Management, (2nd edn.) McGraw-Hill, NY. UTS.
18. Pichtel, J., 2005. Waste Management Practices: municipal, hazardous, and industrial. Boca Raton, FL: Taylor & Francis/CRC Press.
19. Tchobanoglous, G., et al., 1992. Integrated Solid Waste Management, McGraw-Hill, NY.
20. Worrell, W.A. & Vesilind, P.A. 2012, Solid waste engineering, 2nd edn., Cengage Learning, Australia.